101 CAREERS

101 CAREERS

A Guide to the Fastest-Growing Opportunities

SECOND EDITION

MICHAEL HARKAVY

JOHN WILEY & SONS, INC.

New York • Chichester • Weinheim • Brisbane • Singapore • Toronto

Library of Congress Cataloging-in-Publication Data:
Harkavy, Michael David.
    101 Careers : a guide to the fastest-growing opportunities /
Michael Harkavy. — 2nd ed.
      p.   cm.
    Includes index.
    ISBN 0-471-24189-X (paper : alk. paper)
    1. Vocational guidance—United States.   I. Title.
HF5429.3.H37   1999
331.7′ 02—dc21   98-21896

Printed in the United States of America.
10 9 8 7 6 5 4 3 2 1

PREFACE

Future shock has come and gone in the 1990s and left a lot of bewildered people in its wake. As we approach the next century, change comes so fast that reading the daily newspaper can seem an exercise in obsolescence. As for the workplace, don't ask: Who's in? Who's out? Keeping track seems a full-time job. How, you may well ask, *does* one plan for a career in a job market that is so volatile? That is the problem this book sets out to address, and as you will see, the answer lies not so much in specifics as in process. The *way* you prepare yourself for future jobs may be more important than precisely *what* you prepare for.

SEMPER PARATUS: THE KEY TO THE FUTURE?

The 101 jobs covered in this book are remarkably diverse, but they share one common characteristic: All require special training. Jobs requiring the most education and training will be the fastest growing and highest paying in the next 10 years. Almost all require a bachelor's degree, and many require advanced degrees. The few jobs that one can enter with a high school degree (e.g., paralegal, EKG technician, licensed practical nurse) demand special training either on the job or in a classroom setting, and sometimes both.

Most of the jobs presented here are white-collar, prestigious jobs. They represent the wave of future employment because they clearly show that learning how to learn may be the most important ingredient of a successful career. In the future, one industry may blossom and another wither, so workers will have to be able to adjust to change, adapt to new techniques and technologies, and cope with the marketplace's implacable demand for continually upgraded or even new skills. The jobs profiled reflect the general consensus on what the world of work will be like through the first five years of the twenty-first century. Qualified, skilled workers will find many new, well-paying job opportunities. Those with limited educational backgrounds who are either unable or unwilling to learn new skills will find it rough going indeed.

As you read through this book, you will see that a solid, basic education is the cornerstone on which careers in the future will be built. Professional specialty occupations, which require higher educational attainment and offer higher earnings, are expected to increase over the next 10 years at a faster rate than any other occupational group. Education is valuable in itself, but even more important, perhaps, is mastering the learning process; because no matter what profession you choose, you will have to cope with the changes that technology and world economics inevitably will bring. Clearly, the ability to train and retrain—and retrain again—is *the* prerequisite for job success as the twenty-first century begins.

JUST LOOKING: HOW BEST TO USE THIS BOOK

The job profiles in this book give a thumbnail sketch of 101 occupations our research has shown as having strong prospects in the near future. The profiles are collected under nine major industry groupings, giving you an opportunity to survey a number of different occupations in a specific industry. These industries are expected to be in strong demand until 2006, although changes in the economy or government policy or technology may affect demand in one or more of their related occupations.

Each profile begins with an "Occupational Overview" that summarizes the most salient features of the occupation. It is valuable for getting a quick idea of whether the job interests you. Following this, the discussion proper goes into detail about the job—its requirements, remuneration, and probable future. The overview covers such matters as the job description, the job's prospects (giving estimates of job opportunity growth as compared with the general economy), the qualifications and personal skills it requires, and what it pays. These earnings figures come from a number of different sources and surveys, so they are expressed in a variety of ways: median or mean annual earnings; monthly, weekly, or in some cases, hourly earnings; and so forth.

The discussion following the overview, "The Job and the Work Environment," describes some of the most important duties to be performed, the kind of hours per week (regular, irregular, evening or weekend, etc.), the workplace (office, on-site locations, and so on), and any special considerations (e.g., handling dangerous materials, extreme pressures, need for physical strength). This section is designed to help you decide if the occupation entails the kind of work and work environment that appeals to you and in which you think you would do well.

The next section in each chapter, "Training and Qualifications," goes into some detail about the education and training requirements for the occupation. As noted, nearly all the occupations profiled here require at least a bachelor's degree. Special training requirements are also noted, with emphasis on where such training can be obtained—colleges and universities, hospitals, community colleges, vocational or technical schools, and so forth. Professional certification is also covered, with the type of certification and requirements for becoming a candidate discussed.

"Earnings" cites typical earnings figures and remuneration plans for the occupation, using the latest figures and giving as much detail as possible. Where available, figures are given for entry-level jobs in the profession and for experienced workers. Some profiles specify high and low salaries for the occupation, some give mean (average) salaries, and others give median salaries. (A median salary figure is the midpoint amount: half the workers in the profession earned more than this; half, less.)

Finally, "Prospects: Job Outlook" places the occupation in the ongoing life of the economy, giving the expectations for employment opportunities in the occupation and showing how societal trends (such as population demographics) may be reflected in job demand. For instance, the aging of the baby boom generation and the increasing longevity of the general population dictate that medical practitioners in age-related specialties will be in demand. Other occupations may be adversely affected by events. For example, although securities sales representatives (stockbrokers) seem to have a bright future, with a strong demand expected for their services, the occupation is quite sensitive to moves in the general economy. A sharp downturn in economic activity is likely to cause people and institutions to cut back on their investing. When this happens, stock market activity slows; fewer stockbrokers are needed, and those in the profession earn less because their earnings are based on commissions on sales.

Each job profile ends with "Where to Look for Further Information," suggested sources for more information about the occupation. In many cases, a professional group or association is happy to provide information on an occupation—its responsibilities, place in the bigger economic or social picture, and rewards; qualifications needed; schools offering programs to help prepare for the occupation; and sources for jobs.

TRAVEL KIT: WHAT TO PACK IN YOUR CAREER BAGGAGE

You can use the information in this book at any stage of your business life—whether you are soon to graduate from college and are looking for attractive entry-level jobs, considering a midcareer course correction, or looking for new challenges before retiring.

If you know the job you are interested in, the best approach is to get specialized training in the field and acquire as much experience as possible. The "Training and Qualifications" section of each profile offers vital information on the kinds of programs most useful for that profession and where they are available. In addition, many companies are looking for experienced workers in even entry-level jobs, so if you participate in cooperative programs and part-time work while in school, you may have an edge in getting a job after graduation. For many jobs on a managerial level, too, experience counts for more than formal education.

Overspecialization, however, can prove to be a handicap. Companies tend to take on people with specialized training as new hirees, but increasingly they seek generalists with varied experience for their middle and upper-middle managers. Too tight a concentration on technology, for instance, may leave top management with the impression that you are an equipment buff and lack the broad business and people savvy that a line or division manager needs. In a rush to acquire technical training, don't forget the basics. Despite all the talk about technology dominating the job market of the future, the skills most desired across the board in managerial personnel are the ones associated with a liberal arts education: good writing and communication skills, organizational ability, flexibility, open-mindedness, and good analytical and problem-solving skills.

A liberal arts background in this context, however, does not mean a mishmash of courses concentrated at the low end of the intellectual spectrum. For career purposes, a liberal arts background should comprise a rigorous academic program with courses in literature, history, science, mathematics, economics, psychology or other human behavior discipline, and computer science. Such a background gives you the option of going on to specialized training in any number of fields—business, finance, sales and marketing, law, and education, for example. Naturally, if your choice is one of the professions requiring a specialized, advanced degree (e.g., law, medicine, or teaching), you are best advised to take the undergraduate program targeted for that discipline. Even for entry into such specific programs as law or medical school, however, the best strategy may not be to concentrate undergraduate work in one narrow focus. Admittedly, many graduate schools are highly competitive, but they, like private businesses, seek competent candidates with demonstrated abilities in other areas, too. They want to see signs of leadership potential, evidence of interests outside the profession, and indications of initiative. Involvement in sports and other extracurricular activities and part-time employment as an undergraduate carry clout, whether for admittance into a graduate school or acceptance into the training program of the company you've set your sights on.

Communication skills are crucial for success in the marketplace. With foreign competition—and markets—expected to play an ever larger role in the nation's economy, fluency in a foreign language will be a big plus in job hunting. For a long time in the United States, taking a foreign language was something you did in high school (maybe) and then promptly forgot. Those days are gone. We live and compete in a world economy, and there are hundreds of millions of potential customers and clients who don't speak English. As U.S. industries expand abroad, they'll need trained personnel who can communicate easily with people in their new markets. Learning a foreign language can be fun for some, painful for others, but profitable for all.

FITTING IN: THE SHAPE OF THINGS TO COME

Trendy is *not* where it's at. Exotic new jobs will develop, but trying to anticipate the market can lead to misspent time and effort. To guess is cheap; to guess wrong is expensive. There are, however, strong trends that give some clues where the action is likely to be in the next century—as long as you bear in mind that even the best crystal ball is cloudy—and they follow:

- *Demographics.* These provide a solid hint of what's coming. The general population is growing older, so looking in areas that service this large segment of the population makes good sense. The health professions seem particularly attractive here. Employment in health services is expected to grow more than twice as fast as the economy as a whole. The increasing number of elderly will need more care, as will recovering patients discharged from hospitals as insurance companies mandate shorter stays for recovery to contain costs. Also attractive are any of the occupations servicing the over-40 market: financial managers, accountants, travel personnel, and the like. Also likely to be hot are the professions that provide child care, as the family now and in the future is likely to rely on two careers.
- *Small Business.* Predictions are that companies with fewer than 100 employees will generate more than half the new jobs as we head into the next millennium, a turnaround from earlier times when the bulk of new jobs were created by the major corporations. Job hunting will become more fragmented but perhaps easier too. Conventional wisdom has it that the personnel departments of large companies are the least attractive places to begin looking for a job. Smaller companies, where you can make personal contact with a prospective employer, are a better bet. They have relatively underdeveloped bureaucracies, and they are growing and looking for people. For instance, in the last two decades while the Fortune 500 companies have cut millions of jobs from their payrolls, small businesses have added tens of millions. Less is more.
- *Technology.* No, technology is *not* going to run away with all jobs, leaving everyone who isn't an electronic engineer to flip hamburgers. Still, one must know how to work with the computer. The fastest growing occupations reflect growth in computer technology. In the job profiles, again and again, computer literacy is listed as a required skill. Businesses of all sizes have computerized their operations, and almost all workers need to be familiar with working with a computer, manipulating databases and entering, storing, and retrieving information. More important than the equipment you master is learning how to learn these operations. No matter what company you work for, the hardware and software will change, even if you stay at the same job, and you will be obliged (time and again, no doubt) to master new systems. Again, knowing *how to learn* something will be one of the keys to your success. Employment of computer

specialists is expected to grow rapidly to satisfy expanding needs for scientific research and applications of computer technology in business and industry.

- *Geography.* Geography is probably not destiny, but mobility will play an important part in getting and keeping employment in the coming decade. Smart people go where the jobs are (they always have, which is why urban centers are crowded). If the expectations hold up and new businesses are the big job generators, where will most of this activity take place? The betting is that future entrepreneurs will be clustered in the service and technology industries—those that rely on brain power for ideas and marketing. Universities attract brains and provide training; bright, educated people generate ideas; and new companies are formed to exploit these ideas in the marketplace.

  Salaries are generally higher in the West and Northeast and in urban areas. But remember that high-paying areas are usually high-cost areas, too, so a higher paycheck may not always translate into a higher living standard. A lot depends on what you are looking for in a place to live. Economics may not be the final determinant in that decision. Nevertheless, an open mind on location is a trait to cultivate. *Mobility* and *flexibility* are the watchwords of the future.

- *Opportunities for Women.* Women are now and will continue to be major players in the workforce. The goal has enlarged, focusing on cutting the pay gap between men and women and moving into traditionally male-dominated professions that are lucrative and prestigious. Women are projected to represent a greater portion of the labor force in 2006 than in 1994, increasing from 46 percent to 48 percent.

  The best plan is to determine areas in which shortages are expected. Relatively few women enter the sciences and engineering, although these professions (especially the jobs of computer programmers and computer systems analysts) are definitely on the hot list for the immediate future. On the plus side, demand will offer women great opportunities. A Ph.D. in one of these fields gives a woman clout in the job market, in both the private sector and academia. However, the lack of women in these areas may be offputting for many potential candidates. The good jobs are there, though. Women intent on high-paying jobs should take these factors into account when planning their education and tend toward professions that are now male dominated.

  Communications will continue to be a strong employer of women, and, in industry, professions that make for a quick trip up the corporate ladder still are found in the traditional areas—sales, marketing, and finance. All of these are increasingly hospitable to women. The health professions, long a mainstay of employment for women, are expected to be even more desirable as they increase in prestige and earning power. In this area, physical therapists will find themselves in great demand. Law has proved a good profession for women, but anticipated overcrowding will make the field fiercely competitive. Nevertheless, paralegals will be in heavy demand; this occupation is among the brightest spots in the employment picture.

Women would do well to look to entrepreneurial ventures as well. The service sector offers promising opportunities to start one's own business: travel, child care, financial consulting, employment agencies, and others.

MAKING IT: WHICH BRASS RING IS MINE?

Some professions run against the grain. A Scarlatti sonata is rendered today with one instrument and one performer, the same as it was in the eighteenth century. Sure, you go into an occupation to make money. Professionals, after all, differ from amateurs in that they make money at what they do. Even so, choosing an occupation that is likely to engage you for the better part of your adult life has to provide more than bean counting.

Because rapid change is the standard operating procedure of our time, you will have to be nimble and work hard. Long hours, responsibility, stress—each of the jobs profiled here has its share and more. With so much of your life devoted to your work, can you afford to select a profession you don't like?

As you read through the job profiles in this book, put yourself in each one and get a feel for whether it's you (never mind the flashy statistics or the glitz). Does the job sound as if it is something you'd like to do? Do you see yourself in it for the next 10 years—or longer? True, people are more likely to change jobs now than ever before, but normally they find something in the field for which they're prepared. It's quite common to find people who have stayed longer with their professions, alas, than with their spouses. Think about it. Work, for nearly all of us, is not a sometime thing.

✿   ✿   ✿   ✿   ✿

The first edition of this book was published in 1990. This updated version, edited expressly for application during the early years of the 21st century, was based on a variety of sources, the main one being the publication by the Bureau of Labor Statistics, U.S. Department of Labor, of Bulletin 2500, _Occupational Outlook Handbook_, 1998–1999 edition (Superintendent of Documents, U.S. Printing Office, Washington, DC, 1998).

I would like to thank Harry L. Wagner, Edward Ferraro, Ruth Tennenbaum, and Alan Gold for their assistance on this project.

MICHAEL D. HARKAVY

CONTENTS

101 CAREERS

Accounting, Banking, Finance, Insurance, and Management

Accountants and Auditors

OCCUPATIONAL OVERVIEW

Job Description: Accountants and auditors prepare, analyze, and verify financial reports that furnish up-to-date information for business, industrial, and government managers.

Prospects: Employment growth in this occupation is expected to grow about as fast as the average for all occupations through the year 2006.

Qualifications: The minimum requirement is a bachelor's degree in accounting or a closely related field. Many employers require experience, too. Computer literacy is important.

Personal Skills: An aptitude for mathematics; attention to detail; a good sense for numbers; accuracy; the ability to analyze, compare, and interpret facts; and neatness are the hallmarks of this profession.

Earnings: According to surveys by the National Association of Colleges and Employers, in 1995 accountants with limited experience had median earnings of $26,000 and the most experienced had median earnings of $87,400.

THE JOB AND THE WORK ENVIRONMENT

Everyone talks about the bottom line. Accountants and auditors are the people who compute it and work with it. The data that accountants and auditors provide to managers are at the heart of the decision-making process in both the public and the private sectors. The four major fields of accounting are:

Public accountants work for a business or an accounting firm, or they are in business for themselves. Their primary task is financial auditing: verifying that employers' or clients' financial records and reports conform to accepted standards. Public accountants may specialize in tax matters or investments, develop accounting systems, or advise companies on the most efficient use of financial resources.

Management accountants, the largest group of accountants and auditors, work for a single company and are responsible for its financial records. They provide the financial data that company managers need to make informed decisions. They also may prepare financial reports to satisfy stock exchange and other regulatory agency requirements. Some may concentrate on taxation, budgets, investments, costs, and similar areas.

Government accountants maintain and examine the records of government agencies at the federal, state, or local level. They also audit private firms and individuals whose business activities are subject to government regulation.

Internal auditors verify the accuracy of their firm's financial reports and guard against waste or fraud in company operations. They also review their firm's operations for efficiency and for compliance with government regulations, laws, and company procedures.

Accountants and auditors work standard business hours, usually at their firm's offices. Self-employed accountants may work at home, with their hours determined by the needs of their clients. All accountants regularly use a computer and standard accounting programs. Some have developed extensive computer skills, devised software programs for special business needs, and corrected existing software problems.

TRAINING AND QUALIFICATIONS

Accountants and auditors are expected to have a bachelor's degree in accounting. Some firms prefer a master's degree in accounting or in business administration with a concentration in accounting. Experience is an important qualification when job hunting, so job seekers who have held part-time college jobs or participated in part-time internship programs offered by accounting or business firms have an advantage.

Professional certification is valuable for widening job opportunities and career advancement. *Certified public accountants (CPAs)* are licensed by state boards of accountancy. They generally must have a college degree and solid work experience, and they must pass a CPA examination prepared by the American Institute of Certified Public Accountants. *Certified internal auditors (CIAs)* are awarded the designation by the Institute of Internal Auditors upon graduating from an accredited college, completing two years' experience in internal auditing, and passing a four-part examination. Increasingly states are requiring that CPAs and licensed public accountants take continuing education courses to renew their licenses.

EARNINGS

According to a salary survey conducted by Robert Half International, a staffing services firm specializing in accounting and finance, accountants and auditors with up to one year of experience earned between $25,000 and $39,400 in 1997. Those with one to three years of experience earned between $27,000 and $46,600. Senior accountants and auditors earned between $34,300 and $57,800; managers earned between $40,000 and $81,900; and directors of accounting and auditing earned between $54,800 and $109,800 a year. The variation in salaries reflects differences in size of firm, location, level of education, and professional credentials.

PROSPECTS: JOB OUTLOOK

In 1996, over one million accountants and auditors held jobs. Increased demand will generate new jobs into the next century, and most opportunities will come from the replacement of retirees. Because of the large size of the occupation, replacement demands are expected to be substantial. Also, as the economy grows, the number of businesses increases, requiring more accountants and auditors to set up their books, prepare taxes, and provide management advice. Competition for jobs in the major accounting firms will be keen, however, so good academic preparation—and some experience—will be crucial. Applicants with a master's degree in accounting or business administration with a concentration in accounting are increasingly valued, particularly among large firms. Also important will be familiarity with computerized accounting programs, especially in light of the increasing complexity and volume of the accounting needs of businesses.

Junior accountants can expect to advance to intermediate positions in one to two years and to senior positions a few years later. Some may choose to open their own businesses. In accounting firms, the career ladder includes supervisors, managers, and partners. Management accountants may advance to chief plant accountant, chief cost accountant, budget director, and so on. Some move into corporate management as comptrollers, treasurers, and financial vice-presidents. Many corporation executives have backgrounds in accounting and finance.

WHERE TO LOOK FOR FURTHER INFORMATION

To learn more about careers in accounting and about competency tests administered by colleges and accounting firms:

American Institute of Certified Public Accountants
Harborside Financial Center
201 Plaza III
Jersey City, NJ 07311-3881

To learn more about accredited accounting programs:

Institute of Management Accountants
10 Paragon Drive
P.O. Box 433
Montvale, NJ 07645-1760

National Society of Public Accountants
and the Accreditation Council for
Accountancy and Taxation
1010 North Fairfax Street
Alexandria, VA 22314

Institute of Internal Auditors
249 Maitland Avenue
Altamonte Springs, FL 32701

The Information Systems Audit and
Control Association
3701 Algonquin Road
Suite 1010
Rolling Meadows, IL 60008

ACTUARIES

OCCUPATIONAL OVERVIEW

Job Description: Actuaries gather and analyze statistical data to determine quantities such as probabilities of death, illness, injury, disability, unemployment, retirement, and property loss (from accident, fire, theft, and other hazards). Insurance and other business firms and government use the actuarial analysis to assess their risks in areas such as insurance, employee benefits, and retirement programs.

Prospects: Job opportunities for actuaries are expected to grow more slowly than the average for all occupations through the year 2006 due to projected slower growth in the insurance industry. College graduates who have passed at least two of the professional actuarial examinations while in school and have good mathematical backgrounds will be in the best position to take advantage of the opportunities.

Qualifications: A college degree with a major in mathematics or statistics is essential and a degree in actuarial science is even more desirable. Courses in economics, finance, business administration, and computer science are recommended.

Personal Skills: Above-average ability in mathematics is crucial. Aptitude for problem solving, good communications skills, and an interest in general economic and social trends are important, too.

Earnings: Entry-level jobs can start as high as $37,600. Highly experienced actuaries can earn as much as $100,000 a year in salary and bonuses.

THE JOB AND THE WORK ENVIRONMENT

Despite the low profile of the profession, actuaries are eagerly sought by the insurance industry, major corporations, and governmental agencies. Actuaries use quantitative analytical skills to plan for future financial situations. For instance, they may project for a life insurance company how many people age 21 today will die before they reach 65. The company uses this information to determine the amount of monetary risk it faces and plans accordingly. For an automobile insurance company, actuaries may estimate the impact of seat belt laws on automobile losses to determine appropriate rate discounts. For government, they may project the costs of social security benefits for the next 20 years to determine how much money the government needs to collect to meet the forecast outlays. Consultants for a large corporation may need actuaries to design a new retirement program.

Insurance companies—for life, health, and property/casualty—employ over one-half of all actuaries. Actuaries ensure by mathematical analysis that the price charged for the insurance (premium) is enough to allow the company to pay all its claims and expenses as they occur and to make a profit. Moreover, the price must be competitive with other companies offering the same kind of policy. The whole structure of insurance—managing future financial risks—depends on careful and accurate analyses of risks. Hence the insurance industry's great need for trained and skilled actuaries.

Increasing numbers of actuaries work as consultants, either in their own firms or with large, nationwide consulting firms. In this capacity, they advise top company management on matters like financial services, risk management, and health care programs. They also provide actuarial advice to hospitals, labor unions, and government agencies.

Actuaries may find employment in a variety of fields, including education, government, insurance rating bureaus, public accounting firms, large industrial corporations, and labor unions.

All actuaries must be mathematically talented, business-oriented men and women with a broad range of business skills so that they can deal with challenges posed by new legislation, health problems, and social and political trends and developments. Most actuaries specialize in life and health insurance, property and liability (casualty), or increasingly, pension plans.

Actuaries work at their desks in offices that are typically comfortable and pleasant. They work a normal week of 35 to 40 hours, but at peak seasons may have to work overtime. Some travel to company branch offices or to clients may be required.

TRAINING AND QUALIFICATIONS

Despite the technical nature of the job, companies seek candidates who have a rather broad background, but college courses in calculus, statistics, and probability are necessary. Only about 55 colleges and universities offer a degree in actuarial science, but many offer related degrees in math and statistics. In addition, courses in economics, business administration, and finance are strongly encouraged.

Several organizations grant professional recognition to actuaries. The Society of Actuaries (SOA) and the Casualty Actuarial Society (CAS) administer a series of examinations. SOA gives 10 examinations for the life and health and pension field; CAS gives 10 exams for the property and liability field. Exams are given twice a year.

The highest and most widely accepted professional recognition an actuary can achieve is fellowship in either of the groups, gained by passing all 10 tests. Associate status is achieved by passing five examinations in the life insurance series or seven in the casualty series.

The first three examinations cover roughly the same material; thus, candidates are not obliged to choose a specialty until later in the series. It is best to complete the full series as soon as possible, a feat that generally takes 5 to 10 years. Students should try to complete two or more of the exams while still in college, before they are working full time.

The American Society of Pension Actuaries also offers a series of seven exams covering the pension field. Associate membership requires passing two actuarial exams; fellowship status requires passing three actuarial and two advanced consulting exams.

EARNINGS

A 1996 salary survey of insurance and financial services companies, conducted by the Life Office Management Association, Inc., indicated that the average base salary for an entry-level actuary was about $36,500. Associate actuaries, who direct and provide leadership in the design and pricing of products, received a salary of about $78,600. Actuaries with additional experience earned an average of $93,500.

PROSPECTS: JOB OUTLOOK

People think actuaries are even duller than accountants; their reaction is to cry all the way to the bank. There were only about 16,000 practicing actuaries in 1996; more than 1 in 10 were self-employed. Employment of actuaries is expected to grow more slowly than the average for all occupations through the year 2006, due to expected slower growth in the insurance industry.

On the other hand, employment growth of consulting actuaries is expected to be faster than growth in the insurance business, which has experienced downsizing and mergers. There also is a growing need to evaluate catastrophic risks, such as earthquakes and tornadoes.

Once on the job, actuaries advance to more responsible positions primarily on the basis of job performance and the number of actuarial exams they have passed. The ladder goes from assistant, to associate, to chief actuary. Because of their experience in the insurance, pension, and employee benefits fields, actuaries are often tapped for top administrative posts in accounting, underwriting, or data processing.

Success in the profession does not come easily. The testing program is rigorous and long; it takes as much dedication and commitment to become an actuary as it does to become a doctor or lawyer.

WHERE TO LOOK FOR FURTHER INFORMATION

To learn more about actuarial careers and the required qualifications:

Society of Actuaries
475 North Martingale Road
Suite 800
Schaumberg, IL 60173-2226

American Academy of Actuaries
1100 17th Street, NW
7th Floor
Washington, DC 20036

Casualty Actuarial Society
1100 North Glebe Road
Suite 600
Arlington, VA 22201

American Society of Pension Actuaries
4350 North Fairfax Drive
Suite 820
Arlington, VA 22203

*B*ANK ADMINISTRATORS AND MANAGERS

OCCUPATIONAL OVERVIEW

Job Description: Bank administrators and managers oversee bank operations and carry out the policies set by the bank's board of directors. They are part of a larger group of financial managers who occupy positions in just about every business.

Prospects: As of 1996, there were about 800,000 financial managers employed, about one-third by financial institutions. Job opportunities in this area are expected to increase substantially as the global economy expands banking services.

Qualifications: A bachelor's degree is essential for top managerial positions in banking, and most require an M.B.A. also. Sometimes, however, outstanding tellers or clerks with only a high school background work their way up through promotions and are accepted into a bank's management training program. Candidates must possess a thorough knowledge of business, economics, and financial analysis and demonstrate expertise in the banking areas for which they are responsible.

Personal Skills: Excellent interpersonal skills and facility in quantitative analysis are essential. A familiarity with using computers is essential.

Earnings: Earnings vary by geographic region and bank size. The median annual salary of financial managers was $40,700 in 1996. The top 10 percent earned over $81,100.

THE JOB AND THE WORK ENVIRONMENT

Traditionally, bankers were seen as pillars of the community, conservative, and somewhat aloof. Today's banks are still inextricably tied to their communities (they are essential for businesses, consumers, and development), but they are now actively pursuing business and competing vigorously in offering whole menus of services to their customers.

There are two major types of commercial banking: retail consumer banking and wholesale banking. *Retail banking* concentrates on meeting the banking needs of individuals, families, and small businesses. Retail banks offer services such as consumer and small business loans, home mortgages, savings accounts, demand accounts, credit cards, travelers' checks, and financial management advice. *Wholesale banking* concentrates on providing financial services to large corporations, institutions, and government agencies—services such as loans, depository services, cash management assistance, investment advice, advisory treasury services, and systems analysis.

Commercial bank officers and managers have responsibilities in many different areas. *Loan officers* evaluate the credit worthiness of individuals and businesses applying for loans and also work to promote close business relationships with major clients. They are key players in the world of corporate banking. *Trust officers* administer individuals' estates and also manage the money of wealthy individuals, endowments for schools and hospitals, and pension and profit-sharing funds that comprise the retirement funds for corporations. Trust departments in banks also provide financial counseling. *Operations officers* plan and coordinate the bank's procedures and systems. *International officers* take care of the bank's dealings abroad and its foreign customers. *Branch managers* are responsible for the functions of a branch office of the bank. They are especially sensitive to the needs of their local communities and often are active in community civic and business affairs. *Cashiers* are officers responsible for the bank's property. And other officers are in charge of specific departments: auditing, personnel, public relations, and operations research. Smaller banks may have only a few officers, each responsible for several functions or departments.

Bankers' hours are not what they once were. With the increasing competition among banks for customers and loan activities, bank officers and managers frequently must go out to meet prospective clients and involve themselves in community functions, often in the evening and on weekends.

TRAINING AND QUALIFICATIONS

Most commercial banks have extensive management training programs. A bachelor's degree, in almost any major, is generally required for entry into such a program. Candidates for higher level management positions usually need an M.B.A. An ideal background for entry into commercial banking is an undergraduate degree in one of the social sciences and an M.B.A.

Financial management has been revolutionized by computers and data-processing equipment. Knowledge of these developments is vital to enhance advancement opportunities.

Banks generally hire bright, well-rounded people who have good leadership qualities, are comfortable working with numbers, can communicate well on the telephone and in writing, can inspire confidence in others, and work independently. Loan officers and branch managers must have the ability to work closely with people. As the banking industry grows more competitive and aggressive, it needs employees with good marketing skills. Fluency in a foreign language is a big plus for those interested in international dealings.

EARNINGS

According to a 1997 survey by Robert Half International, a staffing services firm specializing in accounting and finance, salaries of assistant controllers range from $41,000 in the smallest firms, to $81,000 in the largest; controllers, $47,000 to $138,000; and chief financial officers/treasurers, $62,000 to $307,000.

PROSPECTS: JOB OUTLOOK

Banking is one of the fastest growing areas of the economy, and demand for experienced bank officers and managers is expected to grow faster than the average for all occupations through the year 2006. The need for skilled management will increase due to the demands of global trade, the proliferation of complex financial instruments, and changing federal and state laws and regulations.

Advancing to senior officer and management positions in commercial banking (the fast track is for investment managers) takes many years. One way to accelerate the promotion process is to gain experience in several banking departments; another is to continue one's education by participating in management-sponsored advanced courses and programs.

WHERE TO LOOK FOR FURTHER INFORMATION

To learn more about careers in commercial banking:

American Bankers Association, Center for
    Banking Information
Bank Personnel Division
1120 Connecticut Avenue, NW
Washington, DC 20036

National Bankers Association
1513 P Street, NW
Washington, DC 20005-1909

Bank Administration Institute
1 North Franklin Street
Floor 10
Chicago, IL 60606

*B*UDGET ANALYSTS

OCCUPATIONAL OVERVIEW

Job Description: Budget analysts study an organization's financial data and help plan the allocation of its resources. They detail the efficient use of limited resources through budgeting; in private industry, they also seek to increase profits through sound budgeting. Budget analysts work for businesses of every size and description and for federal, state, and local governments.

Prospects: Through the year 2006, jobs for budget analysts are expected to increase about as fast as the average for jobs throughout the economy. In addition to employment growth, there will be many openings to replace budget analysts who have left the workforce or changed occupations.

Qualifications: Most candidates for budget analyst positions need a bachelor's degree in business administration, accounting, or economics. Some employers require a master's degree. In some cases, particularly in smaller firms, experience can offset a lack of education. A working knowledge of computers is essential.

Personal Skills: A budget analyst needs an analytical mind and informed judgment, the ability to work well under pressure, and should be well organized, attentive to detail, and good with numbers. Since budget analysts spend a large part of their workday conferring with others, strong interpersonal skills are essential. Familiarity with financial software packages used by most organizations in budget analysis, as well as word processing, is generally required.

Earnings: A survey of workplaces in 160 metropolitan areas in 1995 reported that inexperienced budget analysts had median annual earnings of about $30,100, with the middle half earning between $26,200 and $35,000 a year. Managers in large organizations earned between $47,000 and $83,800.

THE JOB AND THE WORK ENVIRONMENT

Business and government rely on budgets to assess their resources and allocate them efficiently and, in the case of private business, profitably. A well-planned budget is an indispensable managerial tool. It helps keep an organization viable and accountable. Budget analysts gather and analyze financial data and help devise a financial plan for distributing limited resources within the organization.

In small firms, budget analysts, who are typically accountants or controllers, develop budgets for the entire operation. In large firms, each department proposes its own budget, which is combined with the budgets of other departments in drawing up the company's overall financial plan. In the federal government and other extremely large organizations, budget planning is the work of a complex and far-flung bureaucracy.

In all settings, the fundamentals of the job are much the same. Budget analysts begin by reviewing previous budgets and taking stock of a firm's resources. They research economic developments that bear on the firm and review its goals. With the overall picture in hand, they can then consider some fundamental recommendations. Perhaps the most basic is whether a company should take on debt to finance its operations.

In larger organizations, department heads submit plans for their units, detailing their goals and the resources they need to reach them. Budget directors then review the statements for completeness, accuracy, and compliance with procedures and regulations. In both business and government, critical decisions must be made about allocating limited resources. Budget analysts study the proposed allocations and perform cost-benefit analysis, eliminating or combining programs or proposals that duplicate one another, and consider modes of financing. They then draft their findings into preliminary budgets, with accompanying summaries and recommendations that they submit to management. After final financial decisions are made by top-level management, the budget analysts monitor the actual performance of the budget, note any deviations when they occur, and propose necessary adjustments. They keep management and corporate officials up-to-date on the status of the budget and may hold training sessions to instruct personnel in policies and procedures needed to implement and maintain a budget.

Budget analysts must have a background in computers. The larger the organization is, the more budget analysts rely upon computers. Although a majority of budget analysts' time is spent working independently, they must cultivate and maintain good working relations with managers and department heads to ascertain their needs and win their confidence and support. Budget analysts must be able to prepare clear, concise budget proposals.

Budget analysts generally work a 40-hour week in an office. While a budget is being prepared, there is usually a lot of highly stressful overtime to meet budget deadlines. Some analysts are required to travel to their organization's regional offices.

TRAINING AND QUALIFICATIONS

Most private firms and governmental agencies require that candidates for budget analyst positions have at least a bachelor's degree in business administration, accounting, finance, economics, or similar field. A growing number of organizations require a master's degree, and large corporations may employ certified public accountants to do budget analysis. Occasionally, experience can compensate for a lack of formal training.

In smaller companies, a competent accounting or payroll clerk may receive on-the-job training and advance to an entry-level budget analyst position. This opportunity for training is especially likely in companies that prefer to promote from within.

The federal government offers extensive on-the-job and classroom training to entry-level analysts and encourages analysts to continue their education throughout their careers. By contrast, in most private firms, entry-level analysts learn the job by working through one complete budget cycle.

Because the bulk of financial analysis done by organizations is automated, a background in computers, particularly financial software packages, which include electronic spreadsheets and data and graphics software, is important. So is the ability to communicate effectively in writing.

EARNINGS

According to a survey conducted by Robert Half International, starting salaries of budget analysts and other financial analysts in small companies ranged from $24,000 to $33,200 in 1997; in large organizations, from $24,000 to $38,700. In small firms, analysts with one to three years experience earned from $28,000 to $43,100; in large firms, $31,000 to $51,300. Senior analysts in small firms earned from $34,500 to $50,000; in large firms, $39,000 to $60,600. Earnings of managers in this field ranged from $40,000 to $65,000 a year in small firms; in large firms, managers earned between $47,000 and $83,800.

PROSPECTS: JOB OUTLOOK

Budget analysts held about 66,000 jobs in 1996. About 30 percent of those were with federal, state, and local governments. The Department of Defense employed 7 out of 10 budget analysts working for the federal government.

Another 10 percent worked for the educational services industry. A large percentage worked in manufacturing, especially in transportation equipment and electrical and electronic machinery industries. Through the year 2006, job growth in this field should match job growth for the overall economy. Because of the growing complexity of business and the increasing specialization of functions within organizations, more attention is being given to planning and financial control. Most openings are expected to be for replacements of budget analysts who leave the workforce or change occupations.

Budget analysts are essential to the financial well-being of an organization. Generally they are not laid off, even when an organization is in a period of slow growth or affected by a sluggish economy.

The work of budget analysts is being automated. The subsequent increase in productivity of budget analysts is occurring side-by-side with the growing complexity of businesses and organizations and the need for better planning and financial control. Budgets will remain an indispensable part of planning and control. Budget analysts will continue to be needed, but competition will be keen. Experience and formal training, especially in finance and accounting, will become increasingly important.

WHERE TO LOOK FOR FURTHER INFORMATION

For information about employment as a budget analyst for the federal government:

U.S. Office of Personnel Management
1900 East Street, NW
Washington, DC 20415

*F*INANCIAL PLANNERS AND MANAGERS

OCCUPATIONAL OVERVIEW

Job Description: Financial planners and managers work for businesses under a variety of titles: treasurer, comptroller, cash manager. They prepare the financial reports the company needs to conduct its business, to oversee its cash flow, and to manage its assets.

Prospects: Employment for financial managers is expected to increase faster than the average through the year 2006.

Qualifications: A bachelor's degree in accounting, finance, or business administration; an emphasis in accounting or finance is generally required. Most commonly, financial managers gain experience by working as professional technical staff in a company's finance department and are then promoted to a managerial position.

Personal Skills: The ability to work independently and a capacity for analyzing detailed numerical information are essential. Good communication skills are important. Experience in using computers is invaluable.

Earnings: In 1996, the median salary for financial managers was $40,700. The top 10 percent earned over $81,100.

THE JOB AND THE WORK ENVIRONMENT

Business means money, and money needs looking after. Every enterprise must monitor its income and expenses, meet its tax and other legal reporting requirements, and manage its assets to its best advantage. To do this, virtually every business, regardless of its product, service, or size, employs one or more financial managers—and for the same reasons, so do educational, cultural, and even most nonprofit organizations.

In small organizations, the *treasurer*, an officer of the company, generally performs all the financial management functions. In larger businesses, the treasurer oversees the financial management departments, which in turn are headed by highly trained and experienced managers. *Comptrollers* direct the preparation of all financial statements and oversee the accounting, auditing, and budgeting departments. *Cash managers* monitor and control the flow of cash receipts and disbursements and other financial instruments to meet the investment needs of the company. *Risk* and *insurance managers* control programs designed to minimize risks and losses the firm may incur in the course of its financial transactions.

Banks, insurance companies, brokerage houses, mutual funds, and some accounting and law firms employ *financial planners*, money managers who are experienced in advising the firm's clients how best to manage their individual financial resources in the face of changing tax laws and the wide variety of investment options. Financial planners meet with individual clients, study their financial condition and future prospects, ascertain their individual financial goals and needs (increased income now, a retirement nest egg for the future, anticipated funds for a child's college education, and so on), and make investment recommendations designed to accomplish the client's desires.

In 1996, about 800,000 financial managers held positions in virtually every industry, although about one-third were employed in the financial services sector (banks, insurance companies, securities dealers, real estate firms, and related industries). In 1994, about 264,000 people called themselves financial planners, but were more interested in selling a financial product (insurance, securities) than in full-range planning. Steps are being taken to regularize certification and to give the public the same confidence in financial planners that it has in accountants and lawyers.

Financial managers usually work a normal 40-hour week out of their offices, although some overtime may be required in a crisis. Financial planners, depending on their clientele, may have to work some evenings and weekends.

TRAINING AND QUALIFICATIONS

After receiving a bachelor's degree in accounting, finance, or business administration, financial managers usually begin their careers in a company's financial department (accounting, budget analysis, credit analysis, loan supervision, securities analysis, and so on). Promotions are based on technical skill, performance, and experience. Some financial managers continue their formal education in order to broaden their skills and knowledge. An M.B.A. is increasingly valued by employers.

Financial planners may seek certification from the International Board of Standards and Practices for Certified Financial Planners (IBCFP), which offers a certified financial planner (CFP) designation. Applicants must have at least a bachelor's degree and three years of financial planning-related experience, and they must successfully complete six three-hour examinations given by the board.

EARNINGS

Salaries for financial planners depend on the size and location of the company; large institutions in cities generally pay more. Annual salaries are often supplemented by bonuses, which vary according to the size of the firm.

According to a 1997 survey by Robert Half International, salaries of assistant controllers range from $41,000 in the smallest firms, to $81,000 in the largest firms; controllers, $47,000 to $138,000; and chief financial officers/treasurers, $62,000 to $307,000.

PROSPECTS: JOB OUTLOOK

Employment of financial managers is expected to increase about as fast as the average for all occupations through the year 2006 because of the need for expertise in the face of increasing domestic and foreign competition, changing tax laws, and greater emphasis on accurate reporting of financial data. Also, the need for skilled financial management will increase due to the demands of global trade and the proliferation of complex financial instruments. The number of qualified applicants will increase, though, so competition is expected to be keen.

WHERE TO LOOK FOR FURTHER INFORMATION

To learn more about careers in financial management:

International Association for
  Financial Planning
5775 Glenridge Drive
Suite B-300
Atlanta, GA 30328-5364

Institute of Certified Financial Planners
308 East Florida Avenue
Suite 708
Denver, CO 80210-2571

To learn more about a career as a financial planner:

College for Financial Planning
4695 South Monaco Street
Denver, CO 80237-3408

Certified Financial Planner Board
  of Standards
1660 Lincoln Street
Suite 3050
Denver, CO 80264

*I*NSURANCE AGENTS AND BROKERS

OCCUPATIONAL OVERVIEW

Job Description: Insurance agents and brokers advise people with respect to their insurance needs. They sell life, property, liability (casualty), and health insurance policies to individuals, businesses, and public institutions to protect them against financial loss.

Prospects: Slow growth is forecasted for the insurance industry through the year 2006. Most jobs will result from replacement needs for those leaving the profession. (Turnover among agents and brokers is high.) The best opportunities will go to those who like selling and develop expertise in a wide range of insurance and financial services.

Qualifications: It is not necessary, although it is desirable, to have a college degree to enter the field. Brokers and agents must, however, be licensed by the state in which they sell. Most states issue licenses to applicants who pass written examinations on insurance fundamentals and the state's insurance laws.

Personal Skills: Good interpersonal skills and a love of selling are essential. Because competition is keen, ambition and a capacity for long hours and hard work are important. Computer literacy is recommended.

Earnings: Agents and brokers earn commissions on sales. The median annual earnings of salaried insurance sales workers was $31,500 in 1996. The top 10 percent earned over $76,900.

THE JOB AND THE WORK ENVIRONMENT

Insurance is a method of protecting individuals and businesses from financial loss due to accident, ill health, or property damage or loss. Insurance doesn't eliminate risk, but it does help to cover the financial loss that often accompanies one of these unpredictable events. Agents and brokers help individuals, families, and businesses select the right types of insurance policies for their needs. They meet with clients to plan their financial security; advise about insurance protection for automobiles, homes, businesses, or other property; maintain records; and help policyholders settle insurance claims.

Life insurance agents, also known as *life underwriters,* write policies that pay survivors (beneficiaries) when the policyholder dies. Policyholders also may buy whole life insurance policies designed to create retirement income or funds for their children's education.

Casualty agents and *brokers* sell policies that protect individuals and businesses from financial loss resulting from automobile accidents, fire or theft, or other property losses. Commercial and industrial casualty insurance also may cover workers' compensation, product liability, or medical malpractice. In addition, many life and casualty agents sell health insurance policies that cover the costs of hospital and medical care or loss of income because of sickness or injury.

Most agents and brokers work for an insurance company, selling that company's policies. About a quarter of them (as of 1986) were self-employed, representing several companies and receiving commissions on each sale. Here, the broker represents the customer and places business with the company he or she feels best serves the client's needs. While most agents specialize in life or casualty insurance, a growing number (called *multiline agents* MDNM) deal in both types of insurance. Moreover, an increasing number of insurance agents and brokers are offering comprehensive financial planning services to their clients. In this case, the agents and brokers are licensed to sell securities (mutual fund shares, stocks, etc.) and have received special training in helping clients put together a whole financial package, including insurance, savings, and investments.

Agents and brokers work in cities and towns throughout the country. Their hours are often irregular and long—often more than 40 hours per week—as they must arrange to meet clients when it is mutually convenient, often in the evening or on weekends. Considerable local travel is required to keep appointments with clients.

TRAINING AND QUALIFICATIONS

Most employers prefer college graduates (any major) but will hire and train high school graduates with proven sales ability or potential. The common denominator for all successful agents is enthusiasm for selling. Many people come to insurance selling from other occupations. New agents receive training at the agencies where they work and often at the insurance company's home office. All agents and brokers must be licensed by the state in which they work, which generally entails passing a written examination in insurance fundamentals.

As the diversity of financial products sold by insurance agents and brokers increases, continuing education leading to further certification is becoming increasingly valuable. Life insurance agents can qualify for the chartered life underwriter (CLU) designation by passing a series of examinations. The National Association of Health Underwriters awards a registered health underwriter (RHU) designation for the successful completion of a series of courses. Those interested can earn a certified financial planning (CFP) or chartered financial consultant (ChFC) designation; both reflect knowledge of tax laws, estate planning, and other related subjects. Casualty insurance agents and brokers can qualify for the chartered property casualty underwriter (CPCU) by passing a series of examinations.

EARNINGS

New agents generally are paid a moderate salary by the insurance company while they learn the trade and build a clientele. The training period is typically 6 months, although some companies subsidize agents at the training-period level for up to 30 months. Then the agent goes on a full commission basis. Income depends on the kind and amount of insurance sold. Salaried insurance agents earned between $15,000 and $77,000 in 1996.

PROSPECTS: JOB OUTLOOK

Insurance agents and brokers held about 409,000 jobs in 1996. Employment opportunities will grow more slowly than the average for all occupations through the year 2006. Sales of insurance are expected to rise significantly in the last decade of the century, but demand for agents and brokers is not expected to keep pace with sales volume because more policies will be sold to groups and by mail, telephone, and e-mail. In addition, as individual agents and brokers increasingly use computers to perform routine work, thereby becoming more efficient, they will be able to handle more cases than previously. Moreover, the trend to multiline agents will cause employment to rise more slowly than sales volume.

Nevertheless, because most companies and individuals consider insurance a necessity, agents and brokers should not be adversely affected by changes in the economic climate. Bright, ambitious people, good at selling and with a broad expertise in a wide range of insurance and financial services, will have the best chance for success.

WHERE TO LOOK FOR FURTHER INFORMATION

To learn more about a career as a life insurance agent or broker:

National Association of Life Underwriters
1922 F Street, NW
Washington, DC 20006

National Association of Professional
  Insurance Agents
400 North Washington Street
Alexandria, VA 22314

Independent Insurance Agents of America
127 South Peyton Street
Alexandria, VA 22314

For information regarding training for life insurance sales careers, contact:

Life Underwriting Training Council
7625 Wisconsin Avenue
Bethesda, MD 20814

*I*NVESTMENT BANKERS

OCCUPATIONAL OVERVIEW

Job Description: Investment banks help their clients—corporations and governments—to increase their financial value by raising capital. This is accomplished through mergers and acquisitions and other strategies (for example, floating a stock or bond issue). Investment bankers manage the affairs of investment banks. They are primarily responsible for developing new business, structuring transactions, and making client presentations.

Prospects: The high level of financial activity of the 1990s is expected to continue into the next century, and investment banking activity is expected to be high. Demand for investment bankers is expected to be strong, but the occupation is sensitive to economic fluctuations, so reliable forecasting is difficult. In any case, the world of investment banking is small; competition for jobs is fierce.

Qualifications: A bachelor's degree in economics, business, or liberal arts is sufficient for an opening financial analyst position in an investment bank. An M.B.A. is essential for becoming an associate. Excellent academic grades are vital, and the M.B.A. should be from a top business school.

Personal Skills: First-rate quantitative and analytical skills are essential, as are excellent communications and interpersonal skills. Leadership qualities are crucial, and familiarity with using computers is highly recommended.

Earnings: Remuneration for investment bankers usually takes the form of salary plus bonus. The starting salary for analysts is about $30,000; for associates the range is from $50,000 to $70,000. Associates with several years experience make over $200,000, and vice-presidents make from $350,000 to $500,000.

THE JOB AND THE WORK ENVIRONMENT

Investment banking is high finance glamour—wheeling and dealing in the Wall Street corridors of power, major buyouts, takeovers that make the front pages. Behind all the hoopla is a hard-working, fiercely competitive world that makes big money, takes big risks, and, on occasion, gets itself into big trouble.

Investment bankers perform a vital service for businesses. A corporation or government that needs to raise funds to accomplish some desired goal (e.g., to build a new factory) engages the services of an investment banker, who analyzes the client's financial situation, recommends the best method of raising the funds, and implements the agreed-on transaction.

Investment bankers act as the liaison between those with funds to invest and those wishing to put money to use. They put together stock or bond deals, underwrite new stock issues (when a company goes public), and offer advice and expertise to companies interested in buying another company, divesting themselves of an unwanted division, or fighting to avoid a hostile takeover.

Increasingly, investment bankers develop new business for their firms. In the past, most corporations established a relationship with an investment bank and used it for all of its transactions. Today, corporations shop around to find the best deal or the most creative method for raising the needed funds. Investment bankers must now persuade their clients that they can outperform their competitors and that they have more experience, more creativity, more flexibility—more of whatever is needed. Thus, in addition to financial savvy across a broad range of transactions, investment bankers need an ability to sell their solutions to top management people.

The stakes are high and the pressure is enormous. Investment bankers work long and hard—60 and more hours per week is routine, and in a crisis, 100 hours is not unusual. Many analysts and associates wear beepers and are on call. Most work out of their offices, but they also travel a great deal to meet with clients.

TRAINING AND QUALIFICATIONS

A bachelor's degree is required to gain an entry-level job as a financial analyst. This position, however, is only temporary, lasting two (or sometimes three) years. The analyst is then expected to go to law or business school, or leave the field. Working as a financial analyst for a top investment bank is an advantage when applying to a top business school. In addition, some big investment houses offer financial assistance for the M.B.A. or law studies of their financial analysts. (It's all but impossible to get an M.B.A. at night when working in investment banking. Evenings are spent on the job.)

An M.B.A. (from a top-rated school for the best opportunities) is essential for an associate position in an investment bank. Associates can expect to put in three to five years before working their way up through assistant vice-president to vice-president. Getting to the top—managing partner or managing director—generally takes 10 or more years.

Most investment banks offer formal training—in some cases one or two months of classroom study; in others, a series of lectures. Most of the learning comes from on-the-job training, working on one or more project teams comprising three to five people: one or more analysts, one or more associates, a vice-president, and a managing director.

EARNINGS

Managing partnerships in some major privately held investment banks earn $1 million or more; in publicly held companies, they earn in the mid- to high six figures. Earnings are a combination of salary and bonus, the latter depending on individual performance and the firm's profitability for that year. Industry reports have it that an investment banker gets to a six-figure income three years after earning an M.B.A.; after five years, income normally rises to around $250,000.

PROSPECTS: JOB OUTLOOK

As long as economic activity keeps at a normal or faster pace, the demand for investment bankers is expected to be strong. When the market goes down or the economy slows, investment banking feels the downturn in fewer opportunities for making deals and transactions. At such times, investment houses may lay off some personnel and reduce bonuses. On the other hand, large-scale business activities, such as mergers, buyouts, takeovers, and stock and bond issues, could come in waves during the late 1990s and early twenty-first century, creating strong demand and high compensation.

New York City is the main arena of the investment banking world, although there are some smaller, highly regarded firms with regional headquarters in San Francisco and Baltimore. That the best opportunities are in New York is not expected to change in the future—but almost everything else may.

WHERE TO LOOK FOR FURTHER INFORMATION

National Association of Securities Dealers
1735 K Street, NW
Washington, DC 20006

Securities Industry Association
120 Broadway
New York, NY 10271

*L*OAN OFFICERS

OCCUPATIONAL OVERVIEW

Job Description: Loan officers are a bank's primary representatives to its customers or clients. The title, however, is something of a misnomer; loan officers perform many other tasks than approve loans. They foster and, where possible, extend the bank-client relationship, offering the client the bank's full range of financial services and managing the account to maximize customer satisfaction.

Prospects: Demand for loan managers is expected to rise faster than the average for all occupations. As businesses and individuals increasingly use debt leverage to manage their finances, the need for qualified loan officers will grow faster than average through the year 2006.

Qualifications: A bachelor's degree is a minimum requirement for admission to most banks' management training programs. Many banks now require loan officers to have an M.B.A.

Personal Skills: Excellent interpersonal and communications skills are essential. Good analytical and quantitative abilities are valuable. Most banks prefer applicants who are familiar with computers and their applications in banking.

Earnings: Compensation for loan officers varies, depending on the lending institution. The range, according to a survey conducted in 1997, was from $30,600 to about $85,000.

THE JOB AND THE WORK ENVIRONMENT

An old saw has it that banks lend money only to those who can prove they don't need it. On the other hand, bank managers stress to their employees that a bank can't become profitable by just saying no. Today, credit is a way of life for consumers and businesses; loan officers have to steer a narrow path between making credit too easy—and losing money through bad loans, and making it too hard—and losing money through failure to make profitable loans.

There were about 209,000 loan officers and counselors employed in 1996. About three out of five were employed by commercial banks, savings institutions, and credit unions. Others were employed in nonbank financial institutions, such as mortgage brokerage firms and personal credit firms.

The primary business of commercial banks is making loans, and the primary customers of commercial banks are business firms—large and small. Loan officers act as the bank's representatives to these clients as well as to individual clients, and in that capacity, do a lot more than just lend money. They are responsible for establishing working relationships with their clients, learning about their businesses and financial needs, and selling them other banking services, such as cash management, payroll maintenance, and sophisticated trading activities. All this is in addition to their primary charge of researching the creditworthiness of clients seeking loans. In acknowledgment of their many roles, banks often use titles other than loan officer for this position, for example, relationship manager, account officer, and calling officer.

Because they are involved in so many facets of their clients' financial activities, loan officers must be knowledgeable about their banks' services. They frequently work with specialty area staff within their bank to prepare selling presentations to clients. Additionally, they work with loan and credit clerks and credit checkers, who provide the background research necessary for issuing credit. Loan and credit clerks work primarily in banks, either in processing loans or in closing loans.

Lending groups in banks often are organized to service one particular type of client, for instance, foreign governments, foreign corporations, domestic municipalities, or domestic corporations. The groups may be subdivided again, for example, by geographic region or industry.

Loan officers often specialize early in their careers in a particular area—corporate banking, real estate lending, international banking, or institutional banking. Each specialty requires the officer to learn not only about his or her bank's services in the area, but also to become familiar with the problems and opportunities the area presents. Real estate specialists, for instance, must be familiar with zoning laws, appraisal techniques, nationwide trends in development, and building methods and materials.

As commercial banking becomes more competitive, loan officers must be adept at selling and at personal relations. They must be vigilant for new business and work to generate new clients and promote new business from old clients. For the most part, loan officers work a normal workweek, but often they attend meetings with clients in the evenings or on weekends.

TRAINING AND QUALIFICATIONS

Bank management trainee programs generally require applicants to have at least a bachelor's degree. A business major is helpful, but a liberal arts major is sufficient if combined with courses in accounting, mathematics, and economics. M.B.A.'s often go into special training programs that move faster and cover more. Increasingly, the management programs emphasize more areas than the traditional ones of accounting and other skills necessary for credit analysis, such as capital markets activity. Major commercial banks usually have extensive, highly structured training programs.

More generally, loan officers need a comprehensive background in finance that includes accounting, principles of economics, corporate finance, and credit analysis. Perhaps most important is an ability for quantitative analysis. Most of the crucial decisions that loan officers must make require mixing careful numerical analysis with good judgment and a sense of how the economy is going.

EARNINGS

According to a salary survey taken by Robert Half International, residential real estate mortgage loan officers earned between $30,600 and $45,000 in 1997; commercial real estate mortgage loan officers, between $45,100 and $73,000; consumer loan officers, between $28,900 and $48,000; and commercial lenders, between $37,400 and $85,000. Loan officers who are on commission generally earn more than those who are salaried only.

PROSPECTS: JOB OUTLOOK

Expectations are that the demand for loan officers will grow faster than average for all occupations through the year 2006. Prospects for loan and credit clerks also seem exceptionally good. This is due to an increase in applications for consumer, commercial, and mortgage loans as the economy and population grow. Increases in the variety and complexity of loans, and the importance of loan officers to the success of banks and other lending institutions also should assure employment growth.

WHERE TO LOOK FOR FURTHER INFORMATION

To learn more about careers in banking:

American Bankers Association
Bank Personnel Division
1120 Connecticut Avenue, NW
Washington, DC 20036

Bank Administration Institute
1 North Franklin Street
Floor 10
Chicago, IL 60606-3421

National Bankers Association
1513 P Street, NW
Washington, DC 20005-1909

MANAGEMENT CONSULTANTS

OCCUPATIONAL OVERVIEW

Job Description: Management consulting is a service performed for a fee by independent, objective business specialists to help client managers define and achieve their goals. Consultants analyze the problems and opportunities associated with key management functions with an eye to proposing and then implementing solutions.

Prospects: Job opportunities are expected to grow faster than the average for all occupations through the year 2006. Government and private businesses are increasingly turning to outside professional expertise to help them improve organizational performance.

Qualifications: Formal educational requirements for entry-level jobs as management consultants are somewhat vague because of the diversity of their work. A bachelor's degree in business or a business-related subject with several years of experience, or an M.B.A. in business or public administration, or some other advanced degree in a business or technical area represents a minimum requirement.

Personal Skills: Excellent communication and interpersonal skills are essential, as are analytical skills and the ability to manage a variety of projects.

Earnings: Earnings of management consultants vary widely. In 1996, those who were full-time wage and salary workers had median annual earnings of about $39,500. The top 10 percent earned more than $81,500.

THE JOB AND THE WORK ENVIRONMENT

The increasing complexity of society has created a strong demand for specialized expertise and state-of-the-art knowledge in a number of organizational areas. Businesses and government often need to find and employ experts to help them improve performance. Although the range of concerns requiring this kind of outside help is wide, some of the most prominent areas are business management, computer and information sciences, marketing and distribution, and engineering.

Despite the many different kinds of problems that management consultants are engaged to help solve, they ordinarily apply a four-step procedure:

1. _Research:_ Defining the purpose and scope of the engagement, determining the correct approach, deciding on the desired end results, and estimating the time required for fact finding.
2. _Analysis:_ Defining the problems in precise terms, determining the cause of the problem, determining objectives to be achieved, and developing alternative solutions.
3. _Solution:_ Arriving at a specific, detailed plan that the client agrees will answer its needs.
4. _Implementation:_ Implementing the plan or providing guidance to those who will carry out the plan.

Management consulting firms range in size from solo practitioners to large, international firms with hundreds of employees. Services usually are provided on a contract basis, commonly covering a specific project. The most important task of the client and the consultant is ensuring a match-up between the consultant's areas of expertise and the problem at hand. Large firms, with many diverse talents from which to draw, are particularly well suited to this task. Solo practitioners must be especially careful to accept only assignments for which they have the requisite knowledge and experience.

Consultants work in their own offices and also at clients' places of operation, which may entail travel. They normally work at least a 40-hour week, but to meet deadlines, may work extra hours or on weekends. Achieving the required results in the time allotted often makes the work stressful.

TRAINING AND QUALIFICATIONS

A bachelor's degree in a business-related field is the minimum requirement. Important areas of study include computer science, engineering, accounting, management, marketing, and distribution. In recent years, more and more grads with an M.B.A. have chosen to begin their careers in consulting.

Those entering the field directly from school usually join a consulting firm, where they are likely to participate in a formal training program and then work as a member of a consulting team. After several years' experience, they assume more responsible positions—team leader, for instance, or perhaps heading a project. Others go into the consulting business after working successfully for a number of years in a specific occupation or industry. Thus, consulting can be chosen as a career from the start or transferred into after acquiring business or technical experience.

EARNINGS

Salaries for management analysts and consultants vary widely by experience, education, and employer. In 1996, according to the Association of Management Consulting Firms, earnings—including bonuses and/or profit sharing—for research associates in member firms averaged $32,400; for entry-level consultants, $35,200; for management consultants, $50,500; for senior consultants, $74,300; for junior partners, $91,100; and for senior partners, $167,100. The average annual salary for management consultants in the federal government in supervisory, nonsupervisory, and managerial positions was $55,240 in 1997.

PROSPECTS: JOB OUTLOOK

Job opportunities for management consultants are expected to grow faster than the average of other occupations through the year 2006. The demand is due to increasing reliance of industry and government on outside expertise to improve the performance of their organizations. The strongest demand will be in the areas of information systems, human resources and benefits, and compensation and health care.

Foreign competition has caused many American companies to examine their operations more closely. Inefficient businesses or those with underutilized resources risk a loss of market share or lower-than-optimum profits. Thus, companies are turning increasingly to management consultants to address specific problems in reducing costs, streamlining operations, and organizing to take advantage of emerging technologies or business opportunities. A tough, competitive business climate is good for consultants.

The best opportunities are for those with graduate degrees and technical or industry experience. Those who wish to be self-employed additionally need good organizational and marketing skills. The competition for clients is keen; finding the right ones requires skill and perseverance.

WHERE TO LOOK FOR FURTHER INFORMATION

To learn more about careers in management consulting:

ACME, Association of Management
  Consulting Firms
521 Fifth Avenue
35th Floor
New York, NY 10175-3598

Institute of Management Consultants
521 Fifth Avenue
35th Floor
New York, NY 10175-3598

SECURITIES ANALYSTS

OCCUPATIONAL OVERVIEW

Job Description: Securities analysts research and evaluate companies to advise clients on the sale or purchase of securities. A small number of analysts also research and advise on the sale or purchase of bonds. Analysts work for banks, brokerage firms, mutual funds, and insurance companies.

Prospects: Job prospects for securities analysts are tied directly to the stock market. Generally, bull markets increase hirings; bear markets lead to layoffs. A confident projection of the job outlook for securities analysts through the year 2006 is impossible to make. At the end of the 1990s, there was an increase in hiring, reflecting growth in the stock market.

Qualifications: The usual requirement for securities analysts is an M.B.A. The field also is open to one with a bachelor's degree and experience in the financial services industry or statistical research, or in the industry one would specialize as an analyst. Securities analysts also can be chartered.

Personal Skills: Analysts must have a facility for numbers and a good memory. They must have analytical minds, be highly organized, and be able to do thorough and sustained research on their own initiative. They need to be able to inspire confidence in their judgment and must have excellent communication skills, especially writing ability.

Earnings: Recent starting salaries for securities analysts with a bachelor's degree ranged from $15,000 to $30,000 a year. Those with an M.B.A. started at between $30,000 and $50,000 a year. Securities analysts also earn bonuses. Top performers earn in the high six figures, and some have seven-figure earnings.

THE JOB AND THE WORK ENVIRONMENT

Securities analysts advise their clients or employers on which stocks or bonds to buy and sell. Most securities analysts are concerned with stocks. They may work on the sell side, where the objective is to find profitable securities and convince brokers and traders to sell them, or on the buy side, working for businesses that purchase securities. The larger and more lucrative business is on the sell side.

Most securities analysts focus on a particular industry and the companies within it to find good investment opportunities. They study and analyze companies to determine if there is a difference between their real worth and the price of their stock. If a company's real value is undervalued by the stock market, its stock offers a potential opportunity to investors. Analysts also look for indications of expansion and growth in a company's business. Combining these and other types of information, they project the company's future earnings.

Securities analysts learn as much as they can about a company's history, products, and services from books and trade publications, reference services like *Standard and Poor's Outlook,* and financial reports. Based on preliminary research, the analyst arrives at a short list of companies in a particular industry and researches them more thoroughly.

Once an analyst decides that a particular company may be a promising investment opportunity, he or she contacts top management at the company, meets with them, and gathers more detailed information. The analyst then writes a report on the company.

Writing reports is a major part of an analyst's work. The reports must be lucid, concise, and persuasive. The analyst uses marketing skills to sell his or her services to traders, brokers, and investors by alerting them to money-making opportunities and convincing them to buy or sell.

A securities analyst's success depends on performance and reputation. Analysts judge whether a stock should be bought, sold, or held. If their judgments are consistently correct, that is, profitable, they succeed. Their success is measured each year by *Institutional Investor,* which publishes the names of analysts with the more outstanding performance records. A strong showing in the polls secures an analyst's reputation.

Analysts put in long hours, and their work includes a great deal of traveling—visiting companies and attending conferences, conventions, and trade shows. The work is demanding and absorbing, requiring constant attention. The market is mercurial, and analysts must be prepared to make quick decisions when the market takes a sudden and unexpected turn.

TRAINING AND QUALIFICATIONS

The usual prerequisite for securities analysts is an M.B.A., but the educational backgrounds of analysts vary. A bachelor's degree in a subject related to the industry in which an analyst specializes is helpful. Some analysts have prior experience in the financial service industry or statistical research or in the industry on which they focus their research. Many start in business with publications like *Moody's Investor Service, Dun & Bradstreet, Standard and Poor's Corp.,* or *Value Line, Inc.* Analysts without an M.B.A. are encouraged to earn one. They may also continue their studies in programs sponsored by the Financial Analysts' Federation, leading to designation as a chartered financial analyst (CFA). Many mutual funds, investment counseling firms, and bank trust departments require that their analysts earn a CFA, and it is especially valuable to analysts who lack the M.B.A. It takes three years to earn the charter, including the successful completion of three difficult examinations, in essay form, that require extensive reading and concentrated study.

EARNINGS

Earnings depend on performance and the market. Recent starting salaries for analysts with a bachelor's degree often begin at $30,000 a year; with an M.B.A., starting salaries are as high as $50,000. These salaries represent earnings independent of bonuses.

A survey conducted by Frank Pedone Associates of Cliffside Park, New Jersey, shows that analysts with the highest earnings are in energy, market timing, and portfolio strategy.

Earnings also are affected by analysts' showing in the *Institutional Investor* polls. It is believed that certain firms have offered top performers in the polls salaries of up to $500,000 a year.

PROSPECTS: JOB OUTLOOK

Because job prospects for securities analysts are tied to the stock market, it is not possible to accurately forecast job prospects in the field through the year 2006. However, because of recent economic growth, rising personal income, and greater inherited wealth, there are more funds available for investment, and employment for security analysts might be expected to grow faster than average for all occupations.

WHERE TO LOOK FOR FURTHER INFORMATION

Many of the firms that hire securities analysts are listed in the *Money Market Directory.* The names of leading analysts are published in each October issue of *Institutional Investor,* along with other articles that may provide additional information and insight into the field. The personnel departments of brokerage firms, bank trust departments, mutual funds, insurance companies, and investment counseling firms can provide information on select firms' hiring policies and the qualifications and backgrounds they find desirable.

For more information about chartered financial analyst programs:

Institute of Chartered Financial Analysts
5 Boar's Head Lane
P.O. Box 3668
Charlottesville, VA 22903

Financial Analysts' Federation
1633 Broadway
16th floor
New York, NY 10019

*S*ECURITIES SALES REPRESENTATIVES (STOCKBROKERS)

OCCUPATIONAL OVERVIEW

Job Description: Securities sales representatives (also called *registered representatives, account executives,* or *brokers*) work for full-service brokerage houses. Their primary duty is to assist the firm's clients in buying or selling stocks, bonds, shares in mutual funds, and other financial products. In effect, they do much more; however, they are salespeople as well, earning a commission on every transaction. They offer advice to their clients and take an active role in suggesting investment strategies—what and when to buy and sell—and recommending other investments.

Prospects: Demand for brokers is expected to rise faster than the average for all occupations through the year 2006, assuming steady growth in the economy.

Qualifications: Brokers must meet state licensing requirements that generally entail passing an examination and, in some cases, posting a personal bond. They must register as representatives of their firm according to regulations of the securities exchanges where they do business or the National Association of Securities Dealers (NASD). Beginners must pass the General Securities Registered Representative's (Series 7) Examination.

Personal Skills: Excellent sales skills and a capacity for long hours and hard work are essential, as is the ability to handle pressure, competition, and rejection. Skill in the use of computers is recommended since so much of the securities industry is automated.

Earnings: In 1996, median annual earnings of securities and financial service sales representatives was $38,800; the top 10 percent earned more than $98,400.

THE JOB AND THE WORK ENVIRONMENT

The business of securities is selling. Stockbrokers (retail and institutional) provide the means for investors to buy or sell securities. They relay the order through their firm's offices to the floor of a securities exchange (the New York Stock Exchange, for instance). If the security is not traded on an exchange, brokers send the order to their firm's trading department, where it is traded directly with a dealer in an over-the-counter market. Brokers also advise their clients on investments, sometimes giving financial counseling on assembling a portfolio of investments—securities, life insurance, mutual funds, and others.

Brokers are not simply order takers, however. They actively seek investors and regularly confer with their clients about suggested investments. (*Discount brokers* do not give advice to their clients but act only as transaction agents, executing orders for their customers. They are used primarily by investors who do not seek advice.)

Because most stockbrokers are paid by commission, their main activity is drumming up business. New brokers are expected to build their own client base with minimal direct assistance from their firm, so most of their day (and evening, too) is spent *prospecting*—identifying and calling on potential investors to turn them into customers. The drive to find new clients and to sell investing ideas to existing ones is relentless, and brokers must face rejection over and over during the course of a day. Once a broker has established a "book" of satisfied clients, much new business will be generated by referrals. At that point, the broker can spend more time researching investment ideas, and discussing them with clients, and less time on prospecting. As they progress, brokers often specialize, concentrating on stocks, bonds, mutual fund shares, government bills, stock options, or commodity futures.

Although beginners usually start by servicing individual investors, they may be able in time to build a clientele of large institutional accounts (banks, pension funds, and the like) and make large commissions.

Brokers usually work from a desk with a telephone. They arrive to work early, well before trading hours (9:30 A.M.–4:00 P.M.), and leave later, usually around 5:00 P.M. or 6:00 P.M. Often, they plan client meetings or prospecting calls for the evening. Success in this fiercely competitive business requires long days and weeks.

TRAINING AND QUALIFICATIONS

Most brokerage firms prefer but do not require a college degree (any major will do, but concentration in finance or business-related topics is helpful). Many brokers come from other fields, especially those based on commission selling, such as real estate or insurance (the majority of new hires are between 25 and 35 years old).

Most employers provide on-the-job training, including preparation for the state licensing examination and the exam for registered representatives. Some large firms require their brokers to pass the Uniform Securities Agents State Law Examination, so they can do business nationwide. Training normally lasts a few months, but in the larger firms, it can go on for two years, with classroom instruction on securities analysis, public speaking, and the finer points of selling.

EARNINGS

In 1996, median annual salaries of securities and financial services sales representatives were $38,800; the middle 50 percent earned between $24,300 and $73,500. Ten percent earned more than $98,400. New hires begin on salary and may remain on that basis for up to a year, and then go on to straight commission. After that, income is purely a function of successful selling; there is no cap. A broker may be expected to bring in at least $100,000 in commissions a year for the firm, of which he or she may keep 25 or 30 percent. (Larger firms may be looking for at least $250,000 per year.) At $1 million in annual commissions, the broker may keep 45 percent.

PROSPECTS: JOB OUTLOOK

Securities and financial services sales representatives held 263,000 jobs in 1996; securities sales representatives accounted for 8 out of 10 jobs. Although demand for stockbrokers is expected to be strong through the year 2006, the job market is determined by the state of the economy. If an economic downturn causes activity in the securities markets to slacken, jobs may be tight and many brokers may be let go. Even in good times, competition for training slots in brokerage houses is fierce. The first and possibly most difficult selling job a prospective broker has to face is landing a place in the training program of a good firm. Mature individuals with successful experience and a flair for selling stand the best chance. Inexperienced would-be brokers find the best opportunities in smaller houses.

Deregulation has enabled brokerage firms to sell certificates of deposit, offer checking and deposit services through cash management accounts, and sell insurance products, such as annuities; these and other factors point to an expanding market for stockbrokers.

WHERE TO LOOK FOR FURTHER INFORMATION

To learn more about careers as securities sales representative:

Securities Industry Association
120 Broadway
35th Floor
New York, NY 10271-3599

SALES AND MARKETING

ADVERTISING MANAGERS AND ACCOUNT EXECUTIVES

OCCUPATIONAL OVERVIEW

Job Description: Advertising managers work in or with the marketing departments of businesses to supervise the creation of ad campaigns designed to carry out the firm's marketing strategy. *Account executives* work in advertising agencies. Their prime responsibility is to ensure the agency provides the best possible service to the client.

Prospects: Employment of advertising managers is expected to increase faster than the average for all occupations through the year 2006. Advertising agencies expect an abundance of applicants for entry-level positions and anticipate the demand for experienced account execs with track records will remain strong.

Qualifications: Jobs in the advertising field require at least a bachelor's degree, preferably in marketing, business administration, or liberal arts. Some larger agencies and corporations look for an M.B.A. for those in senior positions. Experience in marketing, sales, or advertising is essential for either advertising managers or account executives.

Personal Skills: Excellent communication and interpersonal skills are essential. Creativity, enthusiasm, and good business sense are invaluable, as is the ability to work under pressure.

Earnings: Starting salaries for advertising majors graduating in 1997 averaged about $27,000. The median annual salary of advertising managers in 1996 was $46,000. The top 10 percent earned $97,000 or more.

THE JOB AND THE WORK ENVIRONMENT

The corporate *advertising manager* works closely with the company's marketing department to develop advertising designed to appeal to consumers. In smaller firms, ad managers may run a one-person shop that creates the advertising material and places it in the proper media (newspapers, magazines, radio, and television), as the marketing strategy requires. In larger firms, ad managers may oversee a staff of copywriters, artists, production people, media buyers, and research workers to perform the same function. There, the advertising manager is responsible for monitoring a large budget, coordinating all the activities to meet schedules and deadlines, choosing the appropriate media, and managing the entire advertising department.

Many large corporations with extensive product lines use agencies to create the advertisements and to choose the media mix in which the ads will appear. In this case, the corporate ad manager serves as the company's liaison with the agency and represents the company in its agency dealings. Depending on the company, the ad manager may be responsible for choosing the agency, providing the marketing information the agency needs, deciding how the advertising budget will be spent, and approving the final advertising campaign the agency develops. Usually, top management makes the ultimate decisions on the campaign and budget.

Corporate ad managers are expected to produce tangible results, as manifested in increased sales volume of the company's products or services. The work is high pressure: deadlines are always tight, budgets inadequate, new ideas hard to come by, and competition fierce. Long and irregular hours are often the norm.

Account executives work in ad agencies deploying and coordinating the agency's forces (copywriters, artists, market researchers, and media planners) to give the client company the best advertising for its money. They spend much of their time with clients' advertising managers, helping them set goals and budgets consonant with the company's marketing strategy and translating that strategy into an effective advertising campaign by utilizing the agency's creative, marketing, and media people to its best advantage.

Pressure on account executives can be extreme. Hours are routinely long and irregular, involving meetings with clients, coordinating the work of all the agency's resources, going on location to oversee production of a television or radio ad, and bearing the responsibility of selling the campaign to the client and then seeing that it is brought in on time and on budget. An agency that loses a large account may lay off everyone who worked on that account, including the account executive. Advertising agencies are not for the fainthearted.

TRAINING AND QUALIFICATIONS

Advertising managers and account executives get where they are by proving themselves in the marketplace and amassing good track records. Those seeking an entry-level job in advertising need at least a bachelor's degree. Because ad managers and account executives perform such similar jobs, they have similar ways of gaining experience. Either may begin in one of the advertising specialties—copywriting, art, media planning, research—in a corporate advertising department or at an agency to gain experience in many different facets of advertising. Some agencies offer training programs for account managers, a good entry-level slot for either job candidate.

Persons interested in becoming advertising managers and account executives should be mature, creative, highly motivated, resistant to stress, and flexible, yet decisive. The ability to communicate persuasively—both orally and in writing—with other managers, staff, and the public is vital.

Corporate ad managers learn all about their companies' business, product lines, markets, and competition. Account executives must have the same kind of knowledge about each client. Knowledge of advertising techniques and strategies is not sufficient for success in either position. That is why experience in advertising in the particular industry or market is so important for obtaining either position.

EARNINGS

Surveys show that salary levels vary substantially depending on the level of managerial responsibility, length of service, education, and the employer's size, location, and industry. According to a 1996 survey by *Advertising Age Magazine,* the average annual salary of a vice-president brand manager was $79,000; vice-president product manager, $105,000; vice-president of advertising, $130,000; and vice-president of marketing, $133,000. The median salary of advertising managers in 1996 was $46,000.

PROSPECTS: JOB OUTLOOK

Advertising is closely tied to economic conditions. When times are tough and businesses have low sales or are retrenching, they often slash advertising budgets and lay off personnel. There is great mobility in the advertising industry; advertising managers move easily from one company to another and into and out of advertising agencies. The expectation is that with the increasing competitive markets expected in the 1990s and the high turnover rate in the industry, jobs will be available for experienced ad managers, but competition for the best jobs will be keen. Increasing domestic and global competition in products and services offered to consumers should require greater marketing efforts.

The world of ad agencies is far more hectic. The longevity of agencies is unpredictable. One agency might let go an account management team with the loss of an account, but another agency might hire many new employees because it has landed an account. Experienced account executives are expected to have good opportunities open to them into the next century with advertising agencies as corporate ad managers, owners, or partners in their own agency.

Some industries are expected to have a higher-than-average demand for advertising: computer and data-processing services, radio and television, and travel and entertainment. Many companies that eliminated in-house advertising departments during downsizing in recent years are now relying on advertising firms to provide that service. The education services industry, hospitals, and some manufacturing industries are projected to have only average growth in advertising needs.

WHERE TO LOOK FOR FURTHER INFORMATION

To learn more about careers in advertising:

American Association of
 Advertising Agencies
405 Lexington Avenue
18th Floor
New York, NY 10074-1801

American Advertising Federation
1101 Vermont Avenue, NW
Suite 500
Washington, DC 20005

Association of National Advertisers
155 East 44th Street
New York, NY 10017

American Marketing Association
250 South Wacker Drive
Chicago, IL 60606

PUBLIC RELATIONS SPECIALISTS

OCCUPATIONAL OVERVIEW

Job Description: Public relations specialists seek to project a favorable public image for their clients or employers. They explain programs or policies, articulate goals, and seek to create a climate of opinion favorable to the interests they represent. Public relations workers are employed by government, corporations, industries, and utilities, as well as by hospitals, universities, and charities.

Prospects: Opportunities in public relations are growing as fast as the prevailing norm and are expected to continue to do so through the year 2006.

Qualifications: A college degree combined with work experience is the best preparation for a career in public relations. A major in an area related to a particular firm's business also can be helpful.

Personal Skills: Public relations specialists must have a superior ability to express their thoughts clearly. Creativity and initiative are important in this field.

Earnings: The National Association of Colleges and Employers reported that starting salaries for marketing majors graduating in 1997 averaged from $27,000 to about $29,000. According to a 1996 survey by the Public Relations Society of America, senior public relations managers earned an average of $76,790.

THE JOB AND THE WORK ENVIRONMENT

Public relations specialists gather information about their clients and present it in a novel and persuasive way. They may prepare statements on a client's accomplishments and activities, intended as copy for the news media to publish as is or adapt. They may work on a political campaign or in fund raising, help to represent special interest groups, or develop programs for community or consumer relations. As they acquire experience, many public relations workers specialize, concentrating in areas like investor relations, issues management, corporate communications, or special events.

Jobs in public relations generally are found in counseling firms, the public relations divisions of industries and organizations, and government. Some of the more prominent organizations that employ sizable public relations staffs are public utilities, manufacturing and industrial concerns, banks and insurance companies, special interest lobbies, hospitals, religious organizations, airlines, the branches of the armed forces, vacation resorts, and colleges and universities—all of them hoping that these staffs will present them in a favorable light. Some public relations staffs may be as large as 200 individuals; most are much smaller. The smaller the firm is, the more likely it is that a number of tasks will be combined.

Most people on public relations staffs work a 35 to 40-hour week, but work must often be done against a deadline, with workers on call at all hours. For some assignments, frequent travel may also be necessary. Most public relations work is concentrated in large cities, where press services are available and businesses and associations have their headquarters (for example, New York, Los Angeles, Chicago, and Washington, DC).

TRAINING AND QUALIFICATIONS

The best preparation for a career in public relations is a combination of a college education and work experience. Most workers have earned a degree in communications, journalism, or public relations, although some firms seek those who have majored in a discipline related to their field. Most public relations workers first gain work experience in another field.

In 1996, over 200 colleges and 100 graduate schools offered programs and degrees in public relations. About 300 colleges offered at least one course in the subject. A comprehensive program is likely to include courses in public relations management and administration, public relations theory and techniques, and specialties that concentrate on public relations in government or particular industries. Related areas—advertising, business administration, psychology, sociology, and journalism—also are useful, as are familiarity with word processing and other computer applications. Graduates with a B.A. are eligible for staff positions; those with advanced degrees in public relations are eligible for managerial or administrative positions.

A great deal of the work is learned on the job. Whether their firm has a formal training program or they learn the ropes under the guidance of experienced staff members, entry-level staffers are likely to start out in research. They graduate to writing press releases, drafting speeches, and taking on more important writing assignments. Eventually, they may take part in creating and planning entire campaigns.

Workers who have at least five years' experience and have passed a six-hour examination are accredited by the Public Relations Society of America.

EARNINGS

Surveys show that salary levels vary substantially depending on the level of managerial experience, length of service, education, and the employer's size, location, and industry. For example, manufacturing firms generally pay public relations managers more than nonmanufacturing firms.

The median salary of public relations managers and marketing and advertising managers was $46,000 in 1996. The top 10 percent earned $97,000 or more. According to a 1996 survey by the Public Relations Society of America, senior public managers earned an average of $76,790. Entry-level jobs for marketing majors graduating in 1997 paid, on average, from about $27,000 to $29,000, depending on the industry.

PROSPECTS: JOB OUTLOOK

Public relations specialists held about 107,000 jobs in 1996. Employment in public relations is expected to increase about as fast as the average for all occupations through the year 2006. Recognition of the need for good public relations in an increasingly competitive business environment should spur demand for public relations specialists in organizations of all sizes; however, corporate restructuring and downsizing could limit employment growth. Additionally, most job openings will be for replacements, since public relations work provides good preparation for management positions in other fields.

WHERE TO LOOK FOR FURTHER INFORMATION

For information on schools and their programs in public relations, contact:

Public Relations Society of America, Inc.
33 Irving Place
New York, NY 10003-2376

PR Reporter
P.O. Box 600
Exeter, NH 03833

*P*URCHASING AGENTS AND MANAGERS

OCCUPATIONAL OVERVIEW

Job Description: Purchasing agents and managers buy the goods, materials, supplies, and services organizations in industry or government need.

Prospects: Because of increasing use of computers and the growing reliance on a small number of suppliers (with a gain in efficiency), the increase in employment of purchasing agents and managers is likely to be slower than the average for jobs in the economy as a whole.

Qualifications: Most sizable organizations require at least a bachelor's degree and prefer a master's degree in business administration or management. Continuing education is vital for advancement. Various forms of certification are available.

Personal Skills: Purchasing agents must have excellent analytical ability, a good memory for details, and the ability to work alone and as part of a team.

Earnings: In 1996, the median annual salary for purchasing agents and buyers was $33,200; the middle 50 percent earned between $23,300 and $45,900. The top 10 percent earned more than $63,000. Salaries for agents and contract specialists in the federal government are lower than those of their counterparts in the private sector.

THE JOB AND THE WORK ENVIRONMENT

In 1996, purchasing agents and managers held about 210,000 jobs.

Purchasing agents and managers, or industrial buyers, buy the goods, materials, supplies, and services required by industry and government. Their responsibility includes ensuring the suitability of their purchases. In industry and government, they buy raw materials and finished products, such as machinery, components, vehicles, and furniture; in the media, they buy advertising time and space.

Purchasing agents act under one of three conditions: (1) when stock reaches a reorder point (determined ahead of time), (2) when a department in the organization places a requisition, or (3) when market conditions simply favor a purchase. Computer use is integral to the purchasing agent's job in keeping up with price and product listings, the state of inventory, and suppliers' bids and performance records; they are also used to write purchase orders and process orders.

In the private sector, there has been a trend to sole-source contracting (a single supplier provides a variety of goods and services). In the federal government, the opposite is the case: Rather than seeking one supplier for a wide range of goods and services, agents encourage a large number of suppliers to be competitive for contracts.

In large organizations, *purchasing agents* are responsible for routine assignments, specializing in a commodity or a group of related commodities, such as steel or petroleum products. *Purchasing managers* supervise several purchasing agents and make more complex purchases. In the federal government, *purchasing agents* use simplified methods to make purchases under $25,000. Using sealed bids and negotiation, *contract specialists* handle more expensive contracts. In smaller organizations, there may be only a single purchasing agent with full purchasing responsibility, although agents generally purchase only a narrow range of goods or services.

In some organizations, purchasing is centralized or joint arrangements are made with other organizations. Other organizations may use a systems contractor—a management consultant firm that handles purchasing.

Purchasing agents and managers generally work a 5-day, 40-hour week, but overtime may be required (e.g., when supplies run short). Most work is done in an office, with some travel to suppliers, continuing education seminars, and trade shows.

TRAINING AND QUALIFICATIONS

Generally, a bachelor's degree is the minimum requirement in larger organizations in private industry; a master's degree in business administration or management is preferred. Continuing education, generally through professional seminars, is a necessity for advancement and for keeping up with changes in the field.

Smaller organizations may hire a beginner with an associate's degree and vocational training, and they may promote purchasing clerks and technicians. However, no matter how small the organization, an agent will not advance to a management position without a degree and continuing education.

The federal government requires either a college degree or three years of business experience.

Depending on the organization, a purchasing agent may need technical expertise; for example, in engineering or a natural science. And agents in the private and public sectors alike must be familiar with computers.

Beginners generally work under the supervision of experienced buyers, learning about commodities, pricing, suppliers, and negotiating techniques. At first, they purchase only standard and catalog goods and services, but with experience and promotion they are given responsibility for purchasing custom-made items.

All purchasing agents must have a good memory for details, an analytical mind, and be able to make expensive decisions based on a great deal of technical data. Sometimes agents work alone and unsupervised; when complex negotiations must be made, an agent may work with lawyers, engineers, scientists, and others.

Computers play a major role in the job of purchasers; they handle most of the routine tasks, enabling purchasing professionals to concentrate on the analytical aspects of the job.

In the private sector, the National Association of Purchasing Management confers the title *certified purchasing manager* on those who have passed four examinations and meet educational and experience requirements. The National Institute of Governmental Purchasing confers the title *professional public buyer* on those in state and local government who have passed a two-part written examination and meet education and experience requirements. Those who meet stricter requirements and pass a three-part written examination receive the designation *certified public purchasing officer.*

Specialists in the contractual aspects of purchasing (generally those in the federal government) can receive either the designation *certified associate contract manager* or *certified professional contract manager,* conferred by the National Contract Management Association.

EARNINGS

Median earnings of purchasers and buyers were $33,200 in 1996. The middle 50 percent earned between $23,300 and $45,900. The top 10 percent earned more than $63,600. The average annual salaries for purchasing agents in the federal government in 1995 were about $28,700. Merchandise managers and purchasing managers generally earned more than buyers or agents. As a general rule, those with the most education in their field have the highest incomes.

PROSPECTS: JOB OUTLOOK

Employment growth for purchasing agents and managers may be somewhat slower than the average for the economy as a whole through the year 2006. The use of computers and sole-source contracting has increased the efficiency of agents. Because of cost consciousness in the private and public sectors, though, there may be increased employment of buyers in hospitals, schools, state and local governments, and service organizations.

Because experienced purchasing agents often transfer to sales or management positions, most openings will arise from the need for replacements.

WHERE TO LOOK FOR FURTHER INFORMATION

For information about careers and certification in purchasing:

National Association of Purchasing
  Management, Inc.
2055 East Centennial Circle
P.O. Box 22160
Tempe, AZ 85282

American Purchasing Society
30 West Downer Place
Aurora, IL 60506

National Institute of Governmental
  Purchasing
11800 Sunrise Valley Drive
Suite 1050
Reston, VA 22091

REAL ESTATE AGENTS AND BROKERS

OCCUPATIONAL OVERVIEW

Job Description: *Real estate brokers* are independent businesspeople who sell real estate owned by others and also rent and manage properties, make appraisals, and develop building projects. *Real estate agents* are independent sales agents who generally provide their services to a licensed broker on a contract basis.

Prospects: Growth in employment is expected to be slower than the average for all occupations through the year 2006. While jobs are relatively easy to obtain, the competition in the real estate market is fierce. Turnover is very high.

Qualifications: All brokers and agents must be licensed by the state in which they practice. To qualify for a license, candidates must be at least 18 years old, have graduated high school, and pass a written examination. Most states also require a specified amount of formal training in real estate.

Personal Skills: Agents and brokers must be personable, honest, and enthusiastic. Their main function is to deal with and motivate people. A good memory (for names and faces and for data like taxes and zoning regulations) is very important.

Earnings: Real estate agents derive their income from commissions on sales. In 1996, the median income of brokers and agents working full time was about $31,500. Figures vary widely, depending on types of property sold. Those with an M.B.A. or a B.A. in business administration and work for real estate developers, operators, or consulting firms earn starting salaries from the mid-twenties to $50,000 or more.

THE JOB AND THE WORK ENVIRONMENT

Buying a house is an American dream; agents and brokers are there to prevent it from becoming a nightmare. Buying, selling, leasing, or renting a residential property often is complex, and people are wise to turn to professionals to help them negotiate the deal.

The professionals—brokers and agents—know the housing market in their communities. They know what homes are available at prices that can fit their clients' budgets, and they also know about sources of financing. Brokers arrange for title searches and meetings between buyers and sellers when the basics of the transaction have been agreed on. Brokers also often provide buyers with information on loans to finance their purchases.

Agents and brokers meet with potential buyers to learn what kind of home they want and what their budget is; they then match clients' needs with suitable properties. Generally, the agent takes the client to a number of properties to find the right one. The agent's job is to put the property in the best light and point out its advantages for the client. When negotiating the final price for the property, brokers and agents follow the seller's instructions exactly, but they may present counteroffers from the buyer to arrive at a sale.

Agents also pursue the other side of real estate selling: finding properties to sell. They spend much of their time looking for listings, agreements with owners to place their properties for sale with the firm. They must keep up with developments in the community so that they know what price properties are selling for and thus be aware of the fair market price of a given property. They spend a good deal of time on the telephone following up on advertisements, making contacts, and prospecting for buyers and sellers.

In some large firms and some small specialized firms, brokers and sellers concentrate on certain types of real estate; for example, commercial, industrial, or agricultural properties. This type of selling requires a detailed knowledge of leasing arrangements, business trends, transportation facilities, and the like.

Agents and brokers work out of offices, but most of their activity takes place outside the office, meeting with clients, showing property, evaluating properties, and so on. They often work more than 40 hours a week and frequently during evenings and weekends.

TRAINING AND QUALIFICATIONS

The licensing examination for brokers is more comprehensive than that for agents. Candidates must be at least 18 years old and high school graduates. Most states require 30 hours of formal instruction for a general sales license and 90 hours for a broker's license, plus experience in selling real estate—usually one to three years.

Many people come to real estate selling from other occupations. Homemakers and retired people often obtain licenses to take advantage of the flexible hours. Compensation is based on a commission, so those with a flair for sales or a penchant for establishing personal rapport find this a particularly satisfying and rewarding profession. The real estate market is extremely competitive; only those with determination and perseverance are likely to be successful. Turnover rate is very high among brokers and agents.

Large real estate firms typically look for college graduates with the requisite personality traits to fill their entry-level spots. They often provide formal on-the-job-training programs. Students can take courses in real estate at many colleges, universities, and junior colleges.

EARNINGS

Real estate agents and brokers who usually worked full time had median annual earnings of $31,500 in 1996. The middle 50 percent earned between $20,500 and $49,700. The top 10 percent earned more than $75,400. Independent brokers and agents derive income from commissions, which can vary widely. The rate of commission varies according to the type of property and its value; the percentage paid on the sale of farm and commercial properties or unimproved land is usually higher than that paid for selling a house. Commissions may be divided among several agents and brokers. Beginners should be aware that at the outset, sales may be spotty at best, and they may have some months of little or no income.

PROSPECTS: JOB OUTLOOK

Real estate agents, brokers, and appraisers held about 408,000 jobs in 1996. Many worked part time, combining their real estate activities with other careers. Jobs are easily obtained for the most part; succeeding is another matter. Even salaried jobs in real estate are tied to performance; there is little of the time-and-grade type of compensation found in other industries. Real estate is sensitive to changes in the larger economic picture. During economic downturns or periods of high interest rates, activity slows and market prices may decline, resulting in lower commissions for agents and brokers.

Employment growth in this field will stem primarily from increased demand for home purchases and rental units. Shifts in population distribution over the next decade will result in a large number of persons in the prime working ages (25–54 years old) with careers and family responsibilities, the group that makes most of the home purchases. Although employment of real estate agents and brokers is expected to grow more slowly than the average for all occupations through the year 2006, a large number of job openings will arise due to replacement needs.

Increased use of technology and electronic information may increase the productivity of agents and brokers, as the use of computers, faxes, modems, and databases become commonplace. Use of this technology may eliminate some of the more marginal agents who will not be able to compete with those who have invested in this technology.

WHERE TO LOOK FOR FURTHER INFORMATION

To learn more about opportunities and obtain a list of colleges and universities offering courses in real estate:

American Society of Real Estate Counselors
430 North Michigan Avenue
Chicago, IL 60611

National Association of Realtors
430 North Michigan Avenue
Chicago, IL 60611

The National Association of Real Estate
  Brokers
1629 K Street, NW
Suite 602
Washington, DC 20006

To learn about requirements for licensing of agents and brokers, consult a local real estate organization or your state's real estate commission or board.

SALES AND MARKETING EXECUTIVES

OCCUPATIONAL OVERVIEW

Job Description: Sales and marketing executives are responsible for creating and organizing effective sales programs, devising marketing strategy, identifying customers, and gaining and keeping the largest possible market share.

Prospects: The prospects for this field through the year 2006 vary by industry. Manufacturing, for instance, will see declining employment. The data-processing services industry and the radio and television broadcasting industry, in contrast, should see rapid growth.

Qualifications: Those who aspire to the upper ranks of marketing management should have a bachelor's or a master's degree in business administration with an emphasis on marketing. Those who intend to work for technological industries should have the appropriate engineering or science degree, combined with a degree in business administration.

Personal Skills: To reach the higher levels of the sales and marketing hierarchy, a person must be highly motivated, capable of working under a great deal of stress and absorbing a great deal of information, and able to calculate accurately and rapidly and make sound judgments, sometimes based on intuition. The ability to communicate well and excellent interpersonal skills are indispensable.

Earnings: The median annual income for those in sales and marketing in the mid-1990s was about $40,000. At the executive level, annual salaries of $75,000 to $100,000 are not uncommon, and annual compensation for some executives runs as high as $250,000 to $500,000. To these base salaries, bonuses, profit sharing, stock options, and various perquisites are often added.

THE JOB AND THE WORK ENVIRONMENT

Sales and marketing executives are near the top of the managerial hierarchy. They are responsible for implementing their organization's overall sales and marketing programs; they, in turn, rely on their general managers.

The objective of marketing management is to set a strategy that identifies customers and brings to their attention the company's goods and services. At the topmost level, marketing strategy must take into account the combined capacities of sales, advertising, sales promotion, and public relations. Strategy is defined more precisely by marketing managers, who identify the customer appropriate to the product and devise a competitive pricing strategy. A sound marketing strategy is important not only for new goods and services, but also for established lines because it helps prevent costly price competition.

The sales manager develops and implements a sales program. In some organizations, one executive vice-president oversees both sales and marketing; in others, the two functions remain separate all the way to the top. Sales managers define territories, set sales goals, and oversee training programs for sales staff. They contact and cultivate dealers and distributors. An essential part of the work of executives and managers in sales and marketing involves maintaining good relations with principals in related organizations—government agencies, including foreign governments, other corporations, and manufacturers and suppliers. Sales and marketing managers and executives also monitor customer preferences and oversee product development.

General managers and executive vice-presidents usually occupy comfortable offices and enjoy many perquisites. They work long hours, and in many cases, it is difficult to tell where business ends and private life begins. They often work under considerable stress to meet deadlines and goals. They frequently travel to attend meetings and conferences, where they cultivate potential clients and other contacts and conduct a great deal of business. Transfers abroad or from one branch of the company to another are common.

TRAINING AND QUALIFICATIONS

A bachelor's or a master's degree in business administration with an emphasis on marketing is the best preparation for these fields. A program of study should include courses in business law, economics, accounting, finance, mathematics, and statistics. For high-technology industries, a degree is needed in the appropriate branch of science or engineering, combined with a degree in business administration.

On the job, competition is intense for the top positions. Generally, advancement is from within the company, based on experience and performance. Training programs also can be important in areas like management, international marketing, sales marketing evaluation, telemarketing and direct sales, or marketing communications.

EARNINGS

There is a growing trend nationwide to contain the base salaries of executives and tie a larger percentage of their earnings to the risks of the marketplace. On the whole, though, sales and marketing executives remain well compensated. Annual salaries for some at the executive level are between $75,000 and $100,000, and for a few, the range is between $250,000 and $500,000—and these are salaries independent of valuable perquisites.

In general, the larger the firm, the higher the salary. Until recently, sales commanded higher earnings than marketing, but the recent trend appears to be turning in favor of executives in marketing or in combined sales and marketing. The trend seems particularly noticeable in companies dealing in durable goods.

PROSPECTS: JOB OUTLOOK

Job growth for executives and managers in sales and marketing through the year 2006 promises to be strong. Increasing domestic and international competition increases the importance of marketing research and strategy and all aspects of sales. In addition, replacements are needed for managers who advance, leave, or retire. Competition for high-paying jobs will be keen.

Positions for marketing managers are likely to increase in the data-processing services industry; the radio and television broadcasting industry; and the travel, hotel, amusement, and recreation industries; they are expected to decline in some manufacturing industries. There also appears to be a growing trend in many major firms to shift greater reliance on and compensation toward marketing and, to some degree, away from sales.

WHERE TO LOOK FOR FURTHER INFORMATION

For information about careers in sales and marketing management:

American Marketing Association
250 South Wacker Drive
Suite 200
Chicago, IL 60606-5819

Sales and Marketing Executives,
    International
446 Statler Office Tower
Cleveland, OH 44115

WHOLESALE AND RETAIL BUYERS

OCCUPATIONAL OVERVIEW

Job Description: Wholesale and retail buyers work for various industries; for example, the clothing and apparel, food, and electronic goods industries. They estimate the market for particular goods and then seek the best available merchandise at the lowest possible prices.

Prospects: Through the year 2006, job opportunities for buyers are expected to grow more slowly than average. Because computerization has streamlined this occupation, competition for jobs will be stiff.

Qualifications: The largest stores and distributors prefer applicants with an associate's or a bachelor's degree in marketing and purchasing, but most firms with trainee programs will accept those with a degree in any field. Many firms prefer applicants with experience and promote qualified employees from within.

Personal Skills: Buyers need to be energetic and resourceful. They have to work well under pressure, be able to make quick decisions, and not be afraid to take risks. Good communication skills are essential. Familiarity with computers is important.

Earnings: In 1996, the median annual income for purchasers and buyers was $33,200. Income varies with the volume of business and with the buyer's seniority. Some employers give bonuses and have profit sharing or stock option plans.

THE JOB AND THE WORK ENVIRONMENT

Wholesale and retail buyers are part of the complex system of production, distribution, and merchandising that brings to consumers the vast range of goods they need or want. *Wholesale buyers* are situated between the producers and manufacturers and the retail outlets. *Retail buyers* work for retail outlets and buy from the wholesalers or directly from producers and manufacturers. Buyers work principally for food and apparel retailers and for wholesalers and distributors of machinery, electrical goods, and groceries. They determine what the market needs or wants and find the best available merchandise at the lowest price.

Wholesale buyers usually specialize in one or two lines of merchandise. They must know their commodities well: the manufacturers, product specifications, and other essential characteristics. For this information, they often consult catalogs and computerized directories. They also must know production schedules, production capacities, and the inventories of producers. Against those figures, they calculate the current inventory of a retailer and the size of its order. Wholesale buyers also calculate discounts and must be able to ensure timely delivery.

Much of the work of wholesale buyers is a matter of acquiring information and organizing it. Increasingly, computers are used for this information processing because they offer instant access to the specifications of thousands of commodities, as well as inventories, retailers' purchase records, and manufacturers' deliveries. But a large part of wholesale buyers' work also remains a matter of direct contact, keeping abreast of trends in the industry and among consumers, and they are constantly in touch with producers and retail buyers.

Retail buyers must be attuned to consumers' wants and needs. They study market research reports, monitor sales, keep informed about changes and developments relating to the products with which they deal, and watch economic trends. Like wholesale buyers, they need good communication skills. Perhaps even more than wholesale buyers, they must be able to assess the value of goods and make purchasing decisions quickly. They also discuss merchandising problems with wholesale buyers and sales promotions with advertising departments.

Computers have increased the productivity of retail buyers, too. Many retailers are linked to wholesale distributors through electronic purchasing systems. Known as point-of-sale terminals, cash registers connected to computers give up-to-date sales and inventory records. As a result, more and more retail buyers now work in corporate headquarters.

For the most part, buyers work in comfortable offices in stores, in corporate headquarters, or with wholesale distributors. They often work more than 40 hours a week to meet pressing schedules, and part of the job is attending special sales and conferences. Buyers and merchandise managers often work under great pressure since wholesale and retail stores are so competitive; the work requires quick and confident decision making. It also entails a good deal of travel; most buyers are on the road at least several days a month.

TRAINING AND QUALIFICATIONS

Persons who wish to become wholesale or retail buyers should be good at planning and decision making and have an interest in merchandising.

Businesses prefer to hire applicants who know the merchandise they sell and have some experience in the wholesale and retail businesses. For that reason, some firms try to promote their own employees to assistant buyers. Other firms, including the largest stores and distributors, prefer to hire people with a bachelor's or an associate's degree (preferably in marketing or purchasing) and then train them. The majority of firms look for some combination of education and experience.

After completing a training program, typically combining instruction in merchandising and purchasing with rotations through sales, accounts receivable, and the stockroom, trainees take on basic responsibilities, such as selling merchandise and checking invoices and inventory. After two or three years as assistant buyers, they generally are promoted to buyer. Experienced buyers may eventually become merchandise managers or advance to executive positions.

Since more and more of the record keeping essential to this business is computerized, familiarity with computers is important.

EARNINGS

Income depends on seniority, the amount and type of product purchased, and the company's sales volume, with buyers for large wholesale distributors and mass merchandisers earning the most. Median annual earnings of purchasers and buyers were $33,200 in 1996. The middle 50 percent earned between $23,300 and $45,900. The top 10 percent earned more than $63,000. Other variables affecting income are bonuses, merchandise discounts, profit-sharing plans, and stock options.

PROSPECTS: JOB OUTLOOK

In 1996, purchasers and buyers held some 639,000 jobs. About one-half of all purchasers and buyers worked in wholesale and retail trade establishments, such as grocery or department stores. Through the year 2006, job growth for buyers is expected to be slower than average. As increasing numbers of wholesale and retail businesses centralize their purchasing departments and keep track of record keeping, inventory control, and reorders by computer, fewer staff are needed, particularly assistant buyers. In retail trade, mergers and acquisitions have forced the consolidation of buying departments, eliminating jobs. As a result, most job openings will be to replace buyers who transfer to jobs in sales or management, change occupations, or leave the workforce. Competition will increase for available jobs, and prospects will be best for those with the best qualifications.

WHERE TO LOOK FOR FURTHER INFORMATION

For information on a career in retailing:

National Retail Federation
325 7th Street, NW
Suite 1000
Washington, DC 20004

APPLIED SCIENCES: ARCHITECTURE, ENGINEERING, AND COMPUTER SCIENCE

AEROSPACE ENGINEERS

OCCUPATIONAL OVERVIEW

Job Description: Aerospace engineers design, develop, test, and help to produce commercial and military aircraft, missiles, and spacecraft.

Prospects: Growth in employment of aerospace engineers is expected to be slower than average for all occupations through the year 2006.

Qualifications: The minimum requirement is a bachelor's degree from an accredited engineering program.

Personal Skills: Good mathematical and problem-solving skills are essential. The ability to work with others in teams, creativity, and attention to detail are crucial for success. Computer literacy is important for working with computer-aided design systems.

Earnings: In 1997, the average starting salary for aerospace engineers with bachelor's degrees was $39,957. According to the National Association of Colleges and Employers, engineers with a master's degree averaged about $45,400 upon being hired with no experience; Ph.D.'s entered the workplace at an average salary of $55,300. Median average salaries for all aerospace engineers was $59,200.

THE JOB AND THE WORK ENVIRONMENT

Aerospace: the word conjures up images of high tech, high adventure, and high salaries. Behind the glitz, however, is the reality of demanding work. Because of the complexity of new technologies for commercial aviation, defense, and space exploration, aerospace engineers tend to specialize in certain areas (e.g., structural design, navigational guidance and control systems, instrumentation and communication, or production methods) or in a particular product (e.g., civil aircraft, passenger planes, satellites, rockets, helicopters, or military aircraft).

In 1996, aerospace engineers held about 53,000 jobs. Most aerospace engineers work in the aircraft and parts and guided missile and space vehicle manufacturing industries. The primary employers are the commercial aircraft manufacturers and the U.S. Department of Defense. Other employers are business and engineering consulting firms, manufacturers of communications equipment, and commercial airlines.

Engineers can move into nonengineering jobs in industry, too. Many companies, especially those in technological areas, employ experienced engineers in marketing and sales and even in top management.

TRAINING AND QUALIFICATIONS

All engineers need training in mathematics and one or more of the physical sciences (physics, chemistry, or biology). Typically, they pursue a four-year college engineering program. Some engineering schools allow students to spend three years at a liberal arts college and then two years at an engineering school, earning a bachelor's degree from both institutions; others offer an M.A. in five years. Also available are some five- or six-year cooperative programs in which students combine classroom study for the bachelor's degree with practical work experience, an arrangement that allows for earning while learning, as well as gaining experience.

Aerospace engineers may be experts in aerodynamics, propulsion, thermodynamics, structures, celestial mechanics, acoustics, or guidance and control systems.

Aerospace engineers are on the cutting edge of new technologies. They have to keep up with their field and continue their education if they are not to become redundant later in their careers. They must be flexible enough to change direction if a developing technology is causing great changes in their field.

EARNINGS

Aerospace engineers with a bachelor's degree in 1997 received an average starting salary of $37,957. Median annual earnings for all aerospace engineers in that year were $59,000.

According to the National Association of Colleges and Employers, engineering graduates with a bachelor's degree averaged about $38,500 per year in private industry in 1997. Those with more advanced degrees earned significantly more. Experienced mid-level engineers with no supervisory responsibilities had median annual earnings of about $59,100. Median annual earnings for engineers at senior managerial levels were about $99,200.

Benefit packages vary, with significant differentials for those who advance to management.

PROSPECTS: JOB OUTLOOK

Aerospace is a volatile industry. In the government and defense sectors particularly, funding levels can vary widely from year to year. Current projections are for slower growth in aerospace than the average for all other occupations through the year 2006. But not all aerospace sectors will be down; the major slowdown will be felt in U.S. Department of Defense expenditures for military aircraft, missiles, and other aerospace systems and in plans for National Aeronautics and Space Administration ventures. The civilian aerospace sector, however, has a more positive outlook; it needs new, quiet, fuel-efficient aircraft to replace its aging fleet. Also expected is increased demand among businesses for aircraft and helicopters.

The job market for aerospace engineers will be competitive; most job openings will result from replacement needs rather than growth in the industry. In addition, because the industry will be using more materials, mechanical, or electrical engineers than previously, the number of job opportunities open to aerospace engineers may decline.

Jobs in aerospace engineering will remain in their current geographical distribution. Almost half of the total employment of aerospace engineers and scientists is located in the West (Alaska, California, Hawaii, Oregon, Texas, and Washington). The New England and mid-Atlantic regions account for roughly another 20 percent, with the balance of employment spread more or less evenly over the rest of the country.

WHERE TO LOOK FOR FURTHER INFORMATION

To learn more about careers in engineering:

American Institute of Aeronautics and
  Astronautics, Inc.
1801 Alexander Bell Drive
Suite 500
Reston, VA 20191-4344

Aerospace Industries Association of
  America, Inc.
1250 E Street, NW
Washington, DC 20005

Society of Automotive Engineers
400 Commonwealth Drive
Warrendale, PA 15096

ARCHITECTS

OCCUPATIONAL OVERVIEW

Job Description: Architects design buildings and oversee their construction. Most work for architectural firms, but about one-third of practicing architects are self-employed. Others work for firms related to the construction business or for agencies of the federal government.

Prospects: Through the year 2006, jobs in architecture are expected to grow about as fast as the average for the economy as a whole. However, the outlook is linked directly to the construction industry, which is vulnerable to downturns in the economy.

Qualifications: Architects must have either a bachelor's or a master's degree in architecture. A degree from an accredited architecture program is necessary for those who want to be licensed or registered. All states and the District of Columbia require a license for any architect legally responsible for a building.

Personal Skills: Architects need drafting ability, but it is a skill that most people can be taught. More important for a career in architecture is the ability to visualize spatial relations and an aptitude for solving technical problems. Architects deal closely with clients, engineers, and contractors and should be able to work well as part of a team and have good communication skills.

Earnings: According to the American Institution of Architects (AIA) in a 1996 salary survey, the median compensation for licensed architects who had 8 to 10 years' experience was $45,000. Interns averaged $24,700 a year. Principals or partners earned $75,000 to $100,000. Licensed architects with 3 to 5 years of experience had median earnings of $33,000.

THE JOB AND THE WORK ENVIRONMENT

Architects design buildings ranging from private residences to large public housing projects. No matter what the end product, their basic concerns are the same—to draw up aesthetically pleasing designs for buildings that will be useful, safe, and economical.

A project usually begins when the architect meets with the client and learns what the client needs and wants and how much money is available. The architect then prepares one or more designs calculated to appeal to the client's taste, need, and budget. After discussions, a final design is agreed on, and construction documents showing floor plans, elevations, and building sections and detailing the internal systems of the building (its wiring, plumbing, ventilation, heating, and air conditioning) are drawn up. The architect decides on building materials, and in decisions pertaining to the building, ensures full compliance with relevant building codes and ordinances. The architect also may assist the client in finding contractors.

Thus, the architect is responsible for the building from beginning to end. While construction is in progress, the architect may visit the site to ensure that specifications are being met and that the work is on schedule and within the client's budget. Often, changes in design must be made while construction is in progress; all such alterations are the responsibility of the architect.

About one-third of architects are self-employed, but the majority are employed by architectural firms that vary in size. Generally, they work in offices in pleasant surroundings, but they may visit construction sites. There are also architects working in businesses related to the construction industry, and some work for the federal government.

New architects in a firm are usually assigned to administer construction contracts, research building codes or ordinances, draw up the specifications for building materials, and the like. Eventually, an architect can advance to management and go on to become a partner in the firm.

Increasingly, women are entering the field. One attraction architecture has for women planning both a career and a family is the availability of work for those in part-time practice, although there is still a wide disparity between the earnings of men and women in this field.

TRAINING AND QUALIFICATIONS

Programs in architecture leading to a bachelor's of architecture degree take five years; a master's of architecture takes six years. Students with two years of work in architectural studies at a junior or community college can transfer to a full-degree program. High school students considering a career in architecture should have a good grounding in mathematics, including analytical geometry and trigonometry, and science, especially physics and chemistry.

There are approximately 100 accredited programs leading to degrees in architecture. Accreditation is conferred by the National Architectural Accrediting Board, and architects seeking to be registered must graduate from accredited programs. Though many architects hold jobs without being licensed, all states and the District of Columbia require licensing or registration before individuals can call themselves architects or offer their services as such. In addition to a degree from an accredited program, a candidate for registration must have three years' experience in an architect's office and must pass an examination. Many states require that the three-year apprenticeship match the standards of the Intern Architect Development Program. A registered architect takes legal responsibility for his or her work.

Computer literacy is required as most firms use computers for word processing, specifications writing, two- and three-dimensional drafting, and financial management. A knowledge of computer-aided design and drafting (CADD) is helpful.

EARNINGS

Earnings vary with an architect's education, experience, employer, and region. According to the AIA, in 1996, the median compensation, including bonuses, for, an intern with an architecture degree was $27,000. Licensed architects with 3 to 5 years of experience had median earnings of $33,000. A licensed architect with 8 to 10 years' experience but who was not a manager or principal in a firm earned a median salary of $45,000. A principal or partner earned from $75,000 to $100,000.

PROSPECTS: JOB OUTLOOK

In 1996, there were some 94,000 jobs held by architects. Through the year 2006, job prospects for architects are expected to match the norm, although job growth is tied to the construction industry, whose activity varies with fluctuations in the economy. Prestigious firms will continue to offer good career opportunities, but competition will be keen, and most openings will be to replace those who have retired or moved to other occupations.

WHERE TO LOOK FOR FURTHER INFORMATION

For information on careers in architecture:

Careers in Architecture Program
American Institute of Architects
1735 New York Avenue, NW
Washington, DC 20006

For more information on programs in architecture:

Association of Collegiate Schools of Architecture, Inc.
1735 New York Avenue, NW
Washington, DC 20006

For information on licensing and registration:

National Council of Architectural Registration Boards
1735 New York Avenue, NW
Suite 700
Washington, DC 20006

CHEMICAL ENGINEERS

OCCUPATIONAL OVERVIEW

Job Description: Chemical engineers design equipment, plants, and processes for the manufacturing, production, or treatment of chemicals and chemical-based products.

Prospects: The demand for chemical engineers through the year 2006 will grow as fast as projected trends for overall job growth in the economy. Most projected growth will be in biotechnology and pharmaceuticals, rather than manufacturing.

Qualifications: A bachelor's degree in engineering is a minimum requirement. A graduate degree is required for most teaching posts and management positions.

Personal Skills: Good analytical skills, the capacity for sustained attention to detail, and the ability to work well as part of a team are vital. Good communication skills also are important.

Earnings: According to the National Association of Colleges and Employers, in 1997, starting salaries for chemical engineers with bachelor's degrees averaged $42,817. Experienced mid-level engineers in all categories with no supervisory responsibilities had median earnings of about $59,100, and median earnings for engineers at a senior management level were about $99,200 per year.

THE JOB AND THE WORK ENVIRONMENT

Chemical engineers study and develop the processes and technologies by which chemicals and chemical substances are produced and managed. Most chemical engineers work in manufacturing, chiefly petroleum refining, where they design equipment and plants, test manufacturing processes, and supervise production. The work can be dangerous.

Chemical engineering is a hybrid field. It includes petrochemicals and pharmaceuticals and also electronics and the development of aircraft. Because of increasing complexity, most chemical engineers specialize in a process, such as oxidation or polymerization, or in a specific product, such as plastic or rubber. Chemical engineers also study the properties and effects of dangerous and suspect chemicals and devise processes for neutralizing them. Some work on the development of acceptable substitutes. Pollution control, research into alternative energy sources, and energy conservation are all within the province of the chemical engineer.

In 1996, chemical engineers held over 49,000 jobs. Two-thirds of chemical engineers worked in manufacturing in an industrial setting. Most of the rest worked for engineering services, research and testing services, or consulting firms that design chemical plants.

TRAINING AND QUALIFICATIONS

The minimum qualification for a chemical engineer is a bachelor's degree in engineering. A typical course of study can last from four to six years. The first half provides grounding in physics, chemistry, mathematics, and basic engineering. The second half usually leads to specialization. Those seeking a master's degree pursue a five- to six-year program. Many engineers earn their graduate degrees while on the job, and some five- and six-year courses of study combine classwork and practical work.

Most engineers are likely to undergo additional training in the company. Because of constant and rapid change in technology and the possibility of obsolescence in any specialty, education continues throughout one's career. Postgraduate degrees are essential for most research and teaching posts and for management positions.

All states and the District of Columbia require engineers whose work may affect life, health, and property to have a license, gained by graduating from an accredited engineering school, working in the industry for four years, and passing a state examination. About one-third of all engineers are licensed.

EARNINGS

Earnings for chemical engineers depend on qualifications, experience, and the sector of the economy in which they work.

Chemical engineers with bachelors' degrees started in 1997 at an average salary of $42,817, according to the National Association of Colleges and Employers. Median salaries for all chemical engineers were $56,600. Median annual earnings for engineers in all categories at a senior managerial level were about $99,200. In 1997, the average annual salary for engineers in all categories in the federal government positions was $61,950.

Benefit packages vary, with significant differentials for those who advance to management.

PROSPECTS: JOB OUTLOOK

The overall demand for chemical engineers through the year 2006 is expected to be as great as the average in all occupations as chemical companies research and develop new chemicals and more efficient processes to increase output of existing chemicals. Areas relating to the production of specialty chemicals, pharmaceuticals, and plastics may provide better opportunities than other portions of the chemical industry. The demand for research into alternative synthetic fuels is likely to remain low; pollution control, environmental protection, biotechnology, and pharmaceuticals look promising. Those working in high technology may face greater risks—and greater rewards.

Engineers with business administration and managerial skills and experience are sought by private industry.

WHERE TO LOOK FOR FURTHER INFORMATION

For additional information on academic programs and requirements, as well as career opportunities for chemical engineers:

American Association of Engineering
  Societies
1111 19th Street, NW
Suite 608
Washington, DC 20036

American Chemical Society
Career Services
1155 16th Street, NW
Washington, DC 20036

American Institute of Chemical Engineers
345 East 47th Street
New York, NY 10017-2395

National Society of Professional Engineers
1420 King Street
Suite 405
Alexandria, VA 22314

CHIEF INFORMATION OFFICERS

OCCUPATIONAL OVERVIEW

Job Description: Chief information officers (CIOs), also known as managers of information systems, ensure the efficient operation of a company's entire information-processing system, electronic and human. They must be experts in judging hardware, software, and personnel.

Prospects: With the ever-increasing use of computers to manage, store, and transmit data, not to mention problem solving, demand for CIOs is expected to be strong through 2006.

Qualifications: CIOs do not need a technical degree to qualify for the job. A bachelor's degree in liberal arts or business, plus an M.B.A. with an emphasis on information systems are often enough to begin on this career path.

Personal Skills: Excellent technical skills in information processing are essential, as are good management and communication skills. The ability to lead and motivate others and a capacity to work under pressure are important.

Earnings: Salaries for CIOs vary widely, depending on their experience and the size and location of the companies for which they work. Recently, a typical range ran from about $55,000 to over $300,000 annually.

THE JOB AND THE WORK ENVIRONMENT

The description _manager of information systems_ used to bring to mind a computer hacker toiling in a back office to keep a company's computer network running. Today's CIO is more manager than hacker, more business than computer savvy, and more leader than loner.

Naturally, CIOs need to know about data-processing systems, the capabilities of different hardware and software configurations, and the most recent developments in the field. In addition, they must have a complete understanding of the company's present and probable future data-processing needs. Thus, the job entails more than just technical expertise. The CIO is actually a generalist with a technical background who can manage technical specialists and their supervisors.

The range of activities involving CIOs is a clear indication of their need to be multifaceted. They are responsible for evaluating and purchasing hardware and software, hiring and supervising technical and clerical personnel for their department, assigning individuals to projects, setting work standards, and establishing budgets for all of the computer departments in the company. The computer center is a corporate service center, ready to help any other corporate department in its data-processing or information-processing needs. Thus, CIOs must work closely with other department managers to develop computer-based methods of solving their problems.

In many companies, particularly larger ones, the CIO reports to a vice-president or the chief executive officer. He or she oversees the applications programmers, systems analysts, and operators of the computer network. A CIO in a small company oversees the daily functioning of the firm's information system; those in larger operations work through the managers or supervisors of the system.

CIOs generally work out of their offices in the company's computer or data center. Because they serve several departments, they are often under pressure to deliver projects on short deadlines, and they frequently work overtime. They may travel often (in many cases, up to a third of their time)—to seminars, demonstrations of new products, or their company's other computer installations.

TRAINING AND QUALIFICATIONS

Large companies typically look for a bachelor's degree in computer science or a related field and an M.B.A., plus some management experience. Many CIOs come to their positions after several years of working in programming, systems analysis, or operations planning.

Experience is important because CIOs need a business sense as well as technical expertise. They must be able to lead and motivate people and understand their company's operations and policies so that they can devise ways for the information-processing department to provide maximum support to the company's other departments.

EARNINGS

Most CIOs are well paid. Recent salaries averaged over $90,000 a year, with a range from $55,000 to over $300,000. Salaries depend on the size of the firm and the complexity of its information-processing operations, but because generally larger, more sophisticated companies are looking for CIOs, the position commands a good salary.

PROSPECTS: JOB OUTLOOK

The demand for CIOs is expected to remain strong for the foreseeable future. Individuals with the requisite technical and managerial abilities are in short supply, and as more and more companies, of all sizes, turn to and increase their computerized operations, the demand for CIOs should remain stable. More than half of all the Fortune 500 companies have CIOs, and many smaller companies are beginning to follow suit.

Entry-level jobs are most likely to be found in smaller companies that are just beginning to computerize in a serious way. Such companies are likely to look for less management experience and more technical know-how, choosing, for instance, a senior systems analyst or project leader for the post. The big employment opportunities for CIOs are found in the larger companies or organizations with extensive computer installations, many of which are found in urban areas, suburban business centers, or industrial parks (e.g., banks, hospitals, insurance companies, major wholesale and retail trade establishments, and computer service companies).

Moving from the manager of an information-processing department into general management is often difficult. CIOs, rightly or wrongly, are frequently viewed as having too narrow a technical background for top management positions. Thus, CIOs who feel they have reached an impasse in their careers often turn to consulting (either on a self-employed basis or as part of a data-processing firm). Nevertheless, CIOs have considerable power and influence in their jobs, and they interact with top management on a regular basis.

WHERE TO LOOK FOR FURTHER INFORMATION

To learn more about careers in managing information-processing systems:

Association for Systems Management
24587 Bagley Road
Cleveland, OH 44138-0370

CIVIL ENGINEERS

OCCUPATIONAL OVERVIEW

Job Description: Civil engineers design and supervise the construction of roads, airports, tunnels, bridges, dikes, dams, sewage systems, and buildings. Many work for city, state, or federal agencies. Others hold supervisory, managerial, or consultancy positions in private industry.

Prospects: Job opportunities for civil engineers are expected to increase as fast as the average for all jobs through the year 2006, although the construction industry is vulnerable to fluctuations in the economy. Civil engineers will be needed to maintain and repair existing facilities and structures and to construct new ones.

Qualifications: A bachelor's degree in engineering is the minimum requirement, and a graduate degree is required for most teaching posts and management positions. All states and the District of Columbia require engineers whose work may affect life, health, or property to be licensed.

Personal Skills: A civil engineer needs good analytical and communication skills, the capacity for sustained attention to details, and the ability to work well as part of a team.

Earnings: According to the 1997 National Association of Colleges and Employers survey, civil engineers with bachelor's degrees starting out earned a median annual salary of $33,119. The median average salary for all civil engineers with bachelor's degrees in 1994 was $46,000. Engineers in all categories with a master's degree earned on average $53,200, and those with a Ph.D. earned a median salary of $62,300.

THE JOB AND THE WORK ENVIRONMENT

Civil engineers work in the oldest branch of engineering. In government service and private concerns, civil engineers design and supervise the construction of roads, airports, terminals, tunnels, bridges, dams, reservoirs, dikes, sewage systems, shopping malls, industrial parks, and urban and suburban housing projects. The range of projects to which civil engineering is applied is so broad that most civil engineers specialize; for example, in structural, hydraulic, or transportation engineering.

No matter what the field of specialization, all civil engineers face similar problems in any project. They must design structures to meet specific needs and accommodate specific capacities and analyze building materials for tensile strength, load bearing strength, resistance to fire and corrosion, and insulating properties. Special consideration may have to be taken for building over a water table, on sandy soil, or in an area susceptible to tremors and earthquakes. Civil engineers also must calculate the costs of materials, labor, and equipment and set reasonable construction schedules. They must know and factor in zoning ordinances, health and safety regulations, fire codes, and local, state, and national regulations governing hazardous materials. In civil engineering, the skills of the engineer are combined with those of the supervisor and administrator.

On most projects, civil engineers work in teams and in concert with many other engineers. Their projects may be in remote areas of foreign countries, so travel can be frequent.

Civil engineers who specialize in urban planning or projects requiring public funding, such as bridges, roads, and tunnels, may become managers and administrators in positions of public trust (for example, as head of an interstate port authority or a city's department of public works). Other civil engineers work as independent consultants.

The settings vary, but for the most part, civil engineers work a 40-hour, 5-day week.

TRAINING AND QUALIFICATIONS

The minimum qualification for civil engineers is a bachelor's degree in engineering. A typical course of study lasts from four to six years. The first half provides grounding in physics, chemistry, mathematics, and basic engineering. The second half usually leads to specialization. Those seeking a master's degree follow a five- to six-year program. Many engineers earn their graduate degrees while on the job; some five- and six-year courses of study combine classwork and practical work, making it possible for students to pay their way through school.

An engineer is likely to undergo training in the company for which he or she works. In addition, constant and rapid changes in technology make it necessary for people in the field to continue their education while they work. Graduate degrees are essential for most research and teaching posts and for positions in management and administration. Those interested in careers in management should consider an additional degree in business administration.

All states and the District of Columbia require licensing for engineers whose work may affect life, health, or property. Almost one-third of all engineers are licensed; to become licensed, an engineer must graduate from an accredited engineering school, have four years' experience, and pass a state examination.

EARNINGS

Earnings for civil engineers depend on degree qualifications, experience, and the sector of the economy in which they work. According to the National Association of Colleges and Employers, starting salaries for civil engineers with a bachelor's degree in 1997 averaged $33,119. Median annual salaries for civil engineers with bachelor's degrees were $46,000.

Engineers in all catagories with master's degrees earned on average $56,700 annually, and those with a Ph.D. had median earnings of $64,700. Median average earnings in that year for engineers at a senior managerial level were about $99,200.

Benefit packages vary, with significant differentials likely for those who advance to management.

PROSPECTS: JOB OUTLOOK

In 1994, civil engineers held 196,000 jobs, 39 percent of them in local, state, or federal governmental agencies. The overall demand for civil engineers through the year 2006 is expected to increase as fast as the average for all occupations. Older systems and structures, particularly roads, bridges, tunnels, and other heavily utilized public structures, will need to be maintained and repaired, or replaced. An increasing population will create a demand for new construction projects. Projects funded by the federal government are susceptible to budget cuts, however, and the construction industry is especially vulnerable to economic fluctuation.

WHERE TO LOOK FOR FURTHER INFORMATION

For information concerning careers in civil engineering:

American Society of Civil Engineers
1801 Alexander Bell Drive
Reston, VA 20191-4400

COMPUTER PROGRAMMERS

OCCUPATIONAL OVERVIEW

Job Description: Computer programmers write the detailed lists of instructions—called programs or software—that tell computers what tasks to perform and how to perform them.

Prospects: The demand for programmers at all levels is expected to grow faster than the average for all occupations through the year 2006.

Qualifications: Because each employer's needs are specific to that company, there is no profession-wide training requirements for programmers. Computer programming is taught in high schools, vocational schools, colleges, and universities. The trend among employers is to hire those with more formal educations, with degrees in computer programming and coursework in other business areas, such as accounting.

Personal Skills: Clear, logical thinking is imperative. Patience and the ability to work with abstract concepts are important, and the ability to work with accuracy under pressure is crucial.

Earnings: A survey of workplaces in 160 metropolitan areas in 1995 reported that beginning programmers had median annual earnings of about $27,000; experienced mid-level programmers with some supervisory responsibilities had median earnings of about $40,000. Median earnings for programmers at the supervisory or team leader level were about $55,000.

THE JOB AND THE WORK ENVIRONMENT

Computer programmers generally work according to a job description supplied by a systems analyst or a programmer-analyst, outlining the task to be accomplished in a step-by-step analysis of what the program must do. The programmer translates this description into line-by-line instructions for the computer in the computer's language. These instructions constitute the program.

After creation, the program must be tested and checked for errors, a process called debugging. When the program has tested out successfully by generating the desired information in the required format, the programmer prepares an instruction sheet for the computer operator who will eventually run the program. Simple programs can be written, debugged, and put online in a few days; more complex programs can take a year or more to complete. On very long, difficult programs, several programmers may work for long periods in a team headed by a senior programmer or systems analyst.

Computer programmers are grouped into two general categories: (1) applications programmers and (2) systems programmers. *Applications programmers* work in the business, scientific, or engineering fields, writing software to accomplish specific tasks, such as calculating payrolls or controlling the temperature of an office building. *Systems programmers* work to maintain the software controlling an entire computer system. They must understand how the system's hardware (keyboard, terminals, disk drives, printers, etc.) interfaces with the software. They are especially helpful to applications programmers because their knowledge of the entire computing system can often pinpoint areas that may cause trouble in a program.

Computer use has become a business necessity. Most programmers work for data-processing service organizations such as banks, colleges and universities, manufacturing companies, and government agencies. Applications programmers work for every kind of organization that uses computer systems, which means virtually any enterprise. Systems programmers usually work for organizations large enough to need a computer center to control their information system or for computer hardware and software manufacturers. Much of the programming done today is the preparation of packaged software, one of the most rapidly growing segments of the computer industry.

Programmers generally work in offices and put in a normal 40-hour week. Their hours, however, may be irregular, since major computer users may run their systems around the clock. Thus, programmers may work shifts, come in early or stay late, or work on weekends. Because programmers spend long periods of time in front of a computer monitor typing at a keyboard, they are susceptible to eyestrain, back disorder, and hand and wrist problems.

TRAINING AND QUALIFICATIONS

Because the needs of employers of programmers vary so widely, training requirements for entry-level positions are hard to pinpoint. The level of education and quality of training that employers seek has been rising due to the growth in the number of qualified applicants and the increasing complexity of some programming tasks. The highest levels of training are demanded by scientific organizations, university research groups, and business firms or government agencies that use large, complex data-processing systems; these organizations require a college degree, preferably in computer or information science or in a job-related discipline (mathematics, engineering, etc.) that involves computer science coursework. Some positions at this level require postgraduate degrees.

The business sector is much more varied. Generally, businesses prefer but do not demand a college degree. Increasingly, companies seek people with experience, so the best opportunities go to those who combine formal computer training with part-time work (e.g., college work-study programs or summer internships). To broaden their business background, students may be advised to take courses in accounting, business management, or engineering along with their formal computer training.

Professional recognition for programmers is provided by the Certificate in Computer Programming (CCP), awarded by the Institute for Certification of Computer Professionals. Applicants who take the test must have the equivalent of five years of computing work experience.

In addition, computer programmers at all levels are urged to continue training throughout their careers to keep up with the rapidly developing industry.

EARNINGS

According to the National Association of Colleges and Employers, median earnings of programmers who worked full time in 1996 were about $40,100 a year. The middle 50 percent earned between about $30,700 and $52,000 a year. The top 10 percent earned more than $65,200. Starting salary offers for graduates with a bachelor's degree in the area of programming averaged about $35,167 in private industry. Programmers in the West and Northeast earned somewhat more than those working in the South and Midwest.

PROSPECTS: JOB OUTLOOK

In 1994, computer progammers held about 568,000 jobs. Programmers are employed in almost every industry, and job opportunities for programmers will grow faster than the average for all occupations through the year 2006. Also, government, businesses, schools, and scientific organizations will need programmers as they seek to exploit new users for their hardware and improve their existing software.

Competition for these openings will be keen. Packaged software programs are eliminating some of the need for programmers. College graduates familiar with several programming languages, especially ones relating to computer networking and database management, will have the best chance in job competition. Some work experience also will be important.

A growing number of progammers are employed on a temporary or contract basis, or work as independent consultants as companies demand expertise with newer programming languages or specialized areas of application. For example, a bank offering a new service will need extra programmers to write and debug its software; once the program is in place, the extra help will no longer be needed. Employers are increasingly offering programmers short-term contracts for specific projects, which may last for a few months, a year, or more. There were 20,000 self-employed programmers in 1996, and this number is expected to increase.

WHERE TO LOOK FOR FURTHER INFORMATION

To learn more about careers in computer programming:

Data Processing Management Association
505 Busse Highway
Park Ridge, IL 60068

The Association for Computing
1515 Broadway
New York, NY 10036

Institute for the Certification of
  Computing Professionals
2200 East Devon Avenue
Suite 268
Des Plaines, IL 60018

Association for Computing Machinery
1515 Broadway
New York, NY 10036-5701

IEEE Computer Society
Headquarters Office
1730 Massachusetts Avenue, NW
Washington, DC 20036-1992

COMPUTER SYSTEMS ANALYSTS

OCCUPATIONAL OVERVIEW

Job Description: Computer systems analysts plan and develop methods for computerizing business and scientific tasks or for improving computer systems already in use. They integrate hardware and software into a unified data-processing system. Because computers have proved their usefulness over such a broad range of activities, analysts now specialize in a particular area (e.g., business, scientific, or engineering applications).

Prospects: Expectations are that the occupation of systems analysis will be one of the three faster growing through the year 2006. New technology leads to new applications, and analysts will be needed to devise the most efficient ways to harness computing power to specific tasks.

Qualifications: Employers' requirements for analysts vary, although a college degree is generally a requisite for consideration; a postgraduate degree is preferred for more complex work.

Personal Skills: A capacity for logical, analytical thinking and good communication skills is essential. Also important are the ability to concentrate and a total commitment to detail.

Earnings: Median annual earnings of computer systems analysts who worked full time in 1996 were about $46,300. The middle 50 percent earned between $34,000 and $59,900. The top 10 percent earned more than $76,200.

THE JOB AND THE WORK ENVIRONMENT

Systems analysts are concerned primarily with the technical aspects of data processing (not with the management and business problems of the corporation's information center). Typically, they begin an assignment by discussing the data-processing problem with the involved managers or specialists to determine the nature of their needs. After they have defined the goals of the system, they use mathematical modeling, sampling, cost accounting, or other techniques to design an appropriate system.

When the design has been developed, analysts prepare charts and diagrams that describe it clearly for managers and other users. The analysts may also prepare a cost-benefit and return-on-investment analysis to help management decide whether the proposed system is satisfactory. If the design is accepted, they determine the hardware and software needed and prepare specifications for the programmers. They work with the programmers to debug the system and normally design any forms required to collect data and distribute information.

Throughout the process, the emphasis is on systems—the optimum configurations of hardware and software that will perform the application. Some analysts improve systems already in use; others do research, called advanced systems design, aimed at devising new methods of systems analysis.

The work of analysts has grown in importance as corporations and institutions move to connect all their computers into a companywide network designed to allow the individual PCs of a company to communicate with each other and to tap into the company's mainframe computer and databases, or even to link up with databases provided by libraries or commercial providers of specialized information. Because of the growing complexity of these computer networks and the varied uses to which computers and computer systems can be put, analysts tend to specialize in business, scientific, or engineering applications.

Analysts usually put in a 40-hour week in the office, although occasionally a tight deadline requires evening and weekend work. Urban areas, where there is a heavy concentration of sophisticated computer system users (data-processing service firms, government agencies, insurance companies, banks, manufacturers of durable goods, and the like), provide most of the jobs. Some analysts work on a contract basis; they help a company design and install a new system and then turn it over to staff. Such temporary work might last from several months to two years or more.

TRAINING AND QUALIFICATIONS

Formal education requirements usually include at least a bachelor's and in some instances a postgraduate degree. Employers in business look for people with a background in accounting or business management, and scientifically oriented organizations look for a background in engineering, applied mathematics, or the physical sciences. A degree in computer science, information science, or data processing is helpful. Regardless of background, employers prefer people familiar with programming languages.

Systems analysis is not an entry-level job. Most analysts enter the field from other occupations, such as engineering, management, or computer programming. Certification may also help establish credentials as an experienced computer professional. The Institute for Certification of Computer Professionals confers the designations *certified systems professional* and *certified data processor* on candidates who have five years' experience and pass a five-part examination.

EARNINGS

According to Robert Half International, Inc., starting salaries in 1997 for systems analysts employed by large establishments (more than 50 employees) ranged from $46,000 to $57,500. Salaries for those employed in small establishments ranged from $38,000 to $48,000.

According to the National Association of Colleges and Employers, starting salaries for computer systems analysts with a bachelor's degree can be significantly higher than those offered to other bachelor's degree graduates in many other fields. Starting offers in 1997 for computer systems analysts and designers were about $36,261.

On average, the middle 50 percent of full-time systems analysts earned between $34,000 and $59,000. The highest tenth earned more than $76,200.

PROSPECTS: JOB OUTLOOK

Computer analysis will be one of the three fastest growing occupations through the year 2006. Demand for systems analysts is expected to rise as advances in technology lead to new applications for computers. Also, as computer hardware and software become more sophisticated, they tend to become less expensive, making computerization and networking accessible to medium- and small-sized businesses and institutions—good news for analysts.

The best opportunities will go to college graduates who have had courses in computer programming, systems analysis, and other areas of data processing, and who have training or experience in an applied field. Those without a college degree or who are unfamiliar with data processing will face stiff competition.

WHERE TO LOOK FOR FURTHER INFORMATION

To learn more about the career of systems analyst:

Association for Computing
1515 Broadway
New York, NY 10036

IEEE Computer Society
Headquarters Office
1730 Massachusetts Avenue, NW
Washington, DC 20036-1992

Information about the designation Certified Quality Analyst is available from:

Quality Assurance Institute
7575 Dr. Phillips Boulevard
Suite 350
Orlando, FL 32819

ELECTRICAL AND ELECTRONICS ENGINEERS

OCCUPATIONAL OVERVIEW

Job Description: Electrical and electronics engineers design, develop, and test electrical and electronic equipment and components for a number of industries, including those that do defense-related work. They supervise production and manufacturing processes and oversee installation and maintenance.

Prospects: Through the year 2006, job growth is expected to increase faster than the average for the economy as a whole. Increased production and demand by government and businesses for communications equipment, computers, and military electronics, along with consumer demand and increased R&D on robots and other types of automation, should contribute to the trend. Cutbacks in defense spending may have an adverse effect on job growth, however.

Qualifications: A bachelor's degree in electronics engineering is a minimum requirement, and a postgraduate degree is required for most teaching posts and management positions. All states and the District of Columbia require licensing for engineers whose work may affect life, health, or property.

Personal Skills: Electrical and electronics engineers should have good analytical skills, the capacity for sustained attention to detail, and the ability to work as part of a team. Good communication skills are also important.

Earnings: In 1997, starting salaries for engineering graduates with bachelor's degrees, according to the National Association of Colleges and Employers, averaged $38,500 in private industry; those with master's degrees, $45,400;

and those with Ph.D.'s, $59,200. Electrical and electronics engineers with bachelor's degrees started on average at a salary of $39,513.

THE JOB AND THE WORK ENVIRONMENT

Electrical and electronics engineers constitute the largest branch of engineers in the United States; they held 367,000 jobs in 1996. Most jobs were in engineering and business consulting firms, manufacturers of electrical and electronic equipment, professional and scientific instruments, and government agencies. Their basic work is in the design, development, and testing of electrical and electronic equipment. In electrical equipment, this ranges from power-generating equipment for electric utilities to lighting and wiring for buildings, airplanes, and automobiles; electronic equipment ranges from radar and computers to television sets and stereo components.

They also supervise production and operations or concentrate on maintenance. If they hold administrative positions, they are responsible for cost and quality control and participate in other aspects of the business. Because the field covers such a wide range of systems and products, engineers must specialize (e.g., in power generating equipment used by public utilities or the complex networks of missile guidance systems or aviation electronics). They rely not only on personal expertise, but also on the ability to work as part of a team throughout the process.

Electrical and electronics engineers usually work a 5-day, 40-hour week. They may work exclusively in testing laboratories or divide their time between the office and plant, depending on the industry and their position. Some may also work in administration, management, or sales.

TRAINING AND QUALIFICATIONS

The minimum qualification for electrical and electronics engineers is a bachelor's degree in engineering. A typical course of study lasts from four to six years (the longer program leads to a master's degree). After a grounding in physics, chemistry, mathematics, and basic engineering, the student usually specializes. Many engineers earn postgraduate degrees while working; some five- and six-year courses of study combine classwork and practical work, making it possible for students to pay their way through school.

Once on the job, an engineer is likely to receive training by the company. The learning process never stops. Rapid advances in technology demand continuous education to avoid obsolescence. Postgraduate degrees are essential for most research and teaching posts and for positions in management.

All states and the District of Columbia require licensing for engineers whose work may affect life, health, or property. To be licensed, an engineer must graduate from an accredited engineering school, have four years of experience, and pass a state examination.

Those seeking positions in administration or management will benefit from an additional degree in business administration.

EARNINGS

Earnings for electrical and electronics engineers depend on degree qualifications, experience, and the sector of the economy in which they work. In 1997, the median salary for electric and electronics engineers with a bachelor's degree was $51,700. Starting salaries for electric and electronics engineers with bachelor's degrees were $49,800. For all engineers holding master's degrees, the median annual salary was $56,700; and Ph.D.'s, $64,700. The average annual salary for all engineers in the federal government was $61,950 in 1997.

PROSPECTS: JOB OUTLOOK

Job growth for electrical engineers is expected to be good through the year 2006, although most jobs will come from replacement needs. Due to shortages of electrical engineering faculty and laboratory equipment, enrollments in electrical engineering programs may be lower than the demand for new engineers.

Electrical and electronics engineers will find greater opportunities in the fields of computers and communications due to increased demand on the part of both government and business. Government and business are also likely to contribute to growth by financing more research and development of automated systems. The demand for a wide variety of consumer goods is expected to increase, too. On the other hand, cutbacks in defense spending could result in layoffs of electrical and electronics engineers working for the government or for defense-related industries.

WHERE TO LOOK FOR FURTHER INFORMATION

For information on electrical and electronics engineers:

Institute of Electrical and Electronics Engineers (IEEE)
1828 L Street, NW
Suite 1202
Washington, DC 20036

INDUSTRIAL ENGINEERS

OCCUPATIONAL OVERVIEW

Job Description: Industrial engineers design production, control, and distribution systems, primarily for manufacturing concerns. They are the bridge between management and production.

Prospects: Through the year 2006, the growth of jobs for industrial engineers is expected to grow as fast as the average for all occupations in the economy as a whole.

Qualifications: A bachelor's degree in industrial engineering is a minimum requirement, and a graduate degree is required for most teaching posts and positions in management. For those interested in managerial or administrative positions, a degree in business administration, in addition to the engineering degree, will prove valuable. All states and the District of Columbia require licensing for engineers whose work may affect life, health, or property.

Personal Skills: An industrial engineer needs good analytical skills, the capacity for sustained attention to detail, and the ability to work well as part of a team. Good communication skills are also important.

Earnings: Median annual salaries for industrial engineers who worked full time in 1996 were about $43,700. Starting salaries for industrial engineers with a bachelor's degree were about $38,026 in private industry in 1997.

THE JOB AND THE WORK ENVIRONMENT

In industry and manufacturing, the production process is a combination of people, machinery, materials, information, and energy. Some industries require highly complex processes and pose problems that can be solved only with a novel design, developed with the help of computers. The industrial engineer designs systems that combine all the elements of production efficiently and economically.

Unlike engineers in other specialties, industrial engineers work primarily with people and organizational methods, not products and processes. Although they must understand the specifications and capacities of machinery, their area of expertise is combining machines with other machines and with people who work directly with the machinery. Organizationally, industrial engineers bridge the gap between operations and management.

In the course of solving organizational and production problems, industrial engineers design data-processing systems and apply mathematical analysis. They develop management control systems useful in financial planning and cost analysis, design production planning and control systems used to coordinate plantwide and interplant activities, and enable organizations to maintain effective quality control. They also design and improve distribution systems of goods and services.

Industrial engineers participate in locating and selecting plant sites by conducting surveys to determine which sites have the best access to raw materials, labor, and transportation and which are least burdened with taxes. They contribute to financial organization by developing wage and salary administration systems and job evaluation programs. Much of the work of industrial engineers prepares them for positions in management.

Industrial engineers work in a variety of settings, typically in a 5-day, 40-hour week. Often they spend part of their working time in offices and at computers, another part inspecting plant or work sites, and another part examining or helping to select equipment for incorporation into a production system. The work can entail diverse responsibilities and require travel.

TRAINING AND QUALIFICATIONS

The minimum qualification for industrial engineers is a bachelor's degree in engineering. A typical course of study lasts from four to six years, with the longer program leading to a master's degree. After a grounding in physics, chemistry, mathematics, and basic engineering, the student usually specializes. Many engineers earn postgraduate degrees while working; some five- and six-year courses of study combine classwork and practical work, making it possible for students to pay their way through school. Postgraduate degrees are essential for most research and teaching posts and for positions in management. Most engineers also receive training by the company to keep up with rapid advances in technology.

All states and the District of Columbia require licensing for engineers whose work may affect life, health, or property. To be licensed, an engineer must graduate from an accredited engineering school, have four years of experience, and pass a state examination.

EARNINGS

Earnings for engineers depend on degree qualifications, experience, and the sector of the economy in which they work. Starting salaries for all engineers with a bachelor's degree are significantly higher than for bachelor's degree graduates in other fields. According to the National Association of Colleges and Employers, in 1997, such graduates averaged about $38,500 in private industry. Industrial engineers with bachelor's degrees averaged slightly under that level, at $38,026.

Median annual salaries for industrial engineers in 1996 were $43,700.

The median annual salary for all engineers who worked full time was about $49,200 in 1996. Median annual salaries for all engineers at senior managerial levels were about $99,200.

PROSPECTS: JOB OUTLOOK

In 1996, industrial engineers held about 115,000 jobs. About 73 percent worked in manufacturing industries. Since their skills and expertise can be applied to a variety of industries and organizations, industrial engineers are more widely distributed among manufacturing industries than other engineers. They work in insurance companies, banks, hospitals, and retail organizations, for government agencies, and as consultants.

Through the year 2006, the growth of jobs for industrial engineers should be as fast as the average, although the projected trend depends on several factors: industrial growth and expansion, the increasing complexity of business operations, and the increasing use of automation in plants and offices, along with the need to incorporate it effectively into systems. Industrial engineers will be sought by firms seeking to reduce costs and increase productivity. It is expected that most job openings will be to replace those who have left the workforce or changed occupations.

WHERE TO LOOK FOR FURTHER INFORMATION

For information on career opportunities for industrial engineers:

Institute of Industrial Engineers, Inc.
25 Technology Park/Atlanta
Norcross, GA 30092

MECHANICAL ENGINEERS

OCCUPATIONAL OVERVIEW

Job Description: Mechanical engineers plan and design tools, engines, machines, and other mechanical equipment. They work primarily in manufacturing firms.

Prospects: Through the year 2006, the growth of jobs for mechanical engineers is expected to be as fast as the average for the economy as a whole.

Qualifications: A bachelor's degree in mechanical engineering is a minimum requirement, and a postgraduate degree is required for most teaching posts and managerial positions. For those interested in managerial or administrative positions, a degree in business administration, in addition to the engineering degree, is valuable. All states and the District of Columbia require licensing for engineers whose work may affect life, health, or property.

Personal Skills: Mechanical engineers should have good analytical skills, the capacity for sustained attention to details, and the ability to work well as part of a team. Good communication skills also are important.

Earnings: Starting salaries for mechanical engineers with a bachelor's degree in 1997 averaged $38,113. Median annual salaries for mechanical engineers working full time in 1996 were $43,700. Holders of master's degrees and Ph.D.'s earned significantly more.

THE JOB AND THE WORK ENVIRONMENT

Mechanical engineers design and develop all kinds of power-producing and power-using machinery. Power-producing machines include large steam and gas turbines, internal combustion engines, and jet and rocket engines. The materials used and their tolerances, and the power they generate and their energy sources differ, as do the design problems they pose.

Power-producing machines—refrigerators, air-conditioning and heating machines, robots, and machine tools—are also diverse. In both areas, mechanical engineers specialize.

Mechanical engineering is the broadest engineering discipline, extending across many independent specialties.

Mechanical engineers may also be responsible for maintenance or work in production operations and even technical sales. Their knowledge and experience often provide an excellent foundation for administrative and managerial positions. Increasingly, they rely on computers for their work.

In an industrial setting, mechanical engineers might have to spend some work time near or around the plant; other settings require work in testing and development. Mechanical engineers usually work a 5-day, 40-hour week.

TRAINING AND QUALIFICATIONS

The minimum qualification for mechanical engineers is a bachelor's degree in engineering. A typical course of study lasts from four to six years, with the longer program leading to a master's degree. After a grounding in physics, chemistry, mathematics, and basic engineering, the student usually chooses an area of specialization. Many engineers earn postgraduate degrees while working; some five- and six-year courses of study combine classwork and practical work, making it possible for students to pay their way through school.

Most engineers receive on-the-job training and must work to keep up with advances in technology. Postgraduate degrees are essential for most teaching posts and positions in management.

All states and the District of Columbia require licensing for engineers whose work may affect life, health, or property. To become licensed, an engineer must graduate from an accredited engineering school, have four years of experience, and pass a state examination.

EARNINGS

Earnings for mechanical engineers depend on degree qualifications, experience, and the sector of the economy in which they work. According to the National Association of Colleges and Employers, mechanical engineers with a bachelor's degree in 1997 earned a starting salary of $38,113.

Median annual salaries for mechanical engineers in 1996 averaged $49,700. The median annual salary of all engineers with a master's degree was $56,700, in 1996, and for Ph.D.'s, $64,700.

Benefit packages vary, with significant differentials likely for those who advance to management. In 1995, for example, a survey of 160 metropolitan areas found that the average annual salary for engineers in senior managerial levels was about $99,200.

The average annual salary for all engineers in the federal government in 1997 was $61,950.

PROSPECTS: JOB OUTLOOK

In 1996, mechanical engineers held some 228,000 jobs. Three-fifths worked in manufacturing, especially in machinery, transportation equipment, electrical equipment, and fabricated metal products. Most of the balance held jobs in business and engineering and consulting services and agencies of the government.

Through the year 2006, as industrial processes become more complex and the demand for machinery and machine tools increases, job growth for mechanical engineers is expected to be as fast as the average for the economy as a whole. However, employment of mechanical engineers in business and engineering firms is expected to grow faster than the average as other industries in the economy increasingly contract these firms to solve engineering problems.

WHERE TO LOOK FOR FURTHER INFORMATION

For information on careers as a mechanical engineer:

American Society of Mechanical Engineers
345 East 47th Street
New York, NY 10017

METALLURGICAL, CERAMIC, AND MATERIALS ENGINEERS

OCCUPATIONAL OVERVIEW

Job Description: Metallurgical and ceramic engineers work to develop, respectively, new kinds of metals or varieties of ceramics needed in the manufacture of specific products or to meet the special needs of a structure or mechanism. Materials engineers evaluate a wide range of materials and test and choose those most suitable to particular applications.

Prospects: Through the year 2006, job openings are expected to increase more slowly than the average for the economy as a whole.

Qualifications: A bachelor's degree in metallurgical, ceramic, or materials engineering is necessary for employment in these fields. Postgraduate degrees command higher salaries and are necessary for teaching positions and more challenging research work. For those interested in administrative positions, a degree in business administration, in addition to an engineering degree, is valuable. All states and the District of Columbia require licensing for engineers whose work may affect life, health, or property.

Personal Skills: Those planning to be engineers should have an analytical mind and be good at mathematics. They should have a capacity for careful and methodical work that requires close attention to detail, and they must be able to work as part of a team and have good communication skills.

Earnings: Starting salaries for metallurgical, ceramic, and materials engineers with bachelor's degrees were $38,550 in 1997. The median salary for all engineers who worked full time in 1996 was $49,200. Experienced mid-level engineers with no supervisory responsibilities had median earnings of about $59,100.

THE JOB AND THE WORK ENVIRONMENT

Metallurgical, ceramic, and materials engineers work to develop new materials to meet specific requirements (e.g, heat resistance, strength, or malleability).

The extractive, or chemical, branch of metallurgical engineering studies processes for removing metals from ores and refining and alloying them. *Physical metallurgists* are concerned with the nature, structure, and physical properties of metals and with converting refined metals into final products. *Mechanical* or *process metallurgists* deal with the industrial processes for working and shaping metals. Most metallurgical engineers work in an industrial setting and may divide their time among office and laboratory and the plant. Work in and around the plant requires that engineers, like all other personnel, observe safety precautions around hazardous materials and processes.

Ceramic engineers work with a wide variety of nonmetallic, inorganic materials that require high temperatures in processing: glassware, electronic components, automobile and aircraft engine components, brick, and tile.

Materials engineers test metals, plastics, ceramics, and other materials for technical and economic suitability for a product or application, and develop new materials to meet technological needs.

Metallurgical, ceramic, and materials engineers work a 5-day, 40-hour week. About 20 percent work in the metal-producing industries. Others work in the aircraft, machinery, and electrical equipment industries, business and engineering consulting firms, and various governmental agencies.

TRAINING AND QUALIFICATIONS

The minimum qualification is a bachelor's degree in engineering. A typical course of study lasts from four to six years, with the longer program leading to a master's degree. After a grounding in physics, chemistry, mathematics, and basic engineering, the student usually specializes. Many engineers earn postgraduate degrees while working; some five- and six-year courses of study combine classwork and practical work, making it possible for students to pay their way through school.

Most engineers receive on-the-job training and study to keep up with rapid advances in technology. Postgraduate degrees are essential for most research and teaching posts and managerial positions.

All states and the District of Columbia require licensing for engineers whose work may affect life, health, or property. To be licensed, an engineer must graduate from an accredited engineering school, have four years of experience, and pass a state examination.

EARNINGS

A survey of 160 metropolitan areas in 1997 reported that beginning engineers in all specialties had median annual earnings of about $34,400. Experienced mid-level engineers with no supervisory responsibilities had median earnings of about $59,100. Median earnings for engineers at senior managerial levels were about $99,200.

The average annual salary for all engineers in the federal government in supervisory, nonsupervisory, and managerial positions was $61,950 in 1997.

PROSPECTS: JOB OUTLOOK

For metallurgical, ceramic, and materials engineers, job opportunities are expected to grow more slowly than the average, and most openings will be for replacements. Many of the industries in which they are concentrated, such as stone, clay, and glass products; primary metals; fabricated metal products; and transportation equipment industries are expected to experience little, if any, employment growth through the year 2006. Anticipated employment growth in service industries, such as research and testing services and engineering and architectural services, however, should provide significant job openings as these firms are employed to develop improved materials for their industrial customers.

About 18,000 engineers in this specialty held jobs in 1996.

WHERE TO LOOK FOR FURTHER INFORMATION

For more information on career opportunities in metallurgical, ceramic, and materials engineering:

The Minerals, Metals, and Materials Society
420 Commonwealth Drive
Warrendale, PA 15086-7514

American Society for Metals
9639 Kinsman
Metals Park, OH 44073

American Institute of Mining, Metallurgical
   and Petroleum Engineers
345 East 47th Street
14th Floor
New York, NY 10017

Nuclear Engineers

OCCUPATIONAL OVERVIEW

Job Description: Nuclear engineers design, develop, monitor, and operate nuclear power plants, and work on the research and development of other applications of nuclear power. They work for public utilities, private businesses, and the federal government.

Prospects: Although through the year 2006, it is expected that few, if any, new nuclear power plants will be built, the number of jobs in this field is expected to remain stable.

Qualifications: A bachelor's degree in nuclear engineering is a minimum requirement for nuclear engineers. A postgraduate degree is required for most teaching and research posts and positions in management. For those interested in managerial or administrative positions, a degree in business administration, in addition to the engineering degree, will prove valuable. All states and the District of Columbia require licensing for engineers whose work may affect life, health, or property.

Personal Skills: The nuclear engineer should have good analytical skills, the capacity for sustained attention to details, and the ability to work as part of a team. Good communication skills are also important.

Earnings: Starting salaries for nuclear engineers with a bachelor's degree were about $37,194 in 1997. Median annual salaries of nuclear engineers in 1996 were about $49,700. Median annual salaries for engineers in the federal government are generally lower.

THE JOB AND THE WORK ENVIRONMENT

Nuclear engineers study the practical applications of nuclear power through nuclear technology. For the most part, their work touches on four basic areas: (1) power generating, (2) nuclear waste disposal, (3) nuclear weapons, and (4) the use and application of radioactive materials in medicine. They develop new applications for nuclear power, seek to increase the safe use of nuclear power, and look for ways to dispose of radioactive waste safely.

They also monitor and operate nuclear power plants used by public utilities to generate electricity and on naval ships. Public utilities, for the most part, have ceased design and development work on new nuclear power plants, although the U.S. Navy continues to do this work.

Nuclear engineers whose specialty is the nuclear fuel cycle study the production, handling, and use of nuclear fuel and the crucial problem of how to safely dispose of the waste that nuclear energy produces.

The defense industry uses nuclear engineers to develop and maintain nuclear weapons. Nuclear technology also has medical applications, particularly in the treatment of cancers, and research continues into the medical uses of radioactive materials.

Nuclear engineers work in a variety of settings, ranging from public utilities to the U.S. Navy. In all settings, they must be alert to the hazards of overexposure to radiation and strictly observe all safety procedures.

TRAINING AND QUALIFICATIONS

The minimum qualification for nuclear engineers is a bachelor's degree in engineering. A typical course of study lasts from four to six years, with the longer program leading to a master's degree. After a grounding in physics, chemistry, mathematics, and basic engineering, the student chooses an area of specialization. Many engineers earn postgraduate degrees while working; some five- and six-year courses of study combine classwork and practical work, making it possible for students to pay their way through school.

Most engineers receive on-the-job training and study to keep up with rapid advances in technology. Postgraduate degrees are essential for most research and teaching posts and for managerial positions.

All states and the District of Columbia require licensing for engineers whose work may affect life, health, or property. To be licensed, an engineer must graduate from an accredited engineering school, have four years of experience, and pass a state examination.

EARNINGS

Earnings for engineers generally depend on degree qualifications, experience, and the sector of the economy in which they work. According to the National Association of Colleges and Employers, engineering graduates with a B.S. averaged starting salaries of about $38,500 in 1997; those with an M.S. and no experience, $45,400 a year; and those with a Ph.D., $59,200.

The median annual salary for nuclear engineers in 1996 was $49,700.

In 1996, a survey of 160 metropolitan areas found that the average annual salary for engineers in senior managerial levels was about $99,200.

Benefit packages vary, with significant differentials for those who advance to management.

PROSPECTS: JOB OUTLOOK

Nuclear engineers held about 14,000 jobs in 1996; about 20 percent of them were in utilities, engineering consulting firms, and the federal government. About half of the government jobs were held by civilian employees of the U.S. Navy. The balance of the government jobs were in the Nuclear Regulatory Commission, the U.S. Department of Energy, and the Tennessee Valley Authority. Most nongovernmental jobs were with public utilities or engineering consulting firms, and some nuclear engineers worked for manufacturers of nuclear power equipment.

Through the year 2006, the number of jobs for nuclear engineers is expected to remain stable. Until problems of safety and disposal of hazardous nuclear waste are solved, it is unlikely that any new nuclear power plants will be built; however, nuclear engineers will be needed to maintain and operate existing facilities, working to improve and enforce safety standards. They also will fill defense-related jobs.

Most jobs in this field will be to replace personnel who have changed occupations or left the workforce. Because the number of new graduates with degrees in nuclear engineering has been declining, job opportunities for nuclear engineers should be good.

WHERE TO LOOK FOR FURTHER INFORMATION

For more information on careers in nuclear energy:

American Nuclear Society
555 North Kensington Avenue
LaGrange Park, IL 60525

OPERATIONS RESEARCH ANALYSTS

OCCUPATIONAL OVERVIEW

Job Description: Operations research analysts help organizations coordinate and operate in the most efficient manner by applying scientific methods and mathematical principles to organizational problems. Managers can then evaluate alternatives and choose the course of action that best meets the organizational goals.

Prospects: Employment of operations research analysts is expected to grow much faster than the average for all occupations through the year 2006, due to the increasing importance of quantitative analysis in decision making.

Qualifications: Employers strongly prefer applicants with at least a master's degree in operations research or management science or other quantitative disciplines. A high level of computer skills is also required.

Personal Skills: Operations research analysts must be able to think logically and work well with people, so employers prefer workers with good oral and written communication skills.

Earnings: In 1996, the median salary of operations and systems researchers and analysts was about $42,400 a year. The highest 10 percent earned over $65,500 a year.

THE JOB AND THE WORK ENVIRONMENT

Efficiently running a complex organization or operation such as a large manufacturing plant, an airline, or a military deployment requires the precise coordination of materials, machines, and people. Operations systems analysts help organizations with this coordination. They are sometimes called *management science analysts* and are problem solvers. The problems they tackle are, for the most part, those encountered in large business and government organizations, including strategy, forecasting, resource allocation, facilities layout, inventory control, personnel schedules, and distribution systems. Their methods generally use a mathematical model consisting of a set of equations that explains how things happen within the organization.

Operations analysts use computers extensively in their work. They are typically highly proficient in database collection and management programming, and in the development of and use of sophisticated software programs.

The type of problem they usually handle varies by industry. For example, an analyst for an airline coordinates flight and maintenance schedules, passenger level estimates, and fuel consumption to produce an optimal schedule that ensures safety and produces the greatest profit. An analyst employed by a hospital concentrates on a different set of problems, such as scheduling admissions, managing patient flow, assigning shifts, monitoring the use of pharmacy and laboratory services, and forecasting demand for adding hospital services.

Operations analysts generally work regular hours in an office environment. They are under pressure to meet deadlines, and often work more than a 40-hour week.

TRAINING AND QUALIFICATIONS

A minimum of a master's degree in operations research or management science or some other quantitative discipline is strongly preferred by most employers. A high level of computer skills is also required.

Employers often sponsor skill-improvement training for experienced workers, helping them keep up with new developments in operations research techniques as well as advances in computer science.

Beginning analysts usually do routine work under the supervision of more experienced analysts. As they gain knowledge and experience, they are assigned more complex tasks, with greater autonomy to design models and solve problems. Analysts advance by assuming positions as technical specialists or supervisors. The skills acquired by an operations systems analyst prepare him or her for higher-level management jobs.

EARNINGS

In 1996, the median annual salary of operations research analysts was about $42,400. The middle 50 percent earned between $33,100 and $55,500; the highest 10 percent earned over $65,500 a year.

The average annual salary for operations research analysts in the federal government in nonsupervisory, supervisory, and managerial positions was $66,760 in 1997.

PROSPECTS: JOB OUTLOOK

Those seeking employment as operations research and management science analysts who hold a master's degree or a Ph.D. should find good opportunities through the year 2006. Organizations are increasingly using operations research and management science techniques to improve productivity and quality and to reduce costs. This reflects growing acceptance of a systems approach to decision making by top managers. This trend is expected to continue and should greatly stimulate demand for these workers in the years ahead.

Operations research analysts held about 50,000 jobs in 1996. They are employed in most industries. Major employers include computer and data-processing services, commercial banks and savings institutions, insurance carriers, telecommunications companies, engineering and management services firms, manufacturers of transportation equipment, air carriers, and the federal government, mostly the armed forces.

Employment of operations research analysts is expected to grow faster than the average for all occupations through the year 2006.

WHERE TO LOOK FOR MORE INFORMATION

Information on career opportunities for operations research analysts is available from:

The Institute for Operations Research and the Management Sciences
901 Elkridge Landing Road
Suite 400
Linthicum, MD 21090

For information on careers in the armed forces and U.S. Department of Defense, contact:

Military Operations Research Society
101 South Whiting Street
Suite 202
Alexandria, VA 22304

SURVEYORS

OCCUPATIONAL OVERVIEW

Job Description: Surveyors measure the surface of the earth, from large areas photographed by satellites to mineral or construction sites. They determine boundaries on land and water and provide descriptions of land for legal documents. They work outdoors and in offices.

Prospects: Growth of job opportunities for surveyors may decline slightly compared with the growth of jobs in the economy overall through the year 2006. Most opportunities come about because of the need for replacements and with expected growth in the construction industry.

Qualifications: Most surveyors learn their trade on the job and through coursework after high school. All states require licenses for land surveyors. Because a four-year college degree is required for a license in some states, many surveyors are earning a degree.

Personal Skills: Land surveying can be physically demanding. Surveyors should be physically fit, with good eyesight, hearing, and coordination, and enjoy working outdoors. They need an aptitude for visualizing objects and distances and must have a mind for detail and accurate calculations. They must be able to work well as part of a team.

Earnings: In 1996, the median annual salary for surveyors and mapping scientists was about $36,088. The middle 50 percent earned between $28,444 and $44,148 a year. In 1997, entry-level land surveyors with the federal government earned from $19,520 to $29,850 annually, depending on their qualifications. The average annual salary for federal land surveyors in early 1997 was about $47,850. Benefits are generally good.

THE JOB AND THE WORK ENVIRONMENT

Surveyors measure land, establish boundaries, and record the results of their work in legal documents and land registers and on maps. A surveying party headed by a party chief, who is either a surveyor or a senior survey technician, does the actual measuring and collecting of data. Before a survey party heads for the field, the site is designated, survey reference points are chosen, and the prominent natural or manmade landmarks are located. The party members review information from any previous surveys that may be contained in legal documents pertaining to the site.

The survey party's work may be relatively routine, or it may involve carrying equipment over rough terrain. The actual surveying entails the use of instruments like the theodolite, which measures horizontal and vertical angles between designated points and elevations of points on the earth's surface. The survey party must accurately measure distances, directions, and angles. Survey technicians, who make up the backbone of the group, include the theodolite operator and those who hold tapes and chains. Survey technicians also gather data into note form and make sketches. On some jobs, the survey party may be accompanied by less-skilled workers or apprentices who pound stakes, carry equipment, or clear parts of the site to facilitate measuring. Only after all the data are collected and brought in can the chief surveyor assess and record the results, write reports and prepare maps.

Not all surveyors are land surveyors. *Geodetic surveyors* plot and measure large sections of the globe; their work is based, in part, on satellite data. *Mineral*, or *prospecting, surveyors* mark sites that will be explored for petroleum or valuable minerals and ores. *Marine surveyors* specialize in surveying bodies of water and the topography of the ground under water. Surveying in many of its aspects overlaps with and contributes to the work of cartographers; but whereas most cartographers work chiefly indoors, most surveyors work in the field.

New technology is changing the nature of the work of surveyors and survey technicians. For larger surveying projects, surveyors are increasingly using the Global Positioning System (GPS), a satellite system which precisely locates points on the earth using radio signals transmitted by satellites.

The workweek for most surveyors consists of five eight-hour days. Although surveyors put in office time researching and planning surveys, filing reports, or preparing maps, much of their work entails walking long distances, climbing, and carrying equipment; it can be strenuous.

TRAINING AND QUALIFICATIONS

Most surveyors are trained on the job after completing high school. They combine fieldwork with courses in surveying and advance in skill through experience. All states license surveyors, and some require a bachelor's degree; but in most states, anyone who has 5 to 12 years' experience can take the qualifying examination. High school students interested in surveying should study algebra, geometry, trigonometry, drafting, mechanical drawing, and computer science. After graduating, they can begin work as part of a survey crew and progress to survey technician, party chief, and eventually licensed or registered surveyor. All 50 states license land surveyors. Written examinations are prepared by the state and given by the National Council of Examiners for Engineering and Surveying.

Some four-year colleges offer a bachelor's degree in surveying, and courses in the subject are also available in many community colleges, technical institutes, and vocational schools. The chief advantage to a college degree is that, combined with two to four years' experience, it makes a surveyor eligible for the state licensing examination.

EARNINGS

In 1996, the median annual earnings for surveyors and mapping scientists was about $36,088. The middle 50 percent earned between $28,444 and $44,148 a year. Ten percent earned more than $52,000 a year.

In 1997, entry-level land surveyors with the federal government earned from $19,520 to $29,580, depending on their qualifications. The average annual salary for federal land surveyors in early 1997 was about $47,850.

Most surveyors receive paid sick leave and health and life insurance, though the extent of coverage varied between the public and private sectors.

PROSPECTS: JOB OUTLOOK

Opportunities for work in surveying will see a slight decline compared with the rate of increase in jobs in other sectors of the economy through the year 2006. The widespread use of GPS and remote sensing technologies is increasing both the accuracy and productivity of surveyors. The growth of jobs in the field will result from new openings and replacements for those retiring or changing careers.

In 1996, there were some 101,000 surveyors in the United States. About 8,000 were self-employed, and about one-quarter worked for federal, state, or local governmental agencies. In the federal government, surveyors worked for the U.S. Geological Survey, the Bureau of Land Management, the Army Corps of Engineers, and the Forest Service. Job demand in the public sector may rise, in part, from the need for replacements, as well as from the need for extending and improving the highway system. In general, though, little or no growth is expected in job opportunities within the federal government. The private sector will likely see the effects of increased construction. Surveyors in the private sector will survey land and sites for new housing and factories, shopping malls, and office complexes. Construction work is seasonal, however, and construction projects are highly vulnerable to changes in the overall economy.

WHERE TO LOOK FOR FURTHER INFORMATION

For more information about careers in surveying, schools offering courses in surveying, and licensing requirements:

American Congress on Surveying and Mapping
5410 Grosvenor Lane
Bethesda, MD 20814-2122

NATURAL SCIENCE AND MATHEMATICS

ASTRONOMERS

OCCUPATIONAL OVERVIEW

Job Description: Using the principles of mathematics and physics, astronomers explore the nature and origin of the universe and the celestial bodies. They also apply their knowledge to problems in navigation and space flight. In addition to research, astronomers teach in colleges and universities and work in government agencies and private industry.

Prospects: Astronomy is a small field. Worldwide, there are some 10,000 professional astronomers; and in North America, 3,500. Turnover is slow, and most openings are replacement positions. Reductions in defense-related research and a continued slowdown in the growth of civilian-related research will result in a small decline in employment of astronomers through the year 2006.

Qualifications: Some teaching and research work may be available for those with a master's degree, but most positions in astronomy require a doctorate.

Personal Skills: Astronomers need an aptitude for mathematics and science. Good analytical powers, a temperament and appetite for accurate observation and thorough research, and the ability to combine their efforts with others in larger research projects also are important.

Earnings: The American Institute of Physics reported a median salary of $65,000 in 1996 for astronomers and physicists. Average earnings for managerial .

positions in astronomy and for space scientists in the federal government in 1997 was $71,660.

THE JOB AND THE WORK ENVIRONMENT

Astronomers use the principles of physics and mathematics to learn about the fundamental nature of the universe, including the sun, moon, planets, stars, and galaxies.

In the words of the American Astronomical Society, "Unlike other sciences, astronomy does not 'experiment' with its subject matter. . . . [Astronomers rely on] the careful analysis of the light (electromagnetic radiation) that reaches the earth from . . . objects [in space]. . . . The rest comes from the inventiveness and intellect of the human mind." Astronomers use principles of mathematics, physics, and chemistry to test theories about the nature and origin of the universe and the celestial bodies.

Almost all astronomers do research. They analyze large quantities of data gathered by observatories and satellites, and write scientific papers or reports on their findings.

Some 60 percent of all astronomers work in colleges and universities and combine their research with teaching careers. Another 30 percent, or so, work for the federal government or for observatories or laboratories funded by the government. Governmental agencies that hire astronomers include the National Aeronautics and Space Administration, the Naval Research Laboratory, and the U.S. Naval Observatory. Astronomers also work in national observatories, such as the National Radio Astronomy Observatory, the National Optical Astronomy Observatories, and the Space Telescope Science Institute. Research is less strictly defined at the national observatories than it is with the federal government; it is least restricted for those working in universities.

Some 10 percent of astronomers work in private industry, generally for aerospace or consulting firms. A few put their training in instrumentation and the use of computers to work in industry.

Astronomers who make observations may travel to observatories that are usually in remote locations, and they routinely work at night.

TRAINING AND QUALIFICATIONS

Most teaching and research positions in astronomy require a Ph.D. Preparation begins as early as high school, with mathematics and science courses. A doctorate in astronomy or physics is generally required for a university faculty position and for employment at a federally funded national observatory or laboratory. A Ph.D. is useful but not required for astronomers working in business and private industry, in secondary school (teaching physics), or as technical writers or science journalists. Astronomers also must be proficient with computers.

EARNINGS

According to the National Association of Colleges and Employers, the average starting salary offered to physics doctoral degree candidates in 1997 was $34,700.

According to the American Institute of Physics, in 1996, the median annual salary for its members who had a Ph.D. was $65,000.

Average earnings in 1997 for astronomers and space scientists in supervisory, nonsupervisory, and managerial positions in the federal government were $77,400.

PROSPECTS: JOB OUTLOOK

Of some 10,000 astronomers the world over, about 3,500 work in North America. Each year in North America, there are approximately 150 openings for professional astronomers; competition is expectably stiff. Less than 10 percent of astronomers work in business or private industry (e.g., in the aerospace field and as consultants on government projects, as well as in nontechnical management positions), and reductions in defense-related research will result in a slight decline of employment of astronomers through the year 2006.

WHERE TO LOOK FOR FURTHER INFORMATION

A pamphlet is available describing careers in astronomy and schools that offer astronomy programs from:

American Astronomical Society
Education Office
Adler Planetarium and Astronomy Museum
1300 South Lake Shore Drive
Chicago, IL 60605

Additional information on graduate programs in astronomy is contained in *Graduate Programs in Physics and Astronomy*, available from:

American Institute of Physics
One Physics Ellipse
College Park, MD 20740-3843

BIOLOGICAL SCIENTISTS

OCCUPATIONAL OVERVIEW

Job Description: Biological scientists study life processes at the molecular and cellular levels and in living organisms. They also study the relationships of life forms to their environments. Most biologists work in colleges and universities; many also work in private industry.

Prospects: Through the year 2006, the growth of jobs for biological scientists should be faster than the projected growth of jobs in the overall economy. While significant growth is expected in the areas of genetic and biotechnical research, cuts in government funding of research projects will slow the overall number of grants awarded to medical research.

Qualifications: A bachelor's degree in biology is the minimum requirement. A master's degree is sufficient for some jobs in applied research. For college teaching or research posts and for administrative and managerial positions, a Ph.D. is necessary.

Personal Skills: Biological scientists should have good analytical minds, patience, self-discipline, and keen powers of observation. Those whose research takes them outdoors should be in good physical condition.

Earnings: Median earnings for biological and life scientists were about $36,300 in 1996; the middle 50 percent earned between $28,400 and $50,900. Ten percent earned over $66,000.

THE JOB AND THE WORK ENVIRONMENT

Biological scientists study life in all its forms, from the simplest to the most complex, along with their environments and interrelationships. Advances in genetics and biotechnology have given biological scientists the ability to recombine, duplicate, and otherwise engineer life forms.

Biochemists study the chemical composition of living things. Much of the work of biotechnology is done by biochemists. *Microbiologists* study microscopic forms, such as bacteria, viruses, and molds. Among the subspecialties of this group is *medical microbiology,* which seeks to understand the relationship between microscopic life forms and disease. Other microbiologists study the effects of bacteria on soil fertility; others study immune mechanisms. Many microbiologists use biotechnology in their research into cell reproduction and human disease.

Among the older branches of biological science are botany, zoology, and physiology. *Botanists* study all aspects of plant life, including the biochemistry of plant processes and the causes and cures of plant diseases. *Zoologists—ornithologists, herpetologists,* and *ichthyologists*—study the origin, behavior, diseases, and life processes of animals (birds, reptiles and amphibians, and fish, respectively) in laboratories and zoos, as well as in their natural habitats. *Physiologists* study life functions, such as growth, reproduction, photosynthesis, respiration, and movement. *Ecologists* study the environments in which life forms thrive and the complex interactions among living organisms.

About half of all biological scientists work in research and development. Research may be basic or applied. The newest and most dynamic area of applied research in this field is in biotechnology. Biologists can now recombine the genetic material of animals or plants. For example, they have been able to insert the human gene that codes for the production of insulin into bacteria. The result has been bacteria that produce a much purer form of human insulin for use by diabetics. Research is in progress for new applications of this technology to medicine and agriculture.

Biological research also is carried on outdoors. The work requires patience and keen powers of observation. Because such research may be conducted in remote, inhospitable areas of forest or desert, or underseas, physical stamina is vital.

Biological scientists also work as managers and administrators, for example, testing food and drugs or directing zoos or botanical gardens. They work for government agencies or private firms as consultants and write for technical publications. They may also work in sales and service positions for manufacturers of chemicals, pharmaceuticals, and other products.

Biological scientists work in a variety of settings, including offices, laboratories, and classrooms. Some research may take them outdoors. Laboratory work with dangerous organisms or highly toxic substances requires strict adherence to safety procedures. But for the most part, biological scientists work in clean, well-lit surroundings, and they work regular hours.

TRAINING AND QUALIFICATIONS

The bachelor's degree is a minimum requirement for work as a biologist. With a bachelor's degree, a biologist is likely to start in testing and inspection, or work as a technical sales or service representative. Biological scientists with a bachelor's degree may also become laboratory technicians or high school biology teachers. A master's degree is sufficient for some jobs in applied research, but for teaching or research posts and for positions in administration or management, a doctorate is required.

Most colleges and universities offer at least a bachelor's degree in biology. Advanced degree programs vary by specialization, and not all institutions offer degrees in all specialties. Advanced degree programs include class- and field-work, laboratory research, and a thesis. Biological scientists must be able to write and express themselves clearly and concisely.

For biological scientists, a Ph.D. generally is required for independent research and for advancement to administrative positions. Like all other scientists, biological scientists need good analytical minds; they need patience, self-discipline, and keen powers of observation. Those whose research takes them outdoors should be in good physical condition.

EARNINGS

Median annual earnings for biological and life scientists were about $36,300 in 1996; the middle 50 percent earned between $28,400 and $50,900. In the federal government in 1997, general biological scientists in nonsupervisory, supervisory, and managerial positions earned an average salary of

$52,100; microbiologists averaged $58,700; ecologists, $52,700; physiologists, $65,900; and geneticists, $62,700.

According to the National Association of Colleges and Employers, beginning salaries offered in private industry in 1997 averaged $25,400 a year for bachelor's degree recipients in biological science; about $26,900 for master's degree recipients; and about $52,400 for doctoral degree recipients.

Most biological scientists work in long-term research projects or in agriculture, and are less likely than those in many other occupations to be laid off in a recession.

PROSPECTS: JOB OUTLOOK

In 1996, biological and medical scientists as a group held 118,000 jobs. In addition, many more held faculty positions in colleges and universities. Most of the jobs in private industry were in the pharmaceutical, chemical, and food industries. Another segment held nonfaculty positions at colleges and universities. Another one-third worked for federal, state, and local governments.

Through the year 2006, jobs for biological scientists are expected to increase faster than the average for the economy as a whole. Growth will occur primarily in private industry, especially in biotechnical research and production, where advances have introduced opportunities in many areas of biology, with commercial applications in agriculture and the chemical industries. Opportunities for work on preservation of the environment also are likely to increase. In addition, qualified personnel will be needed to replace biologists who leave the workforce or transfer to other occupations. This growth will be tempered by reductions in government grants due to federal budget cutting.

WHERE TO LOOK FOR FURTHER INFORMATION

For information on careers in biology:

American Institute of Biological Sciences
Suite 200
1444 I Street, NW
Washington, DC 20005

For information on careers in particular specialties:

Biotechnology Industry Organization
1625 K Street, NW
Suite 1100
Washington, DC 20006

American Society for Biochemistry and
   Molecular Biology
9650 Rockville Pike
Bethesda, MD 20841

American Physiological Society
Membership Services Department
9650 Rockville Pike
Bethesda, MD 20841

Botanical Society of America
1725 Neil Avenue
Columbus, OH 43210-1293

American Society for Microbiology
Office of Education and Training—
   Career Information
1325 Massachusetts Avenue, NW
Washington, DC 20005

CHEMISTS

OCCUPATIONAL OVERVIEW

Job Description: Chemists search for and put to practical use new knowledge about chemicals. Some chemists perform basic research, studying the composition of matter and the physical laws governing the reactions of substances. Others perform applied research, in which they create new products or improve existing ones, often utilizing the results of basic research.

Prospects: Employment opportunity growth for chemists is expected to grow as fast as the average for all occupations through the year 2006.

Qualifications: The minimum requirement for a starting job as a chemist is a bachelor's degree with a major in chemistry. Those with postgraduate degrees are more likely to find jobs and to advance in them.

Personal Skills: Most important is an aptitude for science and mathematics. Manual dexterity is also important, as are perseverance, curiosity, and the ability to work independently.

Earnings: The median salary for chemists with a B.S. in 1997 was $49,400; for those with an M.S., $56,200; and for those with a doctorate, $71,000.

THE JOB AND THE WORK ENVIRONMENT

Everyone's life has been touched—and in many ways greatly improved—by the work of chemists. New-and-improved synthetic fibers, paints, adhesives, drugs, electronic components, and many other products have come out of the research laboratories of industrial and pharmaceutical firms. Chemists have developed processes that save energy and reduce pollution, pollution sometimes created by chemical processes in the first place. Thus, if industrial chemistry has been the root cause of certain environmental problems, it also has provided the means to clear them up.

For the most part, chemists work in basic research and development, usually in laboratories, where they investigate the properties, composition, and structure of matter and the laws that govern how elements are combined and interact. Some chemists do purely theoretical research, working in an office with paper, pencil, and computer. Chemists working in manufacturing plants monitor the production processes and ensure that finished products meet government and industry standards.

Some chemists specialize. *Analytical chemists* determine the structure, nature, and composition of various substances, and they develop and improve analytical procedures. For instance, they may identify the presence of pollutants in the air, water, and soil. *Organic chemists* concentrate on studying the substances formed of carbon compounds; their work has given us plastics, fertilizers, and more effective drugs. *Inorganic chemists* examine compounds that consist mainly of elements other than carbon; for instance, those used in electronic components. *Physical chemists* examine the physical characteristics of atoms and molecules and the roles they play in chemical reactions. *Biochemists* study the chemical composition of living things.

The majority of all employed chemists work for manufacturing firms, and of these, most work in the chemical manufacturing industry. Others are employed by state and local governments, primarily in health and agricultural agencies, and by the federal government, principally the U.S. Department of Defense, Health and Human Services, and Agriculture. A number of chemists hold faculty positions.

Chemists are employed throughout the United States, but most job opportunities are clustered in large industrial areas. Chemists more often than not work regular hours, although a special research project may require overtime. Some chemists work with dangerous chemicals that may expose them to health hazards and must adhere to safety procedures.

TRAINING AND QUALIFICATIONS

Beginning jobs are available for chemists with a B.S. in chemistry, but most research jobs require postgraduate training. Faculty positions require a doctorate. In general, there are more opportunities and better pay for those with advanced degrees. In addition to chemistry courses, students planning a career in chemistry usually study biology, physics, mathematics, and some liberal arts.

Chemists with a B.S. usually start their careers in industry or government by analyzing or testing products, working in sales or services, or assisting senior chemists in research. Many employers provide training programs to acquaint new employees with the specialized work of the employer. Chemists with a Ph.D. can go into college teaching, basic research in industry, or management positions in industry.

Computer courses are invaluable, as employers increasingly prefer job applicants to be not only computer literate, but also able to apply computer skills to modeling and simulation tasks. Lab instruments also are computerized, and the ability to operate and understand equipment is essential.

EARNINGS

In 1997, the American Chemical Society reported that the median salary for chemists with a bachelor's degree was about $49,400 a year; with a master's degree, $56,200; with a Ph.D., $71,000. Median salaries were highest for those working in private industry; those in academia earned the least.

Median starting salary for recent B. S. graduates was $25,000 in 1996; for recent M.S. graduates, $31,000; and for those graduating with a Ph.D., $45,000.

In 1997, chemists in nonsupervisory, supervisory, and managerial positions in the federal government earned an average salary of $60,000.

Chemists who become managers earn more than those who remain in research or analytical work. Bonuses are also part of the chemists' income, although they do not show up in the base pay figures. Management personnel receive higher bonuses than research personnel.

PROSPECTS: JOB OUTLOOK

Chemists held about 91,000 jobs in 1996, most in manufacturing firms that produce plastics and synthetic materials, drugs, soaps and cleansers, paints, industrial organic chemicals, and miscellaneous chemical products.

Although there is very little unemployment among chemists, the occupation does not seem to offer much in the way of growth, either. Production in the chemical industry is expected to increase, but much of this will be the result of more efficient technologies and techniques than of an expanded workforce.

Certain segments of the industry, such as biotechnology and pharmaceuticals, are expected to have more growth potential than others. There also should be more opportunities for environmental chemists. These areas offer lower pay than materials science, physical chemistry, work in polymers, and some others—at least now.

WHERE TO LOOK FOR FURTHER INFORMATION

To learn more about career opportunities and earnings for chemists:

American Chemical Society
Education Division
1155 16th Street, NW
Washington, DC 20036

FORESTERS AND CONSERVATION SCIENTISTS

OCCUPATIONAL OVERVIEW

Job Description: Foresters manage forested lands for a variety of purposes. They work in private industry and for state and federal governments, managing public parks and forests. They may also design campgrounds and recreation areas. *Range managers,* also called *range conservationists, range ecologists,* or *range scientists,* manage, improve, and protect rangelands to maximize their use without damaging the environment.

Prospects: Employment of foresters and conservation scientists is expected to grow as fast as the average for all occupations through the year 2006, spurred by a continuing emphasis on environmental protection and responsible land management.

Qualifications: A bachelor's degree in forestry or in range management or science is the usual minimum educational requirement for these jobs. Fourteen states require licensing or registration to acquire the title *professional forester.*

Personal Skills: Foresters and conservation scientists must enjoy working outdoors, be physically hardy, and be willing to move to where the jobs are. They must also work well with people and have good communication skills.

Earnings: In 1997, the average federal salary for foresters in supervisory, nonsupervisory, and managerial positions was $47,600; for soil conservationists, $45,200; and for forest products technologists, $62,200. Salaries in private industry were comparable.

THE JOB AND THE WORK ENVIRONMENT

Forests and rangelands serve a variety of needs: They supply wood products, livestock forage, minerals, and water; serve as sites for recreational activities; and provide habitats for wildlife. Foresters and conservation scientists manage, develop, use, and help protect these and other natural resources.

Foresters working in private industry may procure timber from private landowners. Forestry consultants often act as agents for the forest owner, negotiating timber sales with industrial procurement foresters. Throughout these processes, foresters consider the economics of the purchase as well as the environmental impact on natural resources, a function which has taken on added importance in recent years.

Foresters also supervise the planting and growing of new trees, a process called regeneration.

Foresters who work for the state and federal governments manage public forests and parks, and also work with private landowners to protect and manage forest land outside of the public domain.

Range managers, also called range conservationists, range ecologists, or range scientists, manage, improve, and protect rangelands, which cover about one billion acres of the United States, mostly in the western states and Alaska.

Soil conservationists provide technical assistance to farmers, ranchers, state and local governments, and others concerned with the conservation of water, soil, and related natural resources.

Foresters and conservation scientists often specialize in one area, such as forest resource management, urban forestry, wood technology, or forest economics.

Working conditions vary considerably. Although some of the work is solitary, foresters and conservation scientists also deal regularly with landowners, loggers, forestry technicians, farmers, ranchers, government officials, special interest groups, and the public in general. Some work regular hours in offices or labs.

The work can be physically demanding. Many foresters and conservation scientists work outdoors in all kinds of weather, sometimes in isolated areas. Foresters may also work long hours fighting fires. Conservation scientists are often called to prevent erosion after a forest fire, and they provide emergency help after floods, mudslides, and tropical storms.

TRAINING AND QUALIFICATIONS

A bachelor's degree in forestry is the minimum educational requirement for professional careers in forestry. Fourteen states have either mandatory licensing or voluntary registration requirements, which one must meet to acquire the title *professional forester*. Foresters who wish to perform specialized research or teach should have an advanced degree, preferably a Ph.D.

In 1995, about 60 universities and colleges offered bachelor's or higher degrees in forestry. Curricula stress science, mathematics, communication skills, and computer science, as well as technical forestry subjects.

A bachelor's degree in range management or range science is the usual minimum educational requirement for range managers. In 1996, about 30 universities and colleges offered degrees in these disciplines. Specialized range management courses combine plant, animal, and soil sciences with principles of ecology and resource management. Most soil conservationists have degrees in environmental studies, agronomy, general agriculture, hydrology, or crop or soil science; a few have degrees in such related fields as wildlife biology, forestry, and range management.

Recent graduates usually work under the supervision of experienced foresters or range managers and after gaining experience, may advance to more responsible positions.

EARNINGS

Most graduates entering the federal government as foresters, range managers, or soil conservationists with a bachelor's degree started at $19,500 or $24,200 a year in 1997, depending on academic achievement. Those with a master's degree could start at $24,200 or $29,600. Holders of doctorates could start at $35,800 or, in research positions at $42,900. In 1997, the average federal salary for foresters in supervisory, nonsupervisory, and managerial positions was $47,600; for soil conservationists, $45,200; and for forest product technologists, $62,000. In private industry, starting salaries for students with a bachelor's degree were comparable to those in the federal government, but starting salaries in state and local governments were generally lower.

PROSPECTS: JOB OUTLOOK

Foresters and conservation scientists held about 37,000 jobs in 1996. Employment of foresters and conservation scientists is expected to grow as fast as the average for all occupations through the year 2006. At the state and local levels, demand will be spurred by a continuing emphasis on environmental protection and responsible land management. For example, urban foresters are increasingly needed to do environmental impact studies in urban areas and to help regional planning commissions make land use decisions in major population centers of the country. At the state level, more numerous and complex environmental regulations have created demand for more foresters and conservation scientists to deal with these issues. Job opportunities for soil conservationists also will grow as government regulations, such as those regarding the management of storm water and coastlines, have created demand for persons knowledgeable about erosion—not only on farms, but also in cities and suburbs. In private industry, more foresters will be needed to improve forest and logging practices, increase output and profitability, and deal with environmental regulations.

Certain areas of the country offer greater job opportunities for foresters and range conservationists than others. Employment for range conservationists is concentrated in the West and Midwest, and most forestry-related work is in the South and West.

WHERE TO LOOK FOR FURTHER INFORMATION

For information about the forestry profession and lists of schools offering education in forestry, send a self-addressed, stamped business envelope to:

Society of American Foresters
5400 Grosvenor Lane
Bethesda, MD 20814

Society for Range Management
1839 York Street
Denver, CO 80206

Information about a career as a soil conservationist is available from:

Soil and Water Conservation Society
7515 Northeast Ankeny Road
Rural Route 1
Ankeny, IA 50021-9764

For information about career opportunities in forestry in the federal government, contact:

Chief, U.S. Forest Service
U.S. Department of Agriculture
P.O. Box 96090
Washington, DC 20090-6090

GEOSCIENTISTS

OCCUPATIONAL OVERVIEW

Job Description: Geoscientists—geologists and geophysicists—study the surface and subsurface of the earth. They join in the search for energy sources, aid in construction projects, and contribute to the growing area of hazardous and radioactive waste management. Generally, the work combines outdoor fieldwork and laboratory or office work.

Prospects: Through the year 2006, job growth for geoscientists is expected to grow as fast as the average for the economy as a whole, due in part to the generally improved outlook in the gas and oil industry. Also, prospects in research on the environment, oceans, and climate should grow. As large numbers of those holding tenured academic positions retire in the late 1990s and at the start of the next century, new jobs in academia will open.

Qualifications: A bachelor's degree is adequate for secondary school teaching and some lower-level jobs. A master's degree opens up more opportunities, and a doctorate is needed for most academic teaching and research positions. Geoscientists in the consulting industry also should have a good general background in business, economics, law, and planning.

Personal Skills: The fundamental requirements for geoscientists are an analytical ability and the ability to reason from analogy. Additionally, consultants need excellent communication skills. Fieldwork requires physical stamina. The ability to work as part of a team is important.

Earnings: Salaries for geoscientists vary according to the position held, academic degree, the area of specialization, and employer. The average starting salary for a graduate with a bachelor's degree in the geological sciences in 1997 was about $30,900 a year. The federal government's average salary for geologists in managerial, supervisory, and nonsupervisory positions in 1997 was about $59,700.

THE JOB AND THE WORK ENVIRONMENT

Geologists and geophysicists—collectively, along with those in related disciplines like geological engineering, called geoscientists—share a common basic interest in the history and physical aspects of our planet. They identify and examine rocks, study information collected by remote sensing instruments in satellites, conduct geological surveys, construct maps, and use instruments to measure the earth's gravity and magnetic field. *Geologists* are primarily concerned with the composition, structure, and history of the earth's crust;

geophysicists, applying physics and mathematics, study its surface, interior, and atmosphere and the forces acting on it.

Geological oceanographers gather information about the ocean bottom for basic and applied research. *Physical oceanographers* study the interaction of ocean currents and the atmosphere, as well as other physical aspects of the oceans. *Geochemical oceanographers* study the oceans' chemical composition, its dissolved elements, and nutrients.

Hydrologists study underground and surface water: forms and amount of precipitation, its rate of infiltration into the soil, and its return to the ocean and atmosphere. They play a key role in research into hazardous and radioactive waste management. *Mineralogists* analyze and classify precious stones and minerals. They may work in the highly competitive field of mineral exploration. *Paleontologists* study fossils to understand the evolution of life on this planet and to describe the history of the planet. *Seismologists* and *volcanologists* study and attempt to predict, respectively, earthquake and volcano activity. *Stratigraphers* examine the fossil and mineral content of sedimentary rock layers to increase our knowledge of earth's history and the evolution of life. *Astrogeologists* and *planetary geologists* study the surfaces of planetary bodies.

Knowledge gained from geology and geophysics has practical application. Engineers use information provided by geoscientists in planning the construction of large buildings, dams, tunnels, and highways, as do those searching for petroleum and minerals. Geoscience plays a part in predicting earthquakes and flooding, and, in several federal and state agencies, geoscientists assist in work leading to safe waste disposal.

Geological and geophysical exploration calls for fieldwork that is often strenuous and in remote locations. Beginning geoscientists divide their time between fieldwork and laboratory analysis or writing reports. Even well-established professionals spend at least a month in the field each year.

A number of federal agencies employ geoscientists, among them the U.S. Geological Survey, the Bureau of Land Management, the Bureau of Reclamation, the Mineral Management Service, the Bureau of Mines, and the National Oceanic and Atmospheric Administration. In addition, the U.S. Department of Energy, the Environmental Protection Agency, and the Nuclear Regulatory Commission employ geoscientists in the growing area of nuclear and hazardous waste control.

Geologists teach and conduct research in universities. Some work for consulting firms or as independent consultants for the mining and petroleum industries and for governmental bodies formulating policy on environmental problems.

TRAINING AND QUALIFICATIONS

Hundreds of colleges and universities grant degrees in geology.

A bachelor's degree is necessary for lower-level jobs or secondary school teaching. Generally, an M.S. is the minimum requirement for a professional geoscientist, and a Ph.D. is necessary for those who want to do research, teach at the university level, or advance to the highest-paying positions in the field. Geoscientists working as consultants should have a broad background in business, economics, law, and planning, as well as a grounding in geology or geophysics.

Computer modeling and data-processing skills are important. Since geoscientists often must draw conclusions from limited evidence (e.g., visualizing rock relationships under the earth's surface or reconstructing events that occurred millions of years ago), they need an extremely inquisitive and analytical mind. Good communication skills are essential because they routinely prepare reports.

Geologists often travel to remote field sites by helicopter or four-wheel drive vehicles and cover large areas on foot. Other geoscientists may work overseas or in remote areas, or spend considerable time at sea, and job relocation is not unusual.

EARNINGS

Surveys by the National Association of Colleges and Employers indicate that graduates with bachelor's degrees in the geological sciences received an average starting offer of about $30,900 in 1997. However, starting salaries can vary widely depending on the employing industry. For example, according to a 1996 American Association of Petroleum Geologists survey, the average salary in the oil and gas industry for geoscientists with less than two years of experience was about $48,400. In 1997, the federal government's average salary for geologists in managerial, supervisory, and nonsupervisory positions was $59,700; for geophysicists, $67,100; for hydrologists, $54,800; and for oceanographers, $62,700.

PROSPECTS: JOB OUTLOOK

In 1996, geologists and geophysicists held about 47,000 jobs. Many more individuals held geoscientific faculty positions in universities and colleges. Many jobs for geologists and geophysicists are in or related to the petroleum industry. During the 1980s and early 1990s, low oil prices, higher production costs, improvements in energy efficiency, shrinking oil reserves, and restrictions on potential drilling sites caused exploration activities to decline in the United States. Recently, a growing worldwide demand for oil and gas, and new exploration and recovery techniques, have returned stability to the petroleum industry and increased the demand for geologists and geophysicists. Employment of geologists and geophysicists is expected to grow as fast as the average for all occupations through the year 2006. There will be increased demand for these professionals in environmental protection and reclamation. Because of federal legislation mandating the cleaning of hazardous waste sites, however, geoscientists, especially hydrologists, find more jobs available. State and local governments represent a small but important source of job opportunities. In particular, jobs requiring training in engineering geology, hydrology, and geochemistry should be in demand.

In colleges and universities, most tenured professors in the geosciences will be retiring by the end of the century. This factor and the projected increased enrollments from the late 1990s through 2006 should improve job prospects.

Job forecasts in this field must be tentative because it is so closely connected with the petroleum, gas, and mining industries, which are vulnerable to cyclical changes.

WHERE TO LOOK FOR FURTHER INFORMATION

For more information on career opportunities for geoscientists in private industry and government, as well as a discussion of education requirements:

Geologic Society of America
P.O. Box 9140
3300 Penrose Place
Boulder, CO 80301

For a directory of college and university geoscience departments:

American Geological Institute
4220 King Street
Alexandria, VA 22302-1507

MATHEMATICIANS

OCCUPATIONAL OVERVIEW

Job Description: Mathematicians work in a wide range of capacities, from creating new mathematical theories and techniques to translating economic, scientific, and managerial problems into mathematical terms.

Prospects: Job opportunities are expected to increase more slowly than the average for all occupations through the year 2006 for those whose background is solely mathematics. Those whose background includes the study of a related discipline will have better job opportunities. Most openings will result from replacement needs for those retiring or otherwise leaving the profession.

Qualifications: For academic or research positions in mathematics, a doctorate is required. Some teaching positions may be available with a master's degree. A bachelor's degree in math may be enough for an entry-level job in industry, but advanced degrees are usually necessary for more responsible positions.

Personal Skills: The capacity to work comfortably with highly abstract mathematical concepts and excellent reasoning ability are essential. Good communication skills, the ability to work alone and concentratedly, and experience in using computers to solve complex problems are important.

Earnings: Beginning salaries in 1997, according to a survey by the National Association of Colleges and Employers, for those with a bachelor's degree averaged about $31,800 a year; with a master's, $38,300. In the federal government in 1997, the average annual salary for mathematicians in supervisory, nonsupervisory, and managerial positions was $62,000.

THE JOB AND THE WORK ENVIRONMENT

Work in mathematics falls into two broad and often overlapping categories: (1) theoretical (pure) mathematics and (2) applied mathematics.

Theoretical mathematicians devote themselves to furthering the mathematical sciences by developing new mathematical principles and deepening the understanding of existing ones. Although theoretical mathematicians pursue their interests with little regard to practical use, the abstract knowledge created has time and again led to technological advances.

Applied mathematicians use mathematical principles and techniques to solve practical problems in business, government, engineering, and the natural and social sciences. They have been involved in such diverse areas as analyzing the mathematical aspects of launching communications satellites, the effects of drugs on disease, the aerodynamic properties of different objects, and the distribution costs of major businesses. Much of the work in applied mathematics is performed by people who are not formally labeled mathematicians.

All mathematicians use computers to analyze large quantities of data and to perform complex calculations. Computer science itself, including the study of artificial intelligence, is a subbranch of mathematics.

Mathematicians working for government or industry usually have regular working hours. They often work alone in offices, with computers or calculators. Sometimes teams of mathematicians, engineers, computer scientists, and others pursue special projects. Project deadlines and special requests for information may lead to overtime work, and travel to attend seminars and conferences is also part of the job. Mathematicians on the faculty of colleges and universities have more flexible work schedules, and they may divide their time among teaching, research, consulting, and administration.

TRAINING AND QUALIFICATIONS

An advanced degree in mathematics is required for most beginning teaching jobs and for research positions. A bachelor's degree may suffice for some jobs in private industry or government, but most mathematicians with bachelor's degrees work in fields related to mathematics, such as computer science; they typically assist senior mathematicians by performing computations or solving less-advanced problems. Advanced degrees are necessary for more responsible positions. For full faculty status, a Ph.D. is required; a master's degree may be sufficient for a teaching job in a two-year college or in a small four-year college.

In 1996, about 240 colleges and universities offered master's degrees in mathematics, and some 195 offered the doctorate. Many of these institutions suggest, or even require, that math majors take courses in allied fields such as statistics, computer science, engineering, operations research, or a physical science. Those who work in applied mathematics need training in the field in which the math is to be used—physics, actuarial science, engineering, economics, statistics, chemistry, or the behavioral and life sciences.

Mathematicians should have substantial knowledge of computer programming because most complex mathematical computation and much mathematical modeling is done by computer.

EARNINGS

According to a 1997 survey by the National Association of Colleges and Employers, starting salary offers for mathematics graduates with a bachelor's degree averaged about $31,800 a year; and for those with a master's degree, $38,300. In general, mathematicians in private business earn more than those in government or teaching and research.

In the federal government in 1997, the average salary for mathematicians in supervisory, nonsupervisory, and managerial positions was $62,000; for mathematical statisticians, $65,660; and for cryptanalysts, $56,160.

PROSPECTS: JOB OUTLOOK

Mathematicians held about 16,000 jobs in 1996. In addition, about 20,000 persons held mathematics faculty positions in colleges and universities in 1995, according to the American Mathematical Society. Many nonfaculty mathematicians work for the federal government, primarily the U.S. Department of Defense.

Employment for mathematicians is expected to grow more slowly than the average rate for all occupations through the year 2006. Expected reductions n defense-related research and development will affect mathematicians' employment, especially in the federal government. However, as advancements in technology lead to expanding applications of mathematics, more workers with a knowledge of mathematics will be required.

Business and government will need mathematicians to work in operations research, mathematical modeling, aerodynamics, numerical analysis, computer systems design and programming, information and data processing, robotics, market research, and other areas.

WHERE TO LOOK FOR FURTHER INFORMATION

To learn more about careers in mathematics, contact the following:

American Mathematical Society
Department of Professional Programs and
Services
P.O. Box 6248
Providence, RI 02940-6248

Conference Board of the Mathematical
Sciences
1529 18th Street, NW
Washington, DC 20036

Mathematical Association of America
1529 18th Street, NW
Washington, DC 20036

To learn more about careers in applied mathematics:

Society for Industrial and
Applied Mathematics
3600 University City Science Center
Philadelphia, PA 19104-2688

*M*ETEOROLOGISTS

OCCUPATIONAL OVERVIEW

Job Description: Meteorologists study the atmosphere and the ways in which it interacts with and affects the environment. Most meteorologists work with the federal government.

Prospects: Through the year 2006, the rate of job growth for meteorologists is expected to be slower than average for jobs in the economy as a whole. Most job openings will be in private industry rather than the federal government.

Qualifications: The minimum requirement for a beginner in meteorology is a bachelor's degree with a major in meteorology. Most employers seek employees with advanced degrees. For research and college teaching, as well as for the higher administrative or supervisory positions, a Ph.D. is the usual requirement.

Personal Skills: Meteorologists must have good analytical skills and the capacity for sustained attention to detail. They need to be able to work well alone and as part of a team.

Earnings: The average salary for meteorologists in supervisory, nonsupervisory, and managerial positions in the federal government in 1997 was $57,000.

THE JOB AND THE WORK ENVIRONMENT

Everybody talks about the weather . . . and meteorologists take most of the heat for our inability to do much about it. It is thanks to meteorology, however, that we're able to do as much as we can. Meteorology is the study of the earth's atmosphere—its physical characteristics, motions, processes, and the ways in which it interacts with the rest of our environment, chiefly land and water.

Physical meteorologists study the nature and formation of phenomena like rain, snow, and clouds. They also study the chemical and physical effects of the atmosphere on transmissions of light, sound, and radio waves. *Climatologists* study past records of weather and attempt to develop a long-range profile of the prevailing climate. Their studies are relevant to the design of buildings, effective land use, and the planning of heating and cooling systems. They also study the history of the planet's climate for clues to the fundamental mechanisms governing its various transformations, which we experience as the weather.

Most meteorologists forecast the weather and pursue research designed to improve the accuracy of forecasting. *Operational,* or *synoptic, meteorologists* gather data, organize them into computer models, and make forecasts. Relying on weather stations throughout the world and on data gathered in the atmosphere and also from satellites in orbit, they study readings of air pressure, temperature, humidity, and wind velocity. They interpret the data by applying known relationships and using computer models to project changes in the atmosphere. Then they issue generally short-term, local forecasts.

Meteorologists usually begin their careers by collecting data and doing routine computations and analysis before advancing to computer modeling. More experienced meteorologists may advance to supervisory or administrative positions, in charge of a weather station or a larger research or data-gathering effort. The major research in meteorology is aimed at improving weather forecasting by means of increasingly more sophisticated computer modeling. But most meteorologists in forecasting work in weather stations.

Although most weather stations are in airports or in or near cities, there are some in isolated and remote areas. Weather stations are usually staffed 24 hours a day, all year. In smaller weather stations, meteorologists work alone; in the larger ones, they are part of a group. Meteorologists working in other settings, like consulting services or the media, usually work regular hours and in offices.

TRAINING AND QUALIFICATIONS

For beginning jobs in weather forecasting, a bachelor's degree in meteorology is the minimum requirement. But employers prefer people with advanced degrees, which are necessary for advancement. An advanced degree, preferably a doctorate, is necessary for teaching and research posts and for higher administrative positions.

Because meteorology is a small field, relatively few colleges and universities offer degrees in meteorology or atmospheric science, although many departments of physics, earth science, geography, and geophysics offer atmospheric science and related courses. Many programs are combinations of meteorology and other fields, like agriculture, engineering, or physics.

EARNINGS

The average salary for meteorologists in nonsupervisory, supervisory, and managerial positions employed by the federal government in 1997 was $57,000. An inexperienced meteorologist with a bachelor's degree starting out in the federal government in 1997 earned $19,500 to $24,200 annually, depending on his or her college record. With a master's degree, the starting salary was $24,200 to $29,600; with a Ph.D., it was $35,800 to $42,900.

PROSPECTS: JOB OUTLOOK

In 1996, meteorologists held about 7,300 jobs. In addition, about a thousand people held faculty positions in meteorology. The National Oceanic and Atmospheric Administration (NOAA) is the largest employer of civilian meteorologists. About 90 percent of the 2,700 meteorologists in its employ work at weather stations in the United States and other countries as part of the National Weather Service. The U.S. Department of Defense employs about 280 civilian meteorologists, and thousands of members of the armed forces do forecasting and other meteorological work. Meteorologists also work for private weather consultants, engineering services firms, and nonprofit organizations.

Through the year 2006, jobs for meteorologists are expected to increase slower than the average for the economy as a whole because the National Weather Service has curtailed hiring following an extensive modernization of its weather forecasting equipment. On the other hand, private industry is expected to create a small number of new jobs for meteorologists between 1996 and 2006 as the use of weather forecasting and meteorological services by farmers, commodity investors, utilities, construction and transportation firms, and radio and television stations increases.

WHERE TO LOOK FOR FURTHER INFORMATION

For information on a career in meteorology:

American Meteorological Society
45 Beacon Street
Boston, MA 02108

National Oceanic and Atmospheric
   Administration
Human Resources Management Office
1315 East West Highway
Route Code OA/22
Silver Spring, MD 20910

P_HYSICISTS_

OCCUPATIONAL OVERVIEW

Job Description: Physicists study and do research into the laws governing matter and energy, and they also conduct applied research. Physicists work in colleges and universities, independent laboratories, and for the federal government.

Prospects: Through the year 2006, job opportunities for physicists are expected to decline slightly compared with the growth of occupations in the economy as a whole. Retirements should lead to openings in college and university faculties; on the other hand, cuts in defense spending will have an adverse affect on job growth.

Qualifications: A doctorate is the usual requirement for jobs in physics, although some research and teaching jobs are open to those with a master's degree, and those with a bachelor's degree may qualify for a few jobs in private industry or in the federal government.

Personal Skills: Physicists should have inquisitive minds and good mathematical, computer, and analytical skills. They need to be able to work well on their own and also as part of a team.

Earnings: The median annual salary in 1996, as reported by the American Institute of Physics, for Ph.D.'s was $65,000. Average earnings for physicists in nonsupervisory, supervisory, and managerial positions in the federal government in 1997 were $71,800 a year.

THE JOB AND THE WORK ENVIRONMENT

Physicists do research into the basic properties of matter and energy and attempt to understand the laws governing their formation and interrelations. This broad area of study has many specialties and subspecialties, among them, elementary particle physics, nuclear physics, atomic and molecular physics, solid-state physics, optics, acoustics, and the physics of fluids. Physicists may focus on a narrow subspecialty or their interests may overlap and blend with those of scientists in geology, chemistry, biology, and engineering, creating hybrid disciplines.

The principal work of physicists is research. Taking into consideration current approaches, outstanding problems and questions, and available data, a physicist formulates a hypothesis and then designs and performs experiments to test it. Research may be largely a process of analysis using mathematics, but it also can require work with sophisticated equipment—lasers, particle accelerators, telescopes, mass spectrometers, and others. Much of the research in physics is done in small or medium-size laboratories, where physicists work alone or in small groups. Research in certain areas, however, such as nuclear physics, is elaborate and requires planning; the coordination of research teams; and the use of large, complex, and very expensive equipment.

Most basic research in physics is pursued with practical applications in mind. Physicists also do applied research, seeking to improve the available technology or develop new technologies altogether. Often, the applications are more far-reaching than originally intended; for example, the laser, developed as a tool for research, has been found to have applications in medicine, industry, and defense. Physicists who develop a new product or process sometimes go into business for themselves.

Physicists generally work in laboratories and offices, sometimes traveling in order to use special facilities. Beginners do routine work under supervision. Eventually, they may advance to positions as research directors, project supervisors, or top managers. For the most part, physicists work where heavy industry is concentrated and where there are large research and development laboratories.

TRAINING AND QUALIFICATIONS

Those with a bachelor's degree may qualify for jobs in applied research and development, but prospects will be limited. Those with a master's degree may qualify for research and teaching, but for most jobs in industry, government, and academia, a Ph.D. is required.

Over 500 colleges and universities offer a bachelor's degree in physics. Typical physics courses include mechanics, electromagnetism, optics, thermodynamics, atomic physics, and quantum mechanics. Some 180 institutions offer doctorates, and most graduate students specialize in a subfield, such as elementary particles or condensed matter.

EARNINGS

The American Institute of Physics reported a median salary of $65,000 in 1996 for Ph.D.'s. According to a 1997 survey by the National Association of Colleges and Employers, the average starting salary offered to physics doctoral degree candidates was $34,700.

Average earnings for physicists in nonsupervisory, supervisory, and managerial positions in the federal government in 1997 were about $71,800 a year.

Median salaries in 1996 for master's degree holders were about $55,000; for those holding bachelor's degrees, $50,000.

PROSPECTS: JOB OUTLOOK

In 1994, physicists (including astronomers) held about 18,000 jobs. In addition, a significant number held faculty positions in colleges and universities. About 3 in 10 of all physicists were employed by independent research and development laboratories. Another one-fifth worked for agencies of the federal government, chiefly the U.S. Departments of Defense, Energy, and Commerce. Others held nonfaculty positions at colleges and universities or were employed by noncommercial research laboratories, electrical equipment manufacturers, engineering services firms, or the aircraft and automobile industries.

Through the year 2006, job opportunities for physicists should increase more slowly than for all occupations in the economy. Proposed employment cutbacks and overall budget tightening in the federal government will affect employment of physicists, especially those dependent on federal research grants. Expected reductions in defense-related research and an expected slow-down in the growth of civilian physics-related research will cause employment of physicists to decline through the year 2006. Despite this trend, individuals with a physics degree at any level will find their skills useful for entry to many other occupations.

WHERE TO LOOK FOR FURTHER INFORMATION

For information on careers in physics:

American Institute of Physics
Career Planning and Placement
One Physics Ellipse
College Park, MD 20740-3843

American Physical Society
Education Department
One Physics Ellipse
College Park, MD 20740-3843

SCIENCE TECHNICIANS

OCCUPATIONAL OVERVIEW

Job Description: Science technicians aid scientists working in research and development. They also use scientific principles and procedures to solve practical problems in production, oil and gas exploration, and technical sales. They work in many settings and for a wide variety of businesses and industries, including the chemical, pharmaceutical, petroleum refining, and food-processing industries.

Prospects: Through the year 2006, job growth for science technicians will be about as fast as the average for the economy as a whole. The best opportunities are expected in biotechnology.

Qualifications: Most employers prefer individuals with at least two years of specialized training. Many science technicians have a bachelor's degree. The armed forces offer certain types of training. Some employers have their own on-the-job training programs.

Personal Skills: Science technicians should be good at mathematics and enjoy problem solving. They need to be thorough, patient, and precise, and should be able to work well as part of a team.

Earnings: The median annual salary for science technicians in 1996 was about $27,000. In 1997, the average salary for science technicians working for the federal government was $28,500.

THE JOB AND THE WORK ENVIRONMENT

Science technicians use the principles and theories of science and mathematics to solve problems in research and development and to help invent and improve products.

Work in the sciences can be divided into a few broad categories. *Theoretical science* considers basic principles and proposes hypotheses. *Experimental science* devises experiments to test the validity of hypotheses. *Applied science* does research into the practical uses of scientific knowledge and then develops the applications. These categories are not easy to separate. They all rely on certain tasks: Data must be collected and recorded; instruments must be properly calibrated, operated, and maintained; tests must be conducted. These and other similar tasks are the practical supports of theoretical and experimental science, and are at the very center of applied science. In almost every science and in the many industries that rely on applied science, these responsibilities are the job of science technicians.

Science technicians work in colleges and universities and also participate directly in production in a variety of manufacturing concerns. In support of scientific research, science technicians calibrate and maintain scientific equipment, construct and monitor experiments, and calculate and record results. In a variety of industries, they conduct tests and do analyses, operate technical equipment, conduct experiments, and collect data.

They tend to specialize, with most concentrating on agriculture, biology, chemistry, the nuclear field, or one of several industries. *Agricultural technicians* work with scientists in food research, production, and processing. They conduct tests and experiments to improve crop yields and specialize in animal breeding. *Biological technicians* work on studies of microscopic organisms or analyze organic substances, like blood, food, or drugs. Some biological technicians examine evidence in criminal investigations. *Chemical technicians* assist chemical engineers in research, development, and testing. *Nuclear technicians* assist in modern research by operating nuclear equipment and sometimes manipulating radioactive material by remote control. *Petroleum technicians* measure, record, and monitor conditions in oil or gas wells; collect and examine geological data and test samples; and gather technical information about drilling operations, prospecting, and contracts.

Science technicians work under widely varying conditions and circumstances. In colleges and universities and in most research and development projects, the bulk of their time is spent in the laboratory. Generally, hours are regular, except when experiments have to be monitored beyond the standard workday. Science technicians working in the agriculture and petroleum business do much of their work outdoors and often travel to remote and even inhospitable locations. Chemical and biological technicians sometimes work with toxic substances or infectious organisms, and nuclear technicians may be exposed to radiation; in these cases, technicians must adhere to safety procedures.

At the start, science technicians work under close supervision, but as they gain experience, they are given more responsibility, sometimes advancing to supervisory positions.

TRAINING AND QUALIFICATIONS

Science technicians can prepare for the work in several different ways. Many junior and community colleges offer associate's degrees in a specific technology or a more general education in science and mathematics. Technical institutes also offer training, but it tends to be more specific and teaches less theory. Many science technicians come to their work with a bachelor's degree in science or mathematics, or have studied some science or mathematics during a four-year college program. With the bachelor's degree, a science technician is in a better position to advance to a job as a scientist, manager, or technical sales worker. The armed forces offer training that may qualify an individual for a science technician position. Some companies have on-the-job training programs. Individuals interested in working as science technicians should begin preparing in high school by taking as many mathematics and science courses as they can.

EARNINGS

The median salary for a science technician in 1996 was about $27,000 a year. The middle 50 percent earned between $19,800 and $37,100 a year; the top 10 percent earned more than $49,500; and the bottom 10 percent earned less than $15,500. Chemical technicians earned significantly more than biological technicians.

The average salary for biological science technicians in nonsupervisory, supervisory, and managerial positions with the federal government in 1997 was $28,500; for mathematical technicians, $34,870; for physical science technicians, $35,890; for geodetic technicians, $45,050; for hydrological technicians, $33,230; and for meteorologic technicians, $41,460.

PROSPECTS: JOB OUTLOOK

In 1996, science technicians held about 228,000 jobs. Over one-third worked in manufacturing, especially in the chemical, petroleum-refining, and food-processing industries. About 16 percent worked in education services, and another 15 percent worked in research and testing services. In 1996, the federal government employed about 16,500 science technicians, mostly in the U.S. Departments of Defense, Agriculture, and the Interior.

Through the year 2006, jobs for science technicians will increase at about the same rate as the average for the economy as a whole, with the best prospects for biological technicians (because of anticipated growth in biotechnology). Continued growth of scientific and medical research and development and the production of technical products should spur demand for all science technicians.

WHERE TO LOOK FOR FURTHER INFORMATION

For information on a career as a chemical technician:

American Chemical Society
Education Division, Career Publications
1155 16th Street, NW
Washington, DC 20036

For information on a career as a biological technician:

American Institute of Biological Sciences
730 11th Street, NW
Washington, DC 20001-4521

SOCIAL SCIENCES, THE LAW, AND LAW ENFORCEMENT

ALCOHOL AND DRUG COUNSELORS

OCCUPATIONAL OVERVIEW

Job Description: Alcohol and drug counselors help those who are addicted to or dependent on alcohol or drugs to break their addiction, and they belong to the profession called human services. These counselors work in clinics and treatment programs that are privately funded, government financed, or a combination of the two.

Prospects: It is expected that through the year 2006, drug and alcohol addiction will continue to rise, and with the increase, there will be a need for more treatment programs and qualified personnel to staff them.

Qualifications: Until recently, most counselors for drug and alcohol addiction had themselves undergone treatment but had no formal training. The majority now hold a bachelor's degree, with some preparation in human services, social work, or one of the behaviorial sciences. The number of counselors with master's degrees is increasing. Programs are available at universities, community and junior colleges, and vocational or technical institutes.

Personal Skills: Alcohol and drug counselors must have a desire and the emotional resources to help people. They must be patient and empathetic and able to work toward definite goals in what is typically an emotionally charged process. They must be able to inform and guide without judging or seeming to judge.

115

Earnings: Earnings for alcohol and drug counselors vary with qualifications, setting, and geographic region. In 1997, starting salaries for human services workers ranged from about $15,000 to $24,000 a year. Experienced workers generally earned between $20,000 and $30,000 annually, depending on education, experience, and employer.

THE JOB AND THE WORK ENVIRONMENT

Alcohol and drug addiction threaten society morally and materially. Addiction challenges or breaks many of the rules, written and unwritten, that keep society together. It costs lives, not only of those addicted, but also of addicts' victims. The incidence of deaths in automobile accidents caused by driving under the influence of alcohol amounts to a staggering toll. In economic terms, it costs billions of dollars in lost productivity and the funding of programs to address the problem.

Society has had three basic responses to this growing problem: (1) eliminate the addicting substance, (2) attack the distribution and sale of the substances, and (3) treat the addict. A large number of programs treat addicts; at the center of their efforts are the counselors who work with people trying to overcome their addiction to or dependence on alcohol or drugs.

Some treatment programs are run by nonprofit organizations, such as Alcoholics Anonymous; others are financed entirely or partly by government funds. Programs are usually specific to an addiction and are generally divided between those treating alcohol addiction and those treating drug addiction. Some are inpatient programs, with medically supervised detoxification, and some are outpatient programs. Programs also are divided into subgroups; for example, teenage addicts require treatment strategies that differ from those for adults. Regardless of the program and its particular characteristics, the job of the counselor is basically similar in all settings.

Counselors begin treatment by evaluating the alcoholic or drug addict to determine the appropriate therapy and whether detoxification is necessary. Therapy may be done with an individual, family, or group, and an experienced counselor must be able to conduct all three types. Detoxification requires medical supervision; the counselor refers the patient to a suitable program or facility and assists throughout the process.

At the outset, the counselor must confront the alcoholic or addict with the facts and information about his or her condition. At this stage, the counselor's role is not to judge but to teach, which means that he or she must understand the physiology of addictions and understand the patient's case. The purpose is to overcome the patient's denial of the nature of his or her condition and to win trust and cooperation. Though statistics are not available, many, if not most, counselors have experienced addiction or know people who have. Their experience and empathy enable them to reach their patients.

All counselors must be careful and sympathetic listeners with a good sense of when and how to communicate with patients. Counselors work as part of a team that includes psychologists, social workers, and physicians. The job is emotionally demanding.

Counselors work in varying programs and settings. Even in programs in which they work a standard workweek of 5 days and 40 hours, they are likely to be on call. Supervisory personnel generally work more regular schedules, and their duties are administrative in nature.

TRAINING AND QUALIFICATIONS

In the past, most counselors had little or no formal training. Typically they had overcome addiction or were close to people who were addicted. Now, most employers prefer applicants with some college preparation in the human services, social work, or one of the behavioral sciences.

In 1996, about 380 certificate and associate's degree programs in human services or mental health were offered at community and junior colleges, vocational or technical institutes, and other postsecondary institutions. In addition, about 400 programs offered a bachelor's degree in human services. Some alcohol and drug counselor programs focus on practical experience. No matter what the training program, it is likely to be rigorous to prepare counselors for an emotionally demanding job.

Therapies and approaches effective with one group of alcoholics or drug addicts (teenagers, adults, etc.) may not work with another. Counselors may require special training to be qualified to work with particular groups. Minnesota, for instance, requires that counselors dealing with adolescents have a minimum of 30 hours of undergraduate education in adolescent psychology.

EARNINGS

Pay for alcohol and drug counselors varies with qualifications, setting, experience, and geographic location. Starting salaries for human services workers ranged from about $15,000 to $24,000 a year in 1996. Experienced workers generally earned between $20,000 and $30,000 annually, depending on their education, experience, and employer.

PROSPECTS: JOB OUTLOOK

The number of social and human service assistants is projected to grow much faster than the average for all occupations through the year 2006, ranking among the fastest growing occupations. In 1996, human services workers held about 178,000 jobs, but drug and alcohol counselors amounted to less than 20 percent of that total. It is estimated that there are about 30 million alcoholics and millions of drug addicts in the United States. The federal government recognized the shortage of counselors as long ago as 1970, and created the National Institute on Alcohol Abuse and Alcoholism (NIAAA) and the National Institute on Drug Abuse (NIDA). Organizations like Alcoholics Anonymous recognized and began treating the problem much earlier. The persistence of alcoholism and the spread of drug addiction make it likely that the work of counselors will continue, more trained counselors will be needed, and jobs in this field will increase through the year 2006; however, other factors make it difficult to project the job outlook with any confidence.

Data from the National Alcoholism and Drug Abuse Program Inventory show more than 10,000 treatment programs, public and private, in the United States, and that number has been rising. The government also has been increasing its efforts to stop the production and sale of illegal drugs. Both approaches are costly. At a time when government is cost-conscious, competition for scarcer dollars may eventually confront the government with difficult decisions, which could adversely affect program funding and the number of counselors who can be hired.

WHERE TO LOOK FOR FURTHER INFORMATION

No single list of training programs is available; however, several organizations provide some information. For information on alcohol and drug abuse contact:

National Association of Alcoholism and
  Drug Abuse Counselors (NAADAC)
1911 Fort Meyer Drive
Suite 900
Arlington, VA 22209

National Association of Addiction
  Treatment Providers
1 Massachusetts Avenue, NW
Suite 860
Washington, DC 20001

American Council on Alcoholism
2522 St. Paul Street
Baltimore, MD 21218

ATTORNEYS

OCCUPATIONAL OVERVIEW

Job Description: Attorneys or lawyers perform two functions in our legal system: (1) They are advocates, representing one of the parties in conflict in a lawsuit, and (2) advisers, providing counsel on legal matters for their clients on a variety of personal, professional, and business concerns.

Prospects: Prospects for employment are expected to remain good for attorneys through the year 2006, growing as fast as the average for all occupations.

Qualifications: Attorneys must be admitted to the bar (i.e., licensed) by a state to practice law in that state. To qualify to take a state bar exam, applicants must have at least three years of college and have graduated from a law school approved by the American Bar Association (ABA).

Personal Skills: Integrity and honesty are indispensable, as is the ability to work with people and gain the confidence of clients, colleagues, and the public. Good reasoning ability and an aptitude for culling important information from a variety of documents and other sources, written and verbal, are essential.

Earnings: The median salary for lawyers six months after graduation in 1996 was about $40,000. The average salary of all lawyers in private industry in 1996 was about $60,000. Some senior lawyers who were partners in the nation's top law firms earned over $1 million.

THE JOB AND THE WORK ENVIRONMENT

The long arm of the law seems to grow longer all the time. It would be hard to go through a lifetime of even the most ordinary pursuits without sometime needing the services of an attorney. Laws—federal, state, and local—impinge on our lives constantly (e.g., buying or selling a house, getting a divorce, drawing up business contracts). For both businesses and individuals, legal counsel is not a luxury but a necessity.

Whether as advocates or advisers, attorneys' prime responsibility lies in interpreting the law and its applications to specific situations of interest to their clients. Lawyers research the applicable laws and previous judicial decisions. Using this information, they advise their clients as to the best course of action under the circumstances.

All attorneys admitted to the bar are allowed to represent clients in court. Trial lawyers have to be quick thinking, resourceful, authoritative, and persuasive. Some attorneys never set foot inside a courtroom. They concentrate on the advisory aspect of the profession, providing legal expertise to individuals and companies on matters of taxes, patents, employee benefits, and review of legal instruments, such as contracts, leases, licenses, and real estate sales. Other attorneys specialize in working for government agencies at all levels, in areas like criminal law at the state and local levels, in federal law, or in the lawmaking process itself.

The bulk of attorneys finds its employment in private practice, serving clients in a wide variety of legal matters. Lawyers in large firms tend to concentrate on a particular area, such as litigation (trials), wills, contracts, real estate, or taxes.

Lawyers must adhere to a strict code of ethics, keep their clients' affairs confidential, and be able to communicate clearly and precisely—orally and in writing.

Most lawyers perform their functions in their offices, in law libraries, or courtrooms. They are often under great pressure when preparing for a trial or working on an important business deal, and working more than 40 hours per week is normal. In private practice, especially, they may work long hours.

TRAINING AND QUALIFICATIONS

Almost all states require applicants applying for a license to practice law to pass a written bar examination. To qualify for this exam, candidates must have at least three years of college and a degree from an approved law school. More commonly, the minimum is seven years of full-time study after high school: four years of college and three in law school. Some law schools offer evening or part-time divisions, with a law degree requiring four years of study.

The paper chase begins in college, where the selection of courses has an important bearing on admission to law school. Courses in English, a foreign language, public speaking, government, philosophy, history, economics, and computer science are the best preparation. Acceptance to law school depends on a good undergraduate record and high scores on the Law School Admission Test (LSAT). The competition for admittance to many law schools, especially to the more prestigious ones, is fierce and the three years of law school demanding. The resulting bachelor's of law degree (LL.B.) or juris doctor degree (J.D.) is a highly desired prize, an entrée into a useful, challenging, well-paying career.

Enrollments in law schools are expected to remain at their present level through the year 2006, and competition for admission to the more prestigious schools will remain keen.

EARNINGS

Factors influencing starting salaries for attorneys include academic record; size, type, and geographical location of employer; and area of specialization. Larger law firms and corporations normally pay more than smaller ones. Jobs in New York City, Los Angeles, San Francisco, Washington, DC, Chicago, and Boston offer higher starting salaries than those in other locations. In the federal government in 1997, annual salaries for general attorneys averaged about $72,700. The average salary of experienced lawyers vary widely according to the type, size, and location of their employer. The median annual salary of experienced lawyers in 1996 was about $60,000. Some senior lawyers who were partners of the nation's top firms earned over $1 million.

PROSPECTS: JOB OUTLOOK

It is worth noting that in about 40 years, the number of lawyers has increased from about 220,000 to 622,000. About 7 in 10 of these practice privately, either in law firms or solo practices. Most of the remaining lawyers held positions in government, the greatest number at the local level.

The projection is for strong employment opportunities for law school graduates through the year 2006. The strong demand for lawyers will result from growth in the population and the general level of business activities. Demand also will be spurred by growth of legal action in areas such as employee benefits, health care, intellectual property, sexual harassment, the environment, and real estate. Job growth will be concentrated in the large national and regional law firms, and competition for these spots will be keen. Outstanding students from prestigious law schools will find the best jobs; those with lesser qualifications should find work in smaller law firms or with the legal staffs of corporations and government agencies. The number of self-employed lawyers is expected to decline because of the expense and difficulty of establishing a successful, profitable small practice.

WHERE TO LOOK FOR FURTHER INFORMATION

To learn more about law as a career and legal education:

Information Services
American Bar Association
750 North Lake Shore Drive
Chicago, IL 60611

Association of American Law Schools
1201 Connecticut Avenue, NW
Suite 800
Washington, DC 20036-2605

To learn more about applying to law school contact::

Law School Admission Council
P.O. Box 40
Newtown, PA 18940
Telephone: (215) 968-1001

To learn about admission to the bar, write to the state's Clerk of the Supreme Court or to the State Board of Bar Examiners.

*C*ORPORATE TRAINERS

OCCUPATIONAL OVERVIEW

Job Description: Corporate trainers or human resources specialists work to develop the skills and abilities of employees through means other than their job assignments. The training is designed to improve the employees' performance, productivity, and service to benefit the company's competitiveness and profitability.

Prospects: Forecasts are that human resources management job opportunities will grow faster than the average through the year 2006. More and more companies recognize the impact that trained, motivated personnel have on the bottom line, and they are turning to human resources managers—corporate trainers—to make the most of their employees' abilities.

Qualifications: There are no rigid educational requirements for entry into corporate training, although a bachelor's degree in human resources or some technical, business-related subject is a minimal requirement (about 50 percent of those in training and development have advanced degrees). Adult teaching experience is highly recommended.

Personal Skills: Excellent interpersonal skills are essential, as is a knack for teaching. Skills in technical areas, especially in computers and information processing, are important.

Earnings: In 1996, bachelor's degree candidates majoring in human resources received starting offers averaging $25,300 a year. Personnel supervisors/managers with limited experience had median earnings of $59,000 a year.

THE JOB AND THE WORK ENVIRONMENT

At just the time when most corporate jobs, even at the clerical level, require good reading and organizational skills and the ability to operate a variety of complex equipment, the nation's schools are having trouble imparting basic skills. Companies find they have to shoulder some of the educational burden and run extensive training programs if they are to fill their personnel needs. On-the-job training now resembles school more than the old-style job training, with a foreman saying, "Watch me."

The teachers/trainers who run these programs orient new employees to their jobs, upgrade the skills of veteran workers, and introduce new techniques, technologies, and tactics. They may have to go back to the basic three R's for entry-level workers and then fast forward to advanced word-processing skills or top-level management techniques for senior employees. In all cases, corporate trainers work to develop new skills and competencies, foster an attitude of interest and acceptance, establish a climate of healthy relationships, and promote improved procedures. The goal is to produce more productive, more highly motivated, and more responsible workers for the company, allowing it to compete more effectively.

Trainers identify the needs of the employers, using techniques including questionnaires, interviews, job analyses, and achievement and aptitude tests, and then devise appropriate training programs. They specify desired outcomes from the training, determine program content, and decide on instructional methods and training materials. Finally, they implement the programs, utilizing many different kinds of techniques, such as role playing, simulations, lectures, discussions, and demonstrations. Often trainers also counsel employees on their career and skill development and on other ways of improving their business potential.

Corporate trainers work a normal 35- to 40-hour week, either in their offices or in classroom settings. Because they constantly deal with people, they must possess both tact and patience. They must be able to explain complex procedures or technical materials in easily understood terms, and they must have the skill to develop acceptance, even enthusiasm, for their programs within the organization. After several years of experience, some trainers choose to become self-employed, working on a contract or consulting basis for different corporations. In this case, they need good selling skills as well as training skills.

TRAINING AND QUALIFICATIONS

While a bachelor's degree and some professional experience are minimum requirements, corporate trainers, in many cases, move into training and development from other jobs in the organization. For instance, an experienced programmer may take charge of new programmers, or a top sales representative may break in new sales representatives. In this case, experience in and mastery of the subject at hand are vital.

With the growing complexity of corporate training programs, however, formal education in training is becoming more important. Hundreds of colleges and universities offer human resources degree programs concentrating on training or adult education. These programs teach students how to evaluate and use different teaching methods and materials. Others enter the field with a bachelor's degree in business or a master's or doctorate in business, labor relations, or industrial psychology. Increasingly, trainers are continuing their education by participating in workshops and seminars given by groups that specialize in training, such as the American Society for Training and Development (ASTD) and the National Training Laboratory.

EARNINGS

Salaries and fees vary widely. Skilled trainers, both salaried and self-employed, often have an income par with those working as company executives. According to a salary survey conducted by the National Association of Colleges and Employers, bachelor's degree candidates majoring in human resources received starting offers averaging $25,300 a year in 1996; master's degree candidates, $39,900. According to a survey of workplaces in 160 metropolitan areas, human services specialists with limited experience had median earnings of $25,700 a year in 1995. The middle half earned between $23,700 and $28,500. Personnel supervisors/managers with limited experience had median earnings of $59,000 a year. Directors in 1996 made between $80,500 and $106,100.

PROSPECTS: JOB OUTLOOK

Personnel, training, and labor relations specialists held 544,000 jobs in 1994. They were employed in virtually every industry. The forecast is for continued strong growth in the demand for skilled trainers through the year 2006. As business wrestles with the problem of undereducated and unprepared students coming out of high school, more and more will be forced to institute programs to make up for the deficiencies, generating new job opportunities for trainers. Employers are increasingly concerned about productivity and quality of work, and will devote greater resources to job-specific training programs in response to the growing complexity of many jobs, the aging of the workforce, and technological advances that can leave employees with obsolete skills.

Corporate training as yet does not have its own career ladder. Generally, individuals are cycled into training from other jobs in the company (accounting, data processing, sales, etc.), then after a few years, often no more than three to five, they transfer back to their old departments. The route up the company management ladder does not normally run through the training and development department. Only time will tell if this policy will change as corporations come to view their training supervisors as good management material. For the present, however, those looking for a fast track to the top may want to skip training.

On the bright side, those who enjoy teaching and working with people can find a rewarding, well-paid job in corporate training. Training is not usually the first area to be cut back in an economic downturn. Generally, it is cut no more severely than other departments, and it is not uncommon now to find companies adding to their training and development staffs during times of downsizing. A productive labor force is never more valuable than during hard times.

WHERE TO LOOK FOR FURTHER INFORMATION

To learn more about careers in corporate training:

American Society for Training and Development
1640 King Street
Box 1443
Alexandria, VA 22313

*E*CONOMISTS

OCCUPATIONAL OVERVIEW

Job Description: Economists study how societies use their limited resources of land, labor, and raw materials to produce goods and services to satisfy their people's wants and needs.

Prospects: Employment opportunities are expected to grow about as fast as the average for all occupations through the year 2006. Replacement needs will account for most of the job openings.

Qualifications: Some entry-level jobs in research or administration require only a bachelor's degree with a major in economics or marketing. Postgraduate training is required for more responsible positions.

Personal Skills: Good mathematical and analytical skills are essential. Persistence, objectivity, and creativity in problem solving are important. Computer skills and excellent communication skills are invaluable.

Earnings: The median base salary of business economists in 1996 was $73,000. The highest paid business economists were in the securities and investment industry, which reported a median income of $100,000. The average salary for economists employed by the federal government was $63,870 a year in early 1997. Ninety-two percent of the persons surveyed held advanced degrees.

THE JOB AND THE WORK ENVIRONMENT

All societies face the same basic economic problem: wants are infinite, resources are finite. Economists try to formulate rational bases for making economic choices.

Theoretical economists, employing mathematical models, concentrate on developing theories to examine major economic phenomena, such as the causes of business cycles or inflation or the effects of unemployment, energy prices, or tax laws on the nation's economic posture. Most economists, however, concern themselves with the practical application of economic policy on finance, labor, agriculture, health, and transportation. Using their expertise in economic relationships, they advise private industry and government on how to manage their economic affairs to achieve optimum results. For instance, a business firm's managers may ask its marketing analysts to provide specific information on which to base its marketing and pricing policies. Using econometric modeling techniques, the analysts develop projections of market reactions to various price levels throughout the industry, and on the basis of these projections, the managers can make informed pricing decisions. Informed, rational decision making on economic matters is what economics is all about.

About half of the professional economists are in academic life and the other half are in government or hold jobs in private industry, particularly in economic and market research firms, management consulting firms, banks, securities and investment firms, and insurance companies. Those in government fill a wide variety of positions, primarily in the federal government. Generally, economists who are not in academia work in large cities where there is the highest concentration of major financial and government power; New York City and Washington, DC, are two main centers of employment.

Economists in government and private industry generally work a 35- to 40-hour week. Often they work alone preparing reports, but sometimes they are part of a research team. Frequently, they work under pressure and occasionally to meet a deadline must put in overtime. Faculty economists have flexible work schedules, dividing their time among teaching, research, consulting, and administrative duties.

TRAINING AND QUALIFICATIONS

Although most professional economists hold a master's degree or a doctorate, a bachelor's degree often suffices for an entry-level position in business or government, perhaps in an economics-related area like sales or marketing. The importance of quantitative analysis makes it highly desirable for those planning a career in economics to take courses in mathematics, statistics, sampling theory and survey design, and computer science.

Postgraduate degrees in economics with concentration in areas like economic theory, econometrics, comparative economic systems, and planning are generally required for advancement in government or private industry. For a college or university faculty position, a Ph.D. is normally required. In the federal government, candidates for entry-level economist positions must have a bachelor's degree with a minimum of 21 semester hours of economics and three hours of statistics, accounting, or calculus.

EARNINGS

The highest-paid economists in business are in securities and investment, which reported a median income of $100,000 a year, according to a survey by the National Association of Business Economists in 1996. The lowest-paid economists work in education, nonprofit research institutions, and real estate.

According to a 1997 salary survey by the National Association of Colleges and Employers, persons with a bachelor's degree in economics received offers averaging $31,300 a year. The median base salary of business economists in 1996 was $73,000, according to a survey by the National Association of Business Economists. Ninety-two percent of the respondents held advanced degrees. The highest salaries were reported by those who held a Ph.D., with a median salary of $85,000. Master's degree holders earned a median salary of $65,500, while bachelor's degree holders earned $60,000.

The average annual salary for economists employed by the federal government was $63,870 in early 1997.

PROSPECTS: JOB OUTLOOK

Employment of economists is expected to grow as fast as the average for all occupations through the year 2006. Competition, the growing complexity of the global economy, and increased reliance on quantitative methods for analyzing business trends, forecasting sales, and planning purchasing and production should maintain demand for economists.

Job opportunities for economists should be best in manufacturing, financial services, advertising, and consulting firms. The complexity of modern national and international markets will continue to spur a demand for those skilled in quantitative analysis. In addition, lawyers, accountants, engineers, and urban and regional planners, among others, will continue to need economic analysis. The majority of openings will come as the result of replacement needs for those retiring or otherwise leaving the profession.

Economists with a bachelor's degree will face keen competition in securing jobs in business or industry; some may find positions as management or sales trainees or as research or administrative assistants. Those with master's degrees and a strong background in marketing and finance will have the best prospects in business, banking, advertising, and management consulting.

WHERE TO LOOK FOR FURTHER INFORMATION

To obtain information on schools offering graduate programs:

American Economic Association
2014 Broadway
Suite 305
Nashville, TN 37203-2418

Joint Council on Economic Education
1140 Avenue of the Americas
New York, NY 10036

To learn more about careers in business economics:

National Association of Business Economists
1233 20th Street, NW
Suite 505
Washington, DC 20036

PARALEGALS, OR LEGAL ASSISTANTS

OCCUPATIONAL OVERVIEW

Job Description: Paralegals, or legal assistants, perform support functions for lawyers; they cannot set fees, give legal advice to clients, sign up new clients, or try cases in court.

Prospects: Employment of paralegals is expected to grow faster than the average for all occupations through the year 2006.

Qualifications: Employers generally require formal paralegal training. Some college, preferably with training in legal services or a background in areas of interest to a law firm—tax preparation, estate planning, health care, and so on—is required. As law offices rely more on computers and legal software programs, computer literacy becomes increasingly important.

Personal Skills: Paralegals must be intelligent, organized, able to extract information from available data, have first-rate communication and interpersonal skills, and be detail oriented.

Earnings: Paralegals had an average salary of $32,900 in 1995. The average salary of paralegals who worked for the federal government in 1997 was about $44,400.

THE JOB AND THE WORK ENVIRONMENT

Americans love to go to court. "So sue me," goes the challenge, and as often as not, that's what happens. The increasing rate of litigation, combined with the complex legal needs of businesses and individuals, has brought enormous growth to the legal profession. The resulting demand for legal services has created a relatively new and important career—that of paralegal or legal assistant.

Paralegals have worked in law firms primarily in the areas of litigation, corporate law, real estate, and estate planning. They are increasingly working in labor, tax, employee benefits, bankruptcy, antitrust, banking, municipal financing, and environmental law. The kind of work paralegals may do in law firms is limited only by the legal sanction against unauthorized practice of law; that is, they cannot offer legal advice to a client, represent a client in a court of law, or sign documents for a client. Short of that, they perform a wide array of tasks, chiefly fact gathering. The job is no way secretarial. A good paralegal may even deal with clients but in a nonadvisory, information-gathering capacity.

Paralegals help prepare cases for trial, investigate and collect facts, research reports, summarize records and depositions, handle routine paperwork, and file forms. They also help draft legal documents (contracts, wills, mortgages, etc.), prepare tax returns, plan estates, and even manage some aspects of the law firm's office. In corporate law departments, paralegals may help with employee contracts, shareholder agreements, and annual financial reports, and they may review federal regulations to determine that the corporation is in compliance.

Law firms use trained paralegals to handle much of their clients' routine paperwork at a fraction of the hourly rate of an attorney. Thus, law firms can satisfy many of their clients' needs relatively economically and faster while ensuring the best use of attorneys' valuable—and costly—time.

A growing number of paralegals use computers in their work. Computer software packages and online legal research are increasingly used to search legal literature stored in computer databases and on CD-ROM, organize data, and perform tax computations.

A 40-hour week is usual for paralegals, and generally they work in offices and law libraries. They do not usually get overtime pay but often receive compensatory time. The work may be routine and unexciting at times, but new legal developments keep the atmosphere fresh and challenging.

TRAINING AND QUALIFICATIONS

Although some firms prefer to train paralegals themselves, they are increasingly demanding some formal training. A wide variety of training programs are available, and they generally fall into one of the following categories:

- A two-year course at a community college, usually resulting in a certificate or associate's degree.
- A certificate program at a proprietary school, usually running from 3 to 18 months.
- A four-year college program with a major in paralegal studies.
- A graduate-level program, usually lasting three months to a year, resulting in a certificate.

The American Bar Association (ABA) has approved about 214 of the more than 800 legal assistant programs in the United States using the following standards: (a) The program must be part of an accredited educational institution or an institution eligible for accreditation; (b) the program must offer 60 semester hours or 90 quarter hours of classroom work, with a minimum of 30 semester hours in general education and law-related work and 15 semester hours in legal specialty courses. Although approval is neither required nor sought by many programs, graduation from an ABA-approved program can enhance one's employment opportunities.

EARNINGS

Salaries of paralegals and legal assistant managers depend on education and experience and type of law firm. Paralegals had an average salary of about $32,900 in 1995, according to a compensation survey by the National Federation of Paralegal Associations. Starting salaries of paralegals with one year or less experience averaged $29,300 a year, according to the same survey. In addition to a salary, many paralegals received a bonus, which averaged more than $1,900 in 1995. The average salary of paralegals who worked for the federal government in 1997 was about $44, 400.

PROSPECTS: JOB OUTLOOK

Paralegals held about 113,000 jobs in 1996; private firms employed the vast majority. Employment of paralegals is expected to grow much faster than the average for all occupations through the year 2006. Job opportunities are expected to expand as more employers become aware that paralegals are able to do many legal tasks for lower salaries than lawyers.

Private law firms will continue to be the largest employer of paralegals as a growing population demands additional legal services. The growth of prepaid legal plans should contribute to the demand for the services of law firms. A growing array of other organizations, such as corporate legal departments, insurance companies, real estate and title insurance firms, and banks also will hire paralegals.

Job opportunities for paralegals will expand even in the public sector. Community legal service programs, that provide assistance to the poor, aged, minorities, and middle-income families, operate on limited budgets. They will seek to employ additional paralegals to minimize costs and serve the most people.

WHERE TO LOOK FOR FURTHER INFORMATION

To learn more about paralegals and obtain a list of schools with programs approved by the ABA:

Standing Committee on Legal Assistants
American Bar Association
750 North Lake Shore Drive
Chicago, IL 60611

To learn more about certification and schools offering training programs in specific states:

National Association of Legal Assistants, Inc.
1516 South Boston Street
Suite 200
Tulsa, OK 74119

To learn more about local training programs and job prospects, write to a local legal assistant association. You can obtain a list of these associations from:

National Federation of Paralegal Associations
P.O. Box 33108
Kansas City, MO 64114

POLICE, DETECTIVES, AND SPECIAL AGENTS

OCCUPATIONAL OVERVIEW

Job Description: Police and detectives help maintain public order, protect private property, enforce the law, investigate crimes and accidents, and apprehend lawbreakers. Agents of the Federal Bureau of Investigation (FBI) investigate violations of federal law. Special agents of the U.S. Department of the Treasury also enforce federal law and protect the president and vice president, among others.

Prospects: Through the year 2006, jobs for police in all categories should increase as fast as other jobs in the overall economy. Competition will be keen for available positions, especially with the FBI and the Secret Service.

Qualifications: Police and detectives must meet civil service regulations in almost all states and large cities. Generally, it is required that applicants be high school graduates. For the FBI, requirements include graduation from an accredited law school or a specified equivalent. Secret Service agents must have a bachelor's degree or a specified equivalent.

Personal Skills: Police work requires a sober and responsible individual, able to tolerate routine and tedious work, but with sound judgment and the capacity to be resourceful and levelheaded in action. Personal integrity, good physical condition and bearing, and the ability to communicate clearly and well are essential.

Earnings: In 1996, the median salary of all nonsupervisory police officers and detectives was about $34,700 a year. FBI agents in their first year earned a salary of $42,250, which included automatic overtime.

THE JOB AND THE WORK ENVIRONMENT

Police, detectives, and special agents held about 704,000 jobs in 1996. About 63 percent were employed by local governments, primarily in cities with more than 25,000 inhabitants.

Ours is a government of centralized but distinct authorities, laws, and jurisdictions. We govern at various levels—towns and villages, counties and parishes, cities, states, and the nation. Each governing body has its laws, statutes, ordinances, and regulations. All police maintain public order and enforce the laws. But each department and division has responsibilities and authorities pertaining to the level it protects.

Police in towns and cities include uniformed officers and plainclothes investigators called detectives. In small communities and rural areas, uniformed patrol officers may perform a variety of duties, such as directing traffic in an emergency, investigating theft or assault or other complaints, or giving first aid to accident victims. In larger police departments, specific duties are assigned; most officers are on patrol, while some become experts in microscopic analysis of fingerprint or firearm identification. In large cities, officers may be on canine, horse, motorcycle, or harbor patrol, or they may work for special undercover units, such as narcotics.

Detectives gather facts and collect evidence for criminal cases. They conduct interrogations, examine records, observe suspects, and plan and participate in raids and arrests. In larger police departments, detectives may specialize, for instance, in investigations of homicide, illicit drugs, arson, armed robbery, gambling, or prostitution.

Various regions have *state troopers, highway patrol officers,* or *sheriff's deputies.* Their principal responsibility is enforcing the laws and regulations governing the roadways under their jurisdiction. In a majority of states, they also enforce criminal laws. In communities with a small police force or none at all, state police investigate crimes and often work with city or county police to apprehend lawbreakers and maintain public order.

FBI agents investigate violations of federal laws in connection with bank robberies, theft of government property, organized crime, espionage, sabotage, kidnapping, and terrorism. Agents may specialize; for example, agents with a background in accounting may concentrate on bank embezzlement or fraudulent land deals. FBI agents observe and interview suspects, examine records, and plan and participate in raids and arrests.

Agents of the U.S. Department of the Treasury work for the U.S. Customs Service; the Bureau of Alcohol, Tobacco, and Firearms; the Internal Revenue Service; and the U.S. Secret Service. *Customs agents* prevent smuggling across U.S. borders. *Alcohol, Tobacco, and Firearms agents* investigate illegal sales of firearms or certain classes of tax delinquency. *Internal Revenue Service special agents* collect evidence in cases of tax fraud or tax evasion.

U.S. Secret Service agents protect the president and vice-president of the United States and their immediate families, presidential candidates, former presidents, and foreign dignitaries visiting the United States. As agents of the U.S. Department of the Treasury, they also investigate counterfeiting, the forging of government checks and bonds, and credit card fraud. Besides plainclothes secret agents, the Secret Service also has a uniformed division that protects the president and his immediate family at the White House. They also patrol the Treasury Building, the Treasury Annex, and the offices of the secretary of the treasury.

Police, detectives, and special agents generally work 40 hours a week, but since police protection is usually continuous, night and weekend shifts are required. During emergencies, police must be on call, and investigative work often requires long hours of overtime. FBI and Secret Service agents must be prepared to travel, and some assignments require long absences from home. Police work at all levels often calls for being outdoors in all weather. Police work entails great risk to health and even life.

TRAINING AND QUALIFICATIONS

In almost all states and large cities, and in many small ones, appointment of police and detectives is governed by civil service regulations. There are rigorous physical and personal qualifications, and the applicant must perform well on competitive written examinations. Candidates are interviewed and often tested for drugs and subjected to lie detector tests.

A high school diploma is the usual requirement in large police departments. A few departments accept applicants without a high school diploma, but some departments require a college degree.

New recruits usually go through a period of training that includes instruction in constitutional law and civil rights, state laws and local ordinances, and accident investigation. They receive training and supervised experience in patrol, traffic control, use of firearms, self-defense, first aid, and handling emergencies.

FBI agents must be graduates of an accredited law school or college graduates with a major in accounting, engineering, or computer science. (Alternatively, they must have at least three years of full-time work experience.) They must be fluent in a foreign language. They must be U.S. citizens between the ages of 23 and 35, and they must be prepared to accept an assignment anyplace in the United States. Excellent physical condition is required. Newly hired agents undergo 15 weeks of training at the FBI academy in Quantico, Virginia.

Special agents of the U.S. Department of the Treasury must have a bachelor's degree or a minimum of three years' work experience, at least two of them in criminal investigation, or a comparable combination of education and experience. They must be under 35 years of age and in excellent physical condition. Treasury agents undergo 8 weeks of training at the Federal Law Enforcement Training Center in Glenco, California, and another 8 weeks of specialized training in their particular bureau.

EARNINGS

In 1996, the median salary of nonsupervisory police officers and detectives was about $37,700 a year. The middle 50 percent earned between $25,700 and $45,300; and the top 10 percent, over $56,100.

Sheriffs and other law enforcement officers had a median annual salary of about $26,700 in 1996. The middle 50 percent earned between $20,300 and $37,800; the highest 10 percent earned over $48,400 a year.

In 1996, FBI agents started at a base salary of $33,800 a year, and with guaranteed overtime, earned $42,250 for the year. Other U.S. Justice and Treasury Department special agents started at between $31,300 and $38,400, including guaranteed overtime, and depending on their qualifications; salaries progressed to $55,600, including the automatic overtime, while supervisory agents started at $66,100, including guaranteed overtime.

Payment of overtime can be significant, and most police departments provide special allowances for uniforms and equipment. Police officers generally are covered by liberal pension plans and often can retire at half-pay after 20 or 25 years, thus allowing them to pursue a second career while they are still in their forties.

PROSPECTS: JOB OUTLOOK

Through the year 2006, job growth for police officers, detectives, and special agents is expected to increase about as fast as the average of other occupations. A more security-conscious society and growing concern about drug-related crimes should contribute to the increasing demand for police services. At the local and state levels, growth is likely to continue as long as crime remains a serious concern. However, employment growth at the federal level will be tempered by continuing budgetary constraints faced by law enforcement agencies.

Competition for jobs as police officers and detectives is expected to continue to be keen through the year 2006, especially in the large police departments with higher-paying jobs. The best prospects are for those with college training in law enforcement. Competition for jobs as special agents with the FBI and the U.S. Treasury Department should be extremely keen, and only the most highly qualified candidates will succeed in getting those coveted positions.

WHERE TO LOOK FOR FURTHER INFORMATION

Federal, state, and local civil service commissions or police departments can provide information on entrance requirements. Information on the salary and hours for police and detectives in various cities can be found in *Municipal Yearbook,* published annually by the International City Management Association.

For information on the FBI:

Federal Bureau of Investigation
J Edgar Hoover FBI Building
Washington, DC 20223
Telephone: 202-223-5113

Information on applying for a job as a special agent with the U.S. Department of Treasury is available from any U.S. government Office of Personnel Management Job Information Center. For the telephone number of a nearby center, call toll free, 800-555-1212.

For information on applying for a job with the Secret Service:

U.S. Secret Service
Personnel Division
1800 G Street, NW
Washington, DC 20223

PSYCHOLOGISTS

OCCUPATIONAL OVERVIEW

Job Description: Psychologists study human behavior. They provide mental health services in hospitals, clinics, schools, and private settings, and work in various capacities, ranging from teachers and researchers, to counselors and administrators.

Prospects: Employment of psychologists is expected to grow more slowly than the average of all occupations through the year 2006. However, job opportunities in health care should increase slightly.

Qualifications: For most positions in psychology, a Ph.D. or Psy.D. (doctor of psychology), is necessary. Those with a master's degree qualify for positions as assistants in research, administration, or counseling. Job seekers with a bachelor's degree are likely to find work but have limited opportunities for advancement. Private practitioners must be certified or licensed.

Personal Skills: Researchers need to be scrupulous and detail oriented, and at the same time, they must be able to participate in team projects. Those in counseling and clinical work should be emotionally stable and mature, compassionate but self-controlled, sensitive, and above all patient. Good communication skills are essential.

Earnings: According to the 1995 salary survey of the American Psychological Association (APA), psychologists with a doctorate and five to nine years of experience earned median incomes ranging from $51,000 to $59,000 annually, depending on their specialty and work setting.

In 1997, the average starting salary in the federal government for psychologists with a bachelor's degree was about $19,500. The average salary for all psychologists in nonsupervisory, supervisory, and managerial positions in 1997 was $62,120.

THE JOB AND THE WORK ENVIRONMENT

Psychologists study human behavior—its motivations and how it can be explained or modified. They teach, practice, and do research, or work, in one of the many branches of applied psychology, in settings that range from academia, to hospitals, clinics, and private industry. They also work as private practitioners. Psychologists apply their knowledge and techniques to a wide range of endeavors, including human services, management, education, law, and sports.

As researchers, psychologists proceed like other scientists. They gather data and conduct tests to ascertain the accuracy and validity of a hypothesis. They use laboratory experiments and various kinds of tests, interviews, questionnaires, and surveys.

Experimental psychologists study human and animal cognition and behavior for insights into thinking, learning, and perceptual processes. *Developmental psychologists* study the ways that behavior changes from one stage of life to the next. *Physiological psychologists* investigate the physiological bases for behavior. *Social psychologists* study human interactions and group behavior.

Nearly one-third of all those holding doctorates in psychology are in clinical psychology. *Clinical psychologists* primarily treat the mentally or emotionally disturbed. They work in universities and various clinical settings, and some administer community mental health programs. Relatively new specialties within clinical psychology include cognitive psychology, health psychology, neuropsychology, and geropsychology. *Counseling psychologists* advise people with personal, social, or professional problems. *School psychologists* address students' learning or behavioral problems. *Industrial* and *organizational psychologists* are involved in policy planning, applicant screening, and programs to better train workers or improve their productivity. There are also *health, community, engineering* and *consumer psychologists.*

Psychologists work in various settings. In private practice, they have pleasant, comfortable offices, and their hours are flexible, though organized primarily to accommodate patients. In hospitals and nursing homes, they may have to work evenings or on weekends; in schools and clinics, schedules are more regular. Psychologists who teach also do clinical and research work and may serve as consultants. In academia, psychologists spend a good deal of their time writing articles or books. In all settings, psychologists must keep up with developments in their field.

TRAINING AND QUALIFICATIONS

The highest-paying positions in the field of psychology are held by those with doctorates, either the Ph.D. or the Psy.D. Those with a master's degree work under the supervision of one or more doctoral-level psychologists. Psychologists with a bachelor's degree are eligible for jobs in community health centers and vocational rehabilitation and as administrative assistants.

Most colleges and universities offer degree programs in psychology, and over 600 departments offer doctoral programs.

All states and the District of Columbia require either a license or certification for psychologists who wish to enter private practice. The usual requirements, in addition to the doctorate, are one to two years' experience and a passing grade on an examination that may also include orals and the submission of an essay. In some states, psychologists must continue their education to retain their licenses. Most states restrict a psychologist's practice to an area in which he or she has been trained and proven competent.

EARNINGS

Earnings for psychologists depend on qualifications, area of specialization, and experience. According to APA's 1995 salary survey, the median starting salary of psychologists with a doctorate and five to nine years of experience was $55,000 in counseling psychology; $54,500 in research positions; $51,000 in clinical psychology; and $59,000 in school psychology. The median annual salary of master's degree holders ranged from $38,000 to $60,000. Some psychologists have much higher earnings, particularly those in private practice.

The average salary for psychologists in the federal government in non-supervisory, supervisory, and managerial positions was about $62,120, in 1997.

PROSPECTS: JOB OUTLOOK

Psychologists held about 143,000 jobs in 1996. Educational institutions employed nearly 4 out of 10 salaried psychologists in positions other than teaching, involving counseling, testing, research, and administration. Three out of 10 were employed in health services. Government agencies at all levels employed one-sixth. Over 40 percent of all psychologists were self-employed.

The employment of psychologists is expected to grow more slowly than the average for all occupations through the year 2006. However, job opportunities should increase in health care provider networks, such as health maintenance and preferred provider organizations, and in nursing homes, and alcohol and drug abuse programs. The need to combat alcohol and drug abuse, marital strife, family violence, crime, and other problems plaguing society should maintain employment growth. The growing awareness of the need for better conservation and management of our human resources, including our growing elderly population, is a source of increasing demand.

Though prospects for employment are good, competition will be keen. Posts in universities are expected to decline, putting more Ph.D.'s on the market. Competition for a limited number of jobs will be stiff among those who hold a master's degree. Opportunities for those holding only a bachelor's degree are expected to diminish.

WHERE TO LOOK FOR FURTHER INFORMATION

For information on career opportunities, educational requirements, scholarships and loans, and licensing:

American Psychological Association
Research Office and Education in Psychology and Accreditation Offices
750 1st Street, NE
Washington, DC 20002

For information about school psychologists:

National Association of School Psychologists
4030 East West Highway
Suite 402
Bethesda, MD 20814

For information about state licenses:

American Association of State and Provincial Psychology Boards
P.O. Box 4389
Montgomery, AL 36103-4389

SOCIAL WORKERS

OCCUPATIONAL OVERVIEW

Job Description: Social workers help individuals, families, and groups cope with problems of all kinds, particularly those involving day-to-day living.

Prospects: Forecasts are for more rapid growth in job opportunities than the average for all occupations through the year 2006. The expanding population and the increasing number of older people, among other factors, are expected to spur the demand for social workers.

Qualifications: The minimum requirement for a professional position in this occupation is a bachelor's degree. A master's degree in social work is necessary for positions in the mental health field and general supervisory positions. A doctorate is usually required for teaching jobs and is recommended for some research and administrative slots.

Personal Skills: Emotional stability, objectivity, and sensitivity are essential. Good interpersonal skills, the ability to work alone, and a capacity for decision making are very important.

Earnings: Based on limited information, social workers with M.S.W. degrees had median earnings of about $35,000 in 1997.

THE JOB AND THE WORK ENVIRONMENT

All people have troubles; for some, the troubles become too much and they are unable to cope with daily living. Social workers are the helping hand society extends to those who have been overwhelmed in one way or another, including the homeless, unemployed, ill, and bereaved. It helps those who are too young, too old, too poor, too disadvantaged, or too discouraged to fend for themselves.

Direct counseling is the most common way social workers help their clients put their lives in order. Social workers must be good listeners and know where to find resources to help their clients. For instance, they may tell clients where to find financial counseling; how to apply for public assistance, disability benefits, or child support; where to report suspected cases of abuse; how to get an alcoholic or drug addict into a rehabilitation program; or where to find emergency housing. The needs cover just about every facet of human life, and clients may be individuals, families, or groups.

Providing counseling and referral services is at the heart of a social worker's job. The process is called case management, pulling together the most appropriate package of available services, in consultation with the client, to answer that client's specific needs and then following up to see that the services are actually provided. The case worker reviews eligibility requirements, fills out applications and forms, arranges for transportation or escort services if necessary, visits the client on a regular basis, and steps in during emergencies.

The work calls for tact, sympathy, and expertise. The case worker must be able to determine the facts of the client's situation and establish an atmosphere of trust and openness with the client.

Some social workers specialize in child welfare and family services, mental health services, public assistance, medical social work, community organization, gerontological social work, school social work, planning and policy development, or social welfare administration.

Many social workers are employed by government agencies, mostly at the state and local levels. Others are employed by voluntary social service agencies, religious organizations, hospitals, nursing homes, and home health agencies. They usually work regular 35- to 40-hour weeks; part-time work is available in voluntary nonprofit agencies. Some evening and weekend work is likely. Travel is common; social workers often visit clients in their homes and attend community meetings.

TRAINING AND QUALIFICATIONS

The bachelor's degree in social work (B.S.W.) is the common requirement for employment in this field, but undergraduate degrees in psychology, sociology, or related fields may be acceptable. A master's degree in social work (M.S.W.) is generally required for positions in the mental health field and for supervisory, administrative, or research positions. In 1996, the Council on Social Work Education accredited over 430 B.S.W. programs and 130 M.S.W. programs. There were 55 doctoral programs for Ph.D.'s in social work and D.S.W.'s (Doctor of Social Work). The National Association of Social Workers (NASW) admits those who qualify to the Academy of Certified Social Workers (ACSW). Professional credentials include a listing in the *NASW Register of Clinical Social Workers* or the *Registry of Health Care Providers in Clinical Social Work*—important to those in private practice.

EARNINGS

In 1997, social workers with M.S.W. degrees had median earnings of about $35,000.

According to a Hay Group survey of acute care hospitals in 1997, social workers with a master's degree who worked full-time averaged about $35,000. The middle 50 percent earned between $32,300 and $38,700.

The average annual salary of all social workers in the federal government in nonsupervisory, supervisory, and managerial positions was about $46,900 in 1997.

PROSPECTS: JOB OUTLOOK

Social workers held about 585,000 jobs in 1996. Expectations are that jobs for social workers will increase faster than the average for all occupations through the year 2006. The number of older people, who are more likely to need social services, is growing rapidly. In addition, rising crime and juvenile delinquency as well as increasing concern about services for the mentally ill, the mentally retarded, AIDs patients, and individuals and families in crisis will spur demand for social workers.

Substantial growth is projected in the voluntary sector of the field and also in private practice. The growing number of elderly and the stepped-up need for child protection services, both of which are expected to receive increased funding, will offer job opportunities. An expected decrease in the number of students majoring in social work and earning B.S.W.'s and M.S.W.'s indicates that the supply of prepared professionals in the field will not keep pace with demand. There likely are enough college graduates not specializing in social work to make up the difference at the entry-level position, but those with the requisite training will have the advantage in the keen competition for the more desirable, better-paying openings.

WHERE TO LOOK FOR FURTHER INFORMATION

To learn more about career opportunities in social work:

National Association of Social Workers
IC-Career Information
750 First Street, NE
Suite 700
Washington, DC 20002-4241

To learn more about educational programs in social work:

Council on Social Work Education
1600 Duke Street
Alexandria, VA 22314-3421

URBAN AND REGIONAL PLANNERS

OCCUPATIONAL OVERVIEW

Job Description: Urban and regional planners develop and help implement programs designed to promote growth or revitalization of urban, suburban, and rural areas and regions. About two-thirds of the planners work for local government planning agencies (city, county, or regional).

Prospects: Growth in job opportunities in this profession is expected to grow more slowly than other occupations through the year 2006. Most job opportunities will derive from replacement of those retiring from or otherwise leaving the profession.

Qualifications: Generally, a master's degree in planning is needed for an entry-level job in a federal, state, or local government agency. In some cases, a bachelor's degree in city planning, architecture, or engineering may qualify.

Personal Skills: Good problem-solving and interpersonal skills are essential. The capacity to consider a situation from a variety of viewpoints is important, as is the ability to think in spatial terms and to visualize the effects of proposed designs.

Earnings: The median salary for urban and rural planners with between 5 and 10 years of experience according to one survey in 1995 was about $39,900. Those with more than 10 years experience earned a median salary of about $55,000.

THE JOB AND THE WORK ENVIRONMENT

Communities that do not think about their futures may not have a good one. Planners work to develop plans that show communities how best to utilize their land resources to meet their various needs, both present and anticipated. Urban and regional planners analyze and resolve social, physical, and economic problems of neighborhoods, cities, suburbs, metropolitan areas, and even larger regions.

Planning demands a mix of technical competence and creative vision combined with an ability to mediate conflicts between competing and often equally valid interests. Communities need to accommodate different kinds of uses on their limited land resources: residential, commercial, industrial, recreational, and others. Planners attempt to present the best mix of alternatives based on their study and professional judgment, and they often find themselves enmeshed in many different kinds of community problems and activities. They may be examining rent control legislation one day and preparing an impact report on a proposed industrial park the next.

When working on long-range community development, planners make a detailed study of the present use of resources, including the layout of the streets, highways, water and power lines, and so on; the kinds of industry that sustain the region; the makeup of the community's population; and the economic and financial forecasts for the area. They use this information as they design and propose ways to achieve more efficient use of resources and more attractive communities.

Planners often specialize in land use, transportation, housing and community development, health and human services, economic and resource planning, environment, urban design, or something else. Eventually, though, they need to synthesize these separate concerns and devise a comprehensive plan for the region as a whole.

Planners increasingly use computers to record and analyze information and to prepare their reports and recommendations for government leaders and others.

The great majority of planners work in local government agencies. Some do consulting work, either moonlighting or full time with a firm providing planning services to developers or government agencies. Planners also find employment with architectural and surveying firms, consulting firms, and large land developers.

Urban and regional planners normally work in their offices, but they frequently make site visits. They generally work 40-hour weeks but are often obliged to attend community meetings and make presentations during evenings and on weekends.

TRAINING AND QUALIFICATIONS

Most professionals enter the field by earning a master's degree in planning from an accredited school. In 1997, about 80 colleges and universities offered such programs, the majority of them accredited by the Planning Accreditation Board. The typical program requires two years of study, but undergraduates with majors in planning, architecture, or engineering may complete the program in one year. Students enter these programs from all undergraduate fields, typically directly from college. More and more, however, they enter after gaining some experience in urban or regional planning or in a related field. Courses in related subjects, such as architecture, law, earth sciences, demography, economics, finance, health administration, geographic information systems, and management are highly recommended.

Postgraduate students spend much of their time in workshops or classes learning to analyze and propose solutions to urban problems. They often are required to work in a planning office part-time during their studies or during the summer—experience that is extremely valuable in landing entry-level jobs.

EARNINGS

Earnings of planners vary by educational attainment, type of employer, experience, size of community in which they work, and geographic location. According to a 1995 report by the American Planning Association, urban and regional planners with less than 5 years of experience earned median annual salaries of about $30,000. Those with between 5 and 10 years' experience earned median salaries of about $39,900. Those with more than 10 years' experience earned median salaries of about $55,000.

Salaries of community planners employed by the federal government in nonsupervisory, supervisory, and managerial positions averaged about $57,620 a year in early 1997.

Planners working for the federal government, as consultants, and for large businesses earn the highest salaries at all levels of experience. In the past, planners in large jurisdictions (over 250,000 population) routinely earned more than those in smaller jurisdictions, but the difference is shrinking.

PROSPECTS: JOB OUTLOOK

Urban and regional planners held about 29,000 jobs in 1996. Employment of urban and regional planners is expected to grow more slowly than the average for all occupations through the year 2006. A master's degree from an accredited planning program, or in civil engineering, or landscape architecture coupled with training in transportation, environmental planning, geographic information systems, or urban design, provide the most marketable background.

States experiencing rapid growth need planners to help guide development and protect the environment. Older urban areas continue to employ planners to organize their redevelopment plans and solve housing and transportation problems. Indications are that replacement of retirees or others who leave the profession will account for most of the job opportunities through the year 2006.

WHERE TO LOOK FOR FURTHER INFORMATION

To learn more about careers in urban and regional planning:

American Planning Association
Education Division
122 South Michigan Avenue
Suite 1600
Chicago, IL 60630-6107

To learn more about training in urban and regional planning:

College of Design, Architecture, Art,
   and Planning
University of Cincinnati
Cincinnati, OH 45221

National Planning Association
1424 16th Street, NW
Suite 700
Washington, DC 20036

EDUCATION AND LIBRARY SCIENCE

ADULT AND VOCATIONAL EDUCATION TEACHERS

OCCUPATIONAL OVERVIEW

Job Description: Vocational education teachers prepare people for occupations that do not require a college degree. Adult education teachers conduct programs in continuing education and give courses to help adults update their job skills or adapt to technological advances. Both work in a wide variety of settings.

Prospects: Through the year 2006, job growth in this field is expected to grow faster than the average for the economy as a whole as the demand for adult education continues to rise. Job opportunities in vocational programs for young adults are expected to stabilize, but there is likely to be an increase in programs to upgrade the skills of people already in the workforce, with an increase in adult basic education programs.

Qualifications: Generally, teachers in this field need experience and a license or certificate, but requirements vary from state to state. For teachers of adult basic education, most states and the District of Columbia require a bachelor's degree from an approved teacher education program; some also require certification.

Personal Skills: Adult and vocational education teachers need patience and good communication skills. Above all, they should have the ability to encourage and motivate their students.

Earnings: The earnings of adult and vocational education teachers vary widely. In 1996, those usually working full time had median earnings of about

$31,300 a year. Part-time instructors generally were paid hourly wages and did not receive benefits or pay for preparation time outside of class.

THE JOB AND THE WORK ENVIRONMENT

Adult education teachers work in four main areas: (1) adult vocational-technical education, (2) remedial education, (3) continuing education, and (4) prebaccalaureate training. Some adult education teachers provide instruction for occupations that do not require a college degree, and other instructors help people update their job skills or adapt to technological advances.

Larger numbers of adults are returning to school in order to acquire needed skills, to earn a high school equivalency diploma, or for self-improvement or enrichment. In the first instance, they may enroll in one of many vocational institutes offering programs in computer operations, cosmetology, or automotive mechanics. There are also special programs that prepare adults for the General Educational Development (GED) examination, necessary for a high school equivalency diploma. Finally, there are any number of programs and courses responding to a wide variety of interests and preoccupations, from physical fitness to photography, from amateur astronomy to ethnic dance. Adult and vocational education teachers serve these needs and interests. Within this group of teachers are those faculty in vocational institutes and high schools who educate and train young adults for occupations that do not require a college degree.

Whether teaching adults or young adults, the task of imparting new skills is basically a combination of classwork and hands-on experience. A teacher demonstrates a process or technique, for example, encourages students to try it, then shows them where they need to improve. This kind of teaching requires direct and immediate contact between students and teachers. Knowledge acquired in the classroom is directly applied, and practice improves skills. Teachers must be sensitive to students' difficulties, creative in their approach, and encouraging.

Students who want to earn a high school equivalency diploma vary widely in age and background, but most need a diploma to qualify for a better job or promotion. Qualified teachers instruct these students in adult basic education. The program includes work in reading, composition, and mathematics up to the eighth-grade level for adults, both English and non-English speakers, to prepare students to take the GED examination. Teachers in these programs often deal with students at different levels of development in the same class; conducting the courses can be especially difficult. Instilling self-confidence is an important part of their work, and it often requires patience, caring, and the ability to motivate.

Self-improvement or enrichment courses attract many students and cover an almost inexhaustible range of subjects and interests, from do-it-yourself skills to foreign languages. Many of these courses are conducted at night or during the weekend, and can range from one day to one or two semesters.

Adult and vocational education teachers work in a wide variety of settings, including formally accredited schools, programs, and institutes in which they work full time and many other settings and programs in which work is generally part time, such as institutes offering courses in electronics, bartending, or medical technology; colleges and universities with adult education courses; dance studios; and labor unions and businesses that provide training for their members or employees.

Adult and vocational education teachers must prepare classes, assign homework, grade students, attend meetings, and keep up with developments in their fields. Some may advance to administrative positions in state departments of education, colleges and universities, and corporate training departments.

TRAINING AND QUALIFICATIONS

For the most part, employers seek adult and vocational education teachers who have teaching experience and a license or certificate in their field. In some cases, an advanced degree is needed; in others, a portfolio of past and recent work must be submitted. Formal requirements vary by state and by school or setting. For adult basic education, for instance, most states and the District of Columbia require a bachelor's degree from an approved teacher education program; some also require certification.

All states and the District of Columbia require that public secondary school teachers be certified by the state board of education, the state superintendent of education, or a certification committee. The prerequisites are a bachelor's degree, often with a major in the subject the applicant proposes to teach, completion of an approved teacher education program, and a period of supervised practice teaching. Many states require a certain grade-point average in education courses before granting certification. Certification may also be granted in a specific subject or in special education skills. Information on certification is available from state departments of education or school superintendents.

EARNINGS

In 1996, salaried adult education teachers who usually worked full time had median earnings of around $31,300. The middle 50 percent earned between $19,200 and $44,800. The top 10 percent earned more than $56,600. Setting, subject taught, and region affect earnings. Many adult and vocational education teachers work part time.

PROSPECTS: JOB OUTLOOK

Employment of adult education teachers is expected to grow faster than the average for all occupations through the year 2006, as the demand for adult education programs continues to rise.

In 1996, adult and vocational education teachers held about 559,000 jobs. About half taught part time. Many taught intermittently, and many had other jobs, either as teachers or directly related to the subjects they taught. Demand is increasing for adult and vocational education programs from several sectors of society and the economy. As the population ages, the number of people taking enrichment and self-improvement courses is likely to continue to increase. Adding to this trend will be those who need to upgrade skills or want to change occupations. The 35- to 44-year old population—the largest users of adult education—is expected to grow. Increased demand for adult vocational-technical teachers will result from the need to train young adults for entry-level jobs, and retrain experienced workers who want to switch fields or whose jobs have been eliminated due to changing technology or business reorganization.

Opportunities should be best in fields such as computer technology, automotive mechanics, and medical technology.

WHERE TO LOOK FOR FURTHER INFORMATION

Information on the adult basic education program and certification requirements is available from state departments of education. State departments of vocational education have information on positions for vocational education teachers.

For more information on adult and vocational education:

American Association for Adult and
  Continuing Education
1200 19th Street, NW
Suite 300
Washington, DC 20036

American Vocational Association
1410 King Street
Alexandria, VA 22314

ARCHIVISTS AND CURATORS

OCCUPATIONAL OVERVIEW

Job Description: Archivists and curators seek out, acquire, analyze, catalog, restore, exhibit, maintain, and store and retrieve information and items of lasting value. Such items may include a whole range of artifacts: historical documents, corporate records, collectibles (art, coins, stamps, etc.), minerals, clothing, plants, buildings, and historical sites. They work for government agencies, corporations, educational institutions, museums, and other organizations.

Prospects: Employment opportunities are expected to grow about as fast as the average for all occupations through the year 2006. The private sector is expected to grow faster than the public.

Qualifications: Postgraduate training, usually including an advanced degree, and substantial experience are requisites for the position of archivist or curator.

Personal Skills: Archivists need good organizing and communication skills. Excellent eyesight is important for dealing with poor-quality printed matter (e.g., handwritten manuscripts, old films, photographs). Curators must have an aesthetic sense and manual dexterity for dealing with irreplaceable artwork and artifacts.

Earnings: Salaries vary widely, depending on the type, budget, and geographic region of the employer. In 1997, the annual average salary for all museum curators in the federal government in supervisory, nonsupervisory, and managerial positions was about $55,000.

THE JOB AND THE WORK ENVIRONMENT

It is in the nature of people to collect things, as can be witnessed in closets and attics throughout the land. Archivists and curators bring professionalism and organization to this natural impulse to preserve important artifacts of the past and make them accessible to the present.

Archivists determine what items, from a vast store of information collected by government agencies, corporations, educational institutions, and other organizations, should be made part of a historical record or put on exhibit. They classify such information and store it so that it easily can be located, and they also determine the method of preservation—original documents, microfilm, or computer records. They deal primarily with documents, but, depending on the nature of the institution, may work with blueprints, photographs, or other items. Archivists sometimes specialize in certain areas of history or technology (e.g., in Civil War documents or in nautical designs) or by type of media to be preserved—computerized information, photographs, or ancient documents.

Curators manage collections in museums, zoos, aquariums, botanical gardens, and historic sites. They are responsible for acquiring relevant items through purchase, gift, field exploration, intermuseum loans, and, in the case of plants and animals, breeding. Curators must have an excellent visual sense because they prepare exhibits for the public that should be attractive, interesting, and informative.

Archivists work for the federal government in the National Archives and Records Administration and in the U.S. Department of Defense, where they manage the military archives. The majority of curators employed by the federal government work in the Smithsonian Institution, in military museums operated by the U.S. Department of Defense, and in archaeological and other types of museums operated by the U.S. Department of the Interior.

All state governments maintain archival and historical records agencies that hire archivists, and they also operate numerous historical museums, parks, and zoos that employ curators. Some large corporations maintain archival records centers and thus employ archivists. In addition, religious, fraternal, and professional organizations and some research firms employ archivists and curators.

Archivists generally work in offices, alone or with one or two others. Curators also work chiefly in offices, but depending on the type of museum, they may also be involved in restoring and installing exhibits. Those in botanical gardens, historical sites, zoos, or other outdoor museums may walk a good deal.

TRAINING AND QUALIFICATIONS

Archivists are usually expected to have undergraduate and postgraduate degrees in history or other related fields, with courses in archival or library science. Most have a master's degree, and many have a doctorate or a second master's in library science, in addition to a master's in a particular discipline.

Continuing education is very important. Archivists must keep up with developments in their field, including the use of computers in storing and accessing information, and to this end, they attend meetings, workshops, and conferences sponsored by the Society of American Archivists, the National Archives and Records Administration, and other archival associations.

Curators need, at the least, a bachelor's degree in the discipline of the museum's specialty (for instance, art history or archaeology) and some experience in museum work. Most museums require a master's degree and almost all prefer a doctorate. Degrees in museum studies (museology) are available in many colleges and universities, but many employers believe that thorough knowledge of the museum's specialty is more important. Curators also must have a wide range of knowledge and skills because their duties vary so considerably. For the conservation of artwork, for example, courses in chemistry, physics, and art technique and history are important. Courses in business administration and public relations are valuable for those who work in management.

Many archivists and curators work in archives or museums while completing their formal education, to gain hands-on experience that many employers seek when hiring.

EARNINGS

Earnings vary widely according to the nature of the institution, its region, budget, and size of population served. Average salaries in the federal government, for example, are generally higher than in religious organizations. Salaries of curators in large, well-funded museums may be several times higher than those in small ones.

The average annual salary for all museum curators in the federal government in nonsupervisory, supervisory, and managerial positions was about

$55,000 in 1997. Archivists averaged $53,600; museum specialists and technicians, $36,300; and archives technicians, $31,200.

Median salaries for selected workers in larger art museums in 1996 were reported by the Association of Art Museum Directors to be as follows: director, $103,300; curator, $50,000; senior conservator, $48,500; curatorial assistant, $22,600.

PROSPECTS: JOB OUTLOOK

Archivists and curators held about 20,000 jobs in 1996. About a quarter were employed in museums, botanical gardens, and zoos, and approximately 2 in 10 worked in educational services, mainly in college and university libraries. About 4 in 10 worked in federal, state, and local governments.

Employment of archivists and curators is expected to grow as fast as the average for all occupations through the year 2006. Good employment opportunities are forecast for curators because museums are expected to grow substantially in response to increased public interest in art, history, technology, and culture. However, competition for jobs is expected to be keen, especially for positions in the more desirable institutions. To gain the necessary experience, those wishing for curatorial jobs may have to work part time as interns or as volunteer curatorial staff after graduation.

Archivists will do better to look to private organizations for employment rather than to the government bodies. They can improve their prospects by taking courses in library or information science.

WHERE TO LOOK FOR FURTHER INFORMATION

To learn more about careers as an archivist and schools offering courses in archival science:

Society of American Archivists
600 South Federal Street
Suite 504
Chicago, IL 60605

To learn more about careers as a curator and schools offering courses in curatorial science:

American Association of Museums
1575 I Street, NW
Suite 400
Washington, DC 20005

Association of Art Museum Directors
41 East 65th Street
New York, NY 10021

To learn more about curatorial careers in botanical gardens and in conservation and preservation:

American Association of Botanical Gardens
and Arboreta
786 Church Road
Wayne, PA 19087

American Institute for Conservation of
Historic and Artistic Works
1717 K Street, NW
Washington, DC 20006

COLLEGE AND UNIVERSITY FACULTY

OCCUPATIONAL OVERVIEW

Job Description: Faculty members in colleges and universities teach and advise students, do original research, and take on certain administrative responsibilities. They hold positions in two- and four-year colleges and universities. They may teach full- or part-time undergraduate and postgraduate students.

Prospects: Hirings of faculty at the college and university level are expected to increase about as fast as the average for all occupations through the year 2006, as enrollments in higher education increase but other factors temper the employment picture.

Qualifications: The doctorate is necessary for positions on faculties in four-year colleges or universities. For some fields, an additional period of postdoctoral research is required. Junior faculty at four-year colleges and universities must publish in their fields to advance. For faculty at two-year colleges, a master's degree may suffice.

Personal Skills: College-level teachers should have good oral and written communication skills, the ability to establish good rapport with students, a desire to transmit knowledge, academic integrity, and the ability to work unsupervised.

Earnings: According to a survey by the American Association of University Professors, the average salary for full-time faculty was $51,000 in the 1995–1996 academic year. Positions at four-year colleges and universities pay more than those at two-year colleges. Earnings also vary by discipline, faculty rank, and geographic area.

THE JOB AND THE WORK ENVIRONMENT

Traditionally, colleges and universities have provided a place for professionals committed to the preservation and enhancement of knowledge through study and original research. Faculty members share their learning with colleagues through published papers and papers delivered at conferences and with students through teaching. Faculty members also take on administrative duties in their respective institutions.

Faculty members conduct classes in a variety of settings: large lecture halls, regular classrooms, laboratories, and small, highly focused seminars. Some also teach satellite courses broadcast to students at off-campus sites. Faculty may teach undergraduate and postgraduate students. In general, teachers are responsible for preparing lectures or presentations, assigning and grading papers and examinations, supervising laboratory work, and advising students on programs of study. Increasingly, faculty use technology—including e-mail, the Internet, CDs, and software programs—in their teaching.

Colleges and universities organize their faculties into departments by discipline. Within each department, members specialize (e.g., in the biology department, zoology, botany, physiology, and microbiology are taught). Most faculty members teach courses at different levels, including introductions to or surveys of the field and advanced courses dealing with a member's area of specialization.

Faculty are expected to keep up with developments in their fields by reading, attending conferences, and conducting original studies and research. University faculty spend much of their time doing research; faculty at four-year colleges are required to do less. In two-year colleges, faculty do little research but generally have a heavier teaching load.

Faculty members also perform administrative duties, serving as department heads or deans or working on committees that deal with hiring, budgets, or the expansion of facilities. Some advise and supervise student organizations.

Faculty usually teach from 12 to 16 hours a week. Student consultations usually require 3 to 6 hours' time weekly. Faculty also spend time preparing for class and attending faculty meetings. Most faculty work 9 months of the year and are off during the summer months. Throughout the school year, they work 40 or more hours a week, but there is considerable flexibility in how they schedule their work.

This profession provides the enviable opportunity for developing and sharing with colleagues and students one's ideas and the results of original research one has chosen to pursue. As institutions of higher learning experience budgetary constraints and declining enrollments, however, advancement has become more difficult; many part-time and temporary positions have been substituted for full-time, permanent ones, and research facilities and support services have been reduced. The publish-or-perish pressures, especially on younger faculty, also have traditionally created conflicts over time devoted to teaching versus research.

TRAINING AND QUALIFICATIONS

With few exceptions, a Ph.D. is necessary for a position on the faculty of a college or university. A doctorate generally is not necessary for teaching in a two-year college, and some four-year colleges and universities hire people with a master's degree or doctoral candidates for temporary or part-time positions. Certain departments, such as art, music, and law, may consider outstanding achievement in the profession sufficient for a faculty position.

Faculty are ordered in a hierarchy of full professors, associate professors, assistant professors, and instructors. Tenure, a system that protects academic freedom by eliminating the prospect of losing one's job, is usually granted after a seven-year probationary period teaching under term contracts, if the candidate's record of teaching, research, and general contribution to the institution is deemed acceptable. Those denied tenure generally must leave an institution. Because of budgetary constraints, however, full-time, nontenured, nonprobationary faculty positions have become much more common in higher education, as have part-time and short-term positions. This trend is likely to continue.

Some faculty members advance to managerial or administrative positions, such as department head, dean, or president of an educational institution. A doctorate is essential for such advancement at four-year schools.

EARNINGS

According to a 1995–1996 survey conducted by the American Association of University Professors, full-time faculty averaged $51,000 a year in salary overall. Full professors averaged $65,400 a year; associate professors, $48,300; assistant professors, $40,100; instructors, $30,800; and lecturers, $33,700.

Four-year colleges and universities pay more than two-year colleges; the sciences generally pay more than the humanities, and certain fields with high-paying alternatives outside academia, such as law, medicine, engineering, computer science, and business, exceed average faculty salaries. Faculty on nine-month contracts can earn additional income in the summer from writing, research, or consulting work. Benefits are often good and include tuition waivers for dependents and paid sabbaticals. Part-time faculty, however, have fewer benefits than full-time faculty; they generally do not receive health insurance or retirement benefits nor paid sabbaticals.

PROSPECTS: JOB OUTLOOK

College and university teachers held about 864,000 jobs in 1996, with most of the jobs in public institutions. Employment in this field is expected to grow about as fast as the average for all occupations through the year 2006 as higher-education enrollments increase. College enrollment is projected to grow from 14 million in 1996 to 16 million in 2006, largely in response to the children of baby boomers reaching college age. Many more positions will become available, too, as faculty who were hired in the 1950s and 1960s reach retirement through the year 2006. However, while most of the retirees will be full-time tenured professors, some institutions—to cut costs—will be leaving some jobs vacant or hiring part-time, nontenured faculty as replacements. Competition will, therefore, be intense for available full-time positions.

Continued short-term hiring of faculty also is expected to continue as colleges try to reduce costs and make up for reduced state funding for higher education. With growing enrollments into the new century, the picture may improve. Prospects will be brighter in certain fields—such as law, medicine, computer science, and business—that offer lucrative nonacademic employment, therefore attracting fewer academic candidates. College employment is influenced, too, by the nonacademic job market. The appeal of jobs in computer science in recent decades, for example, led to more students enrolling in computer science courses, thereby increasing faculty needs in the field. Conversely, poor job prospects in a field discourage student enrollments and reduce faculty needs.

WHERE TO LOOK FOR FURTHER INFORMATION

For information on a career in teaching and research at the college or university level, contact one or more of the professional societies in the field of interest.

For information on salaries and working conditions in the profession as a whole:

American Association of University Professors
1012 14th Street, NW
Suite 500
Washington, DC 20005

For information about faculty union activities on college campuses:

American Federation of Teachers
555 New Jersey Avenue, NW
Washington, DC 20001

COUNSELORS

OCCUPATIONAL OVERVIEW

Job Description: Counselors advise and help people with emotional, social, educational, career, and mental health problems. They work in schools and colleges, hospitals, correctional institutions, government agencies, nonprofit organizations, and private practice.

Prospects: Through the year 2006, employment of counselors as a whole is expected to increase about as fast as the average for all occupations. As a large number of counselors enter retirement, replacement needs should be significant.

Qualifications: Generally, counselors must have a master's degree in a counseling specialty, although a bachelor's degree suffices in some cases. Some states require both counseling and teaching certificates for counselors in the public schools. In 1997, 42 states and the District of Columbia required some certification for counselors practicing outside schools.

Personal Skills: Counselors should have a genuine desire to help others. They need to be able to inspire trust, confidence, and respect and also must be able to work both independently and as part of a team. Counselors also must possess high energy to handle the variety of problems presented to them.

Earnings: In 1996, the median annual earnings for full-time vocational and educational counselors were approximately $35,800. According to the Educational Research Service, the average annual salary of public school counselors in the 1995–1996 academic year was about $44,100. Self-employed counselors enjoy the highest incomes.

THE JOB AND THE WORK ENVIRONMENT

Counselors advise people, alert them to choices available to them at important points in their lives, and attempt to help them in times of crisis. Counselors work in schools and in both private and public job-training and vocational rehabilitation centers. They are also employed by nonprofit organizations, such as Goodwill Industries and Lighthouse for the Blind, correctional facilities, hospitals, and halfway houses. The specific work of counselors and the help they offer depend on their training, where they work, and the people they serve.

School counselors work in elementary and secondary schools and in colleges. At the elementary school level, their principal task is to observe children in class and at play and assess their strengths and weaknesses. They confer with educators and parents and help develop programs or courses of study that utilize each child's strengths or address particular problems. Although there is sometimes individual counseling at this level, it is more common in high school, where counselors interview students and help them make decisions about postsecondary education and careers. They offer practical advice and information about college admission requirements, scholarships and loans, trade and technical schools, and apprenticeships or internships in various fields. They also help students deal with social and personal problems, including drug and alcohol abuse. They may work together in consultation with parents, teachers, psychologists, and social workers. At the college level, counselors help students and alumni plan careers and find jobs.

Those forced by a disability to change jobs or careers can seek the help and advice of a *rehabilitation counselor,* who assesses a client's potential and recommends a program of training leading to productive work and greater independence.

Employment counselors use extensive interviews and sometimes aptitude and achievement tests to guide people in making career decisions. They may work in public employment counseling offices or in private counseling firms.

Mental health counselors often work closely with psychiatrists, psychologists, and clinical social workers. Their clients include those struggling with alcohol abuse, drug addiction, family conflicts, suicide, or stress-related problems, and past offenders trying to readjust to society. They work in hospitals, clinics, publicly funded programs, or private practice.

Counselors may work in such other specialized areas as marriage and family, gerontological, or multicultural counseling.

For the most part, school counselors work about the same hours as teachers for the 9- to 10-month school year and are on vacation for 2 to 3 months each year. Rehabilitation and employment counselors usually work a 40-hour week. Mental health counselors employed in hospitals and clinics may work more irregular hours, including evening and weekend shifts. Self-employed counselors also are likely to work less regular hours to accommodate their clients. All types of counselors must have high physical and emotional energy to deal with the wide range of problems presented to them.

Counselors in various settings can advance to supervisory or administrative positions. Some may go into teaching, research, or private or group practice.

TRAINING AND QUALIFICATIONS

Educational level and credentials vary with the type of counseling and the employment setting, but for most positions, a master's degree in one of the branches of counseling is required. Currently, 6 out of 10 counselors hold a master's degree. It is possible to get work with a bachelor's degree in psychology, sociology, counseling, or rehabilitation services, especially if one has some work experience, but one likely will not be eligible for certification or licensing.

In 1996, 111 colleges and universities offered graduate-level programs in counselor education accredited by the Council for Accreditation of Counseling and Related Educational Programs. A master's degree in counseling usually requires about two years of study, including a period of supervised counseling.

Requirements for jobs in counseling differ according to specialty and setting. Those applying for jobs requiring licensing and certification should determine, in advance, the credentials they will need. In some states, counselors in the public schools need certification in both counseling and teaching. Every state requires school counselors to obtain a state school counseling certificate, with certification requirements varying from state to state. Private vocational and rehabilitation agencies generally require a master's degree; many employers also require certification of rehabilitation counselors. Applicants for most state vocational rehabilitation agencies must pass a written examination and be approved by a board of examiners. Mental health counselors need a master's degree or doctorate in mental health counseling.

As of 1997, 42 states and the District of Columbia require some type of counselor licensure, credentialing, or registry for practice outside schools. Requirements vary by state. In some states, a credential is mandatory, while in others it is voluntary.

Counselors can choose to be nationally certified by the National Board for Certified Counselors, from whom they receive a general practice credential after passing an examination. Though this credential is distinct from state certification, some states accept the national examination in place of the state certification exam. To maintain certification, counselors are required to complete 100 hours of continuing education every five years.

EARNINGS

In 1996, the median annual earnings for full-time vocational and educational counselors were about $35,800. The Educational Research Service reports that the average salary of public school counselors in the 1995–1996 academic year was about $44,100.

The highest earnings are to self-employed counselors with established practices and those in group practices, as well as counselors working for private companies.

PROSPECTS: JOB OUTLOOK

In 1996, about 175,000 jobs were held by counselors. (This estimate includes only educational and vocational counselors; employment data was unavailable for other counselors.) Through the year 2006, counselors as a whole can expect jobs in their field to increase about as fast as the average for all occupations. Replacement needs should grow significantly as a large number of counselors enter retirement.

The employment outlook differs somewhat for the various branches of counseling. Job growth for school counselors is expected to increase, in keeping with the projected pace of school enrollments, state laws requiring counselors in schools, and the increasing responsibilities of counselors. Still, school budgetary constraints could affect this growth.

The demand for rehabilitation and mental health counselors is likely to be strong; as insurance companies are increasingly reimbursing counselors, more people are needing rehabilitation services, and more companies are seeking help in complying with disability laws. Greater job growth is expected for mental health counselors specializing in alcohol or drug abuse, aging, stress management, or other personal and social problems. The demand for employment counselors in private job-training services is expected to grow to meet the needs of growing numbers of laid-off workers, homemakers re-entering the workforce, and those seeking career changes. The prospects for employment counselors in local or state government settings may be dampened by budgetary constraints.

WHERE TO LOOK FOR FURTHER INFORMATION

For information about careers in counseling:

American Counseling Association
5999 Stevenson Avenue
Alexandria, VA 22304

For information on programs accredited by the Council for Accreditation of Counseling and Related Educational Programs:

Council for Accreditation of Counseling and Related Educational Programs
American Counseling Association
5999 Stevenson Avenue
Alexandria, VA 22304

For information about national certification requirements and procedures:

National Board for Certified Counselors
3 Terrace Way
Suite D
Greensboro, NC 27403

For a list of accredited graduate programs in rehabilitation counseling:

Council on Rehabilitation Counselor Certification Education
1835 Rohlwing Road
Suite E
Rolling Meadows, IL 60008

State departments of education can supply information on state certifications and licensing requirements.

EDUCATIONAL ADMINISTRATORS

OCCUPATIONAL OVERVIEW

Job Description: Educational administrators provide leadership and daily management for educational institutions.

Prospects: Employment in this field is expected to grow about as fast as the average for all occupations through the year 2006. Job openings largely will result from replacement needs rather than from expansion of the market. Prospects also depend on public funding for education.

Qualifications: The prime qualification is experience in a related field. Because the job encompasses many levels, from primary school principal to university president, educational requirements vary widely. A master's degree or doctorate is needed, along with some teaching experience, usually at the level the administrator is to oversee.

Personal Skills: Motivational skills, leadership qualities, and organizational ability are crucial, as are receptiveness to new ideas and excellent interpersonal skills.

Earnings: The average annual salaries for elementary, junior high, and senior high school principals were approximately $62,900, $66,900, and $72,400, respectively, for the 1996–1997 academic year. The figures for assistant principals were approximately $52,300, $56,500, and $59,700, respectively. The 1995–1996 median salaries for deans of undergraduate medical, education, and mathematics programs were $201,200, $80,000, and $59,900, respectively; for admissions director and registrar, the average salary was $50,700.

THE JOB AND THE WORK ENVIRONMENT

The range for this occupation is enormous. It runs from the current version of the little red schoolhouse to the sprawling campus of a world-class university, and it encompasses every formal learning situation in between. Common to each level is the deployment of educational resources, both personnel and materiel, to achieve maximum results. Managing that deployment is the function of the educational administrator.

Overall, the duties of an educational administrator include, but are not limited to, setting academic goals and developing the procedures for carrying them out; hiring, training, and motivating teaching staffs; managing budgets and overseeing finances; handling relations with students, parents, prospective employers, and the community at large; and administering the routine, nonacademic needs of the institution.

Schools at the elementary and secondary levels are managed by *principals,* whose primary task is to set the academic tone of the institution. Principals hire and assign teachers, oversee their work, and evaluate them. They help select texts and other teaching equipment, prepare budgets, and oversee the procurement and allocation of supplies. They also meet with parents and representatives of community organizations. With tighter school budgets, many principals are initiating fund raising efforts to gain financial support from local businesses. Some also are responding to needs for before- and after-school child care programs and drug, alcohol, and crime prevention programs by seeking help from community organizations.

When enrollment in an elementary or secondary school increases significantly, *assistant principals* often are hired to help principals with administrative duties. Some assistant principals are working toward advancement to principal; others are career assistant principals.

In the public school system, administrators also are employed at the school district level. Among these are administrators who concentrate on curricula and help teachers improve their skills and learn about new methods and materials, as well as directors of district-level programs, such as special education, athletics, counseling, and academic testing.

At the higher education levels, *academic deans* (also known as deans of faculty, provosts, or university deans) assist presidents in formulating academic policies and procedures and in preparing budgets. They coordinate the work of deans and chairpersons of individual colleges and academic departments, and they provide services to students directly by acting as deans of students, registrars, admissions officers, and directors of athletics.

Educational administrators perform many of their duties alone, but, as noted, they also are obliged to meet with academic and other staff personnel, students and parents, alumni, and others. They often work more than a 40-hour week and frequently have duties that keep them busy during evenings and on weekends. Unlike teachers, they normally work 10 or 11 months; some work year round.

TRAINING AND QUALIFICATIONS

Educational administrators are made, not born. They normally come to administration after working in the academic sphere or in some area related to education. Their educational background and experience vary widely, depending on the level at which they perform as administrators. Principals, educational supervisors, and academic deans almost always have taught or held a related position before moving into administration.

Competent and innovative teachers who show good managerial and interpersonal skills are the most likely to be tapped for administrative posts. Principals at the primary and secondary levels throughout the country need at least a master's degree in educational administration, as well as a teaching certificate. Many principals have a doctorate. Most states now require principals to be licensed as school administrators, with licensure requirements varying from state to state. The Interstate School Leaders Licensure Consortium recently created national standards for school leaders (including principals), which states may use as guidelines for their licensure requirements.

In colleges and universities, an academic dean or chairperson usually holds a doctorate. Those holding staff positions, such as registrar, dean of student affairs, admissions director, and the like may begin with a bachelor's degree but find advanced degrees helpful for promotion. Computer literacy and a mathematics background can be assets in financial and admissions positions.

Many colleges and universities offer advanced degrees in educational administration and college student affairs. The National Council for Accreditation of Teacher Education accredits such programs.

Educational administrators usually advance by moving up the administrative ladder in their school system or educational institution, or by transferring to larger schools or systems.

EARNINGS

Educational administrators' salaries vary widely, depending on position, degree of responsibility and experience, and the location and size of the institution.

In a survey of public schools, the Educational Research Service found that the average salaries for elementary, junior high, and high school principals in the 1996–1997 academic year were $62,900, $66,900, and $72,400, respectively. Figures for assistant principals were $52,300, $56,500, and $59,700, respectively.

The College and University Personnel Association reports the following median annual 1995–1996 salaries for select administrators: deans of medicine, education, and mathematics earned $201,200, $80,000, and $59,900, respectively. Admissions and registrar personnel averaged $50,700, and student financial aid directors averaged $45,400.

PROSPECTS: JOB OUTLOOK

There were about 386,000 jobs held by educational administrators in 1996. Employment in the field is expected to increase about as fast as the average for all occupations through the year 2006. Most openings will result from replacement of retiring administrators and those otherwise leaving the profession.

Strong competition is expected for higher education administrators. Many qualified people will seek promotion while the number of openings will be small. Those with the most formal education and the ability to relocate will have the brightest prospects.

Competition is declining for administrative jobs in elementary and secondary schools, however. Many teachers are less inclined to move into principal or assistant principal positions, with their heavier workload and not significantly higher salaries. In addition, as enrollments increase, instead of opening new schools, school systems will add assistant principals and other administrators to help with the workload and enhance the range of services offered to students.

Job opportunities in this area also depend on public funding for education. Pressures to lower taxes may result in fewer administration personnel in school systems; pressures to increase spending to improve the quality of instruction may result in more.

WHERE TO LOOK FOR FURTHER INFORMATION

To learn more about careers in school administration:

American Federation of School
 Administrators
1729 21st Street, NW
Washington, DC 20009

American Association of School
 Administrators
1801 North Moore Street
Arlington, VA 22209

National Association of Elementary
  School Principals
1615 Duke Street
Alexandria, VA 22314-3406

National Association of Secondary
  School Principals
1904 Association Drive
Reston, VA 20190

American Association of University
  Administrators
P.O. Box 2183
Tuscaloosa, AL 35403

American Association of Collegiate
  Registrars and Admissions Officers
One Dupont Circle, NW
Suite 330
Washington, DC 20036-1171

National Education Association
1201 16th Street, NW
Washington, DC 20036

*E*LEMENTARY SCHOOL TEACHERS

OCCUPATIONAL OVERVIEW

Job Description: Elementary school teachers educate children from kindergarten through the sixth or eighth grade in public and private schools. Special training qualifies some to teach children with various physical, emotional, and learning impairments, or students who are gifted or who do not speak English.

Prospects: Through the year 2006, average employment growth is expected in jobs for elementary school teachers. Much depends on the allocation of public funds for education.

Qualifications: Elementary school teachers need a bachelor's degree and must complete an approved teacher education program for licensure that is required in all states and the District of Columbia.

Personal Skills: Elementary school teachers should enjoy working with children. They must be organized, patient, and dependable. Above all, they need the ability to inspire trust and to motivate children to learn, recognizing their individual differences and abilities.

Earnings: According to the National Education Association (NEA), the average annual salary for public elementary school teachers in the 1995–1996 academic year was $37,300. Private school teachers generally earn less than those in the public school system.

THE JOB AND THE WORK ENVIRONMENT

Helping children to focus their natural curiosity and acquire the skills and knowledge that are basic to success in our increasingly complex and demanding culture ranks high among the challenges and rewards of elementary school teachers.

In kindergarten and the lower grades, learning focuses on numbers, language, science, and social studies. As teachers depart from traditional rote-learning approaches, they are employing a more hands-on and interactive focus, as well as using the latest in technology, including computers, CDs, and the Internet. Although elementary school teachers deal primarily with the class as a whole, much of their time and effort is devoted to individual children. Teachers evaluate each student's health, social development, and academic performance and potential, and meet with parents to discuss their children's problems and progress. The teacher must maintain order in the classroom and instill good study habits and an appreciation for learning.

Generally, one elementary school teacher instructs a single class of children in several subjects. Sometimes two or more teachers share the responsibility for a group of students or a subject. A small but increasing number of teachers work in multilevel classes comprised of students at several different grade levels. Special education teachers work with emotionally disturbed, learning-impaired, or physically disabled students. Some teachers work with gifted children; others instruct non-English-speaking students.

Certain responsibilities are common to the job: lessons must be planned, tests made and graded, and homework corrected. Administrative responsibilities include attending faculty meetings, meeting with parents, and supervising extracurricular activities.

Elementary school teachers generally work more than 40 hours a week when school responsibilities outside the classroom are included. For most, the school year is 9 to 10 months long, divided into 2 semesters, with a summer vacation of 2 to 3 months. Year-round schools usually conduct classes in 8-week sessions, with a 1-week break between each session and a 5-week break in midwinter.

Teachers of young children often have to do a lot of kneeling and bending to communicate with students and participate in their activities. Stresses may include having to deal with disruptive students, overcrowded classes, and heavy workloads.

TRAINING AND QUALIFICATIONS

All states and the District of Columbia require that elementary school teachers in the public schools be licensed by the state board of education, the state superintendent of education, or a licensure advisory committee. Teachers in private schools are not required to have a teaching license. The general prerequisites are a bachelor's degree, completion of an approved teacher education program, and a period of supervised practice teaching. Many states require a certain grade-point average in education courses before granting licensure. Licensure may also be specific to the level being taught (e.g., the early childhood grades) or it may be specific to a specialization, such as music, reading, or home economics. Nearly all states test basic skills, teaching skills, or specific subject matter for those seeking licensure, and most require continuing education for license renewal.

Many states have alternative licensure programs for those who hold bachelor's degrees in subjects they want to teach but lack the education coursework needed for a license. Originally, these programs were instituted to ease teacher shortages in certain subjects, but they've been enlarged to attract new groups of people to the profession.

The National Council for Accreditation of Teacher Education (NCATE) accredits more than 500 teacher education programs in the United States. Most programs include courses in psychology of learning, child development, and teaching methods, as well as courses in math, science, social science, art, music, and literature designed specifically for those who want to teach. To maintain certification, programs are now required to offer classes in computers and other technology.

The National Board for Professional Teaching Standards offers voluntary national teacher certification, that may help a teacher find a position in another state. Certified teachers may also earn higher salaries than noncertified teachers, but this varies by state.

EARNINGS

According to the National Education Association, public elementary school teachers earned an average salary of $37,300 in the 1995–1996 academic year. More than half of all public school teachers belonged to a union—most to the NEA or the American Federation of Teachers, which bargained with schools over employment issues.

Many teachers use their summer break to earn additional income by teaching or doing other work. In some school systems, teachers are paid for coaching athletics and working on extracurricular activities with students.

PROSPECTS: JOB OUTLOOK

In 1996, there were about 1.7 million elementary school teachers. Through the year 2006, average job growth is expected in this occupation. Elementary school enrollments are projected to increase through the year 2002 but are then expected to decrease.

Hiring for the public schools also depends on budget appropriations, which depend, in turn, on taxpayers' priorities. Pressures to tighten spending could lead to fewer teacher hirings than expected; pressures to improve the quality of education could increase hirings. As always, education competes with other essential services for scarcer revenue dollars.

Many inner cities and rural areas find it difficult to attract teachers, so prospects in these places are likely to continue to be better than in suburban areas.

WHERE TO LOOK FOR FURTHER INFORMATION

For information on a career in teaching, contact the appropriate local or state affiliate of the NEA. Teacher education programs are accredited by the NCATE. A list of colleges and universities offering accredited programs is available from:

National Council for Accreditation of Teacher Education
2010 Massachusetts Avenue, NW
Suite 500
Washington, DC 20036

For information on teachers' unions and the larger range of issues and challenges affecting the profession:

American Federation of Teachers
555 New Jersey Avenue, NW
Washington, DC 20001

National Education Association
1201 16th Street, NW
Washington, DC 20036

For information on the requirements for voluntary national teacher certification:

National Board for Professional Teaching Standards
26555 Evergreen Road
Suite 400
Southfield, MI 48076

*L*IBRARIANS

OCCUPATIONAL OVERVIEW

Job Description: Librarians gather, organize, and make accessible the resources of libraries. They work with a wide range of materials—books, periodicals, films, records, videotapes, microfiche, and information provided by electronic databases—in schools, public libraries, and government agencies, and, in increasing numbers, for special libraries in the private sector and other information providers.

Prospects: Through the year 2006, jobs for librarians are expected to grow more slowly than the average for all occupations, reflecting increased computerization in the field and budgetary constraints in traditional work settings. However, the number of job openings resulting from librarians retiring is projected to increase. Job prospects will be best outside traditional settings.

Qualifications: A master's degree in library science is necessary. A major in one of the natural sciences or a technical field is indispensable for a librarian specializing in those areas. Librarians must know how to operate computers.

Personal Skills: Librarians must be careful, particular, and precise. Much library work requires constant contact with people, so librarians need an even temperament, a willingness to help, self-assurance, and tact.

Earnings: Earnings vary with library type, size, and location. According to the American Library Association (ALA), beginning librarians holding a master's degree averaged $28,700 in 1996; reference librarians averaged $35,800; and children's librarians in school and public libraries averaged $34,600.

THE JOB AND THE WORK ENVIRONMENT

Since ancient times, libraries have been storehouses of tradition and knowledge; now they have other, more dynamic capacities. School and public libraries maintain and offer access to collections in all kinds of media. They are sources of knowledge and information. Some banks, corporations, and other organizations maintain private libraries focusing on their special needs; they both gather and disseminate information.

The majority of librarians work in school, university, and public libraries. In small school and public libraries, the work is a combination of several functions. Larger libraries require more organization, and the work of librarians is subdivided into specific areas requiring special skills. *Acquisitions librarians* maintain a library's stock and keep it current in all media. They keep abreast of what is being published and deal with wholesalers and suppliers; they spend the library's money and do business on its behalf. *Catalogers* and *indexers* organize material by subject, assign classification codes, and enter material into the library's cataloging system. *Special collections librarians* focus on collections in particular areas, such as genealogy, maps, music, or manuscripts and rare books. They may also arrange special exhibits.

Public libraries serve the public at large. Larger public libraries have on staff children's librarians, young-adult librarians, and adult services librarians. Some libraries maintain community outreach programs and send out bookmobiles staffed by trained librarians. They may also organize storytelling programs for children as well as literacy and book discussion groups for adults.

Nearly all libraries have computerized their catalogs and offer access to various information databases. Librarians help users learn how to search local and remote databases for information through the growing use of e-mail, the Internet, and other computer systems that make greater amounts of reference materials available. Libraries in the private sector, including banking, engineering, and the law, are extensively computerized for quick and efficient access to information. Special librarians are expected not only to provide access to information but also to disseminate it within their organizations. Whereas school, university, and public librarians deal principally with collections of books, special librarians are more likely to deal with collections of technical reports, engineering drawings, patents, laboratory notebooks, and newspaper clippings.

All library work calls for a careful and self-confident command of organization and detail and a tolerance for pressure and routine. Librarians spend most of every day dealing with people. Particularly in school, university, and public libraries, the job requires a lot of time spent standing and often stooping, bending, and reaching. Time spent at a desk in front of a computer monitor may cause headaches or eyestrain. More than 3 out of 10 librarians work part time. Most full-time librarians work a 5-day, 35- to 40-hour week.

Special librarians in the private sector may advance within their particular firms. In school, university, and public libraries, those with training in library administration may advance to positions such as department head, assistant director, or director. Entrepreneurial librarians may start freelance consulting practices, offering services to libraries, government agencies, or businesses.

TRAINING AND QUALIFICATIONS

A master's degree in library science (M.L.S.) is required for most public, college, and special libraries, as well as some school libraries. An M.L.S. (or equivalent in education and experience) is needed to work for the federal government. Although many colleges and universities offer M.L.S. programs, 50 schools of library science are accredited by the ALA; most employers prefer graduates of those programs.

Most M.L.S. programs require a bachelor's degree for admission. The course of study offers a thorough grounding in librarianship and includes training in the use of online and other technologically advanced reference systems and information services. Some librarians also specialize in a specific area, such as reference or children's services. For college teaching or top administrative positions in academic or large libraries, a Ph.D. in library and information science is helpful.

Certification requirements vary from state to state. Some states require certification of public librarians. Most states require that public school librarians be certified as teachers, along with having taken library courses; in some cases, an M.L.S. is required.

EARNINGS

Salaries vary depending on a person's qualifications and the size, type, and location of the library. According to the ALA, the average salary for a beginning librarian with a master's degree was $28,700 in 1996. Reference librarians averaged $35,800, and children's librarians in school and public libraries averaged $34,600 in 1996. The Special Libraries Association reported that the average salary for special librarians with 2 years or less of experience was $33,100 in 1996. The Medical Library Association found that the average salary for medical librarians with less than a year of experience was $25,900 in 1995.

The usual benefits—paid vacations, medical coverage, life insurance, and sometimes dental coverage—prevail for librarians.

PROSPECTS: JOB OUTLOOK

In 1996, librarians held about 154,000 jobs. Employment for librarians is expected to grow more slowly than the average for all occupations through the year 2006. Budget constraints likely will be a factor in the slow growth of jobs in school, public, and college libraries, as will increased computerization in the field. However, the number of librarians projected to retire is expected to increase, which may increase demand.

The best opportunities will lie outside traditional settings and will include jobs with special and research libraries, particularly in medicine, law, business, engineering, and the physical and life sciences. Librarians with computer skills, knowledge of information science, and one or more foreign languages will be sought. Although libraries will be more automated, the skills, judgment, and experience of a trained librarian will continue to be necessary in managing staff, teaching users, and addressing complex reference needs.

Increasingly, library science runs parallel to and even merges with information science and technology. There are opportunities for librarians to market their skills in new fields working in bibliographic co-ops, regional information networks, and information services. The greatest growth potential in the field is likely to be in the combined areas of information management and library automation, with jobs in private corporations and consulting firms, and with information brokers who market information.

WHERE TO LOOK FOR FURTHER INFORMATION

For information on accredited schools of librarianship and scholarships and loans:

American Library Association
Office for Library Personnel Resources
50 East Huron Street
Chicago, IL 60611

For information on a career as a special librarian:

Special Libraries Association
1700 18th Street, NW
Washington, DC 20009

For information on graduate schools of library and information science:

Association for Library and Information Science Education
P.O. Box 7640
Arlington, VA 22207

For federal help for library training:

Office of Educational Research and Improvement
Library Programs
Library Development Staff
U.S. Department of Education
555 New Jersey Avenue, NW
Room 402
Washington, DC 20208-5571

State library associations and boards of education can provide information on their certification requirements and state scholarships.

PRESCHOOL TEACHERS AND CHILD CARE WORKERS

OCCUPATIONAL OVERVIEW

Job Description: Preschool teachers and child care workers take care of infants and young children up to age five whose parents are working or are otherwise away from home during the day. They may be on staff in a nursery school, preschool, or large day care center, or self-employed, working at home.

Prospects: Through the year 2006, jobs for preschool teachers and child care workers are expected to increase faster than the average for all occupations. The percentage of working mothers with young children is expected to continue to increase, adding to the favorable job outlook.

Qualifications: Training and qualifications vary widely. In most cases, a high school diploma and little or no experience are adequate for employment. Some employers provide on-the-job training. Preschool and child care workers can earn certification; in some positions, training and certification are needed for advancement.

Personal Skills: Preschool teachers and child care workers should be mature and responsible, have experience with young children, and enjoy working with them. The job requires physical and emotional stamina, patience, enthusiasm, and the ability to engage children. Preschool and child care workers also must know how to apply fair and firm discipline.

Earnings: Earnings depend on the employer and on the education of the worker. Median weekly pay for full-time, salaried child care workers was $250 in 1996. Benefits vary but are generally minimal. Earnings of self-employed child care workers depend on the number and ages of children cared for, hours worked, clients' incomes, and geographic location.

THE JOB AND THE WORK ENVIRONMENT

Preschool teachers and child care workers look after infants, toddlers, or young children while their parents are at work or otherwise away from home during the day. They work with the children, attending to their basic needs and directing their activities, as well as helping them build skills that will be needed in elementary school.

Preschool teachers and child care workers may be employed by day care centers, nursery schools, preschools, or public schools, or may be self-employed and working in their own homes. In a day care center, nursery school, or pre-school, they work under a supervisor or director, following a structured program with the children and having few, if any, administrative responsibilities. Day care centers, nursery schools, and preschools differ in size and the quality and variety of equipment and activities they offer. Their location ranges from the basement of a local church or synagogue to a separate, specially equipped facility for the children of employees of a private company. About 4 out of 10 child care workers are self-employed; most of these workers are family day care providers who take care of children in their own homes.

In addition to planning and supervising activities for the children, pre-school teachers and child care workers must see that the children are properly fed and regularly rested. They must purchase food and supplies and keep business records. They also must be particularly alert to signs of illness or physical, developmental, or learning disabilities in the children.

Work hours vary widely for preschool and child care workers. Day care centers are usually open long hours year-round to accommodate working parents, and they generally hire full-time and part-time staff to cover their schedules. Full-time staff at day care centers usually work an eight-hour day. Self-employed family day care providers can arrange more flexible hours. Since they work at home, they can combine housework and looking after their own children with their child care responsibilities, but they may have to work long or lopsided hours to accommodate parents' schedules. Moreover, the physical and emotional strains of caring for young children can be stressful for the self-employed child care worker and his or her family.

Child care work calls for direct and sympathetic involvement with children. Part of the work is teaching and stimulating young minds, especially through play activities. Children must learn to dress themselves, clean up after play, form good eating habits, and play well with others. The child care worker provides direction in these areas and encourages activities that will help develop children's self-esteem, skills, and curiosity. Child care workers are responsible for maintaining order, and when necessary, they must be able to discipline children firmly and fairly. The work requires patience and a lot of physical and emotional energy. It can be tiring as well as a source of great satisfaction. Some workers suffer burnout from long hours, low pay, and job stresses, so turnover is high in this field.

TRAINING AND QUALIFICATIONS

Qualifications required of preschool teachers and child care workers vary widely. Individual states have licensing requirements to regulate training, ranging from a high school diploma to a college degree in childhood development or early childhood education. Some states require ongoing education for workers in this occupation. Some private preschool and day care centers have lower educational requirements since they are not bound by state requirements. Often, workers need only a high school education and minimal experience. Some day care centers provide on-the-job training.

Those who plan to work with young children can take high school or college courses in psychology, sociology, child development, and nutrition. Coursework in art, music, drama, and physical education is also good preparation.

For some jobs, formal training and certification are important for employment and advancement. For example, public school programs usually require a bachelor's degree and state teacher certification, and some private schools (e.g., Montessori) require specialized instruction. Many two- and four-year colleges offer programs in child care, early childhood education, child and family studies, and pre-elementary education.

Many states prefer preschool teachers and child care workers to have a Child Development Associate (CDA) credential, offered by the Council for Early Childhood Professional Recognition. Forty-six states and the District of Columbia recognize this credential as a qualification for teachers and directors. Candidates must have a high school diploma, 120 hours of training, and 480 hours of experience. If lacking in experience, a candidate can take a one-year child development training program. When a candidate is ready, CDA professionals assess abilities and performance and, on the basis of their findings, award the CDA credential.

EARNINGS

Earnings depend on the employer as well as the educational level of the worker. Overall, pay is low and benefits are minimal. The median weekly income of full-time, salaried child care workers in 1996 was $250. Preschool teachers in public schools who have state teacher certification usually have the same salaries and benefits as elementary school teachers. Preschool teachers in privately funded centers usually are paid much lower salaries than other equally educated workers.

Earnings for self-employed child care workers depend on clients' incomes, the number and ages of children cared for, the number of hours worked per week, and the region.

PROSPECTS: JOB OUTLOOK

As of 1996, preschool teachers and child care workers held about 1.2 million jobs, many of them part time. More than 40 percent of these workers were self-employed. Through the year 2006, jobs for preschool and child care workers are expected to increase faster than the average for all occupations. Several factors will contribute to a healthy job outlook in this field. There is considerable turnover among child care workers due to stressful conditions and low pay, so many jobs will be available to replace workers who leave the field. The number of working mothers also is expected to continue to increase, with women returning to work sooner after childbirth, therefore increasing the demand for child care. In addition, recently enacted welfare reform legislation requiring more mothers of young children to work may result in an increased demand for child care workers.

The jobs of child care workers are vulnerable to economic change. During periods of increased unemployment, parents who cannot find jobs themselves cannot afford to pay for child care.

WHERE TO LOOK FOR FURTHER INFORMATION

For information about child care careers and issues affecting child care workers:

National Association for the Education of Young Children
1509 16th Street, NW
Washington, DC 20036

For information on the CDA credential program:

Council for Early Childhood Professional Recognition
2460 16th Street, NW
Washington, DC 20009

For information on efforts to improve compensation for child care:

National Center for the Early Childhood Work Force
733 15th Street, NW
Suite 1037
Washington, DC 20005

For information on regulations and training requirements for child care workers, contact individual state human services or social services departments.

SECONDARY SCHOOL TEACHERS

OCCUPATIONAL OVERVIEW

Job Description: Secondary school teachers educate children from middle or junior high school through the twelfth grade. They teach in public and private schools; special training qualifies some to teach students with various physical and learning disabilities, or the gifted, or to teach in a foreign language.

Prospects: Through the year 2006, jobs for secondary school teachers are expected to increase faster than the average for all occupations, as high school enrollments continue to increase in this period. Employment will also depend on state and local spending on education, which cannot be forecast reliably.

Qualifications: Secondary school teachers must have a bachelor's degree, usually with a major in the subject they wish to teach, and also must complete an accredited teacher education program. All states and the District of Columbia require licensure of secondary school teachers in the public schools.

Personal Skills: Secondary school teachers should have a good command of their subject and a continuing and lively interest in it so that they can communicate to their students. Above all, they need the ability to motivate students to learn.

Earnings: According to the National Education Association (NEA), the average annual salary for public secondary school teachers in the 1995–1996 academic year was $38,600. Private school teachers generally earn less.

THE JOB AND THE WORK ENVIRONMENT

Students in junior high school and high school pose special challenges. Those who have not mastered the fundamentals taught in the lower grades require remedial work; others are ready for advanced work. For most young people, these are years of conflict and promise, when they must acquire the knowledge and skills needed to enter the workforce or go on to college. The secondary school teacher provides the education—and fosters the motivation—at this all-important stage of life.

Traditionally, secondary school in the United States has included grades 9 through 12. Recently, rather than junior high school (grades 7 through 9), middle school has been offered (grades 6 through 8). But whatever the grouping of grades, the job of secondary school teachers remains substantially the same. Each teacher specializes in a subject or field and typically teaches several related courses (e.g., a math teacher may teach algebra, geometry, and trigonometry). Special education teachers work exclusively with students who have various physical or learning disabilities or emotional or social problems. Other teachers are responsible for teaching gifted students. Whatever the situation, the usual class period per subject is 45 to 55 minutes.

Science teachers work with students in laboratories, in addition to lecturing. Teachers in technical and vocational schools help students get hands-on experience and training in the tools and techniques of various trades. All secondary school teachers have an opportunity to work with individual students. Especially in the higher grades, teachers encourage independent study and special projects. Because their students come from increasingly diverse backgrounds, teachers need an awareness of different cultures and a multicultural focus in their work. In addition, many teachers use computers for a variety of class activities and for telecommunications to further students' experience of the world around them.

Teachers have a host of duties and obligations: preparing lesson plans and examinations, reading and correcting papers, grading and evaluating students, maintaining order in the classroom, supervising extracurricular activities, attending faculty meetings, counseling students about education or career paths, and meeting with parents.

Secondary school teachers work approximately 50 hours a week. For most, the school year is 9 to 10 months long, divided into 2 semesters, with a summer vacation of 2 to 3 months. Year-round schools usually conduct classes in 8-week sessions with a 1-week break between each session and a 5-week break in midwinter.

Perhaps the most difficult part of secondary school teaching comes in dealing with disgruntled and disaffected students. It is an inevitable part of the job and can cause considerable stress.

TRAINING AND QUALIFICATIONS

All states and the District of Columbia require that public secondary school teachers be licensed by the state board of education, the state superintendent of education, or a licensure advisory committee. The prerequisites are a bachelor's degree (either majoring in the subject the applicant proposes to teach, along with education courses, or majoring in education, along with subject courses), completion of an approved teacher education program, and a period of supervised practice teaching. Many states require a certain grade-point average in education courses before granting licensure. Licensure may also be granted in a specific subject or in special education skills.

Most teacher education programs include courses in psychology of learning, adolescent development, and teaching methods. Almost all states test for competency in basic skills, teaching skills, or specific subject matter for those seeking licensure, and most require continuing education for license renewal. Many require a graduate degree. The National Board for Professional Teaching Standards offers voluntary national certification, which may help teachers to find a position in another state and make them eligible for higher salaries.

Teachers in private schools generally are not required to take courses in teacher education, though other educational requirements for teaching at the secondary school level are similar to those for teachers in the public schools.

EARNINGS

According to the NEA, the average annual salary for public secondary school teachers in the 1995–1996 academic year was $38,600. Some schools pay teachers extra for coaching sports or supervising extracurricular activities. Many teachers use their summer break to earn additional income. In 1996, more than 50 percent of all public school teachers belonged to unions that represented them in contract negotiations. Private school teachers usually earn less than their colleagues in the public schools.

PROSPECTS: JOB OUTLOOK

In 1996, secondary school teachers held about 1.4 million jobs. Through the year 2006, jobs for secondary school teachers are expected to increase faster than the average for all occupations, reflecting the increased high school enrollments expected through this period. Hiring for the public schools also depends on budget appropriations, which depend on taxpayers' priorities. Despite the evident need, education will be competing with other essential services for scarcer revenue dollars.

Many rural areas and inner cities have a problem attracting teachers, so prospects in these areas will be better than in suburban settings. There also should be a strong demand for minority and bilingual teachers, as well as teachers who specialize in the areas of math, science, and computer science.

WHERE TO LOOK FOR FURTHER INFORMATION

For information on a career in teaching, contact the appropriate local or state affiliate of the NEA.

Teacher education programs are accredited by the NCATE. A list of colleges and universities offering accredited programs is available from:

National Council for Accreditation of Teacher Education
2010 Massachusetts Avenue, NW
Suite 500
Washington, DC 20036

For information on teachers' unions and the larger range of issues and challenges affecting the profession:

American Federation of Teachers
555 New Jersey Avenue, NW
Washington, DC 20001

National Education Association
1201 16th Street, NW
Washington, DC 20036

For information on the requirements for voluntary national teacher certification:

National Board for Professional Teaching Standards
26555 Evergreen Road
Suite 400
Southfield, MI 48076

HEALTH CARE

CHIROPRACTORS

OCCUPATIONAL OVERVIEW

Job Description: Chiropractors diagnose and treat health problems related to the musculoskeletal and nervous systems. Manual manipulation of parts of the body, especially the spinal column, constitutes the major form of treatment in chiropractic.

Prospects: Employment prospects are expected to grow faster than the average for all occupations through the year 2006, partly due to increased public demand for complementary medicine and acceptance of the profession.

Qualifications: Chiropractors must be licensed to practice, but the scope of the practice permitted and the educational requirements for a license vary widely among states. All states grant licenses to chiropractors who meet the educational requirements and pass a state board examination.

Personal Skills: Observation skills to detect physical problems and considerable manual dexterity are essential, but unusual strength or endurance is not. The ability to work independently and make decisions is crucial, as are empathy and a desire to help others.

Earnings: The American Chiropractic Association (ACA) reported that the median net income for chiropractors was about $80,000 in 1995.

THE JOB AND THE WORK ENVIRONMENT

Chiropractic entails a holistic approach to health care that stresses the patient's overall health and well-being. Chiropractors encourage the use of natural, nondrug, nonsurgical health treatments and recommend changes in lifestyle (e.g, eating and exercise habits) for their clients. Like other health practitioners, they follow a standard procedure for securing the information required to make a diagnosis and prescribe treatment. They take medical histories, conduct physical and neurological examinations, order laboratory tests, and take x-rays. They also use a postural and spinal analysis unique to chiropractic.

Treatment depends on diagnosis. If a patient's illness can be traced to a weakness of the musculoskeletal structure, chiropractors work to relieve pressure on specific nerves by manually manipulating the spinal column. Most chiropractic offices have physiotherapy machines, such as low-voltage electrotherapy units, ultrasound units, and diathermy units. A majority of chiropractors use traction devices, computed tomography (CT), and magnetic resonance imaging (MRI). Many also use massage and counsel patients on stress management, nutrition, and exercise.

Like other health professionals, chiropractors are subject to state laws and regulations on the kinds of services they are permitted to provide. For example, they do not prescribe drugs or perform surgery. If their type of care seems inappropriate, chiropractors may refer patients to other health practitioners. Some chiropractors specialize in specific areas, such as nutrition, sports injuries, or orthopedics.

Nearly all chiropractors work alone or in group practices. This means that in addition to their professional practice, they must handle the administrative tasks of running their own business, or hire employees to handle this for them. A small number of chiropractors teach or work for hospitals or Health Maintenance Organizations (HMOs).

The average workweek for a chiropractor is 42 hours, and they work in clean, comfortable offices. The work schedule usually includes some evening and weekend hours to accommodate patients; but since most chiropractors are self-employed, they can set their own schedule.

TRAINING AND QUALIFICATIONS

Most state licensing boards require completion of a 4-year chiropractic college course after at least 2 years of undergraduate education. All states recognize academic training in chiropractic colleges accredited by the Council on Chiropractic Education; in 1997, 17 chiropractic programs and colleges in the United States were fully accredited.

The colleges require applicants to have at least two years of undergraduate study, including courses in English, the social sciences, organic and inorganic chemistry, biology, physics, and psychology. (Many applicants have a bachelor's degree; this may eventually become an entry requirement.) The colleges emphasize manipulation and spinal adjustments in their coursework, but all offer a broader curriculum in the basic and clinical sciences along with the chiropractic ones. Students graduating from a chiropractic college earn the degree of doctor of chiropractic (D.C.). For licensure, most states accept all or part of the four-part test administered by the National Board of Chiropractic Examiners, but certain states may supplement the test with a state examination. In addition, some states require chiropractors to pass a basic science examination similar to that required for other health practitioners. Nearly all states require chiropractors to complete a specified number of hours in continuing education per year to maintain licensure.

EARNINGS

According to the ACA, the median net income for chiropractors in 1995 was about $80,000. As in other kinds of independent professional practice, income is low at the outset and then increases as the practice grows. Self-employed chiropractors must provide their own retirement and health insurance coverage.

PROSPECTS: JOB OUTLOOK

In 1996, chiropractors held about 44,000 jobs. Through the year 2006, jobs for chiropractors are expected to grow faster than the average for all occupations as public demand for complementary medicine continues to grow. The demand for chiropractors is dependent on patients' ability to pay, either directly or through health insurance. The increasing acceptance of chiropractic by the public and the acknowledgment by the health insurance industry provide a strong underpinning for the future growth of this occupation. In addition, a rapidly growing senior population, with increasingly likely musculoskeletal problems, will increase the demand for chiropractic. Replacement needs result almost exclusively from retirements in this profession.

WHERE TO LOOK FOR FURTHER INFORMATION

To learn more about chiropractic as a career:

American Chiropractic Association
1701 Clarendon Boulevard
Arlington, VA 22209

International Chiropractors Association
1110 North Glebe Road
Suite 1000
Arlington, VA 22201

To obtain a list of chiropractic colleges:

Council on Chiropractic Education
7975 North Hayden Road
Suite A-210
Scottsdale, AZ 85258

CLINICAL LABORATORY TECHNOLOGISTS AND TECHNICIANS

OCCUPATIONAL OVERVIEW

Job Description: Clinical laboratory technologists and technicians perform the many laboratory tests ordered by physicians as part of the diagnostic process. *Medical technologists* perform the tests, and *medical laboratory technicians* work under a technologist or a laboratory supervisor and assist in routine or less-complex procedures.

Prospects: Employment opportunities for clinical laboratory workers should grow about as fast as the average for all occupations through the year 2006.

Qualifications: Medical technologists generally have a bachelor's degree in medical technology or in one of the life sciences. Medical lab technicians commonly have an associate's degree from a community college, or a diploma or certificate from a trade or technical school.

Personal Skills: A capacity for exacting and detailed work and analytical judgment are essential. Steadiness under pressure caused by the critical nature of the work and often by demands for accurate results quickly is crucial, as is the ability to use computers and other technical equipment.

Earnings: In 1996, the median weekly salary of full-time technologists and technicians was $520. A Hay Group survey of acute care hospitals found the median annual base salary of full-time technologists to be about $35,100 in January 1997; for technicians, the median salary was $26,500.

THE JOB AND THE WORK ENVIRONMENT

Clinical laboratory testing plays a vital role in detecting, diagnosing, and treating diseases. Lab personnel's efforts usually go unsung, but they are certainly not unappreciated.

Medical laboratory technologists use their training to perform a wide variety of chemical, biological, hematological (blood-related), immunological, microscopic, and bacteriological tests. They make microscopic examinations of tissues and blood to detect evidence of disease and chemical tests to determine blood cholesterol levels. They make cultures of body fluids or tissue samples to detect the presence of bacteria, fungi, parasites, or other microorganisms. They also type blood and cross-match blood samples for transfusions and test for drug levels in blood to determine how patients are responding to medications. Technologists perform the tests, verify the results for accuracy (a crucial consideration), and report the results to the physician.

Some laboratories are large, with automated, computerized instruments; others are smaller, with less-sophisticated equipment. In the smaller labs, technologists are likely to perform a variety of tests; in large labs, they tend to specialize in an area such as clinical chemistry (chemical analysis of body fluids), blood bank technology, cytotechnology (study of human tissue), microbiology (study of bacteria and other microorganisms), or immunology (study of the immune system).

Medical laboratory technicians usually work under the supervision of technologists or other senior personnel, performing routine and less-complex tests and procedures and assisting technologists. They may operate automatic equipment and prepare specimens for testing, or may complete manual tests according to detailed instructions. Technicians may perform in all areas of lab work or may specialize.

In large hospitals and laboratories that operate around the clock, the personnel are likely to work assigned shifts and may have to work holidays and weekends. Those in smaller labs that operate around the clock are likely to work rotating shifts. In some cases, personnel may be required to be on call for duty several nights a week.

Labs are usually well lit and clean. Materials and specimens used during the testing process, however, sometimes produce odors. Lab personnel have to exercise special care when handling infectious materials or dangerous chemicals. The work can be stressful and pressured at times, and lab workers may spend a good deal of time on their feet.

TRAINING AND QUALIFICATIONS

A beginning job as a medical technologist typically requires a bachelor's degree with a major in medical technology or one of the life sciences (though it is possible to qualify with combined on-the-job and special training). Programs in medical technology are offered by colleges and universities, as well as by hospitals. The hospitals are usually affiliated with a college or university, and their programs generally lead to a bachelor's degree. A number of universities offer master's programs for technologists who plan to specialize or go into teaching, research, or administration. The Clinical Laboratory Improvement Act requires technologists who perform some highly complex tests to have at least an associate's degree.

Medical laboratory technicians may take courses in junior or community colleges, in hospitals, or in technical or vocational schools, where programs generally last two years and lead to an associate's degree. A small number are trained on the job.

The National Accrediting Agency for Clinical Laboratory Sciences fully accredits 621—and approves 72—programs for medical technologists and technicians; the Accrediting Bureau of Health Education Schools accredits programs for medical lab technicians.

The competency of laboratory technologists and technicians is assured through state licensing and voluntary certification. Some states require laboratory workers to be licensed or registered, and specific licensing information can be obtained from state health departments or boards of occupational licensing.

With certification, a professional society or certifying agency sets standards for professional skills that must be met by individuals seeking certification. With most medical technologist and technician jobs, certification is a requirement, and it is commonly needed for advancement. Groups that certify such workers include the American Medical Technologists, the Board of Registry of the American Society of Clinical Pathologists, and the American Society for Clinical Laboratory Science.

Laboratory technicians can become technologists through further education and work experience. Technologists may advance to supervisory or management positions in labs or hospitals. To become a laboratory director, a doctorate is usually required.

EARNINGS

Salaries for laboratory personnel vary according to the size of the employer and geographic location. Usually, labs in large cities pay the most.

In 1996, the median weekly salary of full-time clinical laboratory technologists and technicians was $520. A Hay Group survey of acute care hospitals found the median base salary of full-time technologists to be about $35,100 in January 1997; the median salary for technicians was $26,500. For medical technologists working for the federal government, the average salary in early 1997 was $40,680; the average salary for technicians was $26,130.

PROSPECTS: JOB OUTLOOK

In 1996, clinical lab technologists and technicians held approximately 285,000 jobs. Through the year 2006, the medical lab field is expected to grow about as fast as the average for all occupations. Growth in older segments of the population is expected to increase the need for diagnostic procedures since seniors usually have increasing health problems. Advances in medical technology will have two opposite effects on job opportunities. New, complex—and more powerful—diagnostic tests will lead to more testing; but advances in automation will increase worker productivity, slowing job growth. Robots may be used to prepare specimens, and more simplified tests may be developed for use by doctors and patients, rather than being performed in laboratories. Finally, labs devoted to research in finding the cause, treatment, and cure of diseases are expected to expand rapidly in response to increased spending by the public and private sectors.

Because of the increased worker productivity due to technological advances in testing procedures, competition for jobs in this field has increased, so individuals must look longer to find employment than in the past.

The greatest growth will likely be in independent labs (to which hospitals are sending more of their testing), with fast growth also expected in doctors' offices and clinics. Slower growth is projected in hospitals. Many openings will result from replacement needs.

WHERE TO LOOK FOR FURTHER INFORMATION

To learn more about medical laboratory careers and certification:

American Medical Technologists
710 Higgins Road
Park Ridge, IL 60068

American Society of Clinical Pathologists
Board of Registry
P.O. Box 12277
Chicago, IL 60612

National Accrediting Agency for Clinical
  Laboratory Sciences
8410 West Bryn Mawr Avenue
Suite 670
Chicago, IL 60631

National Certification Agency for Medical
  Laboratory Personnel
7910 Woodmont Avenue
Suite 1301
Bethesda, MD 20814

To learn more about training programs for medical laboratory technicians:

Accrediting Bureau of Health Education Schools
29089 U.S. 20 West
Elkhart, IN 46514

DENTAL HYGIENISTS

OCCUPATIONAL OVERVIEW

Job Description: Dental hygienists provide preventive dental care, help patients develop good oral hygiene skills, clean teeth, apply fluoride and sealants, and sometimes administer anesthetics.

Prospects: Through the year 2006, employment opportunities for dental hygienists are expected to grow much faster than the average for all occupations.

Qualifications: Dental hygienists must be state licensed. To obtain a license, candidates must complete a program from an accredited dental hygiene school and pass both a written and a clinical examination. Most states also require an examination on the legal aspects of dental hygiene procedures.

Personal Skills: Contact with people is a large part of the job, and the ability to put patients at ease in a stressful situation is very important. Manual dexterity is necessary for performing procedures in the mouth. Personal neatness, cleanliness, thoroughness, and good health are also important.

Earnings: According to the American Dental Association (ADA), the average weekly earnings of a dental hygienist working 32 or more hours a week in a private practice were $759 in 1995.

THE JOB AND THE WORK ENVIRONMENT

The dentist treats what is damaged or diseased. Once the dentist succeeds in restoring oral health, the hygienist shows us how to maintain it. Dental hygienists instruct patients in preventive dental care and good oral hygiene. They clean and scale teeth, apply fluoride treatments and sealants, and instruct patients about the selection of suitable toothbrushes, the use of dental floss, and the proper care of dental prosthetics.

The tasks a dental hygienist may perform vary widely depending on qualifications and the licensing requirements in individual states. Most dental hygienists examine patients and evaluate them, take and develop x-rays, remove calculus, stain, and plaque from above and below the gum line, apply caries-preventive agents, place temporary fillings, remove sutures, apply periodontal dressings, and polish and shape amalgam restorations. If the hygienist is qualified and state licensing permits, he or she may administer local anesthetics and nitrous oxide (i.e., oxygen analgesia).

Nearly all dental hygienists work in private dentists' offices, which are clean and well lit. Some work in public health agencies, clinics, schools, hospitals, or facilities attached to private businesses. Dental hygienists holding advanced degrees may also teach.

The work includes constant contact with people. An outgoing manner and good social skills are important for putting people at ease. The hygienist is likely to work with people from childhood to old age. Hygienists should have manual dexterity for working with dental instruments in patients' mouths and have good personal hygiene and health.

A flexible schedule is a unique aspect of this job. Hygienists are frequently hired to work two to three days a week, and commonly they work for more than one dentist. Those who hold full-time positions work a 35-hour week, which may include evening and Saturday hours.

The work calls for strict adherence to proper radiologic procedures, recommended aseptic technique, and use of appropriate protective devices when administering analgesia. Dental hygienists wear safety glasses as well as surgical gloves and masks to protect against infectious diseases. Hygienists use x-ray equipment, and theirs is one of several occupations covered by the Consumer-Patient Radiation Health and Safety Act of 1981 that encourages uniform standards among the states for training and certification of people who perform medical and dental radiologic procedures.

TRAINING AND QUALIFICATIONS

Dental hygienists are licensed by the state in which they practice. To qualify for a license, a hygienist must graduate from an accredited dental hygiene school and pass a written and a clinical examination. An examination administered by the ADA's Joint Commission of National Dental Examinations is recognized by all 50 states and the District of Columbia. Regional or state agencies administer the clinical examination. In most states, the successful candidate also has to take an examination in the legal aspects of dental hygiene practice.

The Commission on Dental Accreditation accredited 230 programs in dental hygiene in 1997, most of them requiring one to two years of college as a prerequisite and awarding an associate's degree adequate for work in a private dentist's office. Some also offer a bachelor's degree. Master's degrees are awarded by a number of colleges and universities. For teaching, research, or clinical practice in school or public health programs, a bachelor's or master's degree is usually needed.

The course of study for a dental hygienist includes basic and clinical science with laboratory, clinical, and classroom instruction in anatomy, physiology, chemistry, pharmacology, nutrition, histology, periodontology, pathology, dental materials, and clinical and dental hygiene. The curriculum also includes coursework in the liberal arts and social and behavioral sciences.

EARNINGS

Earnings vary with region, practice setting, training, and experience. Those who work for a private dentist may work full or part time and may be paid hourly or per diem; they may be on salary or even work on commission.

According to the ADA, in 1995, the average weekly salary for a dental hygienist working full time (32 or more hours a week) was $759.

Fringe benefits vary considerably and usually are tied to full-time employment.

PROSPECTS: JOB OUTLOOK

In 1996, there were about 133,000 dental hygienists. Several trends are likely to keep job prospects for dental hygienists growing much faster than the average for all occupations through the year 2006: population growth, the aging of the population (with greater retention of natural teeth by middle-age people and seniors), the growth of dental insurance plans, and a general increase in awareness of dental hygiene. The increase in group practice and retail dentistry increases hirings of dental hygienists also. As new dentists, who are trained to use support personnel, open new practices, more hygienists will be hired to perform some of the services previously performed by dentists.

WHERE TO LOOK FOR FURTHER INFORMATION

For information on career opportunities and educational requirements:

Division of Professional Development
American Dental Hygienists' Association
444 North Michigan Avenue
Suite 3400
Chicago, IL 60611

To learn more about accredited programs:

Commission on Dental Accreditation
American Dental Association
211 East Chicago Avenue
Suite 1814
Chicago, IL 60611

For information about licensing, contact the state board of dental examiners in each state or:

American Association of Dental Examiners
211 East Chicago Avenue
Suite 760
Chicago, IL 60611

DENTISTS

OCCUPATIONAL OVERVIEW

Job Description: Dentists diagnose, treat, and prevent problems of the teeth and tissues of the mouth. They use x-rays for diagnostic purposes, fill cavities, apply sealants, straighten teeth, extract teeth, repair fractured teeth, and treat gum diseases.

Prospects: Employment opportunities for dentists are expected to grow more slowly than the average for all occupations through the year 2006. A generally aging population will boost demand for dental care, but dentists will be hiring hygienists and assistants to handle routine services they now perform themselves. Competition in attracting a steady clientele and building a good practice most likely will prove to be keen.

Qualifications: Dentists must be licensed by the state in which they practice. To qualify for a state license, dentists must be graduates of an approved dental school and pass written and practical examinations.

Personal Skills: Manual dexterity, diagnostic ability, good judgment of space and shape, and excellent visual memory are important. Because most dentists work in solo practice, good business sense, communication skills, and self-discipline are desirable.

Earnings: The median net annual income of dentists with private practices was about $120,000 in 1995, according to the American Dental Association (ADA).

THE JOB AND THE WORK ENVIRONMENT

Dentists have come a long way from the days of cutting hair and extracting teeth, both in the same chair. Today's dentists are trained, skilled health practitioners using sophisticated equipment; even the chair is likely to be contoured and ergonomically designed. Most dentists are sole proprietors of their practice and work alone or with a small staff; others may have partners. A few work for other dentists.

Dentists are primarily concerned with caring for teeth and gums and, increasingly, informing their patients on ways to prevent dental problems. They clean teeth, demonstrate proper methods of dental hygiene, and advise on ways of preventing dental disease. They may devote some time to laboratory work, such as making dentures and crowns, although these tasks usually are now done by technicians in a commercial lab. Dentists may employ dental hygienists, assistants, laboratory technicians, and receptionists in their practices, to help in the office, assist in routine chairside duties, and provide therapeutic services under their supervision. Dentists wear surgical gloves, masks, and safety glasses to protect themselves and their patients from infectious diseases.

Most full-time dentists work about 40 hours a week, though a dentist fresh out of school, working to build up a practice, may spend more hours a week in the office. An older dentist with an established practice may work considerably fewer hours. Dentists' offices are usually open four or five days a week and sometimes on weekends and during evenings.

Most dentists are general practitioners; they treat a wide variety of dental problems and provide a wide range of dental care. Others practice in one or another of the eight specialty areas recognized by the ADA. *Orthodontists*, who straighten teeth, make up the biggest group in the specialty area. The next largest group comprises *oral and maxillofacial surgeons*, who operate on the jaw and mouth. The other specialties are *periodontics* (treating gums), *pediatric dentistry* (treating children), *prosthodontics* (artificial teeth or dentures), *endodontics* (root canal therapy), *public health dentistry*, and *oral pathology* (diseases of the mouth).

Some dentists engaged in private practice work in shopping malls, contract with individual companies to provide their employees with dental services, and contract their services to health maintenance organizations. Those not in private practice may work in public and private clinics or hospitals, or in teaching or research.

TRAINING AND QUALIFICATIONS

To qualify for a state license, a dentist must graduate from a dental school approved by the ADA's Commission on Dental Accreditation and pass the required written and practical tests. Candidates can satisfy part of the state licensing requirements by passing the National Board of Dental Examiners' written test.

Dental schools require a minimum of two years of undergraduate-level predental education, though most dental students are college graduates. All require applicants to take the Dental Admissions Test (DAT), which, along with overall grade-point average (GPA), science course GPA, recommendations, and interview results, are used to select students. Dental school is usually a four-year program. For the last two years of the program, students treat patients, usually in clinics and under supervision. The most common degree awarded by dental schools is doctor of dental surgery (D.D.S.); some schools award the equivalent doctor of dental medicine (D.M.D.) degree.

Most state licenses allow dentists to practice as general practitioners and as specialists, but currently about 17 states require a specialty license, which involves 2 to 4 years of graduate education and sometimes a special state examination. Dentists interested in teaching or research generally pursue 2 to 5 additional years of advanced training in hospital or dental school programs.

Some newly graduated dentists begin their careers by working for an established dentist for several years, gaining experience and earning money to equip their own offices. Most purchase an established practice or open a new practice immediately upon graduation.

EARNINGS

Dentists who open their own practices have such large expenditures that they generally earn little more than their expenses in the beginning. Thereafter, earnings normally rise rapidly as the practice takes hold. Specialists do much better than general practitioners. The ADA reports that the median net annual income of dentists in private practice in 1995 was about $120,000. Median net income for specialists was about $175,000; for those in general practice, it was about $109,000. Self-employed dentists must provide their own insurance and retirement benefits.

PROSPECTS: JOB OUTLOOK

In 1996, dentists held about 162,000 jobs. Opportunities for employment are expected to grow more slowly than the average for all occupations through the year 2006, with the majority of employment growth the result of retirements. Although the aging of the population and the maturing of the baby boom generation are expected to swell demand for restorative dentistry, and youngsters will continue to need preventive checkups, the employment of dentists is not projected to increase as rapidly as the demand for these services. That's because, as dentists expand their practices, they're likely to hire hygienists and assistants to perform some of their routine services.

Competition will be keen in some localities, especially in large urban areas, where the practices are more lucrative. Rural areas, although not so lucrative, may be more favorable to those beginning a practice.

WHERE TO LOOK FOR FURTHER INFORMATION

To learn more about dentistry as a career and to obtain a list of fully accredited dental schools:

American Association of Dental Schools
1625 Massachusetts Avenue, NW
Washington, DC 20036

American Dental Association
Commission on Dental Accreditation
211 East Chicago Avenue
Chicago, IL 60611

DIETITIANS AND NUTRITIONISTS

OCCUPATIONAL OVERVIEW

Job Description: Dietitians, sometimes called nutritionists, apply the principles of nutrition to meal selection and preparation. They educate about healthy eating and evaluate and make changes in clients' diets. They set up and manage food service systems for institutions.

Prospects: Employment opportunities are expected to grow about as fast as the average for all occupations through the year 2006. As the public continues to recognize the importance of professional expertise in nutritional matters, the demand for dietitians will increase.

Qualifications: A bachelor's degree with a major in food service systems management, foods and nutrition, or dietetics plus experience are the minimum requirements for entry into the profession. Professional certification as a registered dietitian is also available.

Personal Skills: An interest in food and good health is essential. Good interpersonal skills and administration and organizational ability are important. Computer literacy is highly recommended.

Earnings: Salaries depend on the size and type of institution (for staff dietitians), type of practice, years in practice, size of community, and region. In a January 1997 survey of acute care hospitals by the Hay Group, the median salary of full-time staff dieticians was $34,400.

THE JOB AND THE WORK ENVIRONMENT

A full plate does not always mean good nutrition. Eating properly, rather than overamply, is a necessity if people are to maintain their health and physical fitness. Dietitians promote sound eating habits through education and research, as well as through overseeing the selection and preparation of food services for many different institutions and groups. Some specialize in areas such as obesity, pediatrics, or diabetes.

Clinical dietitians provide food and nutrition services in hospitals, nursing homes, outpatient clinics, research laboratories, and in private practice. They form a vital part of the health team.

Community dietitians advise individuals and families on food selection with respect to lifestyle. They emphasize nutrition awareness and disease prevention and work in such settings as public health agencies, day care centers, home health care agencies, health maintenance organizations, and health and recreation clubs.

Management dietitians coordinate food service systems and clinical management, administer personnel, design and implement training programs, and plan food systems and departmental budgets in health care facilities, schools, prisons, company cafeterias, and restaurants.

Business dietitians work for corporations in product development, food styling, and menu design; act as the sales professionals or purchasing agents representing food, equipment, or nutrition product accounts; and serve as food nutrition or marketing experts in public relations and media.

Education dietitians teach the science of nutrition and food service systems management in colleges, universities, and hospitals; conduct nutrition research; and write articles and books on nutrition and food service systems.

Consultant dietitians, in independent practice, advise the food and pharmaceutical industries; speak at professional seminars; counsel patients in nursing homes and medical and dental centers; plan food service systems; tailor nutritional regimens in fitness programs for athletes, dancers, and others; work for wellness programs; and write articles and books.

Dietitians and nutritionists held about 58,000 jobs in 1996. More than half were employed by hospitals, nursing homes, and physicians' offices and clinics. Others held jobs in local government programs, schools, colleges, and universities. Prison systems, hotel and restaurant chains, and companies that provide food service for their employees employed dietitians also. Consulting, full or part time, is another way for nutritionists to practice their trade.

Dietitians normally work a regular 40-hour week, but those in hospitals sometimes work on weekends. Many dietitians work part time. Jobs in commercial food service systems tend to require irregular hours. Dietitians do spend time in offices and classrooms, but they also may have to work in kitchens and serving areas that are often hot and steamy. Clinical dietitians may have to spend much of the day on their feet, and consultant dietitians may travel.

Dietetic technicians work as members of a food service or health team under the supervision of, or in consultation with, a dietitian. They supervise support staff, monitor cost control procedures, interpret and implement quality control procedures, counsel individuals or small groups, screen patients for nutritional status, and develop nutritional care plans.

TRAINING AND QUALIFICATIONS

There are two basic routes to prepare for a career as a dietitian; both combine classroom work with preprofessional experience:

1. Earn a bachelor's degree in dietetics, foods and nutrition, or food service systems management from 1 of the 231 (as of 1997) programs approved by the American Dietetic Association (ADA). The graduate then completes a dietetic internship that includes a minimum of 900 hours of supervised practice.
2. Earn a bachelor's degree in the required majors from a college or university with an ADA-accredited coordinated program. In this program, students combine classroom study and the necessary work experience.

Dietitians with degrees and completed work experience are eligible to take the registration examination for dietitians given by the ADA's Commission on Dietetic Registration. The successful candidate is granted the title of *registered dietitian* and may use the initials R.D. to signify professional competence.

Dietetic technicians earn an associate's degree by completing an ADA-approved dietetic technician program. Also available is a registration examination for dietetic technicians that allows a successful examinee to use the initials D.T.R. to show professional competence.

Forty states have laws regulating dietetics: 27 require licensure, 12 require certification, and 1 requires registration.

Dietitians may advance to associate or director of a dietetic department or become independent contractors. Some may change occupations and become sales representatives in the food industry.

EARNINGS

Salaries depend on size and type of institution (for staff dietitians), type of practice, years in practice, education, size of community, and geographic location. In a January 1997 survey of acute care hospitals, the Hay Group found the median base salary of full-time staff dieticians to be $34,400.

The ADA reported the following median annual incomes for registered dietitians, by type of practice, in 1995: clinical nutrition, $34,131; food and nutrition management, $42,964; community nutrition, $33,902; consultation and business, $43,374; and education and research, $42,784.

PROSPECTS: JOB OUTLOOK

The expanding need for food services in nursing homes, hospitals, retirement communities, and various social service programs forecasts that job opportunities for dietitians are expected to grow about as fast as the average for all occupations through the year 2006. Openings will result from employment growth as well as from the need to replace dietitians who retire or otherwise change occupations.

Demand seems strong as the public has become more aware of the importance of diet to health and physical fitness. Moreover, the growing numbers of aging people in nursing homes, retirement communities, and home health care organizations will require nutritional services. Growth in independent food services, physicians' offices, and social service settings is expected to be faster than the average for all occupations. Growth in hospitals is projected to be slower as hospitals contract out for food services and experience an expected slow growth of inpatients. Growth also is slowed by limitations in insurance reimbursements for dietetic services. Dietitians with experience and a willingness to relocate to areas of greatest demand will have the best prospects.

WHERE TO LOOK FOR FURTHER INFORMATION

To learn more about academic programs and preparing for a career as a dietitian:

American Dietetic Association
216 West Jackson Boulevard
Suite 800
Chicago, IL 60606-6995

DISPENSING OPTICIANS

OCCUPATIONAL OVERVIEW

Job Description: Dispensing opticians fit people with prescription eyeglasses and contact lenses. Some also fit ocular prostheses. Most work full time for an ophthalmologist or optometrist, or in a retail outlet.

Prospects: Through the year 2006, jobs for dispensing opticians are expected to grow as fast as the average for all occupations. Perhaps the most important factor contributing to this forecast is the aging of the population and the resulting increased demand for corrective lenses.

Qualifications: Dispensing opticians must be high school graduates. They learn their trade through an apprenticeship or formal training. A license is required in 21 states.

Personal Skills: Dispensing opticians must have the patience to do careful work that requires attention to detail. They need deft fingers and good color vision. Since a large part of their work is with the public, a pleasant personality and good communication skills are important.

Earnings: According to a survey cited in the April 1997 *Eyecare Business* magazine, the overall average salary for dispensing opticians was $27,432. The highest earnings went to graduates of opticianry schools and owners and managers of optical stores, as well as those who worked in states requiring licensure.

THE JOB AND THE WORK ENVIRONMENT

Opticians dispense to patients the corrective lenses prescribed by ophthalmologists or optometrists. They help customers select suitable eyeglass frames and make sure they fit properly. In some states, opticians, under the supervision of an optometrist or ophthalmologist, are qualified to fit contact lenses. Still others may specialize in fitting cosmetic shells to blemished eyes. *Ocularists* are opticians trained to fit people with ocular prostheses.

The patient's prescription is the optician's first responsibility. He or she makes certain it is complete, verifies it with the examining physician or optometrist, and, if the patient has a file, compares it with previous prescriptions. The patient's habits, occupation, and pastimes (e.g., whether he or she regularly plays sports) may bear on the selection of suitable eyeglasses. The frames from which a patient can choose are limited by their suitability for the prescribed lenses and by how well they fit the patient. Combining that information with the patient's stylistic preferences, the optician helps the patient make a selection.

The optician makes a number of measurements to ensure that the frame will hold the lenses securely centered and that they fit properly. Once the patient has selected frames that meet the specifications, the optician fills out an order to send to the laboratory, which will grind the lenses and mount them in the frame. (Some dispensing opticians prepare lenses themselves.) In addition to the specifications in the prescription, the order indicates the lens material, any tint or coating, and the type of lens hardening.

When the eyeglasses arrive from the laboratory, the optician checks them against the order and fits them to the patient. Fitting contact lenses requires more care, skill, and patience than fitting eyeglasses. Opticians also routinely repair broken eyeglass frames or temples, replace screws, and refit glasses.

Opticians use optical tools to measure lenses; they also use pliers, screwdrivers, files, and heaters to adjust frames. They maintain records of each patient's prescription. Opticians work in pleasant, well-lit, well-ventilated surroundings. They work in small or large stores or in medical offices. The workweek is usually 40 hours, but in order to cover some evenings and weekends for the convenience of customers, it may extend to 45 to 50 hours. Some opticians work part time.

Opticians who work in retail sales spend most of their time dealing with the public and spend a lot of time standing. They must be patient and tactful. If they do laboratory work, they must take the necessary precautions to guard against the hazards associated with the machinery and materials they handle, including various chemical solutions.

TRAINING AND QUALIFICATIONS

Opticians must be high school graduates. They may learn their trade as apprentices, on the job, or in the armed forces. Employers usually hire people with no opticianry training or who have worked as ophthalmic laboratory technicians and then train them. Large companies usually have formal apprenticeship programs; smaller companies offer informal, on-the-job learning. For the 21 states that license dispensing opticians, persons without postsecondary training must work for 2 to 4 years as apprentices. Apprenticeship programs include studies in optical mathematics and optical physics and training in the use of laboratory equipment and optical tools, in fitting eyeglasses or contact lenses, and in office management and sales. Information on apprenticeships and licensing is available from each state's board of occupational licensing.

Community colleges, vocational and technical institutes, and some colleges and universities offer formal opticianry training. As of 1997, 27 programs were accredited by the Commission on Opticianry Accreditation, with 2-year associate degrees awarded in optometric technology or ophthalmic dispensing.

Opticians can apply to be certified by the American Board of Opticians and the National Contact Lens Examiners. Certification must be renewed every three years with continuing education.

Experienced dispensing opticians may open their own optical stores or become store managers or sales representatives for eyeglass or contact lens manufacturers.

EARNINGS

According to a survey cited in the April 1997 *Eyecare Business* magazine, the overall average salary for dispensing opticians was $27,432. Owners and managers of optical stores and graduates of opticianry schools had higher earnings, along with those who worked in states requiring licensure.

PROSPECTS: JOB OUTLOOK

In 1996, there were 67,000 dispensing opticians; demand for them is expected to increase about as fast as the average for all occupations through the year 2006. As the population ages, more people will need corrective lenses. The increasing popularity of participative sports will require special lenses and frames, and there also is likely to be an increase in the use of safety goggles and glasses. New products and fashion will contribute to increased demand among consumers for novel frames and photochromic and tinted lenses. The number of people using contact lenses is expected to increase with the availability of improved bifocal, disposable, and extended-wear contact lenses.

For opticians with an associate's degree, employment opportunities ought to be excellent, especially in or near large urban areas. However, because fashionable eyeglasses and contact lenses are something of a luxury, the optical industry is vulnerable to economic downturns.

WHERE TO LOOK FOR FURTHER INFORMATION

For information on pursuing a career as a dispensing optician:

National Academy of Opticianry
10111 Martin Luther King, Jr., Highway
Suite 112
Bowie, MD 20720-4299

Opticians Association of America
10341 Democracy Lane
P.O. Box 10110
Fairfax, VA 22030-2521

For a list of accredited training programs:

Commission on Opticianry Accreditation
10111 Martin Luther King, Jr., Highway
Suite 100
Bowie, MD 20720-4299

*E*KG TECHNICIANS

OCCUPATIONAL OVERVIEW

Job Description: EKG technicians use electrocardiographs to record electrocardiograms (EKGs), conducting diagnostic tests and monitoring the heartbeat of patients undergoing treatment or testing. Most EKG technicians work in the cardiology departments of large hospitals.

Prospects: Through the year 2006, job growth for EKG technicians is expected to decline as hospitals train registered nurses, among others, to perform basic EKG tests. Those trained in Holter monitoring and stress testing are expected to have better job prospects than those who can take only basic EKGs.

Qualifications: EKG technicians must be high school graduates and are usually trained on the job for about 8 to 16 weeks. One-year certificate programs also exist for training in basic EKGs, Holter monitoring, and stress testing.

Personal Skills: EKG technicians must have a mechanical aptitude and the ability to follow detailed instructions. They must be mature and reliable and possess presence of mind in emergencies. They must be able to work well with patients and their fellow health care workers.

Earnings: According to a survey of acute care hospitals by the Hay Group in January 1997, the median base salary of full-time EKG technicians was $20,200.

THE JOB AND THE WORK ENVIRONMENT

Health care providers use EKGs, a graphic record of patients' heartbeats, to diagnose heart disease, monitor the effects of drug therapy, and analyze a patient's heart condition over a prolonged period. EKGs are used routinely before most surgery, including outpatient procedures, and for patients who have reached a certain age, and they are common in pre-employment physicals.

The men and women who operate the electrocardiograph, which picks up electrical impulses from the heart during and between heartbeats, are EKG technicians. The equipment is mobile, and the procedure, a relatively simple one, can be done in a physician's office. The technician positions electrodes on the patient's chest, arms, and legs, and manipulates switches on an electrocardiograph machine to get a reading. Knowledge of the anatomy of the chest and heart is necessary for proper placement of electrodes and an accurate reading.

The EKG technician prepares the completed recording for the physician, often a heart specialist. Since equipment is now computerized, the technician enters data via a keyboard, and the computer analyzes the tracing. The technician may bring anomalies to a physician's attention. In general, the technician is responsible for ensuring that the equipment operates properly. Some technicians also schedule appointments, type physician's interpretations, maintain patients' EKG files, and assist in specialized testing.

Techniques for testing the heart are not limited to the standard resting EKG. Technicians may also be trained in Holter monitoring, stress testing, or echocardiography. Holter monitoring, a 24-hour ambulatory monitoring, takes a continuous reading of a patient's heart throughout a day of ordinary activity. Exercise stress testing monitors the heart through various kinds and gradations of physical activity, from ordinary to strenuous. EKG personnel may also be specially trained as invasive or noninvasive cardiovascular technicians. These advanced procedures require a thorough grounding in cardiovascular anatomy and physiology, which is gained through two-year junior or community college programs or, sometimes, through on-the-job training.

EKG technicians usually work a 5-day, 40-hour week. Those who work in hospitals and clinics may also work weekends, holidays, and nights on periodic or rotating shifts. The job entails a lot of walking and standing and includes working in crises. It can be emotionally demanding and requires a stable, self-possessed person who can exercise good judgment in emergencies.

TRAINING AND QUALIFICATIONS

Applicants must be high school graduates. One-year certificate programs exist for training in basic EKGs, Holter monitoring, and stress testing, but most training occurs on the job and is conducted by an EKG supervisor or a cardiologist. For learning the basic, or resting, EKG, 4 to 6 weeks is adequate. More advanced EKG testing techniques and procedures require 12 to 24 months of training, which includes a thorough grounding in cardiovascular anatomy and physiology. EKG technicians do not need a license, but many earn credentials through Cardiovascular Credentialing International. EKG technicians also are trained in the armed forces.

EARNINGS

According to a survey of acute care hospitals conducted by the Hay Group in January 1997, the median base salary of full-time EKG technicians was $20,200. Technicians who can perform more sophisticated tests earn more, as do those in teaching and supervisory positions.

EKG technicians who work in hospitals generally receive benefits that include health insurance, pensions, paid vacations, and sick leave and sometimes also tuition assistance, uniforms, parking, and child care.

PROSPECTS: JOB OUTLOOK

In 1996, EKG technicians held about 16,000 jobs. Most were in the cardiology departments of large hospitals; others worked in cardiologists' offices, cardiac rehabilitation centers, HMOs, and clinics.

Through the year 2006, demand for EKG technicians is expected to decline. Several key factors are shaping the job outlook in this field. Advances in technology make it easier and faster to perform standard EKG procedures. Basic testing that used to take 15 minutes now takes 5 minutes, and computerization also has cut paperwork. Hospitals can increase their savings by cross-training other personnel to perform the relatively simple EKG procedures, even in the emergency room. In some hospitals, EKG departments no longer need to be open 24 hours a day. As a result, job prospects will be better for EKG technicians with a higher level of training and skills, such as those trained in Holter monitoring and stress testing, rather than just basic EKG procedures.

Hospitals are likely to remain the major employer of EKG technicians, but an increase in jobs is expected in cardiologists' offices, cardiology clinics, HMOs, and other outpatient settings. Hospitals will likely prefer technicians with previous training and experience.

Overall, most job openings will rise from replacement needs. Combined job openings from both growth and replacement needs still will be limited, however, since the occupation is small.

WHERE TO LOOK FOR FURTHER INFORMATION

For information on training programs and careers in cardiovascular technology:

Society of Cardiovascular Professionals/Society for Cardiovascular Management
910 Charles Street
No. A
Fredericksburg, VA 22401-5810

For information about acquiring credentials in cardiovascular technology:

Cardiovascular Credentialing International
4456 Corporation Lane
Suite 120
Virginia Beach, VA 23462

*E*LECTRONEURODIAGNOSTIC TECHNOLOGISTS

OCCUPATIONAL OVERVIEW

Job Description: Electroneurodiagnostic technologists use the electroencephalograph machine and other instruments to record electrical impulses transmitted by the brain and nervous system, conducting diagnostic and other tests on patients and subjects of research. Most work for hospitals, but they can be found in other health care settings.

Prospects: Through the year 2006, jobs in this field are expected to grow faster than the average for all occupations, due, in part, to the greater willingness of third-party payers to pay for neurological testing and to the increased numbers of neurodiagnostic tests being developed and performed.

Qualifications: Formal training programs exist, but skills usually are learned on the job. Employers are beginning to prefer applicants with formal training. A trainee must have a high school diploma. Electroneurodiagnostic technologists also can be registered, which is generally necessary for teaching or supervisory jobs.

Personal Skills: Those seeking to enter the field need manual dexterity, good vision, and an aptitude for working with electronic equipment. They need to be able to work well with patients and with other health care professionals.

Earnings: According to a January 1997 Hay Group survey of acute care hospitals, the median base salary of full-time EEG technologists was $26,800.

THE JOB AND THE WORK ENVIRONMENT

The electroencephalograph is an instrument that senses the electrical impulses of the brain and records them in the form of lined patterns on paper, the electroencephalogram (EEG). It is chiefly a diagnostic tool, although it also is used in research. The equipment is used in ambulatory monitoring, evoked potential studies, sleep studies, and brain-wave mapping, as well as the standard resting EEG.

The resting EEG is a basic tool for neurological diagnosis. The physician also uses it to determine the extent of brain damage in patients with brain tumors, strokes, epilepsy, and other disorders and the likelihood of a physiological basis for behavioral aberrations. The electroencephalograph may be used to monitor a patient's condition during surgery. It is standard equipment in intensive care units, monitoring comatose patients and determining brain death.

Ambulatory monitoring follows and records brain activity over a 24-hour period on patients with conditions of varying intensity or conditions that recur sporadically, such as dizzy spells or blackouts. Evoked potential studies are conducted by applying stimuli of progressive strength to patients and measuring sensory and physical responses. This kind of testing can be used for both diagnosis and research. The EEG also has more sophisticated applications in sleep studies and brain-wave mapping, which often require additional equipment.

Those who operate the electroencephalograph were originally called (interchangeably) EEG technicians or technologists. With technological advances and sophisticated new equipment and procedures, the designation *electroneurodiagnostic technologist* has generally replaced that of *EEG technologist*. Operating the electroencephalograph has become an entry-level skill.

Electroneurodiagnostic technologists work directly with patients. They take a short medical history, help the patient relax, and then apply electrodes to the patient's body, simultaneously testing the equipment for its responsiveness. Technologists choose the best combination of electrode placement and machine settings. They account for readings the machine makes of electrical events not originating with the patient. They are responsible for ensuring that their equipment is properly maintained.

Techniques more sophisticated than those required for the resting EEG require more skill and knowledge on the part of the technologist. In ambulatory testing, the technologist must be able to distinguish brain waves from other activity during a long recording period. Evoked potential testing uses machinery for which special training is needed. In the operating room, a technologist must know the effects of anesthesia on the brain and be able to detect abnormalities. For sleep studies, technologists must know how to monitor heart and respiratory as well as brain activity. Electroneurodiagnostic technologists also must know how to recognize and identify medical emergencies, such as a sudden epileptic seizure, and be ready and able to take appropriate action.

Electroneurodiagnostic technologists work in clean, well-lit settings; they spend a good deal of time on their feet. Generally, they work a 5-day, 40-hour week, but in some hospitals, they may be on call. They may have to work night shifts, weekends, or holidays. Sleep studies often require working evenings or nights.

TRAINING AND QUALIFICATIONS

Trainees usually need a high school diploma; generally, training is done on the job. High school students interested in this occupation should take courses in health, biology, human anatomy, and mathematics. Other trainees for this work include those with a background as a laboratory aide or a licensed practical nurse.

In addition to hospital and medical centers, community colleges, vocational-technical institutes, colleges, and universities offer formal training. In 1996, 11 formal programs had been approved by the Joint Review Committee on Education in Electroneurodiagnostic Technology. Programs usually last one to two years, include laboratory experience and coursework, and award associate's degrees or certificates. Some hospitals and other employers prefer applicants with some formal training.

Electroneurodiagnostic technologists can be registered through the American Board of Registration of Electroencephalographic and Evoked Potential Technologists. Technologists may be designated a *registered EEG technologist* or a *registered evoked potential technologist,* or receive a certificate in Neurophysiologic Intraoperative Monitoring. The Association of Polysomnographic Technologists registers sleep disorder studies technologists; the American Association of Electrodiagnostic Technologists offers certification in nerve conduction studies. Registration is necessary for teaching and supervisory positions.

EARNINGS

According to a January 1997 survey of acute care hospitals by the Hay Group, the median base salary of full-time EEG technologists was $26,800. Those employed by hospitals receive benefits, including paid vacations, sick leave, health insurance, and pensions. Some benefit packages also include tuition assistance, uniforms, parking, and child care.

PROSPECTS: JOB OUTLOOK

In 1996, electroneurodiagnostic technologists held more than 6,400 jobs. Most jobs were in hospitals, medical schools, and medical centers, but other settings include neurology laboratories, offices of neurologists and neurosurgeons, group medical practices, HMOs, and psychiatric facilities. Through the year 2006, demand for electroneurodiagnostic technologists is expected to grow faster than the average for all occupations. Job growth is expected to be especially good in offices and clinics of neurologists.

Job growth will be spurred by increasing use of the EEG and new neurodiagnostic procedures and the willingness of health insurers and other third-party payers to cover such testing. In addition, advances in clinical neurophysiology are likely to expand uses of neurodiagnostic testing and will increase the demand for qualified personnel.

Most jobs will arise to replace technicians who leave the workforce; but the openings will be few, since the occupation is very small overall. Job opportunities for those with formal training in EEG technology are expected to be brightest.

WHERE TO LOOK FOR FURTHER INFORMATION

For general information on a career in electroneurodiagnostics and a list of accredited programs:

Executive Office
American Society of Electroneurodiagnostic Technologists, Inc.
204 West 7th Street
Carroll, IA 51401

For job information on specific accredited training programs:

Joint Review Committee on Electroneurodiagnostic Technology
Route 1, Box 63A
Genoa, WI 54632

For information on registration as an electroneurodiagnostic technologist:

American Board of Registration of Electroencephalographic and Evoked Potential
   Technologists
P.O. Box 916633
Longwood, FL 32791-6633

EMERGENCY MEDICAL TECHNICIANS

OCCUPATIONAL OVERVIEW

Job Description: Emergency medical technicians (EMTs) respond to emergency calls to provide efficient and immediate care to the critically ill and injured, and transport such patients to medical facilities.

Prospects: Through the year 2006, jobs for EMTs are expected to grow faster than the average for all occupations. Much of this growth will result from paid EMTs' replacing volunteers, as well as an expanding senior population (who are prone to more health emergencies) and significant replacement needs.

Qualifications: Formal training is required to become an EMT. The EMT-Basic—consisting of 110 to 120 hours of classwork plus 10 hours of internship in a hospital emergency room—is the minimum training necessary to qualify for an EMT job. Further training leads to an EMT-Intermediate or EMT-Paramedic designation. Applicants for EMT training must be 18 years of age and have a high school diploma and a valid driver license. All states require certification for EMTs.

Personal Skills: EMTs must be in good physical condition, emotionally stable, and even-tempered. They should have good dexterity, excellent eyesight and accurate color vision, and be able to lift and carry heavy loads. They must have the ability to think clearly and make decisions under considerable stress.

Earnings: Earnings vary with employment setting and geographic region as well as training and experience. According to a 1996 salary survey by the *Journal of Emergency Medical Services,* average salaries were $25,051 for EMT-Basic and $30,407 for EMT-Paramedic.

THE JOB AND THE WORK ENVIRONMENT

When someone suffers a heart attack at home, is injured in a fire or an automobile collision, or suffers a gunshot wound, the first trained medical personnel on the scene most likely will be the EMTs, who usually work in pairs. The occupation contains three classifications.

EMT-Basics, like all EMTs, are trained to be responsible for the ambulance itself, seeing that it is kept in good operating condition and checking its equipment before beginning each shift. When responding to a call, they determine the extent of the patient's illness or injury, help administer emergency care, or call in for additional guidance or assistance. EMT-Basics are trained to identify various kinds of emergencies but are strictly limited as to the procedures they are trained to administer. They can open obstructed airways to restore breathing, apply bandages to control bleeding, treat for shock, immobilize fractures, assist in childbirth, resuscitate heart attack victims, use automated external defibrillators, and aid victims of burns or poisons. Certain procedures can be done only in special circumstances and under the step-by-step instructions of medical staff. The EMT-Basic transfers the patient to the ambulance, transports the patient to a designated hospital, reports on the patient to the emergency room staff, and sometimes assists in the emergency room. After a run, all EMTs clean the ambulance, put all equipment back in order, resterilize or replace certain equipment, and, if the patient had an infectious disease, ensure that the ambulance is decontaminated and cleared by the authorities before it is used again.

EMT-Intermediates undergo more training than EMT-Basics and are authorized to perform more procedures. Usually, they may assess trauma victims, administer intravenous therapy, use manual defibrillators to start a stopped heart, and use antishock garments and esophageal airways. They are used extensively in rural areas.

EMT-Paramedics are trained in more advanced procedures and can give the most extensive prehospital care. In most states, they may administer drugs orally or intravenously, interpret EKGs, and perform endotracheal intubation; they also are trained in the use of more sophisticated equipment.

EMTs are trained in the equipment and techniques they may need to help patients trapped in vehicular wreckage. In case of patient death, the EMT contacts the proper authorities and secures the personal effects of the deceased.

EMTs are employed by hospitals, private ambulance services, and police and fire departments. Their work exposes them to unpredictable and sometimes dangerous conditions, including diseases such as Hepatitis B and AIDS, and the violence sometimes associated with drug overdose victims and people in psychological crises. They must be ready to work outdoors regardless of the weather. The work, which requires lifting equipment and patients and a lot of standing, bending, and kneeling, can be physically tiring, emotionally draining, and highly stressful.

EMTs who are employed by hospitals often work between 45 and 60 hours a week; those with private ambulance services work 45 to 50 hours. EMTs who work for fire departments often put in a 50-hour week, and those employed by 24-hour ambulance services often must work nights, weekends, and holiday shifts. Since emergency services operate 24 hours a day, EMTs' working hours tend to be irregular, adding to job stress.

TRAINING AND QUALIFICATIONS

The 110- to 120-hour EMT-Basic training program is mandatory for becoming an EMT in all states and the District of Columbia. Applicants for training generally must be high school graduates at least 18 years of age and have a valid driver license. They should have good dexterity and coordination, be capable of lifting and carrying heavy loads, have good eyesight and accurate color vision, and be emotionally stable and able to make decisions under stress. In addition to classwork, training includes 10 hours of interning in a hospital emergency room. The training is offered by fire, police, and health departments; in hospitals; and in colleges and universities (as nondegree courses). EMTs in police and fire departments also must be trained as police officers and firefighters. Graduates of an approved EMT-Basic program who pass written and practical examinations, given by the state certifying agency or the National Registry of Emergency Medical Technicians, receive the title *registered EMT-Basic.*

EMT-Intermediate training varies by state, but it usually includes about 35 to 55 hours of instruction beyond EMT-Basic. To take the EMT-Intermediate examination, candidates must be registered as an EMT-Basic and have completed the necessary classwork and clinical and field internship requirements.

Most EMT-Intermediate graduates take further training to qualify for EMT-Paramedic certification. EMT-Paramedic programs usually require between 750 and 2,000 hours. Because of the intense training, most EMT-Paramedics are paid positions. In most states, registration as an EMT-Paramedic by the National Registry of Emergency Medical Technicians or a state agency requires current registration or state certification as an EMT-Basic, plus completion of EMT-Paramedic training and clinical and field internships, along with passing written and practical examinations. Registration acknowledges an EMT's qualifications and can lead to higher-paying jobs, though it is not a general employment requirement.

All states and the District of Columbia require certification. Registration with the National Registry at some or all levels of certification is required by

38 states and the District of Columbia. Other states offer EMTs the option of taking the National Registry examination or the state's own certification examination.

All EMTs must re-register—usually every two years—to maintain certification. To re-register, a person must be working as an EMT and meet a continuing education requirement.

To advance beyond the EMT-Paramedic level, individuals generally have to leave field work. An EMT-Paramedic may become a supervisor, administrator, or director of emergency services, or an EMT instructor. Some EMTs decide to continue their medical education and become physicians, registered nurses, or other health care workers.

EARNINGS

Earnings vary with employment setting, geographic location, training, and experience. Fire and police departments generally offer higher pay and better benefits and job security than hospitals or private ambulance services. According to a 1996 salary survey by the *Journal of Emergency Medical Services,* average salaries were $25,051 for EMT-Basic and $30,407 for EMT-Paramedic. In this survey, fire departments were found to pay the highest salaries: $29,859 for EMT-Basic and $32,483 for EMT-Paramedic. Private ambulance services paid the lowest salaries: $18,617 for EMT-Basic and $23,995 for EMT-Paramedic.

PROSPECTS: JOB OUTLOOK

In 1996, EMTs held about 150,000 jobs. Through the year 2006, jobs for EMTs are expected to grow much faster than the average for all occupations. Much growth will be due to paid EMT positions replacing volunteers. Adding to the growth will be an increasing population, especially in older age groups that are the most frequent users of emergency services. Many openings will result from the occupation's significant replacement needs. There is high turnover among EMTs due to stress and limited advancement and earnings in the private sector. Finally, openings will result from more states permitting EMT-Paramedics to provide primary care on the scene without taking patients to hospitals.

WHERE TO LOOK FOR FURTHER INFORMATION

A state's emergency medical service director can provide information about that state's job opportunities, training programs, and registration.

For more information about EMTs and their work:

National Association of Emergency Medical Technicians
408 Monroe
Clinton, MS 39056

For information about registration:

National Registry of Emergency Medical Technicians
P.O. Box 29233
Columbus, OH 43229

*E*XERCISE *PHYSIOLOGISTS*

OCCUPATIONAL OVERVIEW

Job Description: Exercise physiologists study functional changes that occur during and after exercise. They are employed in colleges and universities, government laboratories (National Institutes of Health and NASA), research institutes, health, fitness, and gerontological units, rehabilitation centers, and some sports medicine clinics.

Prospects: Since Americans are exercising more and for longer periods of their lives, through the year 2006, there is likely to be an increasing demand for individuals with a background in exercise physiology.

Qualifications: A bachelor's or master's of science degree is needed for employment in laboratories, clinics, and other centers. To teach or to conduct research, however, a Ph.D. is essential.

Personal Skills: An exercise physiologist needs a comprehension of biology, an analytical and critical mind, a concern for detail, patience, and a capacity for careful and accurate observation.

Earnings: Earnings for exercise physiologists vary with education, experience, and type of position. Salaries range from personal fitness trainers with a bachelor's degree who may be paid from $10 to $100 an hour depending on location and clientele, to experienced Ph.D.'s who can earn more than $40,000 a year.

THE JOB AND THE WORK ENVIRONMENT

Exercise physiology is an academic discipline that evolved from physiology and exercise science that seeks to explain and describe the functional changes that occur in the body as a result of exercise. Some of the questions about the body's functions that interest exercise physiologists are:

- How does the heart function to move blood through the body?
- How does a muscle generate force?
- How does the body regulate its internal temperature during exercise?
- How does the body provide the necessary energy to perform the exercise task?

- How does the body function in hot, cold, low oxygen, and microgravity environments?

Other concerns include the components of fitness, the relation of fitness to health and illness, and the influence of exercise in managing body weight.

In addition to teaching and doing research in an academic setting, exercise physiologists work in community organizations that have health maintenance, cardiac risk identification, and rehabilitation programs; corporations that have fitness programs for employees; spas, health clubs, and recreation centers; rehabilitation programs in hospitals, health centers, and rehabilitation clinics; and some sports medicine clinics. They also serve as laboratory technicians or as investigators in laboratories run by NIH, NASA, the U.S. Departments of Defense and Agriculture.

Most exercise physiologists are likely to work a 40-hour, 5-day week. In colleges or universities, they usually work 9 to 10 months a year. In the course of conducting research, human and animal models are used, and in many situations, long hours are devoted to obtaining data and evaluating the results. In certain settings or organizations, the responsibilities of exercise physiologists may be more administrative and managerial.

TRAINING AND QUALIFICATIONS

To teach and conduct research, a doctoral degree generally is required. The same qualification exists for researchers in industry, private foundations, or governmental laboratories. For employment in a commercial setting, as in industry, a bachelor's of science or master's of science degree from a department of exercise and sport science or kinesiology (or equivalent) is desirable. Individuals with a B.S. or M.S. who wish to work in hospitals or clinics as exercise leaders, testers, or supervisors need certification courses offered by the American College of Sports Medicine (ACSM). (Certification is not needed to work as a laboratory assistant or technician). Those who want to work as personal exercise trainers in a health or fitness club must, after receiving a B.S. or M.S., be certified by either ACSM or one of several fitness organizations. If a graduate with a B.S. wants to be a physical therapist, he or she must be accepted into a professional program offered by many institutions. (People with a B.S. in exercise science or kinesiology are well qualified to enter both physical therapy and medical schools.)

Note: A degree with an emphasis in exercise physiology will not enable a person to work as an athletic trainer employed by high schools, colleges, or professional teams. This requires a different preparatory program leading to certification by a professional athletic training organization.

EARNINGS

Salaries for exercise physiologists depend on education, experience, and type of position. Individuals with a Ph.D. and postdoctoral experience can expect to start at a salary of more than $40,000 a year. Personal fitness trainers with a bachelor's degree and professional certification are paid from $10 to $100 an hour depending on their location and the nature of their clientele. Individuals who function as research technicians or exercise testers usually start between $20,000 and $30,000 a year.

PROSPECTS: JOB OUTLOOK

Since an increase in daily exercise has become a national health objective, and more Americans are exercising as they are growing older, there likely is to be an increased demand for individuals with a background in exercise physiology through the year 2006.

WHERE TO LOOK FOR FURTHER INFORMATION

For information on aspects of exercise physiology, doctoral programs, and careers:

American College of Sports Medicine
P.O. Box 1440
Indianapolis, IN 46206-1440

American Physiological Society
Membership Services Department
9650 Rockville Pike
Bethesda, MD 20814-3991

HEALTH INFORMATION TECHNICIANS

OCCUPATIONAL OVERVIEW

Job Description: Health information technicians accurately gather, organize, store, and retrieve medical information. The work is done in a wide variety of settings. In small organizations, tasks may be combined; in large ones, tasks are subdivided, and there may even be specialists.

Prospects: Through the year 2006, employment of health information technicians is expected to grow much faster than the average for all occupations. Although hospitals will continue to employ the most technicians, growth will be faster in physicians' offices and clinics, nursing homes, and home health care agencies.

Qualifications: Beginning health information technicians usually have an associate's degree from a community or junior college. Training also is offered through an Independent Study Program in Health Information Technology offered by the American Health Information Management Association (AHIMA). Most employers favor hiring Accredited Record Technicians (ART), who have passed AHIMA's written examination.

Personal Skills: Gathering, organizing, and maintaining health information requires a person who is scrupulous, responsible, and attentive to detail. It also requires someone who is personable, patient, and thorough under stress.

Earnings: A 1996 survey by the AHIMA found the median salary for accredited health technicians to be $31,200.

THE JOB AND THE WORK ENVIRONMENT

Hospitals and clinics must keep accurate records of every patient they treat. Along with medical histories, physicians' and nurses' notes, diagnoses and treatment plans, and results of tests and procedures, the records provide basic data essential for clinical decision making and documentation for insurance claims and Medicare reimbursements, legal actions, and the training of medical personnel. They provide information the hospital can use in clinical studies and statistical analyses. Health information is managed by a team made up of health information administrators, technicians, and clerks.

Health information administrators direct an entire department and develop systems for documenting, storing, and retrieving information. They are responsible for compiling statistics, assist medical staff with patient care and research, and may be required to testify in court.

Health information technicians organize and evaluate the completeness and accuracy of health information records. They usually work at some point with written records, but eventually all data are computerized using prepackaged systems. Technicians review charts, assigning a code to each diagnosis and procedure; through this coding system, each patient is placed in a diagnosis-related grouping (DRG), which specifies the amount of reimbursement the hospital can expect through Medicare or other insurance programs using the DRG system.

Technicians also tabulate and analyze information on the relations between length of hospital stay and diagnosis, admitting physician, or procedure performed. They maintain health record indexes and statistics for public health officials, administrators, and planners, among others, and they may assemble records at the request of law firms, insurance companies, governmental agencies, researchers, and patients.

In a small medical facility, a single health information technician may be responsible for the health information department. In a large facility, technicians are likely to specialize. Some departments are large enough to include *health information clerks,* who assist the technicians and are usually supervised and trained by them.

Less than 50 percent of health information technicians work in hospitals, with most others employed by group practices, HMOs, nursing homes, insurance and law firms, public health departments, and the manufacturers of health information systems, services, and equipment. The usual workweek is 40 hours; some overtime may be required. In hospitals, there are day, evening, and night shifts; some health information personnel work part time. Work conditions are generally pleasant, but the job, which requires close attention to detail, can be stressful. It often also requires working for long periods at a video display terminal, which may cause eyestrain and musculoskeletal pain.

TRAINING AND QUALIFICATIONS

With a high school diploma, it is still possible to be hired as a health information clerk and eventually to advance to health information technician, but this may be less likely in the future. For the most part, hospitals prefer technicians already trained and with the proper credentials. A technician must graduate from a two-year program in health information technology approved by the Commission on Accreditation of Allied Health Education Programs (CAAHEP) of the American Medical Association, or from the Independent Study Program in Health Information Technology offered by the AHIMA.

The majority of employers prefer hiring ART individuals who have completed the two-year formal training or Independent Study Program and have passed a written examination offered by the AHIMA. (Technicians trained on the job or in nonCAAHEP-accredited programs are not permitted to take the exam.) CAAHEP accredited 157 programs for health information technicians as of 1997. Coursework in these programs includes anatomy, physiology, medical terminology, legal aspects of health information, coding and abstraction of data, computer training, statistics, and database management.

Health information technicians usually advance by specializing or managing. In large health information departments, experienced technicians may become section supervisors. In small facilities, a senior technician with ART credentials may become a director or an assistant director. In larger facilities, directors are health information administrators with a bachelor's degree in health information administration.

EARNINGS

In a 1996 survey, the AHIMA found the median salary for accredited health information technicians to be $31,200. The average salary for technicians working for the federal government in 1997 was $25,570. Benefits for health information technicians usually include paid holidays and vacations, health and life insurance, and retirement benefits.

PROSPECTS: JOB OUTLOOK

In 1996, health information technicians held approximately 87,000 jobs. Through the year 2006, the health care industry will experience an ever-growing need for accurate and readily accessible information, not only to care better for patients, but also to compete more efficiently. Job opportunities for health information technicians are expected to grow much faster than the average for all occupations to meet these needs. Although hospitals still will employ the most technicians, job growth will be faster in other areas, such as in physicians' offices and clinics and in nursing homes and home health care agencies. The job market will be especially good for those who are formally trained and fully credentialed.

WHERE TO LOOK FOR FURTHER INFORMATION

For information about careers in health information technology, including the Independent Study Program, and a list of CAAHEP-approved programs:

American Health Information Management Association
919 North Michigan Avenue
Suite 1400
Chicago, IL 60611-1683

*H*EALTH SERVICES ADMINISTRATORS

OCCUPATIONAL OVERVIEW

Job Description: Health service administrators plan, organize, and coordinate the delivery of health care. They are responsible for facilities, services, programs, staff, budgets, and relations with other organizations.

Prospects: Employment prospects in this profession are expected to increase faster than the average for all occupations through the year 2006, with the continuing expansion and diversification of health services. Hospitals will continue to employ the most administrators, but the fastest job growth will be in long-term care facilities, home health care agencies, and doctors' offices and clinics.

Qualifications: Formal education required for this occupation is at least a bachelor's degree in finance, personnel administration, or public administration; a postgraduate degree in health services administration, nursing administration, or business administration is a decided asset. Work experience in a health care setting is essential.

Personal Skills: The job requires an ability to make effective decisions, be open to differing opinions, and analyze oftentimes contradictory information. Leadership ability, an understanding of finance and information systems, and excellent interpersonal and communication skills are crucial, as are tact and diplomacy.

Earnings: Salaries vary with the type and size of the facility or institution and the administrator's responsibility level. More than half of hospital CEOs earned $190,500 or more in 1997; nursing home administrators had median earnings of $49,500 in 1996; and administrators in small group practices had median earnings of $56,000 in 1996.

THE JOB AND THE WORK ENVIRONMENT

Administrators of health care services have all the problems of managers of other organizations—and more. Competency on the job may literally be a matter of life and death. In almost all instances, managers deal with human fears, pain, and suffering. Good, efficient administration skills are vital; so are empathy and caring.

Hospitals provide more than half the jobs in this field. They are complex organizations, housing many departments, and they require different levels of management: executive, internal (day-to-day management), and specialized staff (e.g., financial management, marketing, strategic planning, systems analysis, and labor relations). The chief administrator or CEO coordinates the activities of the assistant administrators and department heads to ensure that the hospital runs efficiently, provides high-quality medical care, and remains solvent or makes a profit.

Another important employer is the participating health maintenance organization (HMO) or other managed care program. Patients enrolled in these programs must use physicians and facilities affiliated with the HMO. HMO administrators must perform all the functions of those in other large medical practices and in addition, work to establish a medical benefits package with fees low enough to attract adequate enrollments but high enough to operate successfully.

Health services administrators also work in nursing homes; hospices; home health care agencies; rehabilitation centers; community mental health centers; urgent care centers; diagnostic imaging centers; and offices of groups of doctors, dentists, and other health care practitioners. The job is highly complex and the responsibilities are significant. Administrators must respond to consumer expectations, follow good business practices, and develop health care financing.

Health services administrators work long hours. Hospitals and nursing homes operate around the clock, and administrators may need to deal with emergencies. Occasionally, they travel to inspect other health care facilities or attend meetings.

TRAINING AND QUALIFICATIONS

Academic programs in health services administration leading to a bachelor's, master's, or doctoral degree are offered by colleges, universities, and schools of public health, allied health, and business administration. A master's degree in hospital administration, health administration, or public health is regarded as the standard credential for many positions in this field, although educational requirements vary with the size of the organization and job responsibilities. In general, larger organizations require more specialized academic preparation than do smaller ones. Doctors' offices and some other facilities may substitute on-the-job training for formal education.

According to the Accrediting Commission on Education for Health Services Administration, 67 schools had accredited programs leading to a master's degree in health services administration in 1997. Some graduate programs prefer students with business or health administration undergraduate degrees; others seek students with a liberal arts or professional health education.

Competition for entry into postgraduate programs in this area is keen, and applicants need above-average grades to gain admission. Generally, the programs last between two and three years, including up to one year of supervised administrative experience, undertaken upon completion of the coursework. The experience covers areas such as hospital organization and management, accounting and budget control, personnel administration, strategic planning, and management of health information systems. Some programs have students specialize in one type of facility; others promote a generalist approach to health administration education.

New graduates with master's degrees in relevant areas may be hired by hospitals as assistant administrators or, more likely, as department heads or project directors. They also work for HMOs, large group medical practices, and nursing home corporations. Those holding a bachelor's degree in health administration generally start out as administrative assistants or assistant department heads in larger hospitals, or department heads in smaller hospitals or nursing homes. A doctorate may be needed to do research, teach, or consult.

Licensure is not required in most areas of health services administration. However, in most states and the District of Columbia, nursing home administrators must have a bachelor's degree, pass a licensing examination, finish a state-approved training program, and enroll in continuing education.

EARNINGS

Earnings vary by size and type of facility as well as by amount of responsibility. The Medical Group Management Association reported a median salary of about $56,000 for administrators in small group practices (fewer than seven doctors) and a median salary of about $77,000 for those in larger group practices in 1996.

A 1997 survey by *Modern Healthcare* magazine found that half of all hospital CEOs earned compensation of $190,500 or more. Median compensation for heads of select clinical departments included home health care, $62,000; rehabilitation services, $70,400; and nursing services, $97,000.

According to the American Health Care Association's Buck Survey in 1996, the median compensation for nursing home administrators was about $49,500. Assistant administrators made about $32,000.

PROSPECTS: JOB OUTLOOK

In 1996, health services administrators held approximately 329,000 jobs. Through the year 2006, employment in this field is expected to grow faster than the average for all occupations. Although hospitals will continue to employ the most administrators, job growth will be slower than in other areas. The fastest growth will be in long-term care facilities, home health care agencies, and doctors' offices and clinics.

WHERE TO LOOK FOR FURTHER INFORMATION

To learn more about health care administration:

American College of Healthcare Executives
One North Franklin Street
Suite 1700
Chicago, IL 60606

To learn more about opportunities in group medical practices:

Medical Group Management Association
104 Inverness Terrace East
Englewood, CO 80112

To learn more about opportunities in long-term care:

American College of Health Care Administrators
325 South Patrick Street
Alexandria, VA 22314

To receive a list of accredited graduate programs in health services administration:

Accrediting Commission on Education for Health Services Administration
1911 North Fort Meyer Drive
Suite 503
Arlington, VA 22209

INDUSTRIAL HYGIENISTS

OCCUPATIONAL OVERVIEW

Job Description: Industrial hygienists (IHs) identify and help to solve environmental problems faced by government entities and business firms across the country as they work to ensure workplace and community health and safety.

Prospects: Demand for this increasingly important position is expected to be strong through the year 2006 as efforts to clean up toxic waste sites accelerate and more state and local authorities comply with laws and regulations designed to improve air and water quality standards, as well as other health and safety standards.

Qualifications: A bachelor's degree, preferably in a technical area, is essential. A master's degree in industrial hygiene or in geology, hydrogeology, chemistry, or civil engineering is desirable. Also important is certification by the American Board of Industrial Hygiene; this can be obtained after working in the industrial hygiene field for five years, meeting all requirements, and passing a comprehensive examination. Ongoing education is required to maintain certification.

Personal Skills: Excellent interpersonal and communication skills are essential, as is the ability to work independently. A strong commitment to environmental concerns is also important.

Earnings: According to the AIHA's 1997 membership survey, entry-level industrial hygienists generally earned between $35,000 and $40,000; top-level IHs earned between $60,000 and $130,000 or more.

THE JOB AND THE WORK ENVIRONMENT

Air and water pollution, noise pollution, toxic waste disposal, oil spills, and a host of other environmental problems stemming from industrial society are in the news every day. It is the job of the industrial hygienist to keep the workplace and the community safe and sanitary.

IHs plan programs for companies and communities designed to meet statutory and regulatory requirements issued by the Occupational Safety and Health Administration (OSHA) and the Environmental Protection Agency (EPA). They conduct inspection and monitoring programs, which may include performing air sampling and chemical analyses; evaluate environmental programs and plan emergency responses; and train municipal and private sector personnel in ways to forestall industrial accidents. In addition, they evaluate and collect data. In this capacity, they aid risk managers of business firms, who may have data on an environmental problem but no experienced staff to analyze it and draw up a program to solve it. IHs often rewrite hazardous material management data sheets—also called material safety data sheets—to make them clear to risk managers and other key personnel.

IHs often must deal with highly dangerous or toxic substances; however, they are trained to minimize the risks. Many of their tasks—air monitoring, equipment calibrating, and employee training—are more mundane.

Industrial hygienists work in a wide variety of employment settings, including state and federal governmental agencies, public utilities, hospitals, hazardous waste companies, consulting firms, colleges and universities, manufacturing companies, research laboratories, and insurance companies. The job can involve long and irregular hours, and it often means traveling to sites that pose environmental problems.

TRAINING AND QUALIFICATIONS

According to a 1997 member survey by the AIHA, 98 percent of AIHA members have a bachelor's degree, 60 percent have a master's degree, and 11 percent have a doctoral degree. As a rule, those with a master's degree in industrial hygiene, or any technical field, have good job prospects, even if they have little or no experience. Employers generally prefer employees with some graduate school background for most jobs but will hire people who have only an undergraduate degree.

The *Certified Industrial Hygienist* (CIH) designation is available to candidates who have worked in the industrial hygiene field for five years and who meet all requirements and pass a comprehensive examination. Continuing education is required to maintain certification. Many employers use certification as one of their selection and promotion criteria.

EARNINGS

Salaries vary with education level, experience, and employer. According to the AIHA's 1997 membership survey, entry-level industrial hygienists earned between $35,000 and $40,000 annually; mid-level jobs paid between $40,000 and $70,000; and top-level positions paid between $60,000 and $130,000 or more.

PROSPECTS: JOB OUTLOOK

The demand for industrial hygienists is expected to be strong through the year 2006, as environmental health regulations grow stricter and industry and government strive to meet them. Although many industrial hygienists work as salaried employees for businesses or governmental agencies, the fastest growing segment in this field is self-employment and consulting. However, the occupation is sensitive to the economic climate; a downturn in the economy could slow industry's drive to find ways to clean up its environmental problems. The environmental department is generally the first to feel the effects of cutbacks during hard times.

IHs are concerned with career advancement. Their position is sometimes viewed as a technical specialist slot with little opportunity for moving into general management. Nevertheless, the occupation has a built-in plus in the career satisfaction it offers of cleaning up the environment.

WHERE TO LOOK FOR FURTHER INFORMATION

To learn more about careers in industrial hygiene:

American Industrial Hygiene Association
2700 Prosperity Avenue
Suite 250
Fairfax, VA 22031

LICENSED PRACTICAL NURSES

OCCUPATIONAL OVERVIEW

Job Description: Licensed practical nurses (LPNs) perform health care for the sick, injured, disabled, and convalescent under the supervision of physicians and registered nurses (RNs). Their job requires technical skill and training but not to the level of an RN.

Prospects: Expectations are for faster-than-average growth in the demand for LPNs through the year 2006, as a result of long-term care needs of a rapidly increasing elderly population and the overall growth in health care.

Qualifications: LPNs must be licensed to practice. To qualify for licensing, applicants must complete a state-approved program in practical nursing and pass a licensing examination.

Personal Skills: Emotional stability and a sincere commitment to caring for others are essential. Also important are the ability to work under close supervision and a capacity for following orders precisely.

Earnings: In 1996, the median weekly income of full-time salaried licensed practical nurses was $468. The American Health Care Association's Buck Survey found the median wage of LPNs in chain nursing homes to be $12 an hour in 1996.

THE JOB AND THE WORK ENVIRONMENT

LPNs working in hospitals provide basic bedside care: taking and recording temperatures and blood pressures, changing dressings, and helping patients with bathing and personal hygiene. Some assist in the delivery, care, and feeding of infants, and others help RNs monitor the conditions of seriously ill patients in intensive care units or postoperative recovery rooms. LPNs may also, depending on state law and the practices of their institution, administer prescribed drugs and start intravenous fluids. Occasionally, experienced LPNs supervise nursing assistants and aides.

In nursing homes, LPNs perform a wide range of duties. They give routine bedside care and may help assess residents' nursing needs, develop and implement treatment plans, and supervise nursing aides. They often are called on to perform certain complex nursing procedures, such as treating bedsores, administering cardiopulmonary resuscitation, preparing and giving injections, and inserting catheters.

LPNs who work in doctors' offices, walk-in clinics, HMOs, and other out-patient settings perform a variety of clinical and clerical tasks, for example, preparing patients for examination and treatment, administering medications, applying dressings, assisting with procedures, doing laboratory work, and instructing patients in prescribed health care regimens. The specific nature of an LPN's duties in these settings is determined by the size and nature of the practice. Working in private homes, LPNs provide nursing care and also prepare meals, see that patients are comfortable, and teach family members how to perform simple nursing tasks.

LPNs in hospitals work regular shifts, generally 40 hours a week, and usually including some evening and weekend shifts. In short-staffed hospitals, the work-week can be much longer. In nursing homes, which are chronically understaffed, LPNs may have quite heavy workloads. Also, as the duties in nursing homes can be very diverse, reflecting the many different problems and illnesses of the residents, work can become very stressful. LPNs working in private homes usually work 8 to 12 hours a day. Private-duty nursing allows for a great deal of flexibility in setting working hours and the length of the assignment. Such nurses are either self-employed, negotiating their employment directly with their patients, or they are employees of a nurses' registry or temporary help agency.

LPNs are subject to back injuries due to moving patients, hazards from infectious diseases such as hepatitis and AIDS, and stresses that result from dealing with patients who may be confused, agitated, or uncooperative. They often stand for long periods. LPNs should be caring and sympathetic, as well as emotionally stable, to handle such stresses.

TRAINING AND QUALIFICATIONS

In all states, LPNs are required to pass a licensing examination after completion of a state-approved practical nursing program. Applicants for a training program usually must have at least a high school diploma, though some state programs accept applicants without one.

About 1,100 state-approved programs offered practical nursing training in 1997. Almost 6 out of 10 students were trained in technical or vocational schools, 3 out of 10 in junior and community colleges, and the rest in high schools, hospitals, and colleges or universities. The programs include both classroom study—of basic nursing concepts and principles and related basic subjects—and supervised clinical training, generally in a hospital but sometimes in other settings. The course normally lasts for 1 year. Upon completion of the program, graduates can apply to take the licensing examination.

EARNINGS

The earnings for LPNs are a far cry from what one might expect for those involved in the healing profession. However, as demand for their services increases, salaries for LPNs are almost certain to rise. In 1996, the median weekly income of full-time salaried licensed practical nurses was $468. The American Health Care Association's Buck Survey found that the median earnings of staff LPNs in chain nursing homes was $12 an hour in 1996.

PROSPECTS: JOB OUTLOOK

In 1996, licensed practical nurses held about 699,000 jobs. Thirty-two percent worked in hospitals, 27 percent in nursing homes, and 13 percent in doctors' offices and clinics; the rest worked for temporary help agencies, governmental agencies, or home health care services.

Jobs for LPNs are expected to grow faster than the average for all occupations through the year 2006. LPNs seeking jobs in hospitals will face competition as available jobs in this area are expected to decline. Jobs in nursing homes are expected to grow much faster than the average as the number of elderly and disabled individuals in need of long-term care increases rapidly. Employment in home health care services also is expected to grow much faster than the average as a result of a preference for home care, development of technology that enables more complex treatments to be brought into the home, and a growth in the number of elderly persons with functional disabilities.

WHERE TO LOOK FOR FURTHER INFORMATION

To learn more about the career of licensed practical nursing:

National Federation of Licensed Practical Nurses
Aversboro Road
Garner, NC 27529-4547

To learn about nursing careers in hospitals:

American Hospital Association
Division of Nursing
1 North Franklin Street
Suite 27
Chicago, IL 60606

To learn more about training programs and about licensed practical nursing:

Communications Department
National League for Nursing
350 Hudson Street
New York, NY 10014

Nuclear Medicine Technologists

OCCUPATIONAL OVERVIEW

Job Description: Nuclear medicine technologists are trained in the proper use of radiopharmaceuticals (radioactive drugs) for a variety of medical purposes. Mostly, they work directly with patients, performing nuclear medicine procedures designed to diagnose and treat disease.

Prospects: Job opportunities are expected to grow about as fast as the average for all occupations through the year 2006. The number of job openings will be low because the occupation is small. Opportunities will be brightest for technicians who can perform nuclear medicine and radiologic tests.

Qualifications: Nuclear medicine technicians must have formal postsecondary training, available in hospitals, medical centers, community colleges, four-year colleges and universities, and the armed forces. Programs may last one to four years and lead to a certificate or associate's or bachelor's degree; one- and two-year programs leading to an associate's degree are the most common.

Personal Skills: Physical stamina is important; technologists are on their feet much of the time and may be required to lift or turn disabled patients.

Earnings: In a January 1997 survey of acute care hospitals, the Hay Group found the median base salary of full-time nuclear medicine technologists to be $36,100.

THE JOB AND THE WORK ENVIRONMENT

Nuclear medicine is the branch of radiology that uses radionuclides (unstable atoms that emit radiation spontaneously) in the diagnosis and treatment of disease. As in other medical diagnostic procedures, trained nuclear medicine technologists perform the tests and procedures ordered by physicians who are responsible for interpreting the results.

Technologists spend most of their time operating diagnostic imaging equipment. They prepare a radioactive substance (radiopharmaceutical), administer it to the patient, and then operate a camera (scanner) that uses the radiation given off by the radionuclide to create an image. Each radiopharmaceutical is chosen for its affinity for specific organs or tissues; because of its radioactive properties, the radiopharmaceutical can be tracked from outside the patient, and an image of the targeted organs or tissues is created. Nuclides were first used to investigate thyroid function, but now imaging is done of bones, brain, liver, and heart functions as well. When the scan is completed, the technologist views the images on a computer screen or film, examining them for quality and for information the patient's physician can use to arrive at a diagnosis.

Diagnostic imaging is not the only procedure performed by technologists. Nuclear medicine is effective in some laboratory tests, and technologists must be proficient in clinical laboratory procedures. Other job responsibilities include ensuring the adherence to radiation safety procedures by all workers in the laboratory and the completeness and accuracy of patient medical records and records of procedures performed and amounts and types for radionuclides received, used, and disposed of.

Technologists normally work a 40-hour week, including evening and weekend hours if they work in a hospital. They also are required in hospital work to perform on-call duty, usually on a rotation basis. That means that, at specified times, they must be ready to go immediately to the hospital when called for emergency duty. Although nearly 90 percent of technologists work in hospitals, others work in doctors' offices, clinics, and imaging centers. Technologists deal with potentially hazardous radioactive materials, but strict adherence to safety rules and procedures reduces the risk to acceptable levels.

TRAINING AND QUALIFICATIONS

One-year certificate programs in nuclear medicine are designed for individuals who already have some postsecondary education in a health- or science-related field, if not in radiologic technology itself. These may include medical technologists, radiologic technologists, and registered nurses. Those with three or four years of college may choose a certificate program to prepare for a career in nuclear medicine technology.

Two-year associate programs, which accept high school graduates, are usually offered by community colleges. Four-year bachelor's programs are offered in colleges and universities. In 1997, 104 formal education programs were accredited by the Joint Review Committee on Education Programs in Nuclear Medicine Technology.

All nuclear medicine technologists are required to meet minimum federal standards on administering radioactive drugs and operating radiation detection equipment. About half of all states require licensing of technologists. Technologists also can seek voluntary professional certification or registration, which is available from the American Registry of Radiologic Technologists (ARRT) and from the Nuclear Medicine Technology Certification Board (NMTCB). Applicants with credentials from either of these bodies are favored by employers.

Technologists may advance to a supervisory position in the field, or they may choose to specialize in a clinical area, such as cardiology diagnostics or computer analysis. Some become instructors in nuclear medicine technology after gaining a bachelor's or master's degree; others may go to work for research laboratories. Those who leave the occupation may work for radiopharmaceutical companies or become radiation safety personnel in governmental agencies or hospitals.

EARNINGS

In a January 1997 survey of acute care hospitals, the Hay Group found the median base salary of full-time nuclear medicine technologists to be $36,100. The middle 50 percent had earnings of between $33,400 and $39,400.

PROSPECTS: JOB OUTLOOK

In 1996, about 13,000 jobs were held by nuclear medicine technologists, with nearly 9 out of 10 jobs in hospitals. Through the year 2006, the profession is expected to maintain a rate of growth about the same as the average for all occupations. Relatively few job openings are projected since the occupation is a small one.

Job growth will result from a number of factors, including an increase in the number of middle-age and older people who will be the prime users of diagnostic tests. However, to cut costs, some hospitals will be merging nuclear medicine and radiologic technology departments, likely reducing positions. In addition, although technological advances may increase the diagnostic uses of nuclear medicine, cost considerations may make hospitals wary of implementing the more costly of the new procedures.

Competition is keen for nuclear medicine technologist jobs in large urban areas; hospitals and other employers in rural areas offer greater opportunities. The prospects will be best for technologists who can perform radiologic as well as nuclear medicine procedures.

WHERE TO LOOK FOR FURTHER INFORMATION

To learn more about careers in nuclear medicine:

American Society of Radiologic
Technologists
Customer Service Department
15000 Central Avenue, SE
Albuquerque, NM 87123-3917

Society of Nuclear Medicine
Technologists Section
1850 Samuel Morse Drive
Reston, VA 22090

To learn more about certification:

Nuclear Medicine Technology Certification Board
2970 Clairmont Road
Suite 610
Atlanta, GA 30329

To obtain a current list of accredited programs:

Joint Review Committee on Educational Programs in Nuclear Medicine Technology
350 South 400 East
Suite 200
Salt Lake City, UT 84111-2938

OCCUPATIONAL THERAPISTS

OCCUPATIONAL OVERVIEW

Job Description: Occupational therapists help people who are physically, mentally, emotionally, or developmentally disabled achieve or regain more independent and productive lives. Occupational therapists work in hospitals, schools, nursing homes, and, increasingly, patients' homes.

Prospects: Through the year 2006, jobs for occupational therapists are expected to increase much faster than the average for all occupations due to growth in the demand for rehabilitative services. Among the factors contributing to growth are the aging population, medical advances making it possible for more people with critical health problems to survive, and extended services for disabled students in schools where enrollments are rising.

Qualifications: Occupational therapists must hold at least a bachelor's degree from an accredited program in occupational therapy, which includes a period of supervised fieldwork. They also must be licensed. Licensure is granted after completing the accredited training program and passing a national certification examination.

Personal Skills: Occupational therapists should be warm, patient, even-tempered, and friendly. They should have the ability to work well with many different kinds of people in every stage of life from childhood through advanced old age. They need to be imaginative and resourceful and have an aptitude for teaching.

Earnings: Earnings vary with qualifications, years of experience, and setting. In 1996, the median weekly income of full-time salaried occupational therapists was $780. A Hay Group survey of acute care hospitals found the median base salary of full-time occupational therapists to be $42,700 in January 1997.

THE JOB AND THE WORK ENVIRONMENT

For a great many people, ordinary tasks such as washing dishes, shopping, or driving a car can be daunting. Whether because of a birth-related disability, or one that is the result of accident or illness, or due to old age, many people find themselves at a physical, emotional, or mental disadvantage. Occupational therapists work along with other health care professionals to retrain the disabled of all ages and help them achieve levels of independence and self-reliance that make it possible for them to live fuller lives.

A majority of occupational therapists work with patients with physical disabilities; the rest work with those who have mental, emotional, or developmental problems. Those with physical disabilities include a wide range of people—the aged; children; those with disabilities, such as muscular dystrophy and cerebral palsy; and those with disabilities caused by arthritis, hip replacements, or heart surgery. A large number of their patients, many of them young adults or teenagers, are victims of automobile accidents. In addition, occupational therapists also work with the learning disabled and mentally ill and with people suffering from eating disorders, alcoholism, drug abuse, or depression.

In most cases, the occupational therapist works on a team that includes physicians, physical therapists, psychologists, and social workers. Treatment may include retraining patients in commonplace activities, such as cleaning house or making beds, to help patients regain coordination and confidence. The occupational therapist may use toys, games, and simple hobbies and crafts to extend a patient's range of activities. He or she may also use computer programs to help clients improve memory, decision making, problem solving, and perceptual skills—all important for independent living. Throughout the entire course of treatment, the therapist keeps detailed notes that other health professionals use in treating a patient; these documents also provide information required for insurance and Medicare benefits.

The imagination and inventiveness of the therapist is just as important as the patient's motivation, no matter what the disability or the setting. Besides providing the physically disabled with standard equipment (wheelchairs, splints), occupational therapists may help to design individualized equipment. In mental health settings, therapists devise programs to help mentally ill or emotionally disturbed patients cope. Many occupational therapists work in schools, helping to develop programs of study and therapeutic activities for children with disabilities. They may recommend special facilities or equipment for the students and see that students are integrated into the life and activities of the school.

Occupational therapists usually work a 40-hour week, but they may also work evenings and weekends. About one-third work part time. The hours and demands of the job vary with the setting. Therapists in mental hospitals work with patients in wards and on schedules determined by the hospitals' needs; those who work in schools, work in conditions and keep hours similar to those of school teachers. A small number of therapists are in private practice—either as solo practitioners or in a group practice. Occupational therapists spend a good part of their working time on their feet. Using and shifting sometimes bulky and heavy equipment can be physically tiring.

Increasingly, occupational therapists are assuming supervisory roles. To help contain health care costs, third-party payers are encouraging the use of occupational therapy aides and assistants to take on much of the hands-on responsibilities.

TRAINING AND QUALIFICATIONS

Occupational therapists must hold at least a bachelor's degree in occupational therapy from an accredited institution. In 1996, there were 84 bachelor's degree programs for those entering schools to study occupational therapy; 15 programs for those with previously earned degrees in other areas; and 29 master's degree programs. Good high school grades are needed for admission, especially in biology, psychology, and the basic science courses. Admissions offices also favor those with paid or volunteer experience in health care. Most programs are full time. In addition to classwork, those training in occupational therapy must have supervised clinical fieldwork lasting at least six months.

All states, plus Puerto Rico and the District of Columbia, regulate occupational therapists. To gain a license, it is necessary to have a degree from an accredited program and pass a national certification examination, after which the title of *registered occupational therapist* is granted.

EARNINGS

Earnings vary with qualifications, experience, and location. In 1996, the median weekly income of full-time salaried occupational therapists was $780. A January 1997 Hay Group survey of acute care hospitals found the median base salary of full-time occupational therapists to be $42,700.

PROSPECTS: JOB OUTLOOK

In 1996, occupational therapists held about 57,000 jobs. The greatest number worked in hospitals, including rehabilitation and psychiatric facilities, with others working in such settings as offices and clinics, schools, home health care services, nursing homes, and residential care facilities. Through the year 2006, jobs for occupational therapists are expected to increase much faster than the average for all occupations due to projected growth in demand for rehabilitation and long-term care services. There are a number of reasons for this anticipated growth.

Advances in medical technology are saving and prolonging the lives of people consequently in need of rehabilitation, for instance, children born with muscular dystrophy or other health problems or victims of automobile accidents. In addition, as the baby boom generation ages and becomes more at risk for heart attack and stroke, demand for occupational therapy should increase. Furthermore, there are also increasing numbers of older people in the population, a group that suffers a high incidence of disabilities and that will, therefore, require occupational therapy services.

Changes in the health care delivery system also will affect opportunities for therapists as alternatives to extended inpatient hospital treatment are sought. Therapy in hospitals will be more intensive and briefer, and therapists will concentrate on patient evaluation and preparation for rehabilitation on an outpatient basis. There should be increased demand for therapists in subacute outpatient units. Hospitals will seek to achieve greater flexibility by using part-time and contract occupational therapists in the years ahead.

Increasingly, therapists will be finding employment in private practice, contracting for their services in a variety of settings—hospitals, nursing homes, rehabilitation centers, adult day care programs, group homes, industrial settings, and patients' homes.

WHERE TO LOOK FOR FURTHER INFORMATION

For information on a career in occupational therapy, education programs, and certification requirements:

American Occupational Therapy Association
4720 Montgomery Lane
P.O. Box 31220
Bethesda, MD 20824-1220

OPTOMETRISTS

OCCUPATIONAL OVERVIEW

Job Description: Optometrists examine people's eyes to diagnose and, in certain cases, treat existing eye or vision problems. They also test for proper depth and color perception and for proper focus and coordination of the eyes.

Prospects: Job opportunities will grow about as fast as the average for all occupations through the year 2006. As the population ages, optometrists are expected to be in significant demand.

Qualifications: Optometrists must be state-licensed. Applicants for a license must have a doctor of optometry degree from an accredited optometric school or college and pass a written and clinical state board examination. Many states permit applicants to substitute the examinations of the National Board of Examiners in Optometry for all or part of the written exam.

Personal Skills: The ability to deal tactfully and compassionately with people who may be worried or frightened is essential. Good business sense, self-discipline, and manual dexterity are also important.

Earnings: Income varies depending on specialization and location, among other factors. In 1996, according to the American Optometric Association, optometrists overall earned median net incomes of $80,000; optometrists in their first year of practice earned median net incomes of $57,500.

THE JOB AND THE WORK ENVIRONMENT

Optometrists are primary eye care providers; they must not be confused with ophthalmologists (physicians specializing in the diagnosis and treatment of vision disorders) or dispensing opticians (who fit and adjust eyeglasses, and sometimes contact lenses, based on prescriptions from either optometrists or ophthalmologists).

Optometrists prescribe eyeglasses, contact lenses, vision therapy, and low-vision aids. They may also use drugs for diagnosis and the treatment of some eye diseases. When optometrists diagnose diseases that are beyond the scope of their practice, they arrange for consultation with an appropriate health care practitioner.

There are three types of optometric practice: (1) solo, (2) partnership/group, and (3) salaried. According to the American Optometric Association, about two-thirds of optometrists are in private practice. The trend, especially among newly graduated optometrists, has been toward group or salaried practice, chiefly because of the high education-related debt graduates carry and also because of the expense of setting up a private practice. Salaried optometrists work as employees in an established private practice or in health maintenance organizations (HMOs), hospitals, or clinics. Some optometrists who have private practices may moonlight, working part time in a clinic, another practice, or a vision center.

Another option optometrists have is working in retail optical stores rather than in private practice. Not all optometrists in such stores are employees; optometrists may purchase franchises in a chain and operate them as independent businesses.

Optometrists work in their own offices or in the offices of their employer. The work requires great attention to detail and can be exacting. Self-employed optometrists must allow considerable flexibility in setting their working hours to suit the needs of their patients. They may have to arrange for evening hours or work on Saturdays, for instance, and they often work more than 40 hours per week.

TRAINING AND QUALIFICATIONS

All states and the District of Columbia require optometrists to be licensed. Candidates for a license to practice optometry must have a doctor of optometry degree from an accredited school. This degree requires completion of a 4-year professional program at an appropriately accredited school, following at least 2 or 3 years of undergraduate preoptometric studies (most optometry students hold a bachelor's degree). As of 1997, 17 schools and colleges of optometry were accredited by the Council on Optometric Education of the American Optometric Association.

To qualify for optometry school, applicants must have undergraduate courses in English, mathematics, physics, chemistry, and biology or zoology. All applicants also must take the Optometry Admissions Test (OAT). Competition for admission to an accredited optometry school is keen, so a good undergraduate record is crucial. Optometry programs include classroom and laboratory studies, as well as clinical training in diagnosing and treating eye disorders.

One-year postgraduate clinical residency programs are available for optometrists who wish to specialize in certain aspects of optometry (e.g., family practice, pediatrics, geriatrics, low-vision rehabilitation, vision training, contact lenses, hospital-based optometry, or primary care optometry). Those wishing to pursue research or teaching need a master's degree or doctorate.

EARNINGS

Income varies according to specialization, location, and years in practice, among other factors. According to the American Optometric Association, first-year optometrists had median net earnings of $57,500 in 1996; overall, optometrists' median net earnings were $80,000. Net income generally rises annually, peaking at the 20- to 29-year mark. It shows a decline after 30 years of practice, primarily because practitioners reduce their hours.

PROSPECTS: JOB OUTLOOK

In 1996, optometrists accounted for about 41,000 jobs. (The number of jobs is more than the number of optometrists because some optometrists held two or more jobs.) Through the year 2006, jobs for optometrists are expected to grow about as fast as the average for all occupations.

In general, optometrists are looking at the future through rose-colored glasses. As the large baby boom generation ages, demand for optometric services is expected to be strong. The trend is strengthened by the growing awareness on the part of an increasingly educated public of the importance of vision care. In addition, the oldest age group has an increased chance of developing cataracts, glaucoma, and other problems requiring optometric services. Finally, some opportunities will result from retirements.

Job growth would be even more rapid were it not for expected gains in productivity, due to greater use of support personnel and new equipment and procedures, that will enable each optometrist to see more patients.

Competition in the most desirable locations—large metropolitan areas—is expected to be strong.

WHERE TO LOOK FOR FURTHER INFORMATION

To learn more about careers in optometry:

American Optometric Association
243 North Lindbergh Boulevard
St. Louis, MO 63141-7881

To learn more about accredited optometry schools:

Association of Schools and Colleges of Optometry
6110 Executive Boulevard
Suite 510
Rockville, MD 20852

To learn more about licensing requirements, write to the Board of Optometry in the capital of the state in question.

*P*HARMACISTS

OCCUPATIONAL OVERVIEW

Job Description: Working in community pharmacies or chains, independent stores, or hospitals, pharmacists dispense the drugs and medicines prescribed by physicians and dentists. Sometimes they do the actual compounding. They advise laypersons and health professionals about the uses and side effects of pharmaceuticals. They also preserve drugs and medicines. Some pharmacists own and operate their own businesses.

Prospects: Through the year 2006, jobs for pharmacists are expected to grow as fast as the average for all occupations. Many factors are expected to contribute to the trend: (a) an increase in new drug products; (b) the aging of the population; and (c) more cost-conscious insurers, who see pharmacists as providing primary and preventive health services in the form of medications that alleviate conditions that could become worse and, therefore, more costly to the insurers.

Qualifications: Pharmacists must have a bachelor's of science (B.S.) in pharmacy or a doctorate of pharmacy (Pharm.D.) from an accredited college of pharmacy, as well as a state license. Licenses are granted to those pharmacy school graduates who have passed a state board examination, are of good character, and have a certain amount of work experience or have served an internship.

Personal Skills: Pharmacists must be orderly, precise, and detail oriented. The ability to communicate clearly and well, and a desire to help others, are important to gaining the confidence and trust of other professionals and the public.

Earnings: In 1996, a survey by *Drug Topics* magazine found that the average base earnings of full-time, salaried pharmacists were $59,276. Salaries were generally highest in the West and second highest in the East. Women are closer to pay parity in pharmacy than they are in most other professions.

THE JOB AND THE WORK ENVIRONMENT

Health professionals, as well as the lay public, have come to rely increasingly on the pharmacist's expertise with modern drugs. Pharmacists dispense the drugs and medicines prescribed by physicians and dentists, so they must understand the use, composition, and effects of drugs, and they must know how drugs are tested for purity and strength. Occasionally, pharmacists compound the tablets, capsules, or ointments prescribed, but generally the drug manufacturers provide the medication in standard doses. Most pharmacists also create computerized records of patients' drug therapies to help avoid the chance of harmful drug interactions.

Most pharmacists work for community pharmacies or hospitals. A small percentage are self-employed or work for the government. In community pharmacies or chains, in addition to preparing and dispensing drugs, the pharmacist's responsibilities may include purchasing and maintaining inventories of nonmedical goods, hiring and supervising nonprofessional staff, and managing the business. In hospitals, pharmacists advise the professional staff on the selection and effects of drugs and may assist in educating patients about their medications. Some pharmacists monitor and evaluate drug regimens. Pharmacists may also specialize in such areas as drugs for oncology, psychiatric disorders, or intravenous nutrition support.

Radiopharmacists, or *nuclear pharmacists,* prepare and dispense radioactive pharmaceuticals used in diagnosis and therapy.

The pharmacist's workplace is clean, well lit, and well ventilated. Shelves and refrigerators are filled with hundreds of drug products. Pharmacists are responsible for maintaining detailed records of controlled substances that they keep in locked cabinets.

Pharmacists spend much of their day on their feet. They sometimes work with potentially harmful substances and in these situations, take safety precautions. In hospitals and clinics, they likely have to work nights, weekends, and holidays. In the public sector, pharmacists employed by the federal government usually work in the hospitals and facilities of the Veterans Administration or the U.S. Public Health Service. Other federal agencies employing pharmacists include the U.S. Department of Defense and the Food and Drug Administration. State and local governments also employ pharmacists. In the private sector, pharmacists are employed by pharmaceutical manufacturers and professional associations.

Most full-time, salaried pharmacists work a standard 40-hour week. Pharmacists who own their own businesses can expect to put in longer hours—some more than 50 hours a week. Most pharmacists work in or near major population centers.

TRAINING AND QUALIFICATIONS

Pharmacists require a license to practice in all states, the District of Columbia, and U.S. territories. To obtain a license, it is necessary to graduate from an accredited pharmacy program, pass a state's licensing examination, and serve as an intern under a licensed pharmacist.

As of 1997, the American Council on Pharmaceutical Education had accredited the programs in 79 colleges of pharmacy. These programs offer a bachelor's of science (B.S.) in pharmacy, which takes five years of study, or a doctor of pharmacy (Pharm.D.) degree, which usually requires six years of study. Most pharmacists hold the B.S., the minimum requirement for most positions. Recently, however, pharmacy schools voted to proceed toward offering the Pharm.D. as the only professional pharmacy degree, and all accredited schools likely will graduate their last B.S. class by the year 2004.

Entry requirements for pharmacy colleges vary. A few programs admit students directly from high school; most require one or two years of college with an emphasis in the sciences and mathematics as prepharmacy education. Some schools require applicants to take the Pharmacy College Admissions Test.

Most community pharmacy jobs require only a B.S., but more and more hospitals prefer the Pharm.D. degree. A master's or Ph.D. in pharmacy (or a related field) is necessary to do research; a Pharm.D. with additional training, master's, or Ph.D. is needed to teach.

A master's degree or Ph.D. was offered by 60 colleges in the 1996–1997 academic year. In addition to advanced degrees in pharmacy, those who take up further studies may enter a one- or two-year residency or fellowship in such specialties as pharmaceutical chemistry, pharmacology, hospital pharmacy, and pharmacy administration.

In community pharmacies, pharmacists normally begin at the staff level and, with experience and capital, may become part owners or owners. Chain drug store pharmacists can advance to pharmacy supervisor, store-level manager, or go on to district or regional manager positions. In hospitals, advancement is to supervisory or administrative jobs.

EARNINGS

According to a 1996 survey conducted by *Drug Topics* magazine, the base earnings of full-time, salaried pharmacists averaged $59,276. Pharmacists in chain drug stores averaged $61,735 a year; those employed by independent drug stores averaged $52,189; and hospital pharmacists averaged $61,317. Regionally, pharmacists enjoy the highest salaries in the West, with the second-highest salaries in the East. Benefits, especially for those in chains and hospitals, are quite good, including major medical, life insurance, disability insurance, pension plans, deferred income plans, and stock purchase programs. A growing number of pharmacists also receive bonuses.

PROSPECTS: JOB OUTLOOK

In 1996, about 172,000 jobs were held by pharmacists. Through the year 2006, employment of pharmacists is expected to increase as fast as the average for all occupations, primarily because the age of the U.S. population is expected to increase through the period (typically, older people are heavy users of medications). Due to scientific and technological advances, the demand for those with expertise regarding the preparation and administration of drug products should increase. In addition, cost-conscious health insurers see pharmacists as providing primary and preventive care in the form of prescribing medications to alleviate patients' conditions that might worsen if left untreated—and, therefore, be more costly to them.

New prospects will emerge in managed care organizations, where pharmacists will analyze trends in medication use, with fast growth also occurring in research and pharmacoeconomics (determining costs and benefits of drug therapies). Opportunities will be favorable in long-term, ambulatory, and home care settings.

Slower growth is expected in hospitals (due to reduced inpatient stays and cost cutting) and in traditional chain and independent pharmacies.

WHERE TO LOOK FOR FURTHER INFORMATION

For information on career requirements, colleges of pharmacy, and financial aid:

American Association of Colleges of
 Pharmacy
1426 Prince Street
Alexandria, VA 22314

American Council on Pharmaceutical
 Education
311 West Superior Street
Suite 512
Chicago, IL 60610

For information about careers in pharmacy:

American Society of Health-System
 Pharmacists
7272 Wisconsin Avenue
Bethesda, MD 20814

American Pharmaceutical Association
2215 Constitution Avenue, NW
Washington, DC 20037

For information on licensure requirements, contact the Board of Pharmacy of the particular state or:

National Association of Boards of Pharmacy
700 Busse Highway
Park Ridge, IL 60068

PHARMACY TECHNICIANS

OCCUPATIONAL OVERVIEW

Job Description: Pharmacy technicians assist pharmacists, principally in hospitals and clinics. In some hospitals, they are trained to administer certain drugs and are designated *medication administration technicians.*

Prospects: The outlook for jobs for pharmacy technicians is tied to job prospects in pharmacy. Through the year 2006, job growth for pharmacists is expected to be as fast as the average for all occupations.

Qualifications: Pharmacy technicians must be high school graduates. Some employers require completion of a specific training program; others train pharmacy technicians on the job.

Personal Skills: A pharmacy technician should be well organized, precise, and good with details. He or she also should work well as part of a team.

Earnings: Earnings vary depending on training, experience, employment setting, and geographic area. Technicians may have average earnings of $8,000 to $25,000 a year in positions ranging from part to full time.

THE JOB AND THE WORK ENVIRONMENT

Pharmacies store and dispense an ever-growing array of pharmaceuticals. Keeping track of drugs and seeing that they are properly dispensed are jobs that pharmacists often cannot do alone. The work requires a well-trained support staff of pharmacy technicians.

In hospital pharmacies, under the direction and supervision of a staff pharmacist or supervisor, pharmacy technicians are responsible for checking inventory by ascertaining the age, condition, and quantity of pharmaceuticals on hand. They alert the pharmacist of shortages and monitor deliveries, checking them against purchase orders to ensure that the pharmacy has received the correct shipment. Pharmacy technicians help to keep records accurate and up to date. Logs containing the identity, date of dispensation, dosage, prescribing physician, and patient to whom the drug was administered must be accurately filed on computer. The pharmacy technician will assist in this work; keep requisition forms, the pharmacy laboratory, and its equipment in order; and see that all pharmaceuticals are properly arranged and stored.

A small but growing number of pharmacy technicians are being trained for clinical duty. Designated *medication administration technicians,* they administer drugs and medications that require fixed dosages at set intervals. Medication administration technicians are also assigned to medical surgical units, freeing other trained personnel to spend more time administering drugs to patients in intensive care units and to other patients with special needs.

Pharmacy technicians work in clean and orderly settings and in the company of professionals. They can work part or full time. A full-time position involves a 40-hour workweek, and if the job is in a hospital pharmacy, which is open year round and around the clock, the work schedule is likely to include evening and weekend shifts and some holidays.

TRAINING AND QUALIFICATIONS

Pharmacy technicians need a high school diploma. Training can be done on the job. Those planning to work in this field should take high school courses in mathematics, biology, typing, bookkeeping, and computers. The modern pharmacy's records are computerized, so knowing how to use a computer is an essential skill. Secondary and postsecondary vocational schools, community colleges, and the military provide training. Some employers prefer candidates with previous training and experience.

Among the hospitals offering training for medication administration technicians are Detroit Osteopathic Hospital, the University of Wisconsin Hospitals and Clinics, and the University of California at Los Angeles Medical Center.

Voluntary certification is granted by passing an examination given by the Pharmacy Technician Certification Board.

EARNINGS

Earnings vary according to training, experience, employment setting, and geographic location. Pharmacy technicians may earn an average of between $8,000 and $25,000 a year for positions ranging from part to full time. Full-time technicians are likely to enjoy standard benefits, including paid vacation and medical insurance.

PROSPECTS: JOB OUTLOOK

In 1996, pharmacy technicians held 83,000 jobs. Employment prospects for pharmacy technicians are tied to several factors. Perhaps the strongest indication comes from the outlook in job growth for pharmacists, which through the year 2006, should be as fast as the average for all occupations. Many of the same factors favorably affecting pharmacists, such as an aging population that will place increasing demands on the nation's health care system, also should favor pharmacy technicians. In addition, the health care industry, to cut costs and use primary health care providers more efficiently, probably will be expanding support staff.

WHERE TO LOOK FOR FURTHER INFORMATION

For information on a career as a pharmacy technician:

American Society of Health-System Pharmacists
7272 Wisconsin Avenue
Bethesda, MD 20814

For a list of schools offering pharmacy technician education programs:

American Council on Pharmaceutical Education
311 West Superior Street
Suite 512
Chicago, IL 60610

For information on pharmacy technician certification:

Pharmacy Technician Certification Board
2215 Constitution Avenue, NW
Washington, DC 20037

*P*HYSICAL THERAPISTS

OCCUPATIONAL OVERVIEW

Job Description: Physical therapists work to relieve pain, restore functional mobility, and prevent or limit permanent disability for those suffering from a disabling injury or disease.

Prospects: Through the year 2006, physical therapy is expected to be among the fastest growing occupations as the demand for services grows.

Qualifications: All therapists must be licensed to practice. To qualify for a state license examination, applicants must have completed an accredited educational program in physical therapy leading to either a bachelor's or master's degree.

Personal Skills: Because the job can be physically demanding, therapists need stamina and physical strength, as well as manual dexterity. Patients' cooperation is vital to success, so therapists must be able to relate to people and establish a close rapport with them. Above all, perhaps, therapists need patience and the ability to sympathize with another's cares and fears.

Earnings: The median weekly income of salaried physical therapists usually working full time was $757 in 1996. The median base salary for physical therapists working full time in hospitals was $48,000, according to a survey by the American Physical Therapy Association.

THE JOB AND THE WORK ENVIRONMENT

When the drama of recovery from a disabling illness or accident is over, the difficult journey back to functioning in the daily world begins. The journey can be long and arduous with progress measured, often quite literally, step by step. Frequently, it is only the skill, knowledge, and patience of physical therapists that make the journey possible. Physical therapists plan, organize, and administer the treatment necessary for patients to regain as much functioning capacity as possible after a disabling injury or illness. Their patients may include accident or stroke victims as well as those who are disabled, and they may range in age from the very young to the very old. To perform their functions, therapists must have a detailed knowledge of human anatomy and physiology and good clinical problem-solving skills to devise appropriate treatment plans.

Therapists first study the patient's personal background and medical history and work to win the patient's confidence and trust for the proposed treatment. The quality of the therapist-patient relationship can have a profound impact on the treatment's effectiveness.

To arrive at a course of treatment, the therapist conducts a series of tests to evaluate the patient's strengths, weaknesses, and ability to function. He or she then interprets the results and develops a treatment plan designed to help the patient gain the maximum functional independence, muscle strength, and physical skills possible. Often the patient must adjust to a drastic change in his or her physical abilities. To accomplish these goals, therapists work with the patient's family, instructing them in the treatment plan and enlisting their cooperation and aid.

Physical therapists work in a variety of environments, ranging from specifically equipped departments in hospitals to the private homes of patients. They may have to work during the evenings and on weekends, especially if they are in private practice, and must adjust their schedules to their patients' convenience. Therapists work in hospitals (the largest employer of therapists), rehabilitation centers, home health agencies, and nursing homes, either as salaried staff or on a contract basis. A substantial number are in private practice, treating patients referred by physicians.

TRAINING AND QUALIFICATIONS

A state license is required to practice physical therapy. Applicants must have a degree from an accredited physical therapy educational program as a requirement to take the licensure examination. Three types of programs satisfy the requirement: (1) bachelor's degree programs in physical therapy, (2) certificate programs (second bachelor's degrees for those with a bachelor's degree in another subject), and (3) entry-level master's degree programs in physical therapy. As of July 1997, there were 173 accredited physical therapy programs, according to the American Physical Therapy Association. More than twice as many programs offered master's as opposed to bachelor's degrees; and by the year 2001, all accredited physical therapy programs will be at the master's (or above) level.

Competition for entry into these programs is keen. A good record in high school courses in health, chemistry, physics, math, and biology is highly desirable. Most of the education programs also require volunteer summer or part-time work in the physical therapy department of a hospital or clinic.

Physical therapists are expected to keep up with professional developments by taking continuing education courses and workshops. A number of states require this to maintain licensure.

EARNINGS

The median weekly income of salaried physical therapists working mostly full time was $757 in 1996. The American Physical Therapy Association reported that physical therapists working full time for hospitals earned a median salary of $48,000.

PROSPECTS: JOB OUTLOOK

In 1996, physical therapists held about 115,000 jobs, with one in four working part time. About 60 percent worked in hospitals and physical therapy offices. Through the year 2006, physical therapy is expected to be among the fastest growing occupations as demand for services grows. Job opportunities are expected to grow rapidly as the aging population requires rehabilitation and long-term care services. In addition, advances in therapeutic techniques and rehabilitation medicine are likely to fuel demand. The impressive gains of sports medicine and its extraordinary performance in returning athletes to play after severe injuries also has given therapy a high profile to many in the general public. Public interest in maintaining personal health will lead to more demand for therapists, too.

As the health industry expands and diversifies, the use of contract physical therapists by nursing homes and home health care agencies also is expected to increase, creating more job opportunities. Employment would grow even faster except for an emphasis on controlling health care costs that limits use of physical therapy services in some cases.

WHERE TO LOOK FOR FURTHER INFORMATION

For information about careers in physical therapy and to obtain a list of accredited educational programs in physical therapy:

American Physical Therapy Association
1111 North Fairfax Street
Alexandria, VA 22314-1488

*P*HYSICIAN ASSISTANTS

OCCUPATIONAL OVERVIEW

Job Description: Physician assistants, working under the supervision of a licensed physician, interview patients, take medical histories, perform physicals, order and administer tests, make diagnoses, prescribe treatments, and increasingly, prescribe drugs. They work chiefly in hospitals, clinics, and doctors' offices.

Prospects: Through the year 2006, jobs for physician assistants are expected to grow much faster than the average for all occupations because of the projected growth of health services and an ongoing emphasis on containing health care costs.

Qualifications: Forty-nine states and the District of Columbia require that physician assistants be certified to practice. To be certified, a physician assistant must have completed an accredited program and then pass a national certifying examination, meet continuing education requirements, and take a recertifying examination every six years.

Personal Skills: Physician assistants must be dedicated and conscientious. Their education requires a demanding course of studies, and they must continue to study throughout their careers. They must be mature and emotionally stable, and since their work brings them into constant and direct contact with patients, they must be willing and able to deal with all kinds of people.

Earnings: In 1996, the median earnings for physician assistants in clinical practice full time were $60,687. Income varies with experience, specialty, practice setting, and location.

THE JOB AND THE WORK ENVIRONMENT

Physician assistants are adjuncts to licensed physicians; their primary purpose is to relieve doctors of routine chores so they can use their skill and knowledge where the need is greatest. The scope of a physician assistant's activities varies from state to state, but responsibilities usually include the more time-consuming tasks of patient care: interviewing patients, taking medical histories, performing physicals, ordering laboratory tests, diagnosing conditions, prescribing treatment, and in 39 states and the District of Columbia, prescribing drugs. Physician assistants, or PAs, always work under the supervision of a licensed physician. Some physician assistants specialize, working primarily in, for example, neonatology, cardiology, emergency medicine or surgery, psychiatry, or anesthesiology.

Physician assistants work chiefly in hospitals, clinics, and doctors' offices and also in health maintenance organizations (HMOs) and correctional facilities. They have been helping to meet the health needs of rural areas and inner cities, where doctors are in chronically short supply. According to the American Academy of Physician Assistants, nearly 60 percent of all PAs work in communities with fewer than 50,000 residents where physicians may be in short supply. Those who work in clinics where a licensed physician is on duty only one or two days a week bear the major responsibility for patients' health care; they consult with the supervising physician by telephone.

Physician assistants usually work in comfortable, well-lit surroundings, though those in surgery often must stand for long periods of time. Schedules vary according to practice setting. A PA working in a physician's office may have to work some night hours and weekends and be on call. Physician assistants in clinics generally work a standard 40-hour week.

TRAINING AND QUALIFICATIONS

Nearly all states require that physician assistants graduate from an accredited formal program. As of 1997, 96 educational programs existed for PAs, of which 53 offered bachelor's degrees or some other degree option. The others offered a certificate or associate's or master's degree. Bachelor's degrees are held by most PA graduates.

The usual requirements for admission to a program are at least two years of college, with some chemistry and biology, and previous work experience in dealing directly with patients. Former medical corpsmen, emergency medical technicians, and registered nurses have the experience programs seek in applicants.

Most programs take about two years and are found in academic health centers, medical schools, schools of allied health, or four-year colleges, with a few in community colleges, the armed forces, or hospitals. Classwork includes biochemistry, nutrition, human anatomy, pathophysiology, microbiology, clinical pharmacology, clinical medicine, geriatric and home health care, disease prevention, and medical ethics. Beyond classwork, students undertake clinical rotations covering many areas of practice, among them primary care medicine, pediatrics, emergency medicine, obstetrics and gynecology, geriatrics, internal medicine, and surgery. One or more rotations may be headed by a physician seeking to hire a physician assistant. For both the physician and the assistant, the process of selection is crucial since the two will work closely together and rely on each other.

In 1997, 49 states and the District of Columbia had legislation governing the qualifications of PAs (Mississippi did not). These states mandate that PAs pass the Physician Assistants National Certifying Examination open only to graduates of accredited PA programs. To maintain certification, PAs must complete 100 hours of continuing medical education every two years and take a recertification examination every six years.

Some physician assistants pursue further education to practice in a specialized area, such as surgery or emergency medicine. Some, after gaining more clinical knowledge and experience, advance to additional responsibilities and higher earnings.

EARNINGS

Earnings vary according to experience, specialty, practice setting, and location. In 1996, the median earnings for physician assistants in full-time clinical practice were $60,687, according to the American Academy of Physician Assistants; median earnings for first-year graduates were $52,116. A May 1996 Hay Group survey of HMOs, group practices, and hospital-based clinics found the median base salary of full-time PAs to be $54,100.

PROSPECTS: JOB OUTLOOK

In 1996, physician assistants accounted for about 64,000 jobs. Through the year 2006, employment of PAs is expected to grow much faster than the average for all occupations due to expansion and diversification of health services and a continuing emphasis on containing health care costs.

Physicians and institutions are expected to hire more PAs to give primary care and therefore assist physicians in providing health care in a cost-effective manner. Besides traditional office-based settings, PA jobs will be growing in hospitals, public clinics, and academic medical centers. Since states are more commonly imposing legal limits on the number of hours physician residents can work, teaching hospitals are likely to increase their employment of PAs to fill some physician resident services.

Job opportunities will be greatest in states that allow physician assistants the greatest responsibilities, such as the right to prescribe medications.

WHERE TO LOOK FOR FURTHER INFORMATION

For information on a career as a physician assistant:

American Academy of Physician Assistants
Information Center
950 North Washington Street
Alexandria, VA 22314-1552

For information on physician assistant training programs:

Association of Physician Assistant Programs
950 North Washington Street
Alexandria, VA 22314-1552

For information on certification:

National Commission on Certification of Physician Assistants, Inc.
6849-B2 Peachtree Dunwoody Road
Atlanta, GA 30328

*P*HYSICIANS

OCCUPATIONAL OVERVIEW

Job Description: Physicians conduct medical examinations, diagnose illnesses, treat people suffering from injury or disease, and advise patients on preventive health care. They also perform surgery and prescribe drugs and medicines.

Prospects: Expectations are that the demand for physicians will grow faster than the average for all occupations through the year 2006, in keeping with the general forecast for rapid expansion of all phases of the health industry.

Qualifications: All physicians must be licensed to practice medicine. To qualify for licensure, applicants must have graduated from an accredited school of medicine, have successfully passed the licensing examination, and have completed a varying number of years of internship/residency depending on the chosen specialty.

Personal Skills: A strong desire to help the sick and injured is essential. Dedication and excellent study skills are indispensable, especially for the long regimen of study required. Emotional stability and the capacity to make decisions in an emergency are crucial.

Earnings: The American Medical Association reported that in 1995, the median income (after expenses) for allopathic physicians was approximately $160,000. The middle 50 percent earned between $115,000 and $238,000 annually.

THE JOB AND THE WORK ENVIRONMENT

It's easy to understand why novels, movies, and television have dramatized the lives of doctors. Everything about the profession seems outsized: the arduous training, the extreme pressure, the high monetary rewards, and the well-deserved sense of accomplishment.

There are two types of physician: the M.D. (doctor of medicine) and the D.O. (doctor of osteopathy). Doctors of medicine are also known as allopathic physicians. They and doctors of osteopathy employ the full range of medical procedures, including the use of drugs and surgery, but osteopathic physicians put special emphasis on the musculoskeletal system of the body (bones, muscles, ligaments, and nerves) and on holistic care. Moreover, the two types also divide along the kinds of practice in which they engage. About two-thirds of M.D.'s are specialists, and only one-third are primary care providers, while most D.O.'s are general practitioners. Areas of specialization include anesthesiology, internal medicine, obstetrics/gynecology, pathology, pediatrics, psychiatry, radiology, and surgery.

The practice of medicine has changed radically in the past few decades and is expected to change further. Because of the great technological advances in recent years, physicians enjoy whole new arrays of high-tech devices to aid in diagnosis and treatment. These devices are often complex, requiring extensive training and skills. In addition, they are generally quite costly and have profoundly affected the way medicine is practiced. Today, hospitals are the primary sites for advanced medical care because only hospitals or very large clinics or group medical practices can afford to purchase expensive equipment; individual doctors or small groups find them beyond their means. Another ongoing change in medical practice is the shift away from fee-for-service medicine to managed care systems, such as health maintenance organizations (HMOs) and preferred provider organizations (PPOs). Both trends may account for the fact that solo practice among physicians has declined. Physicians are much more likely to work as salaried staff in group medical practices, clinics, or health care networks than in the past.

Physicians in solo or small-group practice usually have long, irregular hours; those in group practice generally work more regular schedules. In 1996, nearly one-third of all full-time physicians worked 60 or more hours weekly. Geographically, the northeastern and western states have the highest ratio of physicians to population; the south central states, the lowest. M.D.s tend to locate in urban areas, near hospital and education centers. D.O.'s are more likely to practice in small towns and rural areas; they tend to locate chiefly in states with osteopathic hospitals. As of 1997, more than half of practicing D.O.'s worked in six states: Florida, Pennsylvania, Michigan, Ohio, New Jersey, and Texas.

TRAINING AND QUALIFICATIONS

Training to become a physician takes many years, including four years of undergraduate school, four years of medical school, and from three to eight years of internship and residency, depending on the specialty. There are 125 schools that teach allopathic medicine and award the M.D. and 17 that teach osteopathic medicine and award the D.O. The minimum educational requirement for entry into medical school is three years of college, but most candidates have a bachelor's degree with a major in the prescribed premedical course of study. Students are selected on the basis of their undergraduate grade-point score, their performance on the Medical College Admission Test (MCAT), and letters of recommendation, but medical schools also consider character, leadership qualities, and extracurricular activities. Most school admissions' committees also interview applicants. Competition for admission is fierce.

Most of the first two years of medical school are spent in classrooms and laboratories in such courses as anatomy, physiology, pharmacology, biochemistry, pathology, medical ethics, and the legal aspects of medical practice. Students learn to take medical histories, conduct patient exams, and diagnose illnesses. In the past two years, students work directly with patients while being supervised by experienced physicians in hospitals and clinics. Through rotations in various medical departments, they gain experience in diagnosis and treatment of a wide range of conditions.

After graduation, almost all M.D.'s complete a residency; nearly all D.O.'s serve a 12-month rotating internship after graduation, followed by a two- to six-year residency. For board certification in a specialty, physicians spend up to seven years, depending on the specialty, in advanced residency training and sometimes two years more of practice in the specialty before taking the specialty board examination.

The investment in time and money to become a doctor is very high, and more than 80 percent of medical students borrow money to cover expenses. Student financial aid has not increased in recent years, but loans and scholarships are still available from federal, state, and private sources.

EARNINGS

Physicians are among the highest-paid individuals in any occupation. Surgeons, radiologists, and anesthesiologists are the highest-paid physicians, while primary care practitioners are at the lower end of the pay scale. In general, earnings also vary depending on years in practice, hours worked, skill, personality, reputation, and geographic location.

According to the American Medical Association (AMA), the median earnings (after expenses) for allopathic physicians in 1995 were $160,000. The middle 50 percent earned between $115,000 and $238,000. Self-employed physicians (owners or part owners of a practice) had higher median earnings than salaried physicians. The AMA reported that from 1996 to 1997, average salaries of medical residents ranged from $32,789 for first-year residents to $40,849 for sixth-year residents.

PROSPECTS: JOB OUTLOOK

In 1996, physicians held approximately 560,000 jobs. Employment of physicians is expected to grow faster than the average for all occupations through the year 2006, in keeping with the general forecast for rapid expansion of the health care industry. The aging and growing population, as well as new technologies, will spur job growth.

Opportunities will be best for primary care physicians, including family practitioners, general pediatricians and internists, and geriatric and preventive health specialists. Specialty services may be in less demand due to health industry cost-consciousness, even though the number of specialists continues to increase. Thus, competition will be stiff for specialist jobs in large urban and suburban areas. Opportunities are likely to be greater for all physicians in rural and low-income areas, because some physicians find the lower income potential and isolation from colleagues unappealing. Managed care arrangements could reduce the demand for physicians if the volume of physician services is constrained either through cost-saving measures of the organization or substitution of nonphysician care providers, such as physician assistants or nurse practitioners.

In addition, the National Academy of Sciences Institute of Medicine, among other groups, has found an oversupply of physicians at the present time and advises that the number of physicians be limited by reducing residency positions. A reduction of physicians entering the profession would help remedy the oversupply problem.

WHERE TO LOOK FOR FURTHER INFORMATION

To learn more about allopathic medical schools and premedical education:

American Medical Association
515 North State Street
Chicago, IL 60610

Association of American Medical Colleges
Section for Student Services
2450 N Street, NW
Washington, DC 20037-1131

To learn more about careers in osteopathic medicine:

American Osteopathic Association
Department of Public Relations
142 East Ontario Street
Chicago, IL 60611

American Association of Colleges of
  Osteopathic Medicine
5550 Friendship Boulevard
Suite 310
Chevy Chase, MD 20815-7321

PODIATRISTS

OCCUPATIONAL OVERVIEW

Job Description: Podiatrists examine, diagnose, treat, and help to prevent diseases and malfunctioning of the foot and lower leg. They provide foot care and perform basic medical and surgical procedures.

Prospects: Through the year 2006, jobs for podiatrists are expected to grow about as fast as the average for all occupations. Rapid growth in the over-65 segment of the population is expected to spur demand for podiatrists.

Qualifications: Podiatrists are required by all states and the District of Columbia to obtain a license to practice podiatric medicine. Applicants for licensure generally must be graduates of an accredited college of podiatric medicine, and they must pass written and oral licensing examinations.

Personal Skills: Good manual dexterity and an aptitude for scientific study are essential. Tact and interpersonal skills are important for a successful practice, as is a good business sense.

Earnings: A survey by *Podiatry Management* found that the median net income of podiatrists in 1996 was approximately $91,400. Income depends on experience and size and location of practice.

THE JOB AND THE WORK ENVIRONMENT

Maybe brain surgeons command the glamour, but the fact is that our feet are far more likely to ache than our brains. Podiatrists deal with mundane matters, but they bring comfort needed by almost everyone at one time or another.

Podiatrists treat the major foot conditions: corns and calluses, ingrown toenails, and bunions. In addition, they treat hammertoes, ankle and foot injuries (more common than ever with the increase in sports and jogging), arch problems, and foot ailments associated with diseases such as diabetes and arthritis.

In the diagnostic process, podiatrists may order x-rays and laboratory tests. As part of the treatment, they may recommend corrective shoes, fit corrective devices such as orthotics, order physical therapy, or perform surgery. Corrective surgery, whether performed in a hospital, a clinic, an outpatient surgery center, or in a podiatrist's office, has assumed an ever-increasing importance in podiatric practice. In addition, many diseases (e.g., diabetes, arthritis, and heart disease) show their first clinical signs in the foot. Podiatrists are trained to spot these and other systemic diseases, so a visit to the podiatrist may be the first step toward a more complete health appraisal.

The vast majority of podiatrists are in private practice, and most are solo practitioners, although multispecialty group practices and partnerships have begun to take on increasing importance. Podiatrists also work in hospitals, nursing homes, clinics, health maintenance organizations (HMOs), and some public health agencies (i.e., federal, state, and local bodies), including the U.S. Department of Veterans Affairs.

Normally, podiatrists work in their offices in a 37- to 40-hour week, scheduling their hours to suit their practice and patients' needs. Those working in hospitals or clinics may work some evenings and weekends. Podiatric practice also is unevenly spread across the country since podiatrists are concentrated in the areas surrounding colleges of podiatric medicine.

TRAINING AND QUALIFICATIONS

All podiatrists must be licensed to practice. Licensure is obtained by graduating from an accredited college of podiatric medicine and passing state written and oral examinations. Some states allow applicants to substitute the examination of the National Board of Podiatric Examiners, given in the second and fourth years of podiatric college, for all or part of the written state examination. Some states grant reciprocity to podiatrists licensed in other states.

Applicants for admission to a podiatric college are required to have completed at least three years of undergraduate study, have an acceptable grade-point average, and have a suitable score on the Medical College Admissions Test (MCAT). Applicants must have eight semester hours each of biology, organic chemistry, inorganic chemistry, and physics, plus six hours of English. More than 90 percent of accepted students hold at least a bachelor's degree.

Podiatric colleges offer a four-year program that includes classwork and clinical rotations in private practices, clinics, and hospitals. The core curriculum is similar to that of medical schools. Graduates earn the doctor of podiatric medicine (D.P.M.) and most complete a one- to three-year residency after receiving a D.P.M. In addition, some podiatrists specialize, and there are certifying boards for the specialties of orthopedics, primary medicine, and surgery; certification requires more advanced training, passing written and oral examinations, and practice experience.

Podiatrists have a number of avenues for advancement. They may become professors at podiatric colleges, health administrators, or hospital department chiefs.

EARNINGS

Earnings normally increase as the practice grows and vary depending on experience and practice size and location. A survey by *Podiatry Management* found that the median net income of podiatrists in 1996 was approximately $91,400.

A survey by the American Podiatric Medical Association reported that the average net income for podiatrists in private practice in 1995 was $108,156, with those in practice less than 2 years earning an average of $44,662, and those in practice 16 to 30 years earning an average of $141,135.

PROSPECTS: JOB OUTLOOK

In 1996, podiatrists accounted for about 11,000 jobs. Through the year 2006, employment is expected to grow about as fast as the average for all occupations. An aging population is expected to experience more severe foot problems than a younger one, but even among the young, sports- and exercise-related injuries are expected to increase demand for podiatric services. Some job growth also will result from replacement needs, but the combined job openings resulting from growth and replacement needs still will be very low because the profession is small.

Particularly important to this field is the widespread access to health care plans among the general population. Medicare and most private plans cover acute medical and surgical foot services, as well as x-rays, fracture casts, and leg braces, whether the services are rendered by doctors of medicine, osteopathy, or podiatric medicine. Routine care, such as removal of corns and calluses, is generally not covered by health insurance, but HMOs and some other prepaid medical plans may provide routine care. As with dental services, podiatric services are more dependent on disposable income than are other health services.

Opportunities will be better for podiatrists who are board-certified because managed care groups require such. New podiatrists will have better opportunities in group practices, clinics, and health networks than in solo practice. Opening a practice will be most difficult near podiatric colleges since podiatrists are clustered in these areas.

WHERE TO LOOK FOR FURTHER INFORMATION

To learn more about careers in podiatric medicine:

American Podiatric Medical Association
9312 Old Georgetown Road
Bethesda, MD 20814-1621

To learn more about education for podiatric medicine:

American Association of Colleges of
   Podiatric Medicine
1350 Piccard Drive
Suite 322
Rockville, MD 20850-4307

American Society of Podiatric Medicine
7331 Collins Avenue
Miami Beach, FL 33141

American Association of Hospital
   Podiatrists
420 74th Street
Brooklyn, NY 11209

RADIOLOGIC TECHNOLOGISTS

OCCUPATIONAL OVERVIEW

Job Description: Radiographers take x-ray films that physicians use to diagnose medical problems. Radiation therapy technologists treat cancer patients. Sonographers, or ultrasound technologists, work with nonradiologic diagnostic imaging equipment. The majority of radiologic technologists are radiographers, and most radiologic technologists work for hospitals.

Prospects: Job growth in radiologic technology is expected to be faster than the average for all occupations through the year 2006. Opportunities will vary by region and specialty. Technologists who are trained in both radiologic and nuclear medicine procedures will have the best job prospects.

Qualifications: Radiographers need at least a high school diploma. They may be trained on the job or in formal programs, though most hospitals prefer hiring applicants with formal training. Prerequisites for training in radiation therapy and sonography vary, but programs prefer individuals with a science background or experience in a health profession. In 1997, 36 states licensed radiologic technologists; none required licensing of sonographers.

Personal Skills: Radiologic technologists ought to be responsible, careful, and precise. They need to be able to work as part of a team and to interact well with patients to win their cooperation. Radiation therapy technologists, in particular, must be compassionate.

Earnings: According to a Hay Group survey of acute care hospitals in January 1997, the median base salary of full-time radiologic technologists was $28,800. Full-time ultrasound technologists earned a median base salary of $36,100; radiation therapy technologists earned $37,300.

THE JOB AND THE WORK ENVIRONMENT

Diagnosis through x-ray films (radiographs) is no longer the only use of radiation in medicine. Radiation is used extensively in the treatment of cancers. A technology of computer-enhanced diagnostic imaging has emerged, too, that does not rely on radiation. Today, the term *radiologic technologist* includes those who work with radiation and those who work with sonographic (ultrasound) or magnetic resonance imaging (MRI) equipment.

Radiographers, the technicians who take x-ray pictures of the human body, often work closely with radiologists, physicians specializing in interpreting radiographs. Radiographers, also called x-ray technicians, take the radiograph (x-ray picture). They prepare and position the patient, mindful of wounds and injuries and minimizing the patient's pain or discomfort, and develop the film. In cases of fluoroscopic examinations, the radiographer prepares a contrast solution for the patient to drink. In many fluoroscopic examinations, the radiographer acts as assistant to the physician.

Radiation therapy technologists work with cancer patients and administer prescribed doses of radiation to specific parts of the body. They operate many kinds of equipment, including high-energy linear accelerators with electron capabilities. The technologist must be attentive to the often unpleasant side effects of the therapy and sympathetic to patients and their families.

Sonographers, or *ultrasound technologists,* use advanced imaging techniques, combining imaging equipment and computers that process great amounts of data. Ultrasound machines, which use sound waves; magnetic resonance scanners, which use radio waves; and positron emission scanners, which use electrons, provide images with more information and detail than x-rays, especially of soft tissue, without the attendant risks of radiation. In addition, the technology provides moving images, especially valuable for examining maternity patients. Sonographers must have a thorough knowledge of physiology and the skills needed to interpret the moving images created by this technology.

Radiologic technologists usually work for hospitals 40 hours a week and may have to work weekend, night, and holiday shifts. Part-time work is widely available. Technologists spend a lot of time on their feet and may often have to lift and position patients who are too weak or ill to move themselves. Those who work with equipment that uses radiation must adhere to safety procedures designed to minimize the risk of overexposure. Radiation therapists are subject to emotional burnout because they treat seriously ill and dying patients every day.

TRAINING AND QUALIFICATIONS

Radiologic technologists can be trained in hospitals or medical centers, or in programs conducted in colleges and universities, trade schools, vocational-technical institutes, or the armed forces. Training includes coursework and clinical instruction in anatomy, physiology, patient care procedures, radiation protection, principles of imaging, and radiobiology. The length of programs varies, but generally two years is the average.

Radiation therapists and sonographers typically have a background in science or experience in one of the health professions. Training can take from one to four years.

One-year certificate programs are available to individuals from other health occupations, such as registered nurses or medical technologists, who wish to change fields.

The Joint Review Committee on Education in Radiologic Technology accredited 629 radiography programs and 97 radiation therapy programs as of 1997, and the Joint Review Committee on Education in Diagnostic Medical Sonography accredited 74 programs in sonography. Radiography programs require applicants with at least a high school diploma or equivalent. For radiation therapy and diagnostic medical sonography programs, applicants with a science background or experience in a health profession usually are preferred.

As of 1997, 36 states licensed radiologic technologists. None require licensing of sonographers. Radiographers and radiation therapists may pursue voluntary registration by the American Registry of Radiologic Technologists (ARRT). Ultrasound technologists are certified by the American Registry of Diagnostic Medical Sonographers (ARDMS). Many employers prefer hiring registered technologists.

Radiographers and radiation therapists must complete 24 hours of continuing education every other year; sonographers must complete 30 hours of continuing education every three years.

To advance to supervisory, administrative, or teaching jobs, a bachelor's or master's degree in one of the radiologic technologies is desirable.

EARNINGS

A January 1997 survey by the Hay Group of acute care hospitals found the median base salary of full-time radiologic technologists was $28,800. Full-time ultrasound technologists earned a median base salary of $36,100; radiation therapy technologists earned $37,300.

Radiologic technologists generally enjoy benefits common to other health care workers, particularly those in hospitals, including paid vacations, sick leave, and health insurance.

PROSPECTS: JOB OUTLOOK

In 1996, radiologic technologists held approximately 174,000 jobs, with most technologists being radiographers and more than half of all technologist jobs found in hospitals.

Through the year 2006, job growth for radiologic technologists should be faster than the average for all occupations as the population ages, leading to increased use of diagnostic imaging and therapeutic procedures. A larger number of technologists will find work in physicians' offices, HMOs, diagnostic imaging centers, and clinics, where employment is expected to increase most rapidly. The rapid growth expected in these facilities is a result of the shift toward outpatient care, encouraged by third-party payers and technological advances enabling more procedures to be performed outside hospitals.

Although hospitals will remain the major employer, growth will be slower. To reduce labor costs, hospitals have been combining radiologic and nuclear medicine departments, so technologists who can perform both kinds of procedures will have the best job prospects. Since there has been an increase in the number of qualified applicants entering the field while hospitals have been trimming staff, competition for openings has intensified.

Sonographers should have somewhat brighter prospects than other radiologic technologists due to the increased use of ultrasound as an alternative to radiologic tests. Ultrasound technologies will continue to increase.

WHERE TO LOOK FOR FURTHER INFORMATION

For information on careers in radiologic technology, send a stamped, self-addressed, business-size envelope with your request to:

American Society of Radiologic
  Technologists
15000 Central Avenue, SE
Albuquerque, NM 87123-3917

Society of Diagnostic Medical Sonographers
12770 Coit Road
Suite 708
Dallas, TX 75251

For a list of accredited programs in radiography and radiation therapy technology:

Joint Review Committee on Education in Radiologic Technology
20 North Wacker Drive
Suite 600
Chicago, IL 60206-2901

For a list of accredited programs in diagnostic medical sonography:

Joint Review Committee on Education in Diagnostic Medical Sonography
7108 South Alton Way
Building C
Englewood, CO 80112

REGISTERED NURSES

OCCUPATIONAL OVERVIEW

Job Description: Registered nurses (RNs) care for the sick; monitor patients' symptoms, reactions, and progress; assist physicians in treatments and examinations; administer medications prescribed by physicians; and help individuals and groups plan how to maintain or improve their health. In staff positions, they also supervise other nursing personnel.

Prospects: Growth in employment for RNs will rise faster than the average for all occupations through the year 2006, a demand fueled in large part by the country's growing and aging population, technological advances permitting a larger number of medical ailments to be treated, and replacement needs.

Qualifications: RNs must be licensed to practice. Individual states issue licenses to candidates who have graduated from an approved school of nursing and pass a national examination administered by the state.

Personal Skills: RNs often work under extreme pressure, frequently under emergency conditions. They must have strong emotional and physical stamina, and they must have genuine sympathy for ill and often frightened people. They must be able to follow directions exactly and work with a very small margin for error.

Earnings: In 1996, full-time, salaried nurses had a median weekly income of $697, with the middle 50 percent earning between $571 and $868. Advanced practice nurses generally have particularly well-paying jobs. In May 1996, a Hay Group survey of HMOs, group practices, and hospital-based clinics, reported that the median base salary of full-time nurse practitioners was $66,800.

THE JOB AND THE WORK ENVIRONMENT

Today's highly trained, professional RNs play a key role in the nation's health care team. The most skilled of all nurses, RNs often take on the supervision of other nursing personnel, as well as providing personal care to patients.

About two out of three nurses are *hospital nurses*. Most are staff nurses responsible for providing bedside care and supervising licensed practical nurses, orderlies, and aides. They often specialize in working with people requiring a particular type of care: postoperative care, pediatrics, maternity care, trauma victims, cancer patients, and so on.

Nursing home nurses perform a wide range of functions for the elderly. They are trained to administer complex treatments, such as starting intravenous fluids. RNs working as *community health nurses* perform their duties in clinics, schools, and other community settings. They also provide care to patients in their homes, following physicians' orders and instructing patients and their families in health care procedures.

Doctors, oral surgeons, clinics, health maintenance organizations (HMOs), and others hire RNs as *office nurses*, who, in addition to their regular nursing duties, may perform routine laboratory and office work. *Occupational health* or *industrial nurses* work in industry and government. They treat minor injuries on the job, arrange for further care when necessary, and offer employees health care counseling. They frequently assist with routine health examinations and inoculations. RNs also can become self-employed *private-duty nurses*, providing care to individual patients in need of constant attention. Private-duty nurses may work in patients' homes, in hospitals, or in nursing homes or rehabilitation centers.

At a more advanced level, *nurse practitioners* provide primary health care, diagnosing and treating common illnesses and injuries. In most states, they can prescribe drugs. *Clinical nurse specialists, certified registered nurse anesthetists,* and *certified nurse-midwives* are other advanced practice nurses.

Work settings vary widely. Most RNs work in hospitals that are generally well supplied and relatively comfortable. Some inner-city hospitals, however, may be overcrowded, with stressful conditions. Community health nurses and private duty nurses may have to travel to patients' homes.

RNs spend a great deal of time on their feet, and they frequently need physical strength to move or otherwise help bedridden patients. On occasion, they must deal with patients with infectious diseases or work in situations requiring extreme care, such as those involving radiation, dangerous chemicals, or gases (in anesthetics). Hospital and nursing home RNs periodically work at night and on weekends. Office, public health, and occupational health nurses generally work regular business hours.

TRAINING AND QUALIFICATIONS

Registered nurses must be licensed to practice in all states. Licensure requires graduating from a nursing program and passing a national licensing examination. As of 1996, there were more than 1,500 entry-level nursing programs, of which there are three basic types:

1. Two-year associate degree in nursing (A.D.N.) programs offered by community and junior colleges.
2. Three-year diploma programs offered by nursing schools connected with hospitals.
3. Four-year bachelor of science in nursing (B.S.N.) degree programs offered by colleges and universities.

All training programs include classroom instruction and supervised practice in hospitals or other health care facilities. RNs who take specialized graduate-level courses leading to a certificate or a master's degree, normally in one or two years, can become nurse practitioners, clinical nurse specialists, nurse clinicians, or nurse anesthetists. These programs are offered by many colleges, and they generally require candidates to be RNs with up to two years' experience in a specialty relevant to the certificate or degree.

In 1995, about two-thirds of RNs were from A.D.N. programs and about one-third from B.S.N. programs. Only a small number came from diploma programs. There have been efforts to raise the minimal education requirement for an RN license to a bachelor's degree; if such a change occurs, it will likely be made state by state. Bachelor's degrees offer more advancement opportunities (e.g., a B.S.N. is usually needed for administrative jobs and is a prerequisite for entering graduate nursing programs in research, consulting, clinical specialization, or teaching).

In management, nurses can advance to head nurse, nursing director, and vice-president of nursing. Management-level jobs increasingly require a graduate degree in nursing or health services administration. Some nurses move into business areas of the health care industry. They may manage ambulatory, home health, and chronic care services or be employed by health care companies in health planning and development.

EARNINGS

Earnings for this occupation are above average, especially for advanced practice nurses with additional education or training. In 1996, the median weekly income of full-time, salaried registered nurses was $697, with the middle 50 percent earning between $571 and $868. In a May 1996 Hay Group survey of HMOs, group practices, and hospital-based clinics, the median base salary of full-time nurse practitioners was $66,800; nurse-midwives earned about $70,100.

Many employers of nurses offer flexible work schedules, educational benefits, bonuses, and child care.

PROSPECTS: JOB OUTLOOK

In 1996, nurses held about 1,971,000 jobs, making nursing the largest health care occupation. Through the year 2006, employment of nurses will grow faster than the average for all occupations. This growth will be due to a number of factors, a primary one being an increasing population with a larger number of seniors, who are more likely than younger people to need medical care. In addition, a large number of new RNs will be hired in home health, long-term, and ambulatory care. Because new technology allows more patients to receive complex ambulatory care in doctors' offices, clinics, and HMOs, RNs will have even greater job opportunities in those settings. Many job openings also will result from replacement needs.

The home health care and nursing home sectors, both rapidly growing users of health care professionals, are expected to offer major employment opportunities for nurses. Hospital employment, the largest sector, is expected to grow more slowly than other sectors. Hospital inpatient stays are declining, so the most rapid hospital growth will be in outpatient departments, such as same-day surgery, chemotherapy, and rehabilitation.

Since RNs now have many more options than traditional hospital nursing positions, flexibility is an advantage. Nurses with advanced education and training will have the best prospects.

WHERE TO LOOK FOR FURTHER INFORMATION

To learn more about the nursing occupation and nursing education, write to the National League for Nursing for a list of its publications:

Communications Department
National League for Nursing
350 Hudson Street
New York, NY 10014

To learn more about career opportunities for registered nurses:

American Nurses Association
600 Maryland Avenue, SW
Washington, DC 20024-2571

To receive a list of B.S.N. and graduate programs:

American Association of Colleges of Nursing
1 Dupont Circle, NW
Suite 530
Washington, DC 20036

RESPIRATORY THERAPISTS

OCCUPATIONAL OVERVIEW

Job Description: Respiratory therapists specialize in the evaluation, treatment, and care of patients with breathing disorders. They are called on to intervene when someone's life is at risk from a failure in the breathing process.

Prospects: Expectation is that the demand for respiratory therapists will increase much faster than the average for all occupations through the year 2006. The growth of the middle-age and elderly segments of the population is certain to bring a higher incidence of cardiopulmonary troubles, increasing the demand for respiratory care services.

Qualifications: Formal training is necessary in this occupation, with programs for respiratory therapy offered at the postsecondary level in hospitals, medical schools, vocational-technical institutes, colleges and universities, trade schools, and the armed forces. Forty-seven states require licensure of respiratory care technologists and technicians.

Personal Skills: Good interpersonal skills with special emphasis on sensitivity to patients' physical and psychological needs are essential. Also important are the ability to work as part of a team, mechanical ability and manual dexterity, and a capacity for paying close attention to detail.

Earnings: A Hay Group survey of acute care hospitals in January 1997, found the median base salary of full-time respiratory therapists to be $32,500, with the middle 50 percent earning between $29,300 and $35,000.

THE JOB AND THE WORK ENVIRONMENT

Few things are more frightening than an inability to breathe. When breathing becomes labored, panic sets in. And there's good reason to be concerned: If one stops breathing for only a few minutes, serious brain damage will occur. Death is the usual result of having oxygen cut off for no more than nine minutes. The breath of life is no exaggeration.

Respiratory therapists generally work in hospitals, where they perform in three major areas: diagnosis, treatment, and patient management. They diagnose by testing and measuring the capacity of lungs and analyzing the oxygen and carbon dioxide concentration and the potential of hydrogen (pH), a measure of the acidity or alkalinity level of the blood. Treatment may range from giving temporary relief to patients with chronic asthma or emphysema to emergency care for heart failure, stroke, drowning, or shock. Therapists who work in patient management monitor patients on oxygen or ventilator equipment. Here, both patients and equipment must be checked regularly, and if the patient appears to be having trouble, or if the oxygen, carbon dioxide, or pH level of the blood is unstable, the equipment setting must be changed.

Respiratory therapists use various kinds of equipment to administer oxygen and oxygen mixtures, including oxygen delivery devices, such as a mask or nasal cannula attached to an oxygen tank, and ventilators, machines that pump air into the lungs. The therapist fits the mask or nasal cannula to the patient and adjusts the flow as prescribed by the physician. The ventilator is for patients unable to breathe on their own. The therapist inserts a tube down the patient's mouth into the trachea; connects it to the ventilator; and sets the rate, volume, and oxygen concentrations of the air being forced into the patient's lungs.

Providing respiratory care at home is a rapidly expanding area of practice for therapists. Increasingly, mechanical ventilators and sophisticated life-support equipment are being used in private homes. Many patients who receive home respiratory care will need it for the rest of their lives, so the therapist must teach patients and families how to use the equipment, visiting several times a month to inspect or clean the equipment and ensure its proper use.

Respiratory therapists generally work a 35- to 40-hour week; however, in hospital settings, this often involves shifts, which means occasional work during evenings or on weekends. Therapists spend long periods on their feet. In emergencies, they are under a great deal of stress. In addition, some of the gases therapists use are potentially hazardous, and therapists are exposed to infectious diseases; but with proper safety precautions, risk of injury or illness is minimal.

TRAINING AND QUALIFICATIONS

Formal training is necessary to become a respiratory therapist, with programs offered by hospitals, medical schools, colleges and universities, vocational-technical institutes, trade schools, and the armed forces. In addition to training programs for therapists, there are shorter programs for respiratory therapy technicians. In 1996, the Commission on Accreditation of Allied Health Education Programs (CAAHEP) of the American Medical Association accredited 210 programs for respiratory therapists; 158 programs for respiratory therapy technicians were accredited.

Formal training programs vary in length and in the credential or degree awarded. Most CAAHEP-accredited therapist programs take two years and lead to an associate's degree; some are four-year programs leading to a bachelor's degree. Technician courses usually last about one year; graduates receive certificates. Respiratory therapy programs include courses in anatomy and physiology, physics, chemistry, microbiology, and mathematics, as well as technical courses dealing with clinical tests, equipment, and procedures.

All states except for Delaware, Nevada, and Washington require respiratory care workers to be licensed. Voluntary certification and registration are offered by the National Board for Respiratory Care to those who have graduated from a CAAHEP-accredited programs. All such graduates—in both technologist and technician programs—can take the examination to receive the *certified respiratory therapy technician* (CRRT) credential. CRRTs who meet training and experience qualifications can take an examination leading to the *registered respiratory therapist* (RRT) credential. Most employers require those in entry-level or generalist jobs to hold the CRRT or be eligible for the CRRT examination. Intensive-care specialties and supervisory jobs normally require the RRT or RRT eligibility.

Respiratory therapy technicians and assistants can advance to the level of therapist by taking the appropriate courses or through on-the-job training. Therapists advance in clinical practice by moving from care of general patients to care of critically ill patients, who have serious problems in other organ systems. Therapists may also advance to supervisory or managerial positions; for example, with additional education or experience, a therapist may become chief of the respiratory department of a hospital. Such administrative posts often require the four-year degree and the RRT.

EARNINGS

In 1996, the median weekly income for full-time salaried respiratory therapists was $636, with the middle 50 percent earning between $506 and $767. A Hay Group survey of acute care hospitals in January 1997, found that the median base salary of full-time respiratory therapists was $32,500, with the middle 50 percent earning between $29,300 and $35,000.

PROSPECTS: JOB OUTLOOK

In 1996, respiratory therapists held approximately 82,000 jobs, with 9 out of 10 jobs in hospitals. Most other jobs were in respiratory therapy clinics, home health care agencies, and nursing homes.

Through the year 2006, employment of respiratory therapists is expected to grow much faster than the average for all occupations, in large part due to the growth in the middle-age and senior population, in which there is a higher demand for respiratory care. In addition, technological advances in treating accident and heart attack victims and premature infants will increase demand. Although hospitals will continue to hire most therapists, a growing number will be working under contract to nursing homes and home health care agencies. Respiratory therapists with cardiopulmonary care skills and experience with infants are expected to have the best job prospects.

WHERE TO LOOK FOR FURTHER INFORMATION

To learn more about careers in respiratory therapy:

American Association for Respiratory Care
11030 Ables Lane
Dallas, TX 75229

To learn about the credentials necessary for respiratory therapy workers:

National Board for Respiratory Care, Inc.
8310 Nieman Road
Lenexa, KS 66214

To receive a list of CAAHEP-accredited programs for respiratory therapy occupations:

Joint Review Committee for Respiratory Therapy Education
1701 West Euless Boulevard
Suite 300
Euless, TX 76040

SPEECH-LANGUAGE PATHOLOGISTS AND AUDIOLOGISTS

OCCUPATIONAL OVERVIEW

Job Description: Speech-language pathologists diagnose and treat those suffering from speech or language disorders arising from a variety of causes. Audiologists identify, evaluate, and treat auditory, balance, and other neural problems.

Prospects: Employment opportunities are expected to grow much faster than the average for all occupations through the year 2006. The aging of the country's population and attendant communication disorders (hearing impairment, speech impairment from stroke, etc.), as well as advances in medical technology, will generate demand for professionals in these disciplines.

Qualifications: The most common certification in this occupation is a master's degree in speech-language pathology or audiology. Most states require practitioners to be licensed, which requires a master's degree. Those practicing in public schools need a certificate issued by the state's education agency. Some practitioners have certification in both speech-language pathology and audiology.

Personal Skills: Compassion, patience, and the ability to take responsibility and work on one's own are essential. Good communication skills also are required because diagnosis, modes of treatment, and instructions must be clearly transmitted to people with various levels of comprehension.

Earnings: According to a survey by the American Speech-Language Hearing Association, the median 1997 salary for full-time certified speech-language pathologists was $44,000; for audiologists, it was $43,000. Salaries vary depending on experience, level of education, certification, employment setting, and geographic location.

THE JOB AND THE WORK ENVIRONMENT

Speech-language pathology and audiology are distinct disciplines, but they are so interrelated that to be fully competent in either means being familiar with both. Basically, both deal with speech, language, and hearing impairments that disrupt the ability to communicate and can present a long-term problem for the sufferer. For instance, children who experience difficulty in hearing, speaking, or understanding language have trouble in school and in every kind of social situation. Adults with such impairments have difficulties on the job and in their private lives. Especially susceptible are the aging, who may expect to sustain some hearing loss as a normal consequence of growing older.

Speech-language pathologists concentrate on those suffering from speech or language problems rising from such conditions as total or partial loss of hearing, brain injury, cerebral palsy, cleft palate, voice pathology, learning disability, emotional problems, or foreign dialect. Patients' problems can be congenital, developmental, or acquired. Speech-language pathologists use a variety of tools in diagnosis and treatment, including audiovisual equipment and computers, as well as less complex devices (e.g., tape recorders to record and play back a patient's speech irregularities and microcomputers to analyze specific characteristics of the speech signal, to provide visual cues to the patient, and to perform other functions).

Speech-language pathologists may also counsel patients and their families to alleviate the stress and misunderstandings that often accompany communication disorders. Teaching how to prevent such disorders is another aspect of the pathologist's job.

Audiologists concentrate on hearing, balance, and related problems that may result from such causes as genetic disorders, birth trauma, viral infections, or exposure to loud noises. Using an audiometer, they test the patient's hearing range, noting the pitches and frequencies of sound the patient can and cannot hear. Based on this assessment, they determine a course of treatment, which may include the fitting and dispensing of a hearing aid or the use of telephone and television amplifiers.

Most practitioners of these occupations work in schools, clinics, and health care facilities, delivering direct services to those with communication disorders, primarily developing and implementing treatment programs. Some do administrative work as well, especially those directing programs in schools, health departments, and other governmental agencies. Record keeping is extremely important.

The work of speech-language pathologists and audiologists is mostly confined to a desk or table in comfortable surroundings and is not physically taxing, but it does demand intense concentration. The workweek is generally about 40 hours, though some pathologists and audiologists work part time. Those who contract out their services may spend considerable time traveling between facilities.

TRAINING AND QUALIFICATIONS

Forty-four states regulate licensing for speech-language pathologists and 47 do so for audiologists; almost all require a master's degree or equivalent. Licensing requirements also include 300 to 375 hours of supervised clinical experience, passing a national examination, and nine months of postgraduate clinical experience. There are continuing education requirements to renew licensure in 34 states. Licensure is usually required by Medicaid, Medicare, and private insurers for practitioners to be reimbursed.

About 230 colleges and universities offer graduate programs in speech-language pathology; about 120 offer graduate programs in audiology in the United States.

The American Speech-Language Hearing Association (ASHA) offers certification to speech-language pathologists and audiologists based on the candidate's obtaining a master's degree or its equivalent, having 375 hours of supervised clinical experience, completing a nine-month internship, and passing a national written examination. The award is a Certificate of Clinical Competence (CCC), given for speech-language pathology (CCC-SLP) or audiology (CCC-A).

EARNINGS

Earnings vary with level of education, experience, specialty, certification, employment setting, and geographic location. According to a survey by ASHA in 1997, the median salary for full-time certified speech-language pathologists was $44,000; for audiologists, it was $43,000. Speech-language pathologists with 22 years of experience earned a median salary of $52,000; audiologists with equivalent experience earned about $55,000.

PROSPECTS: JOB OUTLOOK

In 1996, speech-language pathologists and audiologists held about 87,000 jobs, with about half working in schools. Through the year 2006, employment is expected to grow much faster than the average for all occupations as a result of rapid growth in the elderly population and advances in medical technology. Demand for speech-language pathologists is expected to rise in nursing homes and home health care agencies, with most of these jobs being filled by private practitioners working on a contract basis. Jobs in schools also will increase with higher enrollments and a greater awareness of the importance of early diagnosis of speech, language, and hearing disorders.

Most job opportunities in these occupations will be generated in speech and hearing clinics, physicians' offices, and outpatient facilities. The increased demand will be for rehabilitation services, stemming from anticipated expansion of rehabilitation programs for victims of stroke or head injury. Pathologists and audiologists will continue to be in demand in school systems, which are mandated by law to provide aid to children with disabilities and special education needs. Business and industry will create new demands for audiologists in response to environmental noise problems.

WHERE TO LOOK FOR FURTHER INFORMATION

To learn more about careers in speech-language pathology and audiology:

American Speech-Language Hearing Association
10801 Rockville Pike
Rockville, MD 20852

To learn more about a career in audiology:

American Academy of Audiology
8201 Greensboro Drive
Suite 300
McLean, VA 22102

Information on state licensing is available from individual state licensing boards. To learn about the certification requirements for working in public school systems, write to the education department of the state in question.

VETERINARIANS

OCCUPATIONAL OVERVIEW

Job Description: Veterinarians care for animals—pets, livestock, and zoo, laboratory, and sporting animals—and they help protect the public from exposure to diseases carried by animals. They also do research on animal and human health problems.

Prospects: Through the year 2006, job opportunities for vets are expected to increase faster than the average of all occupations. Job openings resulting from replacement needs will nearly equal those created by growth in the occupation.

Qualifications: Veterinarians must be licensed by the state in which they practice. To obtain a license, candidates must have a doctor of veterinary medicine (D.V.M. or V.M.D.) from an accredited college of veterinary medicine and must pass state board proficiency tests.

Personal Skills: A fondness for animals is essential. Manual dexterity, patience, and a keen sense of observation are equally important. Animals cannot tell what's wrong with them, so the vet must infer the problem from examination and observation.

Earnings: Salaries for veterinarians vary depending on type of practice and location. In 1995, the average earnings of veterinarians in private practice was $57,500. The overall average starting salary of a vet school graduate was $29,900, in 1995.

THE JOB AND THE WORK ENVIRONMENT

Veterinarians may take up one of several different kinds of practice: small animal practice exclusively or predominantly, large animal exclusively or predominantly, mixed animal, or equine exclusively. They diagnose medical problems in their animal patients, perform surgery, and administer vaccines and medicines.

The majority of vets engage in private practice, and most of them specialize in small companion animals (typical household pets). They concentrate on the prevention, diagnosis, and treatment of pet diseases, generally those connected with dogs and cats, as well as birds, rabbits, reptiles, and other small animals kept as pets. They must be familiar with the many breeds of pets and the characteristics of each so they can recommend diets, exercise regimens, and so forth, specific to the breed. These practices are normally found in all urban settings.

Large animal vets specialize in the health needs of cattle, poultry, pigs, fish, and sheep, although they also must be able to treat small animals. They advise ranchers and farmers on the proper care and management of livestock, with emphasis on the prevention of disease and proper growth. A subspecialty of this practice is equine care, which concentrates on the health needs of horses and is of special concern to the sporting community. These practices are normally found in more rural settings.

There has been a growing trend since the 1960s for veterinarians to specialize in an area of medicine or surgery, such as oncology or ophthalmology. Boards of veterinarians award certification or diplomate status to specialists who have passed a series of examinations.

Veterinarians also work in research, food inspection, and education. They may join with physicians and scientists in research at an academic medical center, exploring techniques of organ transplants or the testing of new drugs. Others go into regulatory medicine or public health, inspecting food, investigating outbreaks of disease, and working in laboratories. They are particularly interested in preventing the outbreak and spread of animal diseases, some of which, such as rabies and Lyme disease (spread by the deer tick), can be transmitted to human beings.

The introduction of chemicals (herbicides, pesticides, antibiotics, steroids) into food animals by modern methods of breeding and processing has created a growing need for veterinarians who can deal with the consequences of these additives to the food chain.

Vets generally treat pets in animal hospitals or clinics. Large animals are treated on farms and ranches from well-equipped mobile clinics; hence, large animal vets must be prepared to drive long distances to their patients. In all cases, vets in private practice work long hours, and those in large animal practice often work outdoors in all kinds of weather. Vets may be bitten, kicked, or scratched, and can be exposed to infection and disease during the course of their work. Most vets work 50 hours or more a week, though some may work a standard 40 hours. Self-employed vets set their own schedules and may work evenings and weekends.

TRAINING AND QUALIFICATIONS

Vets must be licensed to practice in all states and the District of Columbia. A doctor of veterinary medicine from an accredited veterinary college and passing a state board examination are essential for obtaining a license. The examination requirement is satisfied by passing the National Board Examination and the Clinical Competency Test. The majority of states also require passing an examination on laws and regulations governing veterinary medicine. There are continuing education requirements for maintaining licensure in 39 states. A master's or doctorate degree is usually required for teaching or research jobs. Certification in a specialty requires a two- to three-year residency plus passing an examination.

The D.V.M. requires a minimum of six years of college, consisting of two years of preveterinary study, with emphasis on the physical and biological sciences, and a four-year veterinary program. Beyond academics, training includes clinical experience in diagnosing and treating animal diseases and in performing surgery and laboratory work. In 1994, all 27 veterinary colleges in the United States were accredited by the American Veterinary Medical Association (AVMA); admission to these schools is highly competitive. Serious applicants should have a *B* average or better, especially in science courses, and must take the Veterinary College Admission Test, the Medical College Admission Test, or the Graduate Record Examination, depending on the preference of the particular college, and show that they have experience and enthusiasm about working with animals.

Veterinary medical school is expensive. Veterinary students, however, often are able to find guaranteed federal government loans to help meet their expenses. After graduation, most veterinarians begin work as an employee or partner in an established practice. Those with sufficient funds for start-up costs may open their own practice or purchase an established practice.

EARNINGS

Annual income depends largely on the type of practice and geographic region. In 1995, the average earnings of vets in private practice was $57,500. The overall average starting salary of graduates of veterinary medical colleges was $29,900, in 1995. In terms of type of practice, select average starting salaries were as follows: large animal (exclusively), $39,500; mixed animal, $31,900; small animal (exclusively), $31,900; equine, $27,500.

PROSPECTS: JOB OUTLOOK

In 1996, veterinarians held about 58,000 jobs. Employment of veterinarians is expected to grow faster than the average for all occupations through the year 2006, fueled in part, by people's willingness to pay for more intensive animal care than before, the demand for farm animal and disease control services, and the replacement needs for retiring vets and those who otherwise leave the profession. Job prospects may be better for vets specializing in farm animals than for small animal practitioners since fewer vet school graduates wish to work in isolated and rural areas.

WHERE TO LOOK FOR FURTHER INFORMATION

For information about careers in veterinary medicine:

American Veterinary Medical Association
1931 North Meacham Road
Suite 100
Schaumburg, IL 60173-4360

For information on veterinary education:

Association of American Veterinary Medical Colleges
1101 Vermont Avenue, NW
Suite 710
Washington, DC 20005

Information on scholarships, grants, and loans can be obtained from individual veterinary schools.

ARTS, ENTERTAINMENT, AND MEDIA

ACTORS, DIRECTORS, AND PRODUCERS

OCCUPATIONAL OVERVIEW

Job Description: Actors, directors, and producers work in entertainment media, including theater, radio, film, and television, to provide audiences with a wide variety of shows. Actors perform roles in the shows; directors and producers plan and supervise the shows and performances.

Prospects: Through the year 2006, employment of actors, directors, and producers is expected to grow faster than the average for all occupations. Increased foreign demand for American productions, along with a growing domestic market, will stimulate demand. Still, even though the entertainment media require an army of creative people for their presentations, competition for jobs is fierce, and employment is uncertain and irregular at best.

Qualifications: Actors need talent, drive, and savvy. Some kind of formal acting training is usual—and experience in performing is crucial. There are no specific training requirements for directors or producers, but a thorough knowledge of the medium, however obtained, is demanded.

Personal Skills: Aside from native talent, perseverance and the ability to withstand rejection are essential for actors and directors. Producers, in addition, need business acumen. Everyone in these occupations must be able to work closely with others.

Earnings: There are various rates and royalties for stage directors, with directors in summer theater usually receiving from $2,500 to $8,000 a week (including royalties) for a three- to four-week run. Salaries also vary for Broadway directors, with top directors typically earning $80,000 plus royalties.

Because some well known actors earn huge salaries, there is a misconception that all actors are highly paid. In fact, the average annual earnings for members of Actors' Equity working on the Broadway stage were $13,700 in 1996. The Screen Actors Guild reported that the average income its members earn from acting is less than $5,000 a year.

Producers rarely receive a salary. They usually receive a percentage of a show's ticket sales or earnings.

THE JOB AND THE WORK ENVIRONMENT

Actors use their skills to play roles in shows designed to inform, educate, or simply entertain. Bringing a role to life and moving an audience to laughter or tears are great rewards in themselves—a good thing because few actors become big stars. Many appear more or less frequently in supporting roles and/or commercials, but most work only now and then and must support themselves doing something else (waiting on tables, temporary office help) while waiting for a part. Patience and perseverance are essential in this occupation.

Actors use voice, gesture, and body motion to communicate with the audience, so they need training in addition to the talent with which they were born. They also need stamina for working long hours, often under great pressure and sometimes under adverse conditions (e.g., under hot lights, on location, or on tour).

Directors interpret screenplays and scripts, using their knowledge of acting and the medium (whether a live presentation or one that is recorded and edited) to bring out the best performances. They generally are responsible for casting and approving sets, costuming, and incidental music. In television and films, the finished show is accomplished through the director's editing (however, movie studios and cable networks often have the final decision on cutting and editing). A director's work is often stressful due to budgeting, schedule, and personnel challenges.

Producers acquire screenplays or scripts, then hire or oversee the selection of the director, cast, and production personnel. They negotiate artists' contracts and coordinate the work of writers, directors, and other staff. Most important, they are responsible for the financing of the project. They determine the project's size and budget, handle difficult personnel problems, and cope with the ever-present problem of funding.

TRAINING AND QUALIFICATIONS

Actors learn their craft by acting. They perform in high school and college plays and participate in community drama groups, regional theaters, and any and all available productions. Some try out for television or radio commercials at an early age. A few high schools offer formal training in acting and the performing arts, and many colleges and universities offer professional training and degrees in drama and theater arts. Dramatic arts schools in New York and Los Angeles also offer training, and private acting classes are given by professionals in many major cities. Singing and dancing lessons are useful, too. The important thing is to keep performing, no matter where.

Directors can benefit from the same training as actors, although there are no specific training requirements. Some formal training is available at colleges and universities.

Producers need to know about finances, be able to work with artistic people, and have a sense of what projects will sell. Some colleges offer programs in arts management; they provide the only formal training readily available for this occupation.

EARNINGS

Earnings for these occupations can range from next to nothing to a bonanza. When working, actors and directors do not do badly; it's the irregularity of the employment that keeps annual earnings down.

To work in movies, actors must belong to the Screen Actors Guild (SAG) or the Screen Extras Guild, and for radio and television, they must belong to the American Federation of Television and Radio Artists (AFTRA). Film and television directors belong to the Directors Guild of America (DGA), and stage directors belong to the Society of Stage Directors and Choreographers (SSDC). To appear on stage, actors must belong to the Actors' Equity Association. These unions bargain collectively with the producers of shows to set minimum salaries; hours; and other terms, including residual rights, for their members. Actors and directors can negotiate with producers directly or through an agent to obtain better terms than the basic contract. Producers generally do not receive a salary; they negotiate a percentage of the project's earnings or ticket sales as their fee.

There are various earnings schedules for directors of musical and dramatic shows in the theater. According to the SSDC, the director of a summer theater production makes anywhere between $2,500 and $8,000 (including royalties) for a three- to four-week run. Regional theaters may hire directors for longer seasons and will increase compensation accordingly. For Broadway productions, the highest paid directors earn $80,000 plus royalties.

Actors' Equity reports that the minimum weekly salary for actors in Broadway shows in 1997 was $1,040. Those in off-Broadway shows earned minimums ranging from $400 to $625 a week, depending on the theater's seating capacity.

Smaller regional theaters paid $375 to $600 a week. In 1996, less than half of dues-paying Actors' Equity members worked on a stage production. Average earnings for those who did find employment were $13,700, in 1996.

The SAG reports that movie and television actors with speaking parts earned a minimum daily rate of $559, or $1,942 for a five-day week, in 1997. Additional compensation may come in the form of contributions to health and pension plans and moneys received for reruns and foreign telecasts. But actors' earnings generally remain low due to the erratic nature of employment; SAG reports that the average income earned by its members from acting is less than $5,000 annually. Most actors have to supplement their professional income by holding other jobs.

PROSPECTS: JOB OUTLOOK

There's no biz like show biz, so predicting job prospects for these occupations means looking into a cloudy crystal ball. In 1996, actors, directors, and producers held an average of about 105,000 jobs in television, radio, stage productions, and movies. With the increasing number of new cable channels and the strong demand for commercials and shows to fill them, increased foreign demand for American shows, a steady stream of new films, and the growth of regional theater, there will be jobs for skilled, talented actors, directors, and producers. Through the year 2006, jobs are expected to grow faster than the average for all occupations. The catch is that there will be more job seekers than there will be jobs. Only the most dedicated and determined will find anything like steady work in this fiercely competitive market. People leaving the field will continue to generate more jobs than will new openings.

WHERE TO LOOK FOR FURTHER INFORMATION

To learn more about regional theaters and grants in the performing arts:

Association for Theatre in Higher Education
200 North Michigan Avenue, NW
Suite 300
Chicago, IL 60601

Theater Communications Group
355 Lexington Avenue
New York, NY 10017

Public Information Office
National Endowment for the Arts
1100 Pennsylvania Avenue, NW
Washington, DC 20506

For information on wages and working conditions for actors:

Screen Actors Guild
5757 Wilshire Boulevard
Los Angeles, CA 90036-3600

BROADCAST TECHNICIANS

OCCUPATIONAL OVERVIEW

Job Description: Broadcast technicians install, operate, and maintain the equipment used to record and transmit radio and television programs. They work with sound and video recorders, television cameras, transmitters, microphones, and equipment used for special effects.

Prospects: Through the year 2006, job opportunities are expected to grow about as fast as the average for all occupations. Competition for openings will continue to be stiff. New jobs resulting from the growth of cable television and other sectors are likely to be offset by the introduction of automated equipment.

Qualifications: For most jobs in television, college or vocational training is needed. Technical schools and colleges offer courses in broadcast technology, engineering, and electronics. Knowing how to operate computers and microprocessors is essential.

Personal Skills: An aptitude for handling mechanical and electronic equipment is basic, as is manual dexterity. Good eyesight and hearing are important. Broadcast technicians work as part of a team and need to be able to work well with others.

Earnings: Salaries depend on the size and type of station, geographic location, and membership in the National Association of Broadcast Engineers and Technicians (NABET). Commercial television pays more than educational television, and television generally pays more than radio.

THE JOB AND THE WORK ENVIRONMENT

Broadcast technicians are trained to do for a living what they may well have enjoyed doing as children—operating and maintaining electronic equipment. In television and radio stations, broadcast technicians operate transmitters, sound and video recorders, computers, special effects equipment, cameras, microphones, and control boards. Working from control rooms, they regulate the signal strength that determines the quality, clarity, and range of the sounds, colors, and images being broadcast or recorded. The work entails the coordination of several technicians—some in the control room, others in the studio, and still others out in the field—all connected by telephones or headsets.

In smaller television and radio stations, the technical staff combine several jobs; but in larger stations, these functions are separate. Supervisory personnel known as *chief engineers,* or *transmission engineers,* oversee the operation of the station. *Transmitter engineers* operate the transmitter and log outgoing and incoming signals. *Maintenance engineers* set up, service, and repair electronic broadcast equipment. *Audio control engineers* are responsible for picking up, transmitting, and switching sound signals. *Video control engineers* work from a console regulating the brightness, contrast, and overall quality of television pictures. *Recording engineers* operate and maintain the equipment used to record sound and video. Approximately the same divisions apply to radio stations, with technicians in charge of transmission, maintenance, setup, and quality control.

Broadcast technicians generally work in studios that are temperature regulated for the sake of sensitive equipment. *Field technicians,* however, often have to set up out of doors under unpredictable conditions. And there are intense, high-pressure assignments, such as television news coverage and special events.

A 40-hour week is common for most technicians, although broadcast deadlines at large networks can be demanding. Small stations routinely require a lot of overtime. Evening, weekend, and holiday work is often needed because most television and radio stations broadcast 18 to 24 hours a day, 7 days a week.

Technicians who are experienced may become supervisory technicians or chief engineers.

TRAINING AND QUALIFICATIONS

Training should begin in high school, with courses in mathematics, physics, and electronics. Building radios and other electronic devices from kits helps lay a strong foundation. Experience can be gained through work in a college radio station or a summer internship at a radio or television station.

Formal training in technical schools and colleges is available. More often, top-level technical slots and supervisory positions require a college degree in broadcast technology, engineering, or electronics. This is especially true for jobs at large stations or the major networks.

Since passage of the Telecommunications Act of 1996, the Federal Communications Commission (FCC) no longer requires the licensing of broadcast technicians. Certification by the Society of Broadcast Engineers now assures the competence and experience of technicians, who must pass an examination to earn such certification.

Thorough familiarity with operating computers and microprocessors is also basic to work in this field.

EARNINGS

Earnings depend on the type and size of station, geographic location, and membership in the NABET. Salaries are highest in New York City, Los Angeles,

Chicago, and Washington, DC. Television generally pays more than radio, and its union wage scales are higher and its benefits better. A survey by the National Association of Broadcasters and the Broadcast Cable Financial Management Association reported that average annual earnings for radio station technicians were $30,251 in 1996; average earnings for chief engineers were $46,602. In television, average earnings for operator technicians were $24,260 a year; for maintenance technicians, $32,533; and for chief engineers, $53,655.

PROSPECTS: JOB OUTLOOK

There were about 46,000 broadcast technicians in 1996. Overall employment is expected to grow about as fast as the average for all occupations through the year 2006. Because of the growing use of automated equipment, opportunities for operating engineers are less plentiful, while openings for maintenance engineers are increasing. Job openings are likely to occur to replace those retiring or changing careers. Cable is expanding, and with it, job opportunities, but this trend is likely to be offset by the increasing use of automated equipment. Competition, especially for beginners, will remain keen; the best breaks are likely to be in smaller cities.

WHERE TO LOOK FOR FURTHER INFORMATION

For information on schools with programs in broadcasting and on careers:

Broadcast Education Association
1771 North Street, NW
Washington, DC 20036

For information on careers for broadcast technicians:

National Association of Broadcasters
  Employment Clearinghouse
1771 North Street, NW
Washington, DC 20036

National Cable Television Association
1724 Massachusetts Avenue, NW
Washington, DC 20036

For certification information:

Society of Broadcast Engineers
8445 Keystone Crossing
Suite 140
Indianapolis, IN 46240

Locations and call letters of television stations are listed in industry directories, such as the *Broadcasting/Cablecasting Yearbook*, commonly available in public libraries.

DANCERS AND CHOREOGRAPHERS

OCCUPATIONAL OVERVIEW

Job Description: Dancers and choreographers work in many different media: classical ballet; modern dance; musical theater; and folk, ethnic, jazz, and rock dances. Choreographers create dances and teach them to performers; they also audition performers for their productions.

Prospects: Expectations are that demand will grow faster than the average for all occupations through the year 2006. The number of professional dancers and choreographers, however, will continue to exceed the openings, making the profession keenly competitive.

Qualifications: Natural talent is the primary requisite for a career in dancing. The training process begins early and never stops. Instruction for girls often begins at about 5 to 8 years of age; boys usually start training between the ages of 10 and 15. Serious professional training usually begins between the ages of 10 and 12.

Personal Skills: Excellent physical condition and exceptional agility, coordination, and grace are essential. A good sense of rhythm and feel for music are vital. Dancers must be highly motivated and able to handle rejection and intermittent employment.

Earnings: Major dance companies normally have union contracts that determine the pay scale for dancers. In 1997, the minimum weekly salary for dancers in ballet or modern productions under the National Dance Basic Agreement was $693. The minimum rate for dancers in theatrical motion pictures was $500 per day of filming. Employment is often irregular, which lowers average yearly income.

Choreographers' rates vary widely. Choreographers of Broadway productions earn more than $30,000 in fees and performance royalties for an 8- to 10-week rehearsal period, as compared with about $1,000 a week in small professional theaters. In television, choreographers make from $8,000 to $12,500 for up to 14 work days; in high-budget movies, they make $3,400 for a 5-day week.

THE JOB AND THE WORK ENVIRONMENT

The language of dance is the human body; its vocabulary is movement. Very few occupations, including those in professional sports, require as rigorous and single-minded a concentration on physical conditioning as does dance. When the body is the medium of the art form, there are no substitutes for native talent, superior training, and innate creativity.

Some dancers decide rather quickly where they will specialize and then concentrate on that form. Classical ballet usually demands such a commitment at an early age. Such dancers begin their training early. They work on only the techniques and styles appropriate to classical ballet and confine their careers to dancing in ballet companies.

Modern dance, a style that began development in the 1920s and 1930s, has a movement vocabulary freer than that of the classical ballet and allowing for more self-expression. Modern dance companies, often headed by one or two outstanding dancer-choreographers, are largely confined to major urban areas. In recent years, the line between classical ballet and modern dance has become blurred, with dancers trained in one style now making appearances with companies of the other form. Some professional dancers and choreographers deplore this trend as a lessening of the purity of each form, but audiences, for the most part, heavily favor it.

Dance also is used in other performance media—opera, musical theater, film, and television. To take advantage of these many opportunities, dancers need to master a variety of styles and be at home with all kinds of music, from delicate baroque sarabands to driving rock ensembles. The same is true for choreographers, as they must create dances for all types of media and music styles.

The life is strenuous. Rehearsal and practice require daily work, including weekends and holidays, and performances usually mean late hours. Dancers begin their careers early; and in the main, they finish them early. Many dancers in their late thirties transfer to related occupations, such as choreographer, dance teacher, or dance therapy teacher, or to other professions altogether. Employment opportunities usually are confined to major urban areas, with many of the major U.S. dance companies situated in New York City.

TRAINING AND QUALIFICATIONS

The first requirement is talent and the correct kind of body. Dancers' body height and weight should not vary much from the average, although most dancers are slender. Feet and normal arches are necessary, as are physical strength and endurance. Students begin training young, and talented teenagers go into advanced professional training in regional ballet schools or schools conducted under the auspices of a major company. The first professional auditions usually take place by age 17 or 18. Preparation for modern dance is similar to but generally does not take as long as that for ballet.

Because dance training begins at such a young age and is so intense, dancers' formal education may be minimal. A broad general education, however, is very desirable, not only for help in interpreting dance roles, but also for a postdancing career. Courses in music, literature, history, and the visual arts are recommended. Many colleges and universities offer bachelor's programs or higher degrees in dance, generally through departments of physical education, music, theater, or fine arts. A college degree is essential for college/university or elementary/high school teaching but unnecessary for teaching dance in a studio, where performance experience is more important than formal education.

With respect to their education, dancers are often between a rock and a hard place. Ballet dancers who postpone entering their careers until they obtain a degree may find themselves at a disadvantage in competing with younger dancers for openings in a company. On the other hand, a degree can be a big asset when one's performing career is over, usually at a relatively early age, and one wishes to enter another field.

Advancement in this field comes with a growing reputation, leading to larger roles, steadier employment, and increased pay.

EARNINGS

Because most dancers are only irregularly employed, their earnings are low. Dancers in the major companies belong to the American Guild of Musical Artists, Inc. Those working in live or videotaped television shows or commercials belong to the American Federation of Television and Radio Artists, and those performing in films and TV belong to the Screen Actors Guild or the Screen Extras Guild. Those working in theater, primarily musical comedies, join the Actors' Equity Association. Unions and producers negotiate basic agreements specifying minimum salary rates, hours, and other conditions of employment. The individual contract a dancer signs with the producer of a show may be more favorable than the basic contract.

The minimum weekly salary for dancers in ballet and modern productions covered by the National Dance Basic Agreement was $693 for 1997 to 1998. First-year dancers under the union contract earned $543 weekly, according to the American Guild of Musical Artists. The minimum rate for dancers in theatrical motion pictures was $500 per day of filming.

Choreographers' rates vary according to the type and size of the production. Earnings in the form of fees and performance royalties range from $1,000 a week in small professional theaters to more than $30,000 for an 8- to 10-week rehearsal period for a Broadway show. Choreographers make $3,400 for a 5-day week on high-budget movies; for television, they make $8,000 to $12,500 for up to 14 work days.

PROSPECTS: JOB OUTLOOK

In 1996, an average of 23,000 jobs were held by professional dancers and choreographers at any one time. Through the year 2006, employment is expected to grow faster than the average for all occupations due to continued interest in this art form. Although the demand for trained and talented dancers is expected to remain strong, competition for jobs will be fierce; only the most talented will find regular employment. In addition, reductions in funds for the National Endowment for the Arts and similar organizations could dampen prospects in this field. The best opportunities are expected to be with national dance companies.

Opera companies also provide some employment openings. Television offers many different kinds of dance opportunities, but the competition is keen, too. The continuing popularity of music videos also will provide some choreography opportunities for highly creative people. Most job openings will occur due to retirement or to dancers and choreographers leaving the field for other reasons.

WHERE TO LOOK FOR FURTHER INFORMATION

To learn about all aspects of dance, including job listings:

American Dance Guild
31 West 21st Street
3rd Floor
New York, NY 10018

To learn about dance courses in colleges and universities:

National Dance Association
1900 Association Drive
Reston, VA 22091

To learn about wages and working conditions in classical ballet and modern dance:

American Guild of Musical Artists
1727 Broadway
New York, NY 10019

To learn about the field of dance therapy:

American Dance Therapy Association
200 Century Plaza
Suite 108
Columbia, MD 21044

For a directory of dance companies and related organizations:

Dance/USA
777 14th Street, NW
Suite 540
Washington, DC 20005

EDITORS—BOOKS AND MAGAZINES

OCCUPATIONAL OVERVIEW

Job Description: *Book editors* are primarily responsible for planning the line of books their company will publish and acquiring the authors to write them.

Magazine editors are responsible for planning the contents of their publications. In both cases, editors often are asked to do some writing and almost certainly some rewriting.

Prospects: Employment for editors, especially in magazines, is expected to grow faster than the average for all occupations through the year 2006.

Qualifications: Generally, a college degree is required. Often a liberal arts major is sufficient, but some specialized publishers may look for a degree in the company's area of specialization.

Personal Skills: Research skills and good judgment in evaluating projects and manuscripts are important for editors. Curiosity, a wide range of knowledge, and self-motivation are also valuable. Excellent writing skills are a must.

Earnings: Publishing salaries are on the low side, especially for entry-level positions. Magazine editors generally earn more than book editors. According to a 1997 salary survey by *Folio* magazine, the average salary of editors/executive editors was about $50,000, with business publications paying an average of $52,000 and consumer publications $48,000. A 1997 salary survey by *Publishers Weekly,* found that the average salaries for book editors include: editorial assistant, $22,336; associate editor, $35,188; editor, $47,838, and senior/managing editor, $63,555.

THE JOB AND THE WORK ENVIRONMENT

Publishing has been called the accidental profession because few individuals plan to become an editor; they fall into some slot in the field while in pursuit of another career—as a writer, perhaps. The truth is that publishing provides satisfying full-time and freelance employment to a diversity of creative people.

Book editors negotiate contracts with authors. They must evaluate the salability of a proposed book, create an acceptable budget for the project, and monitor costs to stay within the approved budget. They may participate intensively in the manuscript revision and book production processes, ensuring the book is correct in form and content.

Magazine editors perform much the same function. They decide what topics will appeal to their magazine's readership, assign topics to writers, and work with production people to make the layout of the publication appealing.

Editors generally must have a wide range of interests because they are likely to be involved with books or articles that cover a broad spectrum of topics. Some editors concentrate on a single area of technical or professional interest (medicine, engineering, data processing, electronics), but even they must be generalists rather than specialists. Editors also must have a strong business sense because they are responsible for setting and staying within the budget for each project. Most editors use personal computers; many use desktop or electronic publishing systems.

For the most part, editors work in offices and put in a normal 35- to 40-hour week. During deadline periods, however, overtime and work on weekends may be necessary.

TRAINING AND QUALIFICATIONS

Generally, editors must have at least a liberal arts degree, usually in English or journalism and less commonly in a specific discipline, such as business, engineering, economics, or history. Many larger publishers have in-house training courses in editing for new hires out of college. The majority of learning in publishing is still on-the-job training, however. Some colleges (notably, Stanford) have formal programs in publishing, ranging from three-day seminars to for-credit courses. Other colleges and universities offer professional courses to those already working in the industry to help them advance in their careers. Many of these concentrate on the technical and business aspects of the industry. For this reason, such courses can prove most useful to those planning a career in editing or writing.

Experience is more important in publishing than educational credentials. It can be gained by working on a college newspaper, yearbook, literary magazine, or other publication. For work in educational publishing, a background in teaching is invaluable.

EARNINGS

Definitely not the fast track, publishing offers many creative challenges but relatively limited lucrative rewards. Earnings vary with the type and size of publisher, experience, and geographic location. Magazines generally pay better than books, technical materials better than general interest areas. Editors also earn more as they advance into senior and management positions.

According to a 1997 salary survey by *Folio* magazine, the average salary of editors/executive editors was about $50,000, with business publications paying an average of $52,000 and consumer publications $48,000.

Book editor salaries vary widely depending on the type and size of publisher (ranging from large commercial houses to small literary presses), geographic location, and the experience and level of responsibility of the editor. A 1997 salary survey by *Publishers Weekly* reported the following average salaries for various types of editors: editorial assistant, $22,336; associate editor, $35,188; editor, $47,838; and senior/managing editor, $63,555.

PROSPECTS: JOB OUTLOOK

Communications is big business, and jobs for editors are expected to increase faster than the average for all occupations through the year 2006.

Competition, however, will continue to be keen as many liberal arts, journalism, and English majors look for entry-level jobs. Opportunities will be best in the business and trade publications areas and in technical publications. Jobs with major book and magazine publishers are concentrated in New York, Chicago, Los Angeles, Boston, San Francisco, Philadelphia, and Washington, DC.

WHERE TO LOOK FOR FURTHER INFORMATION

To learn more about careers in editing:

American Society of Magazine Editors
919 3rd Street
New York, NY 10022

Association of American Publishers
71 5th Avenue
New York, NY 10003-3004

GRAPHIC ARTISTS

OCCUPATIONAL OVERVIEW

Job Description: Graphic artists conceive and produce illustrations and designs for a wide variety of clients. They work in print, film, and electronic media. Whether self-employed or on payroll, most graphic artists work in advertising or publishing; others work for large corporations, the movie and television industries, or large retail stores.

Prospects: Through the year 2006, jobs for graphic artists are expected to increase faster than the average for all occupations. However, computers are creating major changes in this field, including the elimination and redefinition of certain jobs.

Qualifications: Most graphic artists learn their trade by a combination of on-the-job experience and formal coursework offered by a number of art institutes and schools. Computers are now widely used in graphic design and will be used increasingly to produce finished art. Formal training in the use of computers is, therefore, becoming essential in this field.

Personal Skills: Graphic artists need artistic ability, creativity, and a knowledge of techniques for rendering reproducible art in various media. Determination and dependability are essential in this highly competitive career.

Earnings: In 1996, the median income for salaried visual artists working full time was about $27,100. Beginning graphic designers earned between $23,000 and $27,000 in 1997, according to estimates by the Society of Publication Designers.

THE JOB AND THE WORK ENVIRONMENT

Almost everywhere we look, visual images are competing for our attention, entertaining or informing us, or trying to persuade. In contrast to fine artists, who are concerned chiefly with self-expression and with self-determined artistic goals, graphic artists employ their skill and talent for a client.

Graphic designers design the logos, packaging, and promotional material that give companies and their products a distinctive identity. Some work as Webmasters, creating and maintaining a company's Internet home page. *Illustrators* paint or draw the pictures reproduced in books, magazines, and films, as well as on paper products such as calendars and greeting cards. Although some work in a number of related areas, many specialize. *Editorial artists* create illustrations for magazine articles, album covers, and powers. *Medical* and *scientific illustrators,* who render sophisticated, accurate representations for textbooks, journals, and slide presentations, must have formal training in the biological and physical sciences. *Fashion illustrators* represent women's, men's, and children's fashions in a stylish manner.

Illustrators may also help plan television advertisements and movies by creating story boards, which break down scenes into sequences of individual drawings, guiding the choice of camera angles and placement of actors.

Cartoonists create humorous or exaggerated illustrations for books, magazines, and newspapers (including political cartoons and comic strips). *Animators* draw the large number of pictures that are run in sequence to create the animated cartoons in movies and television.

A typical project for a graphic artist who works for an advertising firm begins with a conference with the client for a clear sense of the point to be communicated and the image desired. Design specifications are drawn up, and the designer, working either on a computer or with a paste-up artist, produces a layout for the client's approval. The process usually requires several layouts to incorporate changes in typeface, color, composition, or contents. Finally, camera-ready copy (a finished piece of copy prepared for reproduction) or film is made. Increasingly, versatile computers and software are being used to perform these functions with greater speed and flexibility. A graphics software program can duplicate a design, switch the positions of elements (type, illustrations, etc.) within it, enlarge or reduce it, and change colors or even mimic media without requiring a new layout each time. Computers are also used by graphic artists who design typefaces.

Graphic artists who are salaried and on staff generally work in spacious but hectic and often noisy studios. In publishing, they are likely to work in an office. More than 60 percent of graphic artists work as freelancers. For those on salary, the workweek is usually standard, though overtime may be necessary to meet deadlines. Freelancers' hours are more flexible, but freelancers must spend a good part of their time, especially at the beginning of their careers, looking for clients and work.

TRAINING AND QUALIFICATIONS

Training of graphic artists varies. Usually a graphic artist who has completed a four-year postsecondary art school program is best prepared for a career in commercial art. A bachelor's degree in fine arts is less relevant to this field. Some art schools offer a two-year associate's degree, and more and more art schools and graphic arts institutes are offering varied and comprehensive programs and training in computer graphics; some even offer postgraduate degrees in the field. For those who want to work in specialized areas, such as technical or medical illustrating, formal training in the sciences is a corequisite.

In addition to formal training and job experience, a graphic artist must develop a portfolio containing samples of his or her work in a range of styles and media.

Artists in graphic design studios and advertising agencies begin with relatively routine work but move on to more creative responsibilities as they improve their skills. The most talented may advance to art director, becoming responsible for all the visual aspects of the books, publications, or other products being created. Others may become skillful enough to set up their own business and work on a freelance basis. Those most confident in their ability often begin as freelance graphic artists directly out of art school.

EARNINGS

In 1996, the income of salaried visual artists (including graphic and fine artists) who worked full time varied considerably, with median earnings of about $27,100 a year. The top 10 percent earned more than $43,000; the bottom 10 percent, less than $15,000; and the middle 50 percent earned between $20,000 and $36,400 annually. Beginning graphic designers earned between $23,000 and $27,000 a year in 1997, according to the Society of Publication Designers. Staff designers who become art directors or production supervisors earn significantly more. Earnings are higher for specialists known for the quality of their work (e.g., in medical or technical illustration). Work in this field tends to be cyclical: Busy years and good money can be followed by slow periods and a drop in income. This is especially true of freelancers. And, of course, freelancers do not receive fringe benefits, such as paid sick days and holidays, health insurance, or pension benefits.

PROSPECTS: JOB OUTLOOK

In 1996, there were 276,000 jobs in the visual arts, including the graphic arts. Through the year 2006, jobs in this field are expected to grow faster than the average for all occupations. Advertising agencies and graphic arts studios, in particular, will be seeking talented workers to help meet increasing demands from many sectors of the economy to create visual appeal in selling their products. The growth of the Internet will likely provide many opportunities. Competition will be stiff, however, for both salaried positions and freelance work, and increased computerization will give a decisive edge to those with training in computer graphics.

WHERE TO LOOK FOR FURTHER INFORMATION

For information on graphic arts careers in publishing:

Society of Publication Designers
60 East 42nd Street
Suite 721
New York, NY 10165-1416

For information on careers in illustration:

Society of Illustrators
128 East 63d Street
New York, NY 10021–7392

For a list of schools offering graphic design programs:

American Institute of Graphic Arts
164 5th Avenue
New York, NY 10010

MUSICIANS

OCCUPATIONAL OVERVIEW

Job Description: Musicians play musical instruments; sing, write, or arrange musical compositions; or conduct instrumental or vocal performances. They often specialize in classical or popular music, though the distinction between the two is not always firm. They may perform as soloists or as part of a group, and may appear on stage, in concert halls, or on radio, television, and film.

Prospects: Employment prospects are expected to grow faster than the average for all occupations through the year 2006. The large number of people desiring to be professional musicians makes competition for available jobs especially keen. Only the most talented have a chance of finding regular employment.

Qualifications: Musicians need extensive and prolonged training to acquire the necessary skill, knowledge, and ability to interpret music. Sources of this training include private study, college and university programs, and music conservatories.

Personal Skills: Innate musical talent is essential. Also important are creative ability, poise, and stage presence.

Earnings: Musicians' earnings vary widely, depending on the artist's reputation and area of specialty. In 1996 to 1997, minimum salaries in major orchestras ranged between about $22,000 and $90,000 per year. Soloists generally negotiate fees with managers and producers, as do pop and rock groups.

THE JOB AND THE WORK ENVIRONMENT

Music is probably the most pervasive art form; practically everyone makes music, if only in whistling or singing in the shower. The chances of becoming a professional musician are very slight, the training is long and arduous, and the demands are enormous; but the dream, for multitudes, is there.

Instrumentalists play a musical instrument in an orchestra, band, or smaller group. Classical instrumentalists play string, brass, woodwind, or percussion instruments. Pop musicians usually play brass, woodwind, or one of the rhythm instruments—piano, string bass, drums, guitar, or one of the many electronic synthesizers.

Singers, who interpret music using their voices, are classified according to their voice range (soprano, alto, tenor, baritone, or bass) or by the type of music they sing (e.g., opera, folk, rock, rap, or country and western). They may sing character parts, as in opera or the musical theater, or they may perform in their own individual styles.

Composers create original musical works, writing in varied forms—symphonies, sonatas, operas, stage musicals, jazz, or pop music. They write their works using musical notation and must be thoroughly familiar with the musical qualities of harmony, rhythm, melody, and tonal structure. In addition, they must know the special characteristics of each of the musical instruments for which they write, including the human voice. Many composers now create and edit their music using computers.

Orchestral conductors lead orchestras and bands. They audition and select musicians and direct rehearsals and performances. They are especially concerned with choosing and interpreting musical works. *Choral conductors* direct choirs and glee clubs and work with the choruses used in opera houses.

Musicians find the most opportunity for work in those cities where entertainment and recording activities are concentrated, including Los Angeles, New York, and Nashville. They find employment in the nation's many symphony orchestras, opera and ballet companies, and musical productions in the theater and films and on television. Organists play in churches and synagogues. (In fact, two out of three musicians who are paid a salary work for religious organizations.) Instrumentalists also give recitals in small chamber music groups, and singers give solo *lieder* recitals. Pop groups and musicians perform in stadiums, large theater auditoriums, nightclubs, cabarets, and restaurants. The military also offers careers in bands and other musical groups.

For the most part, musicians perform in the evenings and on weekends, with rehearsals and practice accounting for much of their work time in addition to performing. They are also likely to travel a good deal to fulfill engagements. Work is often irregular, and many musicians must supplement their professional income with other types of jobs.

TRAINING AND QUALIFICATIONS

In general, classical musicians begin studying an instrument while very young. Combined with this private study, they also participate in school bands or orchestras and in school plays or choirs. Professional musicians continue their training in conservatories or in college or university programs. They study with teachers who have an established reputation in the specialty they are pursuing. Training and practice are ongoing throughout a professional musician's career.

Pop musicians must have an innate feel for the kind of music they play, but classical training may help expand their employment opportunities. Although many successful pop singers have untrained voices, voice training can be an asset for them, too. Singing in school musicals, glee clubs, or choirs offers good experience. Singing techniques are quite different for those working, unmiked, in the classical repertoire, compared with those working in studios or in live musical comedies, where miking is essential or predominant.

Many colleges and music conservatories offer bachelor's and higher music degrees, as well as graduate degrees in music education that qualify graduates for a state certificate to teach music in elementary and secondary schools. A bachelor's or higher degree is also needed for college teaching.

Musicians must have self-discipline and physical stamina to maintain high-quality performances through grueling tours and periods of heavy bookings. They also must be ready for the anxiety that accompanies intermittent employment and rejections at auditions.

EARNINGS

The American Federation of Musicians reported that in 1997, the minimum salaries in major orchestras ranged from about $22,000 to $90,000 a year, with the performing season running from 29 to 52 weeks. Minimum salaries in regional orchestras ranged between $8,000 and $22,000 per year, with a season lasting from 7 to 48 weeks, and an average season of 35 weeks. Musicians working in movie or television recording and those employed by recording companies earned a minimum ranging from $120 to $250 per 3-hour session in 1996. Famous opera or pop singers and bands may command many thousands of dollars (or more) per performance. Many musicians, however, face long periods of unemployment, so they often will give private lessons or take nonmusic jobs to supplement their income.

PROSPECTS: JOB OUTLOOK

About 274,000 musicians had jobs in 1996. (Since many musicians are between jobs at a given time, the total number employed during the year could have been higher.) Through the year 2006, overall employment of musicians is expected to grow faster than the average for all occupations. The many metropolitan and regional symphony orchestras in the country attest to the growing popularity of classical music, as does the proliferation of ballet and modern dance companies and regional theater companies. All this growth, however, rests on a somewhat fragile base. When the economy takes a downturn, patronage of the arts does, too. Cutbacks in the past have resulted in the shortening of an opera or orchestra season to save money or the abandoning of plans for new works. Thus, an already insecure employment picture is made worse by its vulnerability to overall economic activity.

Nearly all new salaried jobs for musicians will arise in religious organizations, orchestras, bands, and other musical groups; a decline in jobs is expected for salaried musicians in bars and restaurants. Many job opportunities will occur to replace musicians who retire or otherwise leave the occupation. Competition for those slots will be fierce since there are bound to be more applicants than openings. Only the truly talented and dedicated will have a chance at making a successful career as a professional musician.

WHERE TO LOOK FOR FURTHER INFORMATION

To learn about wages and working conditions for musicians:

American Federation of Musicians of the United States and Canada
1501 Broadway
Suite 600
New York, NY 10036

To learn about wages and working conditions for singers:

American Guild of Musical Artists
1727 Broadway
New York, NY 10019

For a directory of accredited music teacher programs:

National Association of Schools of Music
11250 Roger Bacon Drive
Suite 21
Reston, VA 22091

To learn about certification of private music teachers:

Music Teachers National Association
441 Vine Street
Suite 505
Cincinnati, OH 45202-2814

To learn more about careers in orchestra management:

American Symphony Orchestra League
1156 15th Street, NW
Suite 800
Washington, DC 20005

*P*HOTOGRAPHERS

OCCUPATIONAL OVERVIEW

Job Description: Photographers use cameras to capture people, places, and events on film. The final products can be used as historical records, a means of communication, instruction media, or pieces of art significant in themselves.

Prospects: Job opportunities are expected to grow as fast as the average for all occupations through the year 2006. Competition for jobs and clients is intense, however.

Qualifications: Formal education is not especially important for a career as a photographer, except in technical, scientific, and industrial specialties and perhaps photojournalism. Skill in the use of camera techniques is the main requirement, and this can be learned through practical experience or in postsecondary courses.

Personal Skills: Good eyesight—a keen eye for what makes a striking image—and excellent color perception are essential. An aesthetic sense, creativity, patience, and manual dexterity for operating the photographic equipment are also required.

Earnings: Salaried photographers (including camera operators) in 1996, earned a median annual income of $30,600. About 4 out of 10 photographers are self-employed, though, and their earnings vary widely. Some earn more than salaried photographers; many do not.

THE JOB AND THE WORK ENVIRONMENT

Photographers have given our century a record of its political and social upheavals, natural disasters and technological achievements, the enduring responses to the challenges and joys of life, and the fads and celebrities of the moment. It would be hard to exaggerate how much the camera has taught us to see things.

Photographers work for many different kinds of employers, each interested in a specific type of photography. *Advertising* photography uses photos to sell products or services. The client (the company or its ad agency) maps out the ad and assigns the task of creating the visual to a photographer. Work in this field also includes promotional and publicity shots, which are portrait or action shots of celebrities used for promotion purposes.

Industrial or *corporate* photography uses photos in a variety of ways: in brochures, promotional literature, product catalogs, audiovisual programs, annual reports, and in-house publications. Clients may include corporations, government agencies, and educational and similar institutions.

Editorial photography and *photojournalism* use photos to help tell a story or illustrate a text. Newspapers, magazines, and book publishers hire photographers or contract with them on a fee basis to cover stories or to illustrate a piece of writing. Just about any subject in the world can be covered—current events, travel, food, history—anything that can be written about and illustrated.

Scientific photography uses photos to illustrate and document scientific publications, research reports, and textbooks; the photos and slides also may be used for educational purposes. Special photographic techniques used in this branch of photography include time-lapse photography, photomicrography (involving magnification of the subject) and photogrammetry (aerial photography).

Portrait photography includes taking pictures of individuals and groups of people (clubs, school classes, weddings). Many portrait photographers own studios and may hire and train staff to work in the business.

Photographers use a variety of equipment besides cameras. They must be knowledgeable about different kinds of film, filters, lighting equipment, and backdrops. Some photographers equip and operate a darkroom so they can develop film. Increasingly, photography involves the use of computers for scanning photos and transferring the images into digital form, manipulating them, and compiling images on compact disks (CDs).

Photographers work in settings ranging from their own studios to locations selected by their clients. Photojournalism can be dangerous, as, for example, when an assignment is on a natural disaster or a military conflict. The work is frequently stressful, and photographers are often under great pressure to meet deadlines and keep the project on budget.

TRAINING AND QUALIFICATIONS

Photography requires creativity as well as technical expertise. Formal education is less important than photographic training, although beginning jobs in photojournalism or technical, scientific, or industrial photography may well require a college degree in photography with courses in the field being photographed. Many colleges; universities; vocational-technical schools; junior colleges; and private, trade, and technical schools provide photographic training. Art schools offer valuable instruction in design and composition but often do not include the technical training necessary for professional photographers.

A new and growing area involves digitizing photographic data and using computers to print out photographic images. Once used primarily in scientific photography, this technique is becoming a valuable tool for creating images in many other fields, most notably special effects for advertising or educational purposes. This skill is likely to be important in the future.

Choosing a specific area of photography in which to specialize and working for a photographer, newspaper, or magazine are ways to gain entry into this field. On-the-job training may be the most important source of experience. People often begin their careers by working for two or three years as assistants in a commercial studio. They usually start in the darkroom, learning to mix chemicals, develop film, and doing photo printing and enlarging. Later, they may help a professional photographer set up lights and cameras and take pictures.

Some photography requires special knowledge. For instance, scientific work may require some knowledge of a discipline, such as biology, medicine, engineering, architecture, or physics. Most commercial photography demands creativity and imagination in thinking. Action photography requires excellent visual judgment and quickness in execution. In addition, photographers who own their own business need business skills as well as photographic talent. All photographers should be able to work on their own, as well as with others, since this occupation entails both kinds of situations.

EARNINGS

Most salaried photographers can be found in commercial or portrait photography studios; others work for magazines, newspapers, ad agencies, or government agencies. In 1996, the median annual income for salaried photographers (including camera operators) was $30,600, with the lowest earnings at less than $14,500 and the highest over $75,000.

About 4 out of 10 photographers are self-employed. Earnings for self-employed photographers depend on the number of hours they work, the type and size of their clientele, and the kind of work they do. Many license use of their photographs through stock photo agencies.

PROSPECTS: JOB OUTLOOK

Photography is highly competitive since there are more people who want to be photographers than there is work to support them; this is especially true in commercial photography and photojournalism. Only those photographers with the keenest skills and business sense, plus the best industry reputations, are able to find salaried positions or support themselves as freelancers.

In 1996, photographers and camera operators held about 154,000 jobs. Jobs for photographers are expected to grow as fast as the average for all occupations through the year 2006. The use of visuals in so many aspects of modern life—education, communication, entertainment, marketing, and research and development—is expected to spur the demand for experienced, creative photographers. In addition, many jobs will open up as people leave the field. Jobs also will be created in portrait studios as a result of increased demand from a larger and more affluent population and from the maturing of the baby boomers, who have become parents and want pictures of their children at various stages of life.

WHERE TO LOOK FOR FURTHER INFORMATION

To learn more about careers in photography and colleges offering courses or degrees in photography:

Professional Photographers of America, Inc.
57 Forsyth Street
Suite 1600
Atlanta, GA 30303

Advertising Photographers of America
7201 Melrose Avenue
Los Angeles, CA 90046

American Society of Media Photographers
14 Washington Road
Suite 502
Princeton Junction, NJ 08550-1033

RADIO AND TELEVISION ANNOUNCERS AND BROADCASTERS

OCCUPATIONAL OVERVIEW

Job Description: *Radio announcers* report the news, act as disk jockeys (DJs), do commercials, and perform other duties at the studio, depending on the size and nature of the station. *TV newscasters* and *announcers* deliver the station's news and events programming.

Prospects: The number of announcers' jobs is expected to decline slightly through the year 2006. The job is perceived as glamorous, and competition will be tough. Announcers with specialized knowledge may have an edge. Most openings will result from replacement needs.

Qualifications: Formal education, especially a college degree or training in a technical school, is helpful. More important is a good audition tape and, in television, one's appearance and presence on camera. Computer literacy is important since stories are written and edited on computer.

Personal Skills: A pleasant, well-controlled voice is essential. Also crucial are excellent diction and pronunciation and a good command of standard English usage. For television work, a relaxed, persuasive manner in front of the camera is vital. Good communication skills, including writing, are also important.

Earnings: The average annual salary for a radio news announcer in 1996 was $31,251. Averages for television news anchors, weathercasters, and sportscasters were $65,520, $52,562, and $48,704, respectively.

THE JOB AND THE WORK ENVIRONMENT

TV newscasters are glamorous figures. In the big network news programs, the anchor of the evening news is a household name, and announcers on radio seem like old friends to millions. The job of announcer or broadcaster is, in good part, show business, but it also involves journalism, marketing, and selling.

At small radio stations, the announcers double in brass as DJs announcing the recorded musical selections. They also give the news, weather, and sports; do the commercials; report on community activities; represent the station at promotional events, and interview local and national public figures. They may run the control board (often assisted by an engineer), sell commercial time to advertisers, and write commercial and news copy.

Announcers at large radio and television stations usually specialize in a particular area: sports, weather, general news, arts criticism (film, books, music, theater). They need expertise in the area and may have to research and write scripts.

Some newscasters become highly paid national figures. Large news programs use specialized on-camera personnel—anchorpersons, news reporters, and news analysts. The anchor (or coanchor) is responsible for presenting the day's important news stories, introducing videotaped news or live transmissions from on-the-scene reporters, and providing a wrap-up of the news presentation.

News analysts, called commentators, also present news stories, but with an emphasis on interpreting them or discussing how a specific event may affect the world, nation, region, or individual listeners. Smaller television stations may have only an anchor reading accounts of the day's events and introducing background visuals or reports supplied by a network or television news service.

Announcers and newscasters usually work out of a station's well-lit, temperature-controlled broadcast studio but sometimes travel to on-site breaking news locations or interviews. Because many radio and television stations are on the air 24 hours a day, beginning announcers generally are given the least desirable shifts—weekends, nights, and holidays. Working time includes both time on the air and preparation time. Announcers usually work a 40-hour week but at small stations, may work a fair amount of overtime. In the newsroom, life can be hectic, with split-second timing and last-minute changes the rule. The work is stressful and demanding, but the rewards of public recognition and personal satisfaction (working in a creative, high-profile industry) are always present.

TRAINING AND QUALIFICATIONS

A liberal arts degree is excellent preparation for a career as an announcer, and many universities offer courses of study in broadcasting and electronic journalism, as do private broadcasting schools. Students can gain valuable experience by working on the campus radio or at local stations. For those interested in newscasting, courses in journalism are particularly helpful, especially in the areas of interviewing and writing. Work on a college newspaper can provide experience in one of the newscasting areas, such as sports, general news, news analysis, or criticism.

Performance in school drama groups and participation in debate groups and student government can be useful. Announcers will almost certainly encounter situations where they will have to ad lib, and the ability to think on one's feet in front of a camera or mike is a major asset. Taking speech or elocution courses is also recommended, as the voice, even on television, is the announcer's major resource. Computer literacy is essential since stories are written and edited on computers.

Announcers usually get their first jobs at small stations, where pay is low but where the best opportunities exist for beginners. Experience is especially valuable in securing employment at one of the major stations or networks. Usually, a college degree and several years of experience are required before one of the big radio or television networks will grant a candidate an audition.

EARNINGS

Salaries vary widely. Television pays better than radio; major markets pay better than smaller ones; and commercial broadcasting is more lucrative than public broadcasting. A survey by the National Association of Broadcasters and the Broadcast Cable Financial Management Association found that the average salary for radio news announcers was $31,251 in 1996, with sportscasters' average salary at $43,646. In television, news anchors' average salary was $62,520; weathercasters' average was $52,562; and sportscasters' average was $48,704. In the network news programs, salaries can go into six and even seven figures.

PROSPECTS: JOB OUTLOOK

In 1996, there were about 52,000 jobs for radio and television announcers. Competition for starting jobs as announcers is expected to remain keen because broadcasting is a high-visibility profession that normally attracts many more job seekers than there are openings. Radio is a better bet than television for beginners because there are more radio than television stations. Many of them, however, are small, and the pay is low. Still, experience is a valuable commodity, and major stations and networks are always looking for highly skilled announcers and newscasters with proven success in attracting and keeping audiences. Competition in major metropolitan areas is fierce, but good people are needed.

Through the year 2006, employment of announcers is expected to decline slightly, with most openings arising from replacement needs. Special knowledge (e.g., in health, consumer, or business areas) may give an edge in this highly competitive field.

Employment in this occupation tends not to be significantly affected by downturns in the economy. If economic slowdowns and/or falling advertising revenues occur, stations are more likely to cut behind-the-scenes people, with on-camera and on-mike personnel largely unaffected.

WHERE TO LOOK FOR FURTHER INFORMATION

To learn more about the broadcasting industry in general:

National Association of Broadcasters
1771 North Street, NW
Washington, DC 20036

To learn more about careers in broadcast news:

Radio-Television News Directors Association
1000 Connecticut Avenue, NW
Suite 615
Washington, DC 20036-5302

To learn more about careers in the cable industry:

National Cable Television Association
1724 Massachusetts Avenue, NW
Washington, DC 20036

To obtain a list of schools offering programs in broadcasting:

Broadcast Education Association
1771 North Street, NW
Washington, DC 20036

REPORTERS AND CORRESPONDENTS

OCCUPATIONAL OVERVIEW

Job Description: Reporters and correspondents research and report on local, state, national, and international events and issues for newspapers, magazines, television, and radio. Seven out of 10 work for newspapers.

Prospects: Jobs for reporters and correspondents are expected to decline through the year 2006. The profession is highly competitive, especially for positions with one of the major newspapers or networks.

Qualifications: Most reporters and correspondents have four years of college with a major in journalism. Some editors look for people with a liberal arts bachelor's degree and a master's in journalism, though most editors are less interested in advanced degrees than they are in practical experience. Good writing skills and computer literacy are essential.

Personal Skills: Reporters and correspondents must be committed to accurate and impartial news and possess a natural curiosity—a nose for news—that motivates them to search out facts and get at the truth. They must be persistent, resourceful, and able to work well under pressure—at times under noisy, distracting, and even dangerous conditions.

Earnings: In 1996, the median minimum salary for newspaper reporters was about $448 a week; for those on the job after three to six years, the median minimum salary was about $742 a week. The 1996 median salary for radio reporters was $32,356 a year; for television reporters, $31,235.

THE JOB AND THE WORK ENVIRONMENT

Reporters and correspondents work in three media: print, radio, and television. By far, the majority work for newspapers or magazines. The work can be demanding. Though some reporters may work in private offices, many work in large newsrooms that are usually crowded and noisy, and a good journalist has to be able to produce copy on deadline despite the distractions. Generally, the workweek is 35 to 40 hours long, with compensation for overtime. Reporters for morning papers work from late afternoon to midnight; those on afternoon or evening papers are on the job from morning until late afternoon. Radio and television schedules are similarly divided to cover days and nights. Journalists in all media must be ready to cover events as and when they happen.

The work is not confined to an office. Many reporters work in the field, where conditions can be hazardous. Foreign correspondents often work under difficult and dangerous conditions, particularly when covering conflicts or on assignment in remote areas. To meet deadlines, they must work lopsided hours so that dispatches are on time despite different time zones.

The work of reporters and correspondents requires determination and the ability to remain objective under even extreme and provocative circumstances.

TRAINING AND QUALIFICATIONS

Most reporters and correspondents are graduates of a four-year college and hold a bachelor's degree in journalism. More than 410 colleges and universities offer this degree. The usual program consists of studies in the liberal arts, along with courses in basic reporting and copyediting, studies in mass media, and the history, ethics, and law of journalism. Students planning to go into broadcast journalism take courses in radio and television newscasting. Those who want careers in news media, such as online publications, must merge traditional journalism skills with new ones. Although some prospective reporters earn a bachelor's degree in one of the liberal arts and then a master's degree in journalism, the advanced degree does not necessarily give an applicant an edge in winning a job. However, if an applicant wants to report on a specific subject (e.g., economics), a bachelor's degree in that subject may make a difference. Many community and junior colleges also offer courses in journalism, with credits that may be transferable to a four-year program, but applicants without at least a bachelor's degree are at a disadvantage.

Though the principles of journalism can be learned in school, the craft can be learned only by practice. Experience can begin quite early, with work on high school and college newspapers and publications. Internships or summer or part-time jobs with news organizations are especially useful.

Computer skills are also essential for reporters and correspondents. In addition, knowledge of a foreign language is needed for some positions. Broadcast reporters should be comfortable on camera. All reporters should feel at ease with unfamiliar places, people, and situations.

Most journalists find their first jobs as part-time reporters for smaller newspapers and gain experience before advancing to larger newspapers, of which almost all require that applicants have at least several years' experience.

EARNINGS

The Newspaper Guild negotiates reporters' salaries with individual newspapers. In 1996, the median minimum salary for newspaper reporters was about $448 a week; for reporters on the job after three to six years, the median minimum salary was about $742 a week.

A 1996 survey by the National Association of Broadcasters found that the median annual salary for radio reporters was $32,356. The median annual salary for television reporters was $31,235.

PROSPECTS: JOB OUTLOOK

In 1996, reporters and correspondents held about 60,000 jobs. Employment is expected to decline through the year 2006, due to mergers and closures of newspapers and decreases in circulation and advertising profits. Competition for jobs with large newspapers, magazines, or major television and radio networks will continue to be stiff. The best opportunities for beginners will be with small town and suburban newspapers.

The major newspapers look for graduates of the better journalism programs who have solid work experience. Those who specialize in reporting on scientific and technological subjects are also in demand. Online magazines and newspapers, which are expected to continue to grow rapidly, will be a source of many new jobs. Most opportunities, however, will arise due to the heavy turnover in this demanding profession, which can be hectic and highly stressful. People with degrees in journalism can and often do leave the field to pursue careers in the related fields of advertising and public relations. Others extend their scope and take jobs in related careers in law, business, and public administration.

WHERE TO LOOK FOR FURTHER INFORMATION

For information on careers in journalism:

Association for Education in Journalism and Mass Communication
LeConte College, Room 121
University of South Carolina
Columbia, SC 29208-0251

For information on careers, scholarships, and internships in journalism:

The Dow Jones Newspaper Fund, Inc.
P.O. Box 300
Princeton, NJ 08543-0300

A list of schools with accredited programs in journalism is available by sending a stamped, self-addressed envelope to:

Accrediting Council on Education in Journalism and Mass Communications
University of Kansas School of Journalism
Stauffer-Flint Hall
Lawrence, KS 66045

For information on union wage rates for reporters:

The Newspaper Guild
Research and Information Department
8611 Second Avenue
Silver Spring, MD 20910

For a list of newspapers as well as schools and departments of journalism, see *Editor and Publisher International Year Book*, available in most public libraries.

TRANSLATORS AND INTERPRETERS

OCCUPATIONAL OVERVIEW

Job Description: Translators and interpreters take information printed or spoken in one language and re-create its sense—and perhaps more than simply its sense—in another language. They work in many different settings (governmental agencies, multinational corporations, publishing, the United Nations, and research institutions) and in most cases, are self-employed.

Prospects: The ever-increasing amount of scientific, technological, and cultural information promises a growing need for those able to facilitate international communications.

Qualifications: The American Translators Association (ATA) proposes knowledge of a source language "equivalent to at least 4 years of intensive and 10 years of sporadic study" and writing ability in the target language "equivalent to that of . . . educated native speakers." Translators of scientific and technical material should be familiar with the subject matter and terminology. ATA also has an accreditation program.

Personal Skills: Translators must be intellectually honest and disciplined. They must have excellent communication skills in a source language. Often they need stamina and an even temper to meet tight deadlines.

Earnings: Translators are generally very well paid, and this allows many to work only part time. Technical translators earn the best rates; some earn more than $60,000 a year. Those working in exotic foreign languages that are in great demand can earn into the six figures.

THE JOB AND THE WORK ENVIRONMENT

Translators work full or part time, on staff or self-employed, working on a project-by-project basis. In many positions, they may not be designated translators, but their skills as translators are an indispensable part of their work. As a result, translators can be found in many positions in a wide variety of fields.

The principal employers of many full-time translators are the U.S. government and its agencies and international organizations, such as the United Nations. Multinational corporations and their subsidiaries rely on translators and staff members with translating skills, as do large and small export and import firms. Pharmaceutical and chemical companies, computer and electronics firms, international engineering firms, and companies that buy and sell machinery require the services of technical translators. In these businesses, it is important to keep abreast of opportunities and competition in foreign markets and to translate manuals and specifications. As the world economy becomes increasingly interdependent, patent attorneys are important clients for translators. Other opportunities exist in the publishing industry, news media, and graduate schools and universities.

Generally found in large cities, translation agencies provide work in technical or commercial subjects for freelance translators.

Translators are often under pressure to meet demanding deadlines.

TRAINING AND QUALIFICATIONS

The chief qualification for translators is command of and facility in their native and acquired languages. In the native language, this means the ability to write clearly and effectively at the level of educated readers. A 1996 survey of its members by the ATA found that 44 percent of those responding had a master's degree, and 14 percent had a Ph.D.

Courses in an area of specialization (mathematics, science, literature, economics, finance) are needed for technical translation. These should be combined with writing courses in one's native language. For those who plan to become technical translators, preparation at the college level can lead to better opportunities and higher earnings.

Translators are accredited by the ATA. Examinations for accreditation are given in Arabic, Dutch, Finnish, French, German, Hungarian, Italian, Japanese, Polish, Portuguese, Russian, and Spanish. The Federal Bureau of Investigation, along with local, state, and federal courts, among others, also certify translators. Foreign governments and associations offer accreditation as well, including the courts of the Netherlands, Rome, and United Nations.

Most translators spend at least one year abroad learning their acquired language. In order to keep abreast of the field, the better translators continue their studies and attend advanced workshops throughout their careers.

EARNINGS

Translators are generally very well paid, allowing many to work only part time in this occupation. Of all translators, those dealing with technical subjects and the more exotic languages are the highest paid. Technical translators can earn more than $60,000 a year. Those working in an exotic foreign language that is much in demand can earn into the six figures. Salaried translators receive benefits depending on their position and employer. Work for self-employed translators may be irregular, and time between contracts usually is spent looking for the next job.

PROSPECTS: JOB OUTLOOK

In a world economy that is increasingly interdependent, the need for good translators should grow, and it will be felt in all areas—commerce, the arts, technology and science, and industry. The most lucrative opportunities probably will continue to be in technical translating. Research and development continues in translation technology, and advances may affect the amount of routine translation available. But technology is unlikely to displace skilled and qualified translators altogether. On the other hand, the world over, more people in business, finance, science, and technology are learning to speak, read, and write English as a second language. The long-term effects of this development on professional translators has yet to be assessed; however, it still will take a skilled translator to deliver a professionally completed project.

WHERE TO LOOK FOR FURTHER INFORMATION

For information on careers in translating, opportunities, earnings, and suggested programs of study:

American Translators Association
1800 Diagonal Road
Suite 220
Alexandria, VA 22314

AIR TRANSPORTATION

AIRCRAFT MECHANICS

OCCUPATIONAL OVERVIEW

Job Description: Most aircraft mechanics service aircraft for airlines. Some work for the federal government, some are general aviation mechanics, and some work for independent repair shops. Aircraft mechanics service and repair all aircraft systems and the body of the aircraft, as well as completing FAA-required inspections.

Prospects: Through the year 2006, employment opportunities for aircraft mechanics are expected to increase about as fast as the average for all occupations. Prospects will vary among different types of employers, with most openings arising from replacement needs.

Qualifications: Mechanics are certified by the Federal Aviation Administration (FAA) as airframe mechanics, powerplant mechanics, technicians (repairmen), or combination airframe-powerplant mechanics. To qualify for certification, candidates must possess at least a high school diploma or equivalent, have a specified amount of experience, and pass written and oral tests.

Personal Skills: High mechanical aptitude is essential, as is the ability to perform precision work thoroughly and carefully—and often under pressure. Agility and a certain amount of physical strength are also important.

Earnings: Beginning aircraft mechanics working for airlines earn from $18.00 an hour (at smaller, turbo-prop airlines) to $22.00 an hour (at major airlines). Estimated earnings for experienced mechanics range from $25.00 to $32.00 an hour.

THE JOB AND THE WORK ENVIRONMENT

Aircraft mechanics service the nation's fleet of commercial aircraft in accordance with the schedule of maintenance required by the FAA, ensuring passenger safety and comfort. The confidence of most travelers boarding airline flights day in and day out is a tribute to the efficiency and skill of these mechanics.

Planes are kept on a strict schedule of maintenance based on the number of hours flown, calendar days, cycles of operations, or a combination of all three. Mechanics specializing in maintenance inspect and service all systems of an aircraft (engines, electronic and hydraulic systems, instruments, landing gear, pressurized areas, door and hatch openings, etc.). They use sophisticated equipment, such as x-ray and magnetic inspection devices, to check for wear and cracks invisible to the naked eye. They also repair sheet-metal surfaces, measure the tension of control cables, and check for corrosion, distortion, or cracks in the fuselage, wings, and tail section. Ongoing technological changes have led to mechanics' spending more and more time working on electronic systems, including computerized controls.

Mechanics specializing in repair work troubleshoot problems brought to their attention by pilots. Repair work often is performed under trying conditions and great pressure to accomplish the job promptly so the plane can return to service and maintain flight schedules.

Mechanics may work on all kinds of aircraft—jets, propeller-driven planes, and helicopters—or they may specialize in one area of a particular kind of aircraft, such as the engine or the electrical or hydraulic system. The growing complexity of modern aircraft and the increasing sophistication of their operating systems make specialization particularly desirable as an efficiency measure in the large airports that service airline fleets. In smaller, independent repair shops and in airports servicing general aircraft, mechanics are more likely to work on different types of airplanes.

Maintenance and repair work is generally carried out in hangars or other indoor areas. When hangars are full or when minor repairs must be made quickly, mechanics may have to work outdoors at the terminal, occasionally in inclement weather. They frequently have to work in stooped or awkward positions and sometimes in precarious positions, such as on ladders or scaffolds. The great responsibility of maintaining safety standards while working under time pressures can be stressful, as can exposure to the vibration and noise involved when testing engines. Aircraft mechanics generally work a 40-hour week, in 8-hour shifts around the clock, with frequent overtime.

TRAINING AND QUALIFICATIONS

Training and experience are the crucial factors for this occupation. Most mechanics working on commercial aircraft are certified by the FAA as powerplant mechanic, airframe mechanic, or technician (also called repairman). *Powerplant mechanics* are authorized to work on engines and do limited work on propellers. _Airframe mechanics_ work on all parts of the aircraft except the instruments, powerplant, and propellers. _Technicians_ are confined to work on instruments and major work on propellers. Mechanics with both airframe and powerplant certification can work on any part of the plane, and those with an inspector's authorization can certify the inspection work of other mechanics. Uncertified mechanics are supervised by those who are certified.

The FAA requires at least 18 months of work experience for an airframe, powerplant, or technician certificate and 30 months with airframes and engines for a combined airframe-powerplant certificate. An inspector's authorization requires holding an airframe-powerplant certificate for at least three years. Most airlines require mechanics to have both a high school diploma and an airframe-powerplant certificate.

About 200 aircraft mechanic schools certified by the FAA are operating currently, offering 2-year to 30-month courses in preparation for the FAA examinations. For an FAA certificate, attendance at such schools may substitute for the work experience requirement, but the schools do not guarantee either a job or certification. In the past, many mechanics got their training in the armed forces, but this pool is drying up since the military now uses fewer mechanics and offers those in its employment more incentives to stay in the service. Furthermore, the FAA currently requires broader experience than military jobs generally entail, so most mechanics trained in the armed forces must still complete a trade school program. Trade school graduates who do have military experience have an edge.

As more sophisticated aircraft are being produced, employers are requiring mechanics to enroll in ongoing training. A solid background in electronics is needed to get and then retain a job in this occupation. New certification requirements by the FAA make continuing training mandatory. Mechanics can take training offered by manufacturers or their employers (generally through independent contractors).

With experience, a mechanic can advance to crew chief, inspector, or shop supervisor. Given broad overhaul and maintenance background, a mechanic may become an FAA inspector.

EARNINGS

The median annual salary of aircraft mechanics was about $35,000 in 1996. For beginning aircrafts mechanics, the average hourly pay ranged from $18.00 an hour (at smaller turbo-prop airlines) to $22.00 per hour (at major airlines); experienced mechanics earned from $25.00 an hour to $32.00 an hour.

About half of all aircraft mechanics, including those at some major airlines, are covered by union contracts.

PROSPECTS: JOB OUTLOOK

Aircraft mechanics held about 137,000 jobs in 1996. Through the year 2006, job opportunities in this field are expected to increase about as fast as the average for all occupations. Prospects vary depending on the employer. Competition will be greatest with major airlines due to higher wages and travel benefits. The best opportunities likely are to be with small regional or commuter airlines, which have lower wages and, therefore, fewer applicants. As the armed forces are reduced, job openings with the federal government likely will decline. Job applicants with significant experience and who have kept up with technological advances will have an edge.

Overall, most openings will arise from replacement needs. The job remains vulnerable to economic conditions; any downturn can reduce the number of air travelers and, therefore, the number of flights and mechanics needed.

WHERE TO LOOK FOR FURTHER INFORMATION

To learn more about the career of aircraft mechanic:

Aviation Maintenance Foundation
  International
P.O. Box 2826
Redmond, WA 98073

International Association of Machinists and
  Aerospace Workers
9000 Machinists Place
Upper Marlboro, MD 20772

Professional Aviation Maintenance
  Association
1200 18th Street, NW
Suite 401
Washington, DC 20036-2598

To obtain the addresses of airline companies and information on salaries and job opportunities:

Federal Aviation Administration
800 Independence Avenue, SW
Washington, DC 20591

AIRCRAFT PILOTS

OCCUPATIONAL OVERVIEW

Job Description: Aircraft pilots fly a variety of airplanes and helicopters to accomplish many different tasks, such as transporting passengers, carrying cargo and mail, crop dusting, traffic monitoring, and aerial photography. The majority of commercial aircraft pilots work in the airline industry.

Prospects: Through the year 2006, job opportunities for pilots are expected to grow about as fast as the average for all occupations. The best prospects should be for pilots who have flown the most hours in the more sophisticated planes, with regional airlines and international service segments expected to grow faster than other areas.

Qualifications: All pilots must be licensed by the Federal Aviation Administration (FAA). To fly passengers or cargo, pilots must have a commercial pilot's license in addition to a pilot's license. Helicopter pilots must have a commercial pilot's license with a helicopter rating. Other requirements are necessary for airline pilots.

Personal Skills: Airline pilots must meet strict health requirements and take frequent medical examinations to ensure compliance. Physical dexterity and mental alertness are essential. The ability to function under great stress and responsibility is crucial.

Earnings: According to figures from the Future Aviation Professionals of America (FAPA), the 1996 average starting salary for airline pilots ranged from about $15,000 (at smaller turbo-prop airlines) to $26,290 (at the major airlines). Average earnings for those with six years' experience ranged from $28,100 (turbo-prop airlines) to $76,800 (largest major airlines). Salaries of $200,000 a year were earned by some senior captains on the largest airlines. Pilots working outside the airlines earn less; pilots who fly nonjet aircraft usually earn less than those who fly jets.

THE JOB AND THE WORK ENVIRONMENT

Pilots have exciting jobs and great pay. On commercial airlines, all but the smallest planes require two pilots in the cockpit; larger airliners sometimes have three. All three positions—captain, first officer, and second officer—require FAA and medical certification.

The *captain* is responsible for the entire flight: passengers, crew, cargo, and aircraft. The captain is senior in command and supervises all other crew members.

The *first officer (copilot)* assists the captain in operating the aircraft, handling communications with the ground, and monitoring the craft's instruments. In airlines flying only two-pilot aircraft, the first officer is the starting position for new pilots.

The *second officer (flight engineer)* assists in operating the flight, checks the craft's mechanical and electronic devices, makes minor inflight repairs, and watches for other planes. Second officers do not fly the aircraft but are required to have a valid pilot's license. New technologies, however, are taking over many of the second officer's tasks, and nearly all new aircraft fly with only a two-man crew. The job of flight engineer will be eliminated in the future.

Airline pilots' duties begin on the ground, where they check the plane before takeoff, request information on expected weather conditions, and file flight plans. Takeoffs and landings are the most difficult and dangerous part of flying, requiring alertness and quick response. The actual flight itself, except in bad weather, is relatively routine and requires little physical activity. In low visibility, pilots must rely on instrument flying. After the flight, pilots are responsible for filing records of the trip with their company and the FAA.

Airline pilots are forbidden by law to fly more than 100 hours a month or 1,000 hours a year. The average is 75 hours a month flying and 75 hours fulfilling other duties. Half of all pilots work more than 40 hours a week. Most flights involve layovers away from home, and as flights occur at all times, pilots' schedules are erratic. Seniority determines flight assignments.

Pilots not employed by airlines also have irregular schedules. They may fly 30 hours one month and 90 the next, according to the needs of clients or employers. They also generally have more nonflying duties (e.g., supervising refueling and loading the plane) and thus less free time than airline pilots. Helicopter pilots working for the police or fire departments or other emergency services face especially dangerous conditions. Some pilots are instructors, teaching students at flight schools or serving as "check pilots" to test pilots' license applicants for proficiency. Others work for federal, state, or local governments, or large businesses.

Stresses include the mental demands of being responsible for a safe flight under any conditions and the jet lag affecting pilots who fly long hours across time zones.

TRAINING AND QUALIFICATIONS

Applicants for a commercial pilot's license must be at least 18 years old and have 250 hours or more flying experience. They must pass a strict physical examination, showing that they have 20/20 vision with or without glasses, good hearing, and no physical disabilities that could impair performance. Applicants must pass a written test covering material on principles of safe flight, navigation, and FAA regulations, and they must demonstrate their flying skills to FAA or designated examiners.

To fly in bad weather, pilots must have an FAA rating for instrument flying. Airline flight engineers must pass FAA written and flight tests for a license. Captains and first officers must have an airline transport pilot's license, which requires applicants to be 23 years old and have 1,500 hours of flying experience, including night and instrument flying. In addition, they may be given psychological and aptitude tests to determine their ability to make quick, accurate decisions under pressure. All licenses are valid as long as a pilot can pass the periodic physical and flight tests required by the government and company regulations.

Traditionally, the armed forces have been an invaluable source of trained pilots for civilian employment. Their extensive experience make them preferred candidates. Training also can be pursued at any of the approximately 600 FAA-certified flight schools. With federal budget reductions projected to decrease military pilot training, FAA-certified flight schools will train a larger percentage of pilots in the future.

Most airlines require applicants to have finished two years of college but prefer to hire college graduates. High school graduates are accepted by some small carriers. Since most people now entering the occupation have a college diploma, employers may make this a requirement in the future.

New airline pilots begin as either first officers or flight engineers. Every new pilot is trained in classrooms and simulators before receiving a flight assignment. Advancement in the airlines normally follows the seniority provisions found in union contracts, with movement from flight engineer to first officer and then captain. For all pilots, advancement is usually to other flying jobs.

EARNINGS

The skies are friendly to airline pilots, whose earnings are among the highest in the United States. The FAPA reported that, in 1996, the average starting salary for airline pilots ranged from about $15,000 (at smaller turbo-prop airlines) to $26,290 (at larger major airlines). Average earnings for pilots with six years' experience ranged from $28,100 (turbo-prop airlines) to $76,800 (largest airlines). Pilots who work outside the airlines usually earn lower salaries; those who fly jets earn more than those who fly nonjet aircraft.

Airline pilots usually have insurance plans through the airlines, receive retirement benefits, and are entitled to per diem expenses for the time they are away from home. Pilots and immediate family members usually also receive free or discounted airfares from their own and other airlines.

PROSPECTS: JOB OUTLOOK

In 1996, civilian pilots held about 110,000 jobs, with 60 percent working for airlines. Through the year 2006, employment of pilots is expected to grow as fast as the average for all occupations. While passenger and cargo traffic is projected to grow, increasing the demand for pilots, computerized flight systems will eliminate the need for flight engineers, thus slowing pilot employment. Competition will continue to be keen as mergers during recent industry restructuring have created a pool of unemployed pilots. Reductions in military spending also have resulted in pilots leaving jobs in the armed forces. Pilots who have flown the greatest number of hours on sophisticated aircraft will have the best employment opportunities.

Growth will vary according to industry segments. Helicopter pilot jobs are expected to grow more rapidly, while demand for business pilots is likely to decrease as companies choose to fly with small and regional airlines instead of buying and operating their own private aircraft. Since regional airlines and international services are expected to grow faster than other industry segments, job prospects in these areas will be greater.

Finally, the airline industry will continue to experience bumpy times periodically, as it is vulnerable to economic swings. In downturns, when air travel slows, airlines will reduce the number of flights and may temporarily lay off some pilots.

WHERE TO LOOK FOR FURTHER INFORMATION

To learn more about the occupation of airline pilot:

Airline Pilots Association
1625 Massachusetts Avenue, NW
Washington, DC 20036

Air Transport Association of America
1301 Pennsylvania Avenue, NW
Suite 1100
Washington, DC 20004-7017

For information about job opportunities and qualifications at a particular airline, write to that airline's personnel manager. For addresses of airlines and job information:

Future Aviation Professionals of America
4959 Massachusetts Boulevard
Atlanta, GA 30337

To receive a copy of *List of Certified Pilot Schools:*

Superintendent of Documents
U.S. Government Printing Office
Washington, DC 20402

*A*IR TRAFFIC CONTROLLERS

OCCUPATIONAL OVERVIEW

Job Description: Air traffic controllers use radar, radio communications, and visual observation to monitor aircraft and provide flight crews with the information they need to take off and land safely. They also monitor and guide aircraft during their flight. They work in towers and control centers at airports and in other locations around the country.

Prospects: Through the year 2006, employment of controllers is projected to show little or no change, so competition is expected to remain keen. Job growth is not expected to keep pace with overall growth in the airline industry due to the introduction of a new air traffic control system, with more sophisticated computer equipment, over the next decade.

Qualifications: Three years of work experience, four years of college, or a combination, are generally required to become an air traffic controller trainee. Candidates must pass a civil service examination. For airport tower or enroute center posts, applicants must be under 31 years of age and pass physical, aptitude, and psychological examinations.

Personal Skills: The successful controller is able to absorb and interpret information quickly and give clear instructions or commands. Air traffic controllers must be able to perform under extreme stress.

Earnings: Salaries for air traffic controllers vary with responsibilities and the complexity of the airport or station. Air traffic controllers starting with the Federal Aviation Administration (FAA) in 1997 earned approximately $29,500 a year. They receive good benefits, including eligibility for retirement earlier than other federal employees.

THE JOB AND THE WORK ENVIRONMENT

The two most critical operations for aircraft are taking off and landing. Air traffic controllers are the ground-based navigators who guide aircraft arriving at and departing from civilian and military airports all over the country. Through a nationwide network of enroute centers, they also guide aircraft through the often crowded airways between their points of departure and destinations.

The primary concern of air traffic controllers is safety. They keep track of the weather, as well as the altitude, speed, and flight path of an aircraft and its relation to all other aircraft in its vicinity. Using radar, the controller gives the flight crew information about flight conditions, instructions they need to keep a safe distance from nearby aircraft, and warnings of bad weather. When necessary, controllers assign an aircraft a holding pattern and then prepare it for landing by indicating the approach and runway to use. Controllers also keep an orderly and regular flow of traffic so that planes take off and land on schedule.

At airport towers, where controllers are responsible for guiding planes into and out of the airport and its surrounding airspace, the work is done in stages by several controllers. A controller in the radar room beneath the tower either guides a plane directly to a runway or turns it over to a controller in the tower if the airport is busy. The tower controller, working with radar, puts the plane in a holding pattern until a runway is available. Once the plane has landed, a ground controller has it in sight and directs it to its assigned gate. When a plane takes off, the ground controller guides it to the runway; the local controller clears it for takeoff; and the departure controller guides it to the edge of the airport's airspace.

The air traffic control system is a kind of relay with 21 enroute control centers located around the country. When an aircraft leaves the airspace of the airport, it is passed from one enroute control station to another throughout its flight until it is picked up by the airport tower at its final destination. Enroute controllers work in teams of up to three members keeping the pilot informed of weather conditions and the location of other aircraft. The radar controller watches for potential hazards and approves course corrections or adjustments, such as a change in altitude to avoid bad weather.

Both enroute and airport tower controllers usually monitor and guide several planes at once. The larger and busier the airport and the more complex its traffic patterns, the more stressful and demanding the job. At any moment a controller may be guiding one plane to its landing and radioing airport conditions to other aircraft just entering the airport's airspace. At the same time, the controller is watching other aircraft in the vicinity and keeping them at safe distances from one another. The FAA is now creating and implementing a new automated air traffic control system with more powerful computers that will aid controllers in handling increased air traffic duties.

Air traffic controllers may also work at one of more than 100 flight service stations around the country that provide aircraft with information about weather, terrain, and suggested routes in and around a particular location.

Controllers work a 40-hour week; they may well put in overtime. Most airport control towers and enroute centers are run 24 hours a day, 7 days a week, and weekend and night-shift work is rotated.

TRAINING AND QUALIFICATIONS

Air traffic controllers are employees of the FAA and are selected through the federal civil service system selection process. Applicants must pass a written examination that tests, among other things, their aptitude for abstract reasoning and three-dimensional visualization. Candidates must have three years of work experience, four years of college, or a combination. They must be less than 31 years old for airport tower or enroute positions. Older applicants are eligible for work at flight service stations. All candidates have to pass physical examinations whose requirements include vision correctable to 20/20 and psychological examinations. Successful candidates also must pass drug screening tests.

Controllers must be able to give directions clearly and quickly. They must have intelligence and a good memory, be able to absorb and process information immediately, and have the capacity to concentrate and make quick decisions in the midst of distractions.

Successful applicants are trained on the job and in an intensive program that lasts seven months at the FAA Academy in Oklahoma City. Several more years of classwork and experience are required to qualify fully as an air traffic controller.

Every controller must pass an annual physical examination and a semiannual job performance examination, as well as submit to periodic drug screening.

Controllers can transfer to different locations or advance to supervisory jobs, including management positions in air traffic control and high-level administrative jobs with the FAA. Limited opportunities exist for transfers from enroute center to tower positions.

EARNINGS

Salaries vary, depending on job responsibilities and the complexity of the specific facility; busier facilities pay more. Air traffic controllers starting with the FAA in 1997 earned approximately $29,500 annually. In 1997, the FAA implemented a new pay classification system, with more grade levels and pay based on how many airplanes a controller monitors, increasing the base pay of controllers at some of the FAA's busiest facilities.

Controllers receive from 13 to 26 days of paid vacation, 13 days of paid sick leave per year, life insurance, and health benefits, and they can retire with a full pension at a younger age and with fewer years of service than other federal employees.

PROSPECTS: JOB OUTLOOK

In 1996, air traffic controllers held about 22,000 jobs. Competition for jobs will continue to be stiff since employment of air traffic controllers is projected to change little or not at all through the year 2006. Openings for controllers are not likely to keep pace with the growth of jobs in the rest of the airline industry due to low turnover (because of generous pay and retirement benefits), minimal retirements expected until at least 2006, and the introduction of a new, more sophisticated air traffic control system that will automate more controller tasks. Controllers who continue to meet the demanding standards of their profession can expect to be relatively secure in their positions.

WHERE TO LOOK FOR FURTHER INFORMATION

For information on a career as an air traffic controller:

National Association of Air Traffic
   Specialists (NAATS)
11303 Amherst Avenue
No. 4
Wheaton, MD 20902

National Air Traffic Controllers Association
1150 17th Street, NW
Washington, DC 20036

*F*LIGHT ATTENDANTS

OCCUPATIONAL OVERVIEW

Job Description: Flight attendants work on passenger aircraft and are responsible for the safety and comfort of passengers. They check safety equipment on board the aircraft before flights, serve meals and supply other amenities during flights, and submit logs on each flight. They are trained in emergency and first aid procedures.

Prospects: Through the year 2006, jobs for flight attendants are expected to grow faster than the average for all occupations as the number of airline passengers increases. Most jobs will arise from replacement needs. As always, the airlines' susceptibility to downturns in the economy may adversely affect job security.

Qualifications: A high school diploma or equivalent is the main academic requirement, but some college education is preferred. Applicants generally must be 19 to 21 years of age, have excellent health and good vision, meet height requirements, and be able to speak clearly. A foreign language is necessary for those who wish to work on international routes.

Personal Skills: Flight attendants enjoy working with people and have excellent social and communication skills. They tend to be outgoing, have a positive attitude, and are able to maintain poise and presence of mind under stress. Good grooming and the ability to work well in a team are also very important.

Earnings: According to the Association of Flight Attendants, beginning flight attendants had median earnings of about $12,800 a year in 1996; those with six years' experience had median yearly earnings of about $19,000; and some senior attendants earned $40,000 a year. Flight attendants get free or reduced-fare flights. Other benefits vary with the airline.

THE JOB AND THE WORK ENVIRONMENT

Looking after the safety and comfort of passengers means a combination of busy activity and public relations that requires a thorough knowledge of in-flight safety procedures. Flight attendants begin work before the flight with a briefing from the captain on the destination and flight path, expected weather conditions, and a list of passengers with special needs (e.g., infants or individuals with disabilities). Flight attendants must ensure that everything passengers might need is on board, including meals, beverages, blankets and pillows, reading materials, and headsets for movies. They also must confirm that safety gear is in working order. When these preliminaries are over, attendants are ready to greet passengers, check tickets, and assist with carry-on luggage and seating.

An important part of the flight attendant's job is to establish order and put passengers at ease by means of a set and familiar routine. This begins before takeoff, with directions to make all seats upright and fasten seat belts and demonstrating the use of oxygen masks and indicating the location of emergency exists and flotation devices. During the flight, attendants spend most of their time on their feet, offering reading materials, blankets and pillows, and other types of assistance to passengers, serving cocktails and other beverages, and preparing, serving, and busing meals. In the event of an emergency, flight attendants keep passengers calm and implement appropriate procedures. They may also provide first aid to passengers who become sick.

Most flight attendants put in 75 to 85 hours a month in the air and an equal amount of time on the ground preparing planes for flight, writing reports after completed flights, or waiting for late arrivals. Airlines operate around the clock, all year long, and the schedules are demanding. Beginning flight attendants with no seniority must be ready to report to work on short notice or none at all. But due to variations in scheduling and limits on flying time, many attendants have 11 or 12 days off each month.

The work includes a lot of opportunity for free or discount travel, but it has its difficult aspects. Short flights with meal service can be hectic. During rough flights, attendants must remain courteous and pleasant, no matter how tired they may be or how rude and unreasonable the passenger. They stand during much of a flight and are prone to back and other injuries as a result of job demands in a moving airplane.

TRAINING AND QUALIFICATIONS

Candidates must be high school graduates. Ideally, they should have taken courses in geography, sociology, psychology, and health science. Extracurricular activities such as public speaking, drama, modeling, or debating are helpful, as is participation in team sports. Candidates with several years of college or experience in working with the public will enjoy an edge. Since flight attendants are the face an airline shows to the public, personality and attitude weigh heavily in the selection of applicants.

To qualify for admission to a training program, most applicants must be 19 to 21 years old, meet height requirements, and have good vision and excellent overall health. Men and women are equally eligible. Some airlines have special qualifications. International carriers, for instance, look for candidates who can speak an appropriate foreign language (some prefer two).

Applicants accepted by an airline attend a flight attendants' training school for four to six weeks. The program has a dual purpose: it trains applicants to present the image an airline wants to project, and it trains them to cope with any situation. Training includes instruction in company policies, grooming and appearance, attitude and personality, first aid and safety procedures, and service. Those being trained for service on international routes also receive instruction on dealing with terrorism and passport and customs rules. The airline seeks not only to inculcate but also to maintain the standards set during training by means of testing and evaluation during the program and with retraining and testing throughout the flight attendant's career. Attendants receive 12 to 14 hours of training in emergency procedures and passenger relations every year.

EARNINGS

According to the Association of Flight Attendants, beginning flight attendants had median annual earnings of $12,800 in 1996; those with six years' flying experience had median earnings of $19,000; and some senior attendants earned $40,000 annually. Flight attendants are compensated for increased hours and night and international flights. While they are away from their home base, the airlines provide attendants with hotel rooms and meal allowances. Additionally, flight attendants and their immediate families are entitled to free airfare on their own airline and discounted fares on most other airlines.

PROSPECTS: JOB OUTLOOK

There were 132,000 flight attendants in 1996. Through the year 2006, employment of flight attendants is expected to grow faster than the average for all occupations, with most job openings arising from replacement needs. The outlook is favorable since the number of airline passengers is expected to increase with growing population and incomes. Because airlines meet rising demand by increasing the size and number of their planes—and the Federal Aviation Administration (FAA) requires one attendant for every 50 seats—more flight attendants will be needed. Those applicants with at least two years of college and some experience in dealing with the public will have an edge in being hired. The industry, however, is vulnerable to economic swings; in a downturn, flight attendants are put on part-time status or laid off until demand increases again.

WHERE TO LOOK FOR FURTHER INFORMATION

For individual airlines, write to the personnel department of the company. For information about being a flight attendant:

Association of Flight Attendants
1625 Massachusetts Avenue, NW
Washington, DC 20036

*T*RAVEL AGENTS

OCCUPATIONAL OVERVIEW

Job Description: Travel agents make travel arrangements and sell tickets for all kinds of transportation and other services travelers need. They may be employed by large firms or own their own businesses.

Prospects: Jobs for travel agents are expected to grow faster than the average for all occupations through the year 2006. Spending on business and leisure travel is expected to increase significantly in this period. Though the outlook is good, the industry is vulnerable to losses due to recession, a weakening currency, or political turmoil.

Qualifications: The minimum education requirement is a high school diploma or equivalent. A travel agent needs knowledge in many areas, including geography, history, and accounting. A foreign language is often valuable, as is some personal experience in traveling. Knowledge of computers is essential. Formal training is becoming more important.

Personal Skills: Above all, the successful travel agent must be able to communicate effectively with people from all walks of life. He or she should have excellent sales skills, enjoy doing multiple tasks, and be well organized and good with numbers.

Earnings: According to a survey conducted for *Travel Weekly,* 1996 median yearly earnings for agents on straight salaries ranged from an average of $16,400 for beginners to an average of $32,600 for agents with more than 10 years' experience. Earnings for all travel agents depend on commissions received by their companies.

THE JOB AND THE WORK ENVIRONMENT

Travel agents help their clients prepare for trips. Their services may be limited to finding a cut-rate airline fare, or they may include making hotel reservations, arranging car rentals, getting rail passes, or helping to organize an entire group tour, right down to meals and sightseeing itineraries. For international travel, agents advise clients on passports and visas, exchange rates, and vaccinations.

Travel agents rely heavily on computers to access information on schedules and fares. Computers are also equipped with directories and reference sources with the most up-to-date information on hotels. As agents gain experience in the business and through their own travels, they are better able to advise their clients about the services and facilities of hotels, resorts, and restaurants.

In the course of their work, travel agents fill several roles and combine various tasks. More and more, they must be pro-active salespeople to be successful. With some clients, they are close advisers; with others, only ticket agents. The job also entails some accounting and bookkeeping.

Travel agents work almost entirely at their desks. From time to time they may give slide shows or present movies to groups, assist in developing advertising displays, or meet with business clients planning company-sponsored trips. Some travel agents make it a point to visit some of the hotels and resorts whose services they sell. They are then in a better position to recommend a facility they think will best meet a client's needs.

The work tends to be seasonal, and busy agents often work under a great deal of pressure. Self-employed agents frequently put in long hours. At all times, the job requires working closely with people of every kind and description: support staff, colleagues, and clients.

TRAINING AND QUALIFICATIONS

Although some employers look for prospective agents with college degrees, the minimal requirement is a high school (or equivalent) diploma. Whether in high school, community college, or college, courses in geography, history, computer science, a foreign language, business management, and accounting are good preparation. With computerization's pervasive impact on the travel industry, specialized instruction is becoming more important. Basic training in the travel industry is available at many vocational schools, with the usual course lasting 6 to 12 weeks. Adult education programs, community colleges, and colleges also offer courses in the travel industry. Home study courses are available, and the American Society of Travel Agents conducts a correspondence course. Prospective travel agents can prepare in one of these programs or combine coursework with an entry-level job or internship to gain experience. In addition, many travel agencies train their own employees. Working as an airline ticket reservation agent is another avenue for breaking into the business.

Advanced study courses are also available to experienced agents through the Institute of Certified Travel Agents (ICTA), leading to the *Certified Travel Counselor* (CTC) designation. The ICTA also offers programs to develop sales skills and specialized knowledge of specific geographic areas.

Travel agents spend their workdays dealing with people. The job can be interesting and stimulating but also trying. An agent must enjoy working with people and be courteous and professional even with the most difficult clients. A successful career is built on the confidence of clients and other travel professionals. On the strength of these associations, some agents eventually go into business for themselves. Agents in business for themselves usually need the approval of a formal supplier or corporation (organizations of airlines, ship lines, or rail lines) before they can receive commissions.

Many sellers of travel are independent contractors, working out of their homes and assisting their own client base. Typically, an independent contractor works with a single agency as a source of brochures, tickets, and information. The earned commission is then split between the sponsoring agency and the independent contractor. This work arrangement is growing rapidly.

A federal license is not required for travel agents, but nine states require some kind of certification or registration: California, Florida, Hawaii, Illinois, Iowa, Ohio, Oregon, Rhode Island, and Washington.

EARNINGS

According to a survey conducted for *Travel Weekly* in 1996, travel agents on straight salary with less than 1 year of experience had median earnings of $16,400. With 3 to 5 years' experience, salaries averaged $22,300 a year; with 5 to 10 years' experience, $26,300; and with more than 10 years' experience, $32,600 a year. The better the agent is at selling travel services and earning commissions for the agency, the higher the agent's earnings. Salaried agents generally receive standard benefits. When agents travel for personal reasons, they usually receive discounted rates for accommodations and transportation.

Self-employed travel agents depend for their earnings on commissions from airlines and other carriers, hotels, tour operators, and other sectors of the travel industry. Commissions for domestic travel arrangements are about 7 to 10 percent and for international travel about 10 percent of the total sale. Agents may charge service fees for making more complicated arrangements and itineraries.

PROSPECTS: JOB OUTLOOK

There were more than 142,000 travel agents in 1996, and their numbers are growing. Employment is expected to grow faster than the average for all occupations through the year 2006.

Many factors are likely to contribute to an increase in business for travel agents. Spending on travel is expected to rise, with increased business travel, more leisure travel due to rising incomes, and a deregulated and expanding airline industry with more flights, scheduled and charter. Automated reservations systems have not weakened the demand for travel agents.

A number of factors could reduce future job opportunities. On-line computer systems and electronic ticketing machines now enable people to make their own arrangements. In addition, airlines are putting caps on commissions paid to travel agents. And, no matter how much it prospers, the travel business will remain seasonal and vulnerable to downturns in the economy.

WHERE TO LOOK FOR FURTHER INFORMATION

For information on training:

American Society of Travel Agents
1101 King Street
Alexandria, VA 22314

For information on certification:

Institute of Certified Travel Agents
148 Linden Street
P.O. Box 812059
Wellesley, MA 02181-0012

APPENDIX A

TRADE AND PROFESSIONAL JOURNALS

ACCOUNTING, BANKING, FINANCE, INSURANCE, AND MANAGEMENT

ABA Banking Journal
Accounting Review
Actuary
American Banker
American Economic Review
Bank Administration
Bank Marketing
Banker's Magazine
Banker's Monthly
Best's Review (Life/Health Insurance Edition)
Best's Review (Property/Casualty Insurance Edition)
Consultants News
CPA Journal
Financial Analysts Journal
Financial Management
Financial Planner Magazine
Fund Raising Management
Fund Raising Review
Independent Agent
Insurance Week
Internal Auditor

Investment Dealers' Digest
Journal of Accountancy
Journal of Economic Literature
Journal of Financial Planning
Journal of Management Consulting
National Underwriter (Life and Health Insurance Edition)
National Underwriter (Property/Casualty Edition)
Risk Management
Securities Week

SALES AND MARKETING

Advertising Age
Adweek
Adweek's Marketing Week
American Agent and Broker
Business Marketing
Direct Marketing
Journal of Property Management
Marketing and Media Decisions
Marketing News
National Real Estate Investor
O'Dwyer's PR Services Report
Public Relations Journal
Public Relations Quarterly
Public Relations Review
Real Estate Review
Real Estate Today
Sales and Marketing Management

APPLIED SCIENCE, ENGINEERING, ARCHITECTURE, AND COMPUTER SCIENCE

Aerospace
AIAA Journal (Aeronautics and Astronautics)
AIChE Journal (Chemical Engineering)
American Industrial Hygiene Association Journal
Architectural Record
Architecture
Automotive Engineering
Aviation Mechanics Journal
Aviation Week and Space Technology
Bulletin of the American Meteorological Society
Bulletin of the Society of Economic Geologists
Byte
Chemical Engineering
Chemical and Engineering News
Chemical Engineering Progress

Chemical Marketing Reporter
Chemical Week
Civil Engineering
Computer Decisions
Computer Industry Report
Computer Reseller News
Computer and Software News
Computer Systems News
Computers in Industry
Computers and Security
Computerworld
Datamation
Digital Review
Electronic Engineering
Engineering in Medicine
Engineering and Mining Journal
ENR (Engineering News Record)
Geological Society of America Bulletin
Ground Water
IBM Systems Journal
IEEE Communications Magazine
IEEE Computer Graphics and Applications
IEEE Spectrum
Industrial Ceramics
Industrial Chemist
Industrial Design
Industrial Engineering
InfoWorld
Interior Design
Journal of the American Planning Association
Journal of the American Society for Information Science
Journal of the Association for Computing Machinery
Journal of Climate and Applied Meteorology
Journal of Electronic Engineering
Journal of Hazardous Materials
Journal of Structural Engineering
Journal of Surveying Engineering
Journal of Systems Management
Journal of Urban Planning and Development
Journal of Water Resources Planning and Management
MacWEEK
Management of World Wastes
Mechanical Engineering
MIS Week
Monthly Weather Review
Occupational Hazards
Operations Research
P.O.B. (surveyors)
PC

PC Computing
PC Magazine
PC Tech Journal
PC Week
Personal Computing
Planning
Planning Review
Site Selection and Industrial Development
Surveying and Mapping
UNIX Review
VARBUSINESS
Wall Street Computer Review
Waste-to-Energy Report

NATURAL SCIENCE AND MATHEMATICS

American Zoologist
Geology
Journal of the American Chemical Society
Journal of Geology
Mathematics
Physics Today
Scientific American

SOCIAL SCIENCES, THE LAW, AND LAW ENFORCEMENT

Administrative Management
American Bar Association Journal
American Lawyer
Arbitration Journal
Compensation and Benefits Management
Compensation and Benefits Review
Employee Benefit Plan Review
Employee Benefits Journal
Human Resource Management
Human Resource Planning
Industrial and Labor Relations Review
Journal of Sociology and Social Welfare
Journal of Vocational Behavior
Labor Law Journal
Legal Assistant Today
Management Review
Occupational Outlook Quarterly
Paralegal
Pensions and Investment Age
Personnel
Personnel Administrator

Personnel Management
Social Casework: The Journal of Contemporary Social Work
Social Work

EDUCATION AND LIBRARY SCIENCE

Academe
ATA Chronicle (translators)
Executive Educator
Library Journal
NEA Today
School-Administrator
Serials Librarian
Special Libraries
Today's Education

HEALTH CARE

American Journal of Hospital Pharmacy
American Journal of Nursing
American Journal of Occupational Therapy
American Journal of Physiology
American Pharmacy
American Psychologist
ARMA Records Management Quarterly
ASHA (American Speech and Hearing Association)
Clinics in Sports Medicine
Drug and Cosmetic Industry
Drug Topics
Healthcare Financial Management
Health Care Management Review
Health Services Manager
Hospital and Health Services Administrator
Hospital Formulary
Hospitals
Hospital Week
JAMA (Journal of the American Medical Association)
Journal of the American Animal Hospital Association
Journal of the American Dental Association
Journal of the American Dietetic Association
Journal of the American Medical Record Association
Journal of the American Optometric Association
Journal of the American Osteopathic Association
JAPCA (Journal of the Air Pollution Control Association)
JAVMA (Journal of the American Veterinary Medical Association)
Journal of Cardiovascular Pulmonary Technology
Journal of Counseling Psychology
Journal of Emergency Medical Services

Journal of Employment Counseling
Journal of Long Term Care Administration
Journal of Nursing Administration
Journal of Occupational Medicine
Journal of Pharmacy Technology Insurance
Journal of Psychology
Long Term Care Management
Medical World News
Modern Healthcare
New England Journal of Medicine
Nurse Practitioner
Nursing Homes
Nursing Homes and Senior Citizen Care
Optometric Management
Physical Therapy
RESNA News (rehabilitative medicine)
Respiratory Care
Sports Medicine Bulletin

ARTS, ENTERTAINMENT, AND MEDIA

American Cinematographer
Art Direction
Billboard
Broadcasting
Cable Marketing
Cable Television Business
Cable Vision
Columbia Journalism Review
Communications News
Computer Graphics News
Computer Graphics World
Editor and Publisher, The Fourth Estate
Folio: The Magazine for Magazine Management
Graphic Arts Monthly
Industrial Photography
Journalism-Educator
JQ (Journalism Quarterly)
Music Trades
News Photographers
Photo Marketing
Professional Photographer
Publishers Weekly
Publishing News
SPTME Journal (Society of Motion Picture and Television Engineers)
Technical Communication
Television/Radio Age

AIR TRANSPORTATION

Air Line Pilot
Air Transport
Air Transport World
ASTA Travel News
Business Travel
Journal of Travel Research
Plane and Pilot Magazine
Tour and Travel News
Travel Age
Travel Agent
Travel and Leisure
Travel Weekly

GENERAL BUSINESS

Barron's
Business Month
Business Week
Corporate Financing Week
Forbes
Fortune
Harvard Business Review
Industry Week
Institutional Investor
Monthly Labor Review
The Wall Street Journal

APPENDIX B

THE RESUME AND THE INTERVIEW

THE RESUME

Your resume is often all that stands between an interview and you. A resume is a listing of one's credentials, including experience, and other qualifications. Don't expect a job offer simply because your resume is good. It's a given that you have the right credentials and qualifications for the job you're seeking—but so do many other applicants, who have also listed them on their resumes. It's the impression you make, face to face, with an interviewer that will most likely clinch the job. Getting face to face with him or her is the problem. Your resume is what convinces the interviewer to set up that meeting.

Interviewers generally scan many more resumes than they could hope to follow up on in the time they have for filling an opening. They have to do some weeding out, and you make that job all too easy for them if you submit a careless, gabby, or otherwise unprofessional resume.

If you use a professional resume-writing service, be sure that the resume is something you feel comfortable about. Does it sound like you? Does it get the facts straight? If the resume is wrong, will you have trouble getting it corrected?

If you plan to write your own resume, here are some don'ts you must avoid at all costs.

- *Don't be sloppy, cheap, or oddball.* If you type your resume yourself, use good-quality typing paper and a new ribbon or a truly letter-quality printer. Don't submit a photocopy (the resume may get photocopied several more times down the line, and by the fourth generation, the characters start looking fuzzy), and never pencil in a correction. If you find an error you can't live with, redo the whole resume. Don't use dark-colored paper or any size other than 8½″ × 11″ (remember, it's probably going to get photocopied). If you pay for professional typesetting (a smart investment), don't let your resume get too typographically flamboyant (unless you're a designer and you planned the resume to show your talents).

- *Don't submit a resume with typos.* There isn't much you can do to put yourself in a worse light than misspelling a word, omitting a phrase, or punctuating in a truly illiterate fashion. If you have your resume professionally typeset, proofread it as though you typed it yourself, because the person reading it will see it as coming directly from you.

- *Don't say too much.* Leave out all but the pertinent details. Don't mention jobs involving vacuuming or floor buffing or licking envelopes unless there's something about them that relates to the job you're now seeking. And don't describe at length something almost anybody is sure to be familiar with. Remember, the interviewer doesn't have much time to spend on any one candidate. Get right to the point and catch his or her interest immediately. A one-page resume is the rule. If you include a second page, you'd better be talking about some pretty impressive achievements. If you can't fit everything in two pages, start over. That third page shows you're not yet ready for a serious interview.

- *Don't say too little.* Terseness is a virtue, but don't be mysterious. If you held a position with real responsibilities or otherwise stood out in a job, club, or team, spell out your accomplishments—briefly—especially if you think they're relevant to the job for which you are applying.

- *Don't blow your own trumpet.* Let the facts speak for themselves. Don't crow about being "a born leader," "self-starter," or "truly well-rounded individual." Keep the harder sell for your interview; leave it out of your resume. Take it for granted that whoever is reading your resume has enough savvy to read between the lines.

- *Don't omit a cover letter.* The person screening resumes usually only skims them to reject those clearly unacceptable. It's the cover letter that grabs your reader's attention and makes you memorable enough to win an interview. Let the reader know what job you seek, and promise to call in a week if you don't receive an interview appoint. (Keep that promise. The reader may be waiting for that call to see if you're serious about the opening.)

The don'ts that apply to your resume apply to your cover letter, too. Make it neat, literate, concise, complete, and modest. And let your voice come through in your writing. Give it a personal touch by typing it yourself.

Now that you're clear about what to avoid, you'll want to *include* the following on your resume:

- *Your name, address, and telephone number(s).* Make this information prominent. You want the company to get back to you, so make the job easy. You're not required to give your sex, health, marital status, race, or religion on your resume (and you can't be asked about them at your interview either), but you can include them if you wish.
- *Your job goal(s).* Express this clearly and briefly—in one sentence if possible, two sentences at most. Use proper English, but don't be ponderous, solemn, or pretentious. And be specific: Spell out the job you want and the track you think you will pursue.
- *Your education.* Give this section of your resume a heading: "Education." Include dates of attendance (months and years), the name of each school (generally don't go back past high school), the address of each, your curriculum (major and minor), and the highest grade reached or diploma or degree awarded. Don't keep a degree with honors a secret.

  Work this section backward from the highest level of education attained, and give each school its own block. If your major was in the humanities, you might want to mention the fact that you took a respectable number of courses in business and accounting, too. (Many employers are looking for well-rounded beginners.)
- *Your job experience, paid or volunteer.* Give this section a title, too: "Job Experience." List a few relevant jobs, from most to least recent (use the same style you did for education). Include the dates of employment, your job titles, and the names and addresses of your employers. Give a brief job description if it's not something obvious. Mention (modestly) your achievements, if any.

  You don't want to account for every month of your adult life in this section, but do mention full-time employment and any military experience, including highest rank attained.
- *Your achievements.* Special skills, knowledge of equipment or procedures, honors received (other than academic), awards, or membership in organizations belong here.
- *Special interests.* Cite creative pastimes, involvement in sports, and so on that indicate your originality, drive, and/or ability to work as part of a team.

Be prepared to supply a list of references upon request. If you want to submit this list before it's requested, type it on a separate sheet. Include each person's name; title, if applicable; address; and telephone number. Be sure your contact people are willing to give a reference that will help you get that job.

THE JOB INTERVIEW

Assuming your resume looks and sounds professional and you have the right credentials and qualifications for the job, it's the impression you make in your job interview that will get you on board—or send you back to scouring the classifieds. There are certain preliminaries to getting that interview. They're mostly a matter of common sense, but you won't be ready for the interview until you've taken care of them:

- *Find out at least the basics (even better, a lot more than the basics) about the organization.* This often means time (well spent) in the library. Keep up with current events applying to the profession, industry, or specialty. Read the company's annual report. Look into trade papers and journals (there's a generous listing in Appendix A). Talk to people in the know.
- *Know what job for which you're applying and what track you're on.* The first serious item to come up in your interview will most likely touch on one point: Why do you think you're right for this job? Before the interview, try to work out well-phrased answers to likely questions, but don't go overboard; you don't want your answers to sound forced or rehearsed. You simply want to give the correct impression that you've given thought to your career.

  You probably also will be asked to enlarge upon the points the interviewer finds most interesting or most relevant to the job.
- *Be on time for the interview.* Better still, be 15 minutes early. Very little else makes a worse impression than showing up late (even with a plausible excuse). Give yourself time to catch your breath and compose yourself.
- *Dress neatly and appropriately.* For most of the jobs in this book, that means conservatively—except possibly in the entertainment industry. (Of course, you won't have gum in your mouth.)

At the interview, a few more common-sense rules should be followed:

- *Respond to every question briefly and promptly.* Remember, you've practiced answering likely questions already. (And you should know enough about the job and your qualifications to answer unexpected questions, too.) Don't be chatty or familiar or bring up irrelevant information. The interviewer has to cover a certain amount of territory within a time limit.
- *Good manners and proper English are expected.* Be well poised and well spoken, not stuffy and pretentious. And don't try so hard to please that you start to twitch. On the other hand, don't be so self-restrained that you hide your enthusiasm for the job. Make your eagerness clear.
- *Ask about the job and the organization.* Yes, you've done your homework, but there's only so much you can learn from hearsay and secondary sources. After giving you a standard job description and a summary of benefits, along with a look at the nature, goals, and strengths of the organization, the interviewer probably will ask whether you have any questions about the job. Surely, you will have some, so ask them; they'll show you're interested.

- *Bring another copy of your resume and three references.* The resume you sent with a cover letter will probably be on file, but you may be asked to provide another one at the interview and provide references, too. Give a phone number and a mailing address for each reference. Be sure—ahead of time—that your references are prepared to sing your praises.

After the interview, do one more thing:

- *Write a follow-up letter.* And do it soon—the day after the interview. Make it brief and to the point. Thank the interviewer for his or her time on such-and-such a date in regard to such-and-such a job. Mention again why you find the job appealing (show that you were paying attention to the job description given by the interviewer). If you can think of additional qualifications you forgot or were unable to bring up at the interview, mention them now (but don't sound immodest).

If all else fails, remember the Internet is an invaluable tool in your search for employment. Increasingly, jobs are sought and found through the Internet. At the time of this writing, a search through Yahoo using the words "Employment Online" found 396 World Wide Web sites.

Here are a few examples. The Virtual Job Fair Library & Career Resources lists the following databases to search: General Employment, Law/Medical Employment, International Employment, USA Daily Newspaper Employment, Academic/College Employment, as well as High-Technology Employment. Another, Monster Board, offers the user the opportunity to post and revise his or her resume, and the jobs described come directly from employers, not newspaper ads, so jobs may be offered that are not published elsewhere. Another feature of Monster Board is a database of more than 4,000 company profiles. Another site is CareerPath, whose slogan is "where employers and employees click." It provides a search of want ads drawn from leading newspapers around the country, as well as research into career resources and information on selected employers.

You can even find Web sites that offer articles on future trends and career management. In addition to job seekers utilizing the Internet, companies can review qualified employment prospects in the job categories they need to fill by searching out resumes that have been posted on appropriate Web sites.

INDEX